FIDIC 施工合同条件

黄 莺 主编

中国建筑工业出版社

图书在版编目(CIP)数据

FIDIC 施工合同条件/黄莺主编. —北京：中国建筑工业出版社，2018.1
ISBN 978-7-112-21617-8

Ⅰ.①F… Ⅱ.①黄… Ⅲ.①建筑施工-经济合同-研究 Ⅳ.①D913.6

中国版本图书馆 CIP 数据核字(2017)第 304076 号

FIDIC 系列合同条件是国际通用的工程合同范本，其中施工合同条件（新红皮书）在土木工程和房屋建筑工程项目中被广泛采用。本书主要分为两部分，第一部分简介 FIDIC 及其施工合同条件，对 FIDIC（国际咨询工程师联合会）、FIDIC 系列合同条件及其应用、FIDIC 施工合同条件的主要内容及国际其他施工合同文本进行了介绍；第二部分阐述了 FIDIC 施工合同条件的主要内容，该部分分为 20 章，采用英文条款论述、中文综合解释的方法对 FIDIC 施工合同条件的 20 章内容进行了分析和解释，主要内容包括：FIDIC 条件概述；合同的谈判与订立；雇主、监理、承包商三方责权利；风险管理及合同担保；工程承包合同的履行；合同价格与付款；工程分包管理；工程延期管理；工程变更管理；工程索赔等。

本书力求对 FIDIC 施工合同条件的各条款解释详尽，使读者全面深入地掌握 FIDIC 施工合同条款的内容及应用时的注意事项。本书既可以作为普通高等学校土木工程专业、工程管理专业、建筑类院校英语专业等学生的双语教材或教学参考用书，也可供建筑施工单位、工程咨询及监理单位的合同管理和项目管理人员及相关从业人员初学 FIDIC 合同条件时参考使用。

责任编辑：刘瑞霞　武晓涛
责任设计：李志立
责任校对：李欣慰

FIDIC 施工合同条件
黄　莺　主编

中国建筑工业出版社出版、发行（北京海淀三里河路 9 号）
各地新华书店、建筑书店经销
北京红光制版公司制版
北京盈盛恒通印刷有限公司印刷

*

开本：787×1092 毫米　1/16　印张：15¼　字数：378 千字
2018 年 1 月第一版　2018 年 1 月第一次印刷
定价：**42.00 元**
ISBN 978-7-112-21617-8
(31267)

版权所有　翻印必究
如有印装质量问题，可寄本社退换
（邮政编码　100037）

前　言

随着全球经济一体化的进程加快，我国建筑业在更宽更广的层面上进一步加快融入国际承包市场的进程。参与国际建筑市场竞争，学习国外建设法规知识至关重要。这些需求对于土木工程类人才的培养提出了新的要求。土木工程专业法律教学知识体系包括国内建设法规专业知识和国外建设法规专业知识两个方面，FIDIC 施工合同条件是工程建设领域国际通用的合同条件，也是国外建设法规的集中反映。《FIDIC 施工合同条件》一书加强国外原版教材内容和信息的渗透和融合，及时吸收国外专业法规的最新内容，兼容并蓄，能够适应对土木类专业复合型人才专业法规知识的要求。

本书与目前国内现有同类教材相比，编制中更加注重与英文原版"FIDIC 施工合同条件"相结合，还原原版合同内容，从介绍 FIDIC 历史背景及 FIDIC 合同条件内容出发，以充实的内容、清晰的结构，将合同管理理论和实践有机地结合。主要内容分为两个部分：第一部分介绍 FIDIC 及其施工合同条件；第二部分为本书的核心内容，对 FIDIC 施工合同条件进行详细解读和分析。本书可作为高等学校土木工程专业、英语专业的本科生教材，也可作为工程管理专业及其他相关专业的本科教材乃至研究生教材，可以同时满足中文授课和双语教学两种授课方式，同时可作为土木工程建设领域企事业单位经营管理人员的学习培训教材和专业工作手册。

本书由西安建筑科技大学黄莺主编，赖锦翌统稿。研究生赖锦翌、郑夏飞、景泳皓参与了部分章节的编写。其中，第一部分由黄莺、景泳皓、郑夏飞编写，第二部分第 1 章至第 4 章由黄莺和郑夏飞编写，第二部分第 5 章至第 14 章由黄莺和景泳皓编写，第二部分第 15 至第 20 章由黄莺和赖锦翌编写。

由于编者水平有限，书中不足之处在所难免，敬请广大专家、同行和读者批评指正。在编写过程中，参考了许多专家的著作和兄弟院校的有关教材和文献资料，在此一并向他们表示衷心的感谢。

编　者

2017 年 10 月于西安

目　　录

第一部分　FIDIC 及其施工合同条件简介 ········· 1
Ⅰ　FIDIC 简介 ········· 1
Ⅱ　FIDIC 合同条件及其应用 ········· 3
Ⅲ　FIDIC 施工合同（新红皮书）的主要内容 ········· 12
Ⅳ　国际其他施工合同文本 ········· 16

第二部分　FIDIC 施工合同条件解读与分析 ········· 21
1　Generally Provision（一般规定） ········· 21
1.1　Definitions（定义） ········· 21
1.2　Interpretation（解释） ········· 53
1.3　Communications（通信交流） ········· 54
1.4　Law and Language（法律和语言） ········· 55
1.5　Priority of Documents（文件的优先次序） ········· 55
1.6　Contract Agreement（合同协议书） ········· 57
1.7　Assignment（权益转让） ········· 58
1.8　Care and Supply of Documents（文件的保管和提供） ········· 59
1.9　Delayed Drawings or Instructions（延误的图纸或指示） ········· 60
1.10　Employer's Use of Contractor's Documents（雇主使用承包商文件） ········· 61
1.11　Contractor's Use of Employer's Documents（承包商使用雇主文件） ········· 63
1.12　Confidential Details（保密事项） ········· 63
1.13　Compliance with Laws（遵守法律） ········· 64
1.14　Joint and Several Liability（共同的与各自的责任） ········· 64

2　The Employer（雇主）
2.1　Right of Access to the Site（现场进入权） ········· 67
2.2　Permits，Licences or Approvals（许可、执照或批准） ········· 69
2.3　Employer's Personnel（雇主人员） ········· 70
2.4　Employer's Financial Arrangements（雇主的资金安排） ········· 70
2.5　Employer's Claims（雇主的索赔） ········· 71

3　The Engineer（工程师） ········· 73
3.1　Engineer's Duties and Authority（工程师的任务和权力） ········· 73
3.2　Delegation by the Engineer（由工程师付托） ········· 74
3.3　Instructions of the Engineer（工程师的指示） ········· 76

  3.4   Replacement of the Engineer（工程师的替换） …………………… 77
  3.5   Determinations（确定） ……………………………………………… 77
4 The Contractor（承包商） …………………………………………………… 79
  4.1   Contractor's General Obligations（承包商的一般义务） ………… 79
  4.2   Performance Security（履约担保） ………………………………… 81
  4.3   Contractor's Representative（承包商代表） ……………………… 82
  4.4   Subcontractors（分包商） …………………………………………… 83
  4.5   Assignment of Benefit of Subcontract（分包合同权益的转让） … 84
  4.6   Co-operation（合作） ………………………………………………… 85
  4.7   Setting Out（放线） …………………………………………………… 86
  4.8   Safety Procedures（安全程序） ……………………………………… 87
  4.9   Quality Assurance（质量保证） ……………………………………… 87
  4.10 Site Data（现场数据） ……………………………………………… 88
  4.11 Sufficiency of the Accepted Contract（中标合同金额的充分性） … 89
  4.12 Unforeseeable Physical Conditions（不可预见的物质条件） …… 90
  4.13 Rights of Way and Facilities（道路通行权和设施） ……………… 92
  4.14 Avoidance of Interference（避免干扰） …………………………… 92
  4.15 Access Route（进场通路） ………………………………………… 93
  4.16 Transport of Goods（货物运输） …………………………………… 93
  4.17 Contractor's Equipment（承包商设备） …………………………… 94
  4.18 Protection of the Environment（环境保护） ……………………… 94
  4.19 Electricity, Water and Gas（电、水和燃气） ……………………… 95
  4.20 Employer's Equipment and Free-Issue Material
       （雇主设备和免费供应的材料） …………………………………… 95
  4.21 Progress Reports（进度报告） ……………………………………… 96
  4.22 Security of the Site（现场保安） …………………………………… 99
  4.23 Contractor's Operations on Site（承包商的现场作业） ………… 100
  4.24 Fossils（化石） ……………………………………………………… 101
5 Normited Subcontractors（指定的分包商） ……………………………… 103
  5.1   Definition of "nominated Subcontractor"（"指定的分包商"的定义） … 103
  5.2   Objection to Nomination（反对指定） ……………………………… 103
  5.3   Payments to nominated Subcontractor（对指定的分包商付款） … 104
  5.4   Evidence of Payments（付款证据） ………………………………… 105
6 Staff and Labour（员工） …………………………………………………… 108
  6.1   Engagement of Staff and Labour（员工的雇用） ………………… 108
  6.2   Rates of Wages and Conditions of Labour（工资标准和劳动条件） … 108
  6.3   Persons in the Service of Employer（为雇主服务的人员） ……… 109
  6.4   Labour Laws（劳动法） ……………………………………………… 109
  6.5   Working Hours（工作时间） ………………………………………… 109

- 6.6 Facilities for Staff and Labour（为员工提供设施） …… 110
- 6.7 Health and Safety（健康和安全） …… 110
- 6.8 Contractor's Superintendence（承包商的监督） …… 111
- 6.9 Contractor's in Personnel（承包商人员） …… 111
- 6.10 Records of Contractor's Personnel and Equipment（承包商人员和设备的记录） …… 112
- 6.11 Disorderly Conduct（无序行为） …… 112

7 Plant, Materials and Workmanship（生产设备、材料和工艺） …… 114
- 7.1 Manner of Execution（实施方法） …… 114
- 7.2 Samples（样品） …… 114
- 7.3 Inspection（检验） …… 115
- 7.4 Testing（试验） …… 116
- 7.5 Rejection（拒收） …… 117
- 7.6 Remedial Work（修补工作） …… 118
- 7.7 Ownership of Plant and Materials（生产设备和材料的所有权） …… 119
- 7.8 Royalties（土地（矿区）使用费） …… 119

8 Commencement, Delays and Suspension（开工、延误和暂停） …… 120
- 8.1 Commencement of Works（工程的开工） …… 120
- 8.2 Time for Completion（竣工时间） …… 121
- 8.3 Programme（进度计划） …… 122
- 8.4 Extension of Time for Completion（竣工时间的延长） …… 124
- 8.5 Delays Caused by Authorities（当局造成的延误） …… 126
- 8.6 Rate of Progress（工程进度） …… 127
- 8.7 Delay Damages（误期损害赔偿费） …… 128
- 8.8 Suspension of Work（暂时停工） …… 129
- 8.9 Consequences of Suspension（暂停的后果） …… 131
- 8.10 Payment for Plant and Materials in Event of Suspension（暂停时对生产设备和材料的付款） …… 132
- 8.11 Prolonged Suspension（拖长的暂停） …… 133
- 8.12 Resumption of Work（复工） …… 133

9 Tests On Completion（竣工试验） …… 136
- 9.1 Contractor's Obligations（承包商的义务） …… 136
- 9.2 Delayed Tests（延误的试验） …… 137
- 9.3 Retesting（重新试验） …… 138
- 9.4 Failure to Pass Tests on Completion（未能通过竣工试验） …… 138

10 Employer's Taking Over（雇主的接收） …… 140
- 10.1 Taking Over of the Works and Sections（工程和单位工程的接收） …… 140
- 10.2 Taking Over of Parts of the Works（部分工程的接收） …… 141
- 10.3 Interference with Tests on Completion（对竣工试验的干扰） …… 143

10.4　Surfaces Requiring Reinstatement（需要复原的地面） …………… 144

11　Defects Liability（缺陷责任） ……………………………………… 146
11.1　Completion of Outstanding Work and Remedying Defects
　　　（完成扫尾工作和修补缺陷） …………………………………… 146
11.2　Cost of Remedying Defects（修补缺陷的费用） ………………… 147
11.3　Extension of Defects Notification Period（缺陷责任期限的延长） … 148
11.4　Failure to Remedy Defects（未能修补缺陷） …………………… 148
11.5　Removal of Defective Work（移出有缺陷的工程） ……………… 149
11.6　Further Tests（进一步试验） ……………………………………… 150
11.7　Right of Access（进入权） ………………………………………… 150
11.8　Contractor to Search（承包商调查） ……………………………… 151
11.9　Performance Certificate（履约证书） ……………………………… 151
11.10　Unfulfilled Obligations（未履行的义务） ……………………… 152
11.11　Clearance of Site（现场清理） …………………………………… 153

12　Measurement and Evaluation（测量和估价） ……………………… 155
12.1　Works to be Measured（需测量的工程） ………………………… 155
12.2　Method of Measurement（测量办法） …………………………… 157
12.3　Evaluation（估价） ………………………………………………… 158
12.4　Omissions（删减） ………………………………………………… 159

13　Variations and Adjustment（变更和调整） ………………………… 162
13.1　Right to Vary（变更权） …………………………………………… 162
13.2　Value Engineering（价值工程） …………………………………… 164
13.3　Variation Procedure（变更程序） ………………………………… 165
13.4　Payment in Applicable Currencies（以适用货币支付） ………… 166
13.5　Provisional Sums（暂列金额） …………………………………… 167
13.6　Daywork（计日工作） ……………………………………………… 168
13.7　Adjustments for Changes in Legislation（因法律改变的调整） … 169
13.8　Adjustments for Changes in the Cost（因成本调整的改变） …… 170

14　Contractor Price and Payment（合同价格和付款） ……………… 174
14.1　The Contractor Price（合同价格） ………………………………… 174
14.2　Advance Payment（预付款） ……………………………………… 175
14.3　Application for Interim Payment Certificates（期中付款证书的申请） … 177
14.4　Schedule of Payments（付款计划表） …………………………… 179
14.5　Plant and Materials intended for the Works
　　　（拟用于工程的生产设备和材料） ……………………………… 180
14.6　Issue of Interim Payment Certificates（期中付款证书的颁发） … 182
14.7　Payment（付款） …………………………………………………… 183
14.8　Delayed Payment（延误的付款） ………………………………… 184
14.9　Payment of Retention Money（保留金的支付） ………………… 184

14.10　Statement of Completion（竣工报表） ……………………………… 185
14.11　Application for Final Payment Certificate（最终付款证书的申请）…… 186
14.12　Discharge（结清证明） …………………………………………………… 187
14.13　Issue of Final Payment Certificate（最终付款证书的颁发） …………… 187
14.14　Cessation of Employer's Liability（雇主责任的终止） ………………… 188
14.15　Currencies of Payment（支付的货币） …………………………………… 189

15　Termination by Employer（由雇主终止） ……………………………… 192
15.1　Notice to Correct（通知改正） ……………………………………………… 192
15.2　Termination by Employer（由雇主终止） ………………………………… 192
15.3　Valuation at Date of Termination（终止日期时的估价） ………………… 194
15.4　Payment after Termination（终止后的付款） …………………………… 195
15.5　Employer' Entitlement to Termination（雇主终止的权利） ……………… 195

16　Suspension and Termination by Constractor（由承包商暂停和终止） … 197
16.1　Contractor's Entitlement to Suspend Work（承包商暂停工作的权利）… 197
16.2　Termination by Contractor（由承包商终止） …………………………… 198
16.3　Cessation of Work and Removal of Contractor's Equipment
　　　（停止工作和承包商设备的撤离） ………………………………………… 199
16.4　Payment on Termination（终止时的付款） ……………………………… 200

17　Risk and Responsibility（风险与职责） …………………………………… 201
17.1　Indemnities（保障） ………………………………………………………… 201
17.2　Contractor's Care of the Works（承包商对工程的照管） ………………… 202
17.3　Employer's Risks（雇主的风险） …………………………………………… 203
17.4　Consequences of Employer's Risks（雇主风险的后果） ………………… 204
17.5　Intellectual and Industrial Property Rights（知识产权与工业产权） …… 205
17.6　Limitation of Liability（责任限度） ………………………………………… 207

18　Insurance（保险） ……………………………………………………………… 209
18.1　General Requirements for Insurances（有关保险的一般要求） ………… 209
18.2　Insurance for Works and Contractor's Equipment
　　　（工程和承包商设备的保险） ……………………………………………… 212
18.3　Insurance against Injury to Persons and Damage under to Property
　　　（人身伤害和财产损害险） ………………………………………………… 215
18.4　Insurance for Contractor's Personnel（承包商人员的保险） …………… 216

19　Force Majeure（不可抗力） ………………………………………………… 217
19.1　Definition of Force Majeure（不可抗力的定义） ………………………… 217
19.2　Notice of Force Majeure（不可抗力的通知） …………………………… 218
19.3　Duty to Minimise Delay（将延误减至最小的义务） ……………………… 219
19.4　Consequences of Force Majeure（不可抗力的后果） …………………… 219
19.5　Force Majeure Affecting Subcontractor（不可抗力影响分包商） ……… 220
19.6　Optional Termination, Payment and Release

（自主选择终止，付款和解除） ………………………… 220
　19.7　Release from Performance under the Law（根据法律解除履约） ………… 221
20　Claim, Disputes and Arbitration（索赔、争端和仲裁） ……………… 223
　20.1　Contractor's Claims（承包商的索赔） ……………………………… 223
　20.2　Appointment of the Dispute Adjudication Board
　　　（争端裁决委员会的任命） ……………………………………… 226
　20.3　Failure to Agree Dispute Adjudication Board
　　　（对争端裁决委员会未能取得一致） …………………………… 227
　20.4　Obtaining Dispute Adjudication Board's Decision
　　　（取得争端裁决委员会的决定） ………………………………… 228
　20.5　Amicable both Settlement（友好解决） ……………………………… 229
　20.6　Arbitration（仲裁） …………………………………………………… 230
　20.7　Failure to Comply with Dispute Adjudication Board's Decision
　　　（未能遵守争端裁决委员会的决定） …………………………… 231
　20.8　Expiry of Dispute Adjudication Board's Appointment
　　　（争端裁决委员会任命期满） …………………………………… 231
参考文献 ……………………………………………………………………… 233

第一部分　FIDIC 及其施工合同条件简介

Ⅰ　FIDIC 简介

FIDIC 是国际咨询工程师联合会 Fédération Internationale des Ingénieurs－Conseils 的法文缩写，其英文名称是 International Federation of Consulting Engineers。中文音译为"菲迪克"。

FIDIC 是国际上最有权威的被世界银行认可的国际咨询工程师组织，1913 年 FIDIC 在比利时根特成立，最初的成员是欧洲境内的法国、比利时等 3 个独立的咨询工程师协会。1949 年，英国土木工程师协会成为正式代表，并于次年以东道主身份在伦敦主办 FIDIC 代表会议，一般历史学家将这次会议描述成当代国际咨询工程师联合会的诞生。1959 年，美国、南非、澳大利亚和加拿大也加入了联合会，FIDIC 从此打破了地域的划分，成为了一个真正的国际组织。FIDIC 总部设在瑞士洛桑，2002 年迁往日内瓦，主要职能机构有：执行委员会（TEC）、土木工程合同委员会（CECC）、雇主与咨询工程师关系委员会（CCRC）、职业责任委员会（PLC）和秘书处。

截至 2016 年，FIDIC 已有 97 个成员国，分属于四个地区性组织：即亚洲及太平洋地区成员协会（ASPAC）、欧共体成员协会（CEDIC）、非洲成员协会集团（CAMA）、北欧成员协会集团（RINORD）。

FIDIC 组织创立之初的最重要的职业道德准则之一是咨询工程师的行为必须独立于承包商、制造商和供应商之外，他必须以独立的身份向委托人提供工程咨询服务，为委托人的利益尽责，并仅以此获得报酬。FIDIC 成立以来，对国际工程建设项目的实施，以及促进国际经济技术合作的发展起到了重要作用。由该组织编制的《雇主与咨询工程师标准服务协议书》（白皮书）、《土木工程施工合同条件》（红皮书）、《电气与机械工程合同条件》（黄皮书）、《工程总承包合同条件》（桔黄皮书）被世界银行、亚洲开发银行等国际和区域发展援助金融机构作为实施项目的合同和协议范本。这些合同和协议文本、条款内容严密，对履约各方和实施人员的职责义务做了明确的规定；对实施项目过程中可能出现的问题也都有较合理规定，以利遵循解决。这些协议性文件为实施项目进行科学管理提供了可靠的依据，有利于保证工程质量、确保工期和控制成本，使雇主、承包人以及咨询工程师等有关人员的合法权益得到尊重。此外，FIDIC 还编辑出版了供雇主和咨询工程师使用的业务参考书籍和工作指南，帮助雇主更好地选择咨询工程师，使咨询工程师更全面地了解业务工作范围和根据指南进行工作。该组织制订的承包商标准资格预审表、招标程序、咨询项目分包协议等都有很实用的参考价值，在国际上受到普遍欢迎，得到了广泛承认和应用。

作为一个国际性的非官方组织，FIDIC 的宗旨是要将各个国家独立的咨询工程师行业组织联合成一个国际性的行业组织；促进还没有建立起这个行业组织的国家也能够建立起这样的组织；鼓励制订咨询工程师应遵守的职业行为准则，以提高为雇主和社会服务的质量；研究和增进会员的利益，促进会员之间的关系，增强本行业的活力；提供和交流会员感兴趣和有益的信息，增强行业凝聚力。

　　FIDIC 规定，要想成为它的正式会员，须由该国的一家"全国性的咨询工程师协会"（以下简称"全国性协会"）提出申请，"全国性协会"应当达到以下要求：应为雇主和社会公共利益而努力促进工程咨询行业的发展；应保护和促进咨询工程师和私人业务方面的利益和提高本行业的声誉；应促使会员之间在职业、经营方面的经验和信息交流。FIDIC 还对"全国性协会"的主要任务提出建议：要使社会公众和雇主了解本行业的重要性和它的服务内容，以及作为一个独立咨询工程师团体和个人的职能；要制订出严格的规则和措施，促使会员保证遵守职业道德标准，维护本行业的声誉；致力于开展国际交流，并为会员开展业务，获取先进技能，提供国际接触通道；了解和发挥本国工程咨询的某些优势和特点；广泛地建立会员与其他工程组织机构和教学单位的联系，充实咨询内容和明确新的方向；促进使用标准程序、制度和合约（如以上所说的有白皮书、红皮书、黄皮书等）；向政府报告本行业的共同性问题并提出需要政府解决的问题；传递 FIDIC 提供的各种信息和其他国家同行业协会的经验；研究会员收取咨询服务合理报酬的办法；提倡按能力择优选取咨询专家，避免单纯价格竞争，导致降低工程咨询标准和服务质量。

　　中国工程咨询协会于 1996 年 10 月正式加入 FIDIC，取得在 FIDIC 的发言权和表决权。随着中国加入 WTO 和全球经济一体化模式的逐步形成，越来越多的外国公司必将进入中国工程咨询业市场。这预示着我国工程咨询业作为建筑业的服务行业，其市场格局、服务体系、法律法规环境等将会在短时间内发生巨大而深刻的变化。如何完善有关的法律法规，尽快与国际惯例接轨，按照国际工程咨询业的行业规范管理我国的工程咨询公司已成为我国咨询业发展的当务之急。FIDIC 组织作为业界最大的协会，其影响已遍及世界各地。FIDIC 所制定的通用标准合同条件也在国际上得到了广泛应用和普遍认可。在中国外资贷款项目均普遍采用 FIDIC 合同条件，在国内采用 FIDIC 合同条件的工程项目将会越来越多。因此，雇主、承包商和咨询工程师都需要对该组织进行比较全面的了解。

Ⅱ FIDIC 合同条件及其应用

FIDIC 合同条件是由国际咨询工程师联合会组织编撰的一系列合同的总称。FIDIC 合同条件体系不仅被 FIDIC 成员国在世界范围内广泛使用，也被世界银行、亚洲开发银行、非州开发银行等世界金融组织在招标文件中使用。有人称 FIDIC 合同是国际承包工程的"圣经"。可以说，FIDIC 合同是集工业发达国家土木工程建筑业上百年的经验，把工程技术、法律、经济和管理科学等有机结合起来的一个合同条件。为了适应国际工程业和国际经济的不断发展，FIDIC 对其合同条件要进行修改和调整，以令其更能反映国际工程实践，更具有代表性和普遍意义，更加严谨、完善，更具权威性和可操作性。尤其是近十几年，修改调整的频率明显增大。

一、FIDIC 早期出版的主要合同条件

FIDIC 系列合同范本经历了较长的发展过程。在 1998 年之前，FIDIC 出版的主要合同文件有五种：

（1）土木工程施工合同条件（1957，1965，1977，1987，1992（DAB））

1957 年针对海外土木工程，FIDIC 与国际房屋建筑和公共工程联合会（欧洲国际建筑联合会）（FIEC）正式发布了第一版 FIDIC 合同条款——《土木工程施工合同条件（国际）》（俗称"红皮书"），常称为 FIDIC 条件。该合同条件是在英国咨询工程师联合会（ACE）颁布的《土木工程合同文件格式》的基础上编写而成的，条件分为两部分，第一部分是通用合同条件，第二部分为专用合同条件。

随后于 1963、1977、1987 年分别出了第二、三、四版。1963 年的第二版加了第三部分，"疏浚和填筑工程专用条件"。1977 年 FIDIC 和欧洲国际建筑联合会（FIEC）联合编写的《Federation Internationale Europeenne de la Construction（巴黎）》是红皮书的第三版。1987 年 9 月红皮书出版了第四版，将第二部分（专用合同条件）扩大了，单独成册出版，但其条款编号与第一部分一一对应，使两部分合在一起共同构成确定合同双方权利和义务的合同条件。第二部分必须根据合同的具体情况起草。为了方便第二部分的编写，其编有解释性说明以及条款的例子，为合同双方提供了必要且可供选择的条文。1988、1992 年又两次对第四版进行了若干编辑方面修改，这些修改不影响有关条款的涵义，只是澄清了其真正意图。

（2）机电设备安装合同条件（1963，1980，1987）

1963 年，FIDIC 出版了适用于雇主和承包商的机械与设备供应和安装的《电气与机械工程标准合同条件格式》即黄皮书。1980 年，黄皮书出了第二版。1987 年出版了黄皮书第三版《电气与机械工程合同条件》，分为三个独立的部分：序言，通用条件和专用条件。

（3）土木工程施工分包合同条件（1994）

土木工程施工分包合同条件的各项条款是由国际咨询工程师联合会（FIDIC）编制的，并被推荐与《土木工程施工合同条件》（1987年第四版，1992年再次修订后重印）配套使用。分包合同条件稍加修改同样适用于分包商由雇主指定的情况。

（4）设计-建造与交钥匙合同条件（1995）

考虑到某些雇主希望以承包商做设计的包干方式为基础进行项目工程施工的采购，1995年FIDIC编制并出版了相应的合同模式"设计-建造和交钥匙工程合同"，后来称之为桔皮书。桔皮书可以成为提供由承包商设计的设施的所有合同的基础，这里的设施包含建筑工程、土木工程、化学工程、电气工程、机械工程或任何联合工程。桔皮书编写过程中编入了适用于房屋建筑、道路、炼油设施、发电机、水轮机、污水处理工程等的各项规定。桔皮书不适用于由雇主和其咨询工程师设计的项目。

（5）雇主与咨询工程师标准服务协议书（1979，1990，1998）

1979年，FIDIC编写出版了《设计和施工监督协议书国际范本及通用规则》；1980年FIDIC编写出版了《雇主与咨询工程师项目管理协议书国际范本及通用规则》。1990年，在上述文件的基础上，FIDIC编写出版了《雇主与咨询工程师标准服务协议书》，该协议书又称为白皮书。白皮书适用于国际工程的投资前研究、可行性研究、设计及施工管理、项目管理等，是国际通用的雇主与咨询工程师之间标准服务的协议书。

以上的红皮书（1987）、黄皮书（1987）、橘皮书（1995）和《土木工程施工合同—分合同条件（1994）》、蓝皮书（《招标程序》）、白皮书（《顾客/咨询工程师模式服务协议》）、《联合承包协议》、《咨询服务分包协议》共同构成FIDIC彩虹族系列合同文件。

二、新版FIDIC施工合同条件及其特点

1999年9月，FIDIC出版了一套4本全新的标准合同条件：

（1）《施工合同条件》（新红皮书），即：由雇主设计的房屋和工程施工合同条件（Conditions of Contract for Construction for Building and Engineering Works Designed by the Employer）。新红皮书与原红皮书相对应，但其名称改变后合同的适用范围更大。该合同主要用于由雇主设计的或由咨询工程师设计的房屋建筑工程（Building Works）和土木工程（Engineering Works）。在这种合同形式下，承包商一般都按照雇主提供的设计施工。但工程中的某些土木、机械、电力等建造工程也可能由承包商设计。该合同条件与原来的土木工程施工合同条件（红皮书）相对应，其名称的改变并不是出于简化目的，而在于其适用的工程范围扩大，不仅可以用于土木工程（engineering应理解为civil engineering），也可以用于房屋建筑工程。总的来说，新红皮书适用的工程范围为：

① 各类大型或复杂工程，主要工作为施工；
② 雇主负责大部分设计工作；
③ 由工程师来监理施工和签发支付证书；
④ 按工程量表中的单价来支付完成的工程量（即单价合同）雇主承担的风险较大。

（2）《设备与设计-建造合同》（新黄皮书），即：由承包商设计的电气和机械设备安装与民用和工程合同条件（Conditions of Contract for Plant and Designed—Build for Electrical and Mechanical Plant and Building and Engineering Works Designed by the Contractor）。该合同条件被推荐用于电力和/或机械设备的提供，以及房屋建筑或土木工程的设计和实施。在这种合同条件形式下，一般都是由承包商按照雇主的要求设计和提供设备和/或其他工程（可能包括由土木、机械、电力和/或建造工程的任何组合形式）。该合同条件与原来的电气与机械工程合同条件（黄皮书）相对应，其名称的改变在于从名称上直接反映出该合同条件与"新红皮书"的区别，即在"新黄皮书"的条件下，承包商的基本义务是完成永久设备的设计、制造和安装。Plant 一词原来译为工程设备，现改译为永久设备，旨在与"新红皮书"中的永久工程一词相对应。总的来说，新黄皮书适用的工程范围为：

① 机电设备项目、其他基础设施项目以及其他类型的项目；

② 雇主只负责编制项目纲要（即："雇主的要求"）和工程设备性能要求，承包商负责大部分设计工作和全部施工安装工作；

③ 工程师来监督设备的制造、安装和施工，签发支付证书；

④ 在包干价格下实施里程碑支付方式，在个别情况下也可能采用单价支付，风险分担均衡。

（3）《EPC/交钥匙项目合同条件》（银皮书），即：EPC/交钥匙项目合同条件（Conditions of Contract for EPC/Turnkey）。银皮书又可译为"设计－采购－施工交钥匙项目合同条件"，它与桔皮书相似但不完全相同。它适于工厂建设之类的开发项目。是包含了项目策划、可行性研究、具体设计、采购、建造、安装、试运行等在内的全过程承包方式。承包商"交钥匙"时，提供的是一套配套完整的可以运行的设施。该合同条件适用于在交钥匙的基础上进行的工厂或其他类型的开发项目的实施，这种合同条件所适用的项目：对最终价格和施工时间要求较高；承包商完全负责项目的设备和施工，雇主基本不参与工作。在交钥匙项目中，一般情况下由承包商实施所有的设计、采购和建造工作，即在"交钥匙"时，提供一个配套完整、可以运行的设施。该合同条件与原来的设计-建造和交钥匙（工程）合同条件（桔皮书）有一定的相关性，但 FIDIC 并无意以"银皮书"取代"桔皮书"。该合同条件中的 EPC 为 Engineering Procurement and Construction 或 Engineer, Procure and Construct 的缩写，其中 Engineering 一词不能译为工程，建议译为设计，但其内涵比一般意义的设计（Design）大得多，可能包括项目的规划或策划、可行性研究、具体的设计工作等。因此，该合同条件的名称完全译为中文应为：设计-采购-施工交钥匙项目合同条件。总的来说，银皮书适用的工程范围为：

① 私人投资项目，如 BOT 项目（地下工程太多的工程除外）固定总价不变的交钥匙合同，并按里程碑方式支付；

② 雇主代表直接管理项目实施过程，采用较宽松的管理方式，但严格竣工检验和竣工后检验，以保证完工项目的质量；

③ 项目风险大部分由承包商承担，但雇主愿意为此多付出一定的费用。

（4）《简明合同格式》（绿皮书），即：适合于小规模项目的简明合同格式（Short Form of Contract）。该合同条件主要适于价值较低的或形式简单、或重复性的、或工期短的房屋建筑和土木工程。根据工程的类型和具体条件的不同，此格式也适用于价值较高的工程，特别是较简单的、或重复性的、或工期短的工程。在这种合同形式下，一般都是由承包商按照雇主或其代表——工程师提供的设计实施工程，但对于部分或完全由承包商设计的土木、机械、电力和/或建造工程的合同也同样适用。

FIDIC1999 新版合同条件具有许多特点：

（1）适应国际工程承包方式的新发展

自 20 世纪 70 年代以来，国际工程承包市场的承包方式有了迅速发展，我国习惯上所称的项目总承包方式得到较多运用，且有多种表现形式。应当承认，FIDIC 原有的合同条件体系在适应国际工程承包方式发展和需要方面不是特别及时，例如，"桔皮书"（1995年版）和土木工程施工分包合同条件（1994 年版）的出版均远远落后于美国 AIA 和英国 JCT 的相应合同条件。但是，FIDIC 于 1999 年所推出的"银皮书"却实现了领先一步，对在国际工程承包市场出现的 EPC 承包方式及时进行了总结，这对规范 EPC 合同条件下承发包双方的行为、明确双方的权利和义务，从而使 EPC 承包方式能健康发展，无疑将起到积极作用。同时，这也有利于扩大 FIDIC 组织以及 FIDIC 合同条件在国际工程界的影响。

（2）结构体系统一

在 FIDIC 原有的合同条件体系中，几个主要的合同条件文本的结构体系不统一，如"红皮书"有 25 大类 72 条 194 款，"黄皮书"有 32 大类 51 条 197 款，而"桔皮书"则为 20 条 160 款。显然，这三个合同条件的内容分类和条款设备不统一，同一内容在不同合同条件文本中的位置不同，甚至具体表述也不统一。这对于各合同条件的实际运用是非常不利的，尤其是对于能够运用多种方式承包工程的承包商来说，必须对各个合同条件文本进行深入的分析和比较研究，才能避免失误。而 1999 年新版 FIDIC 合同条件实现了结构体系的统一，取消了原来没有编号的"类"，且三个合同条件文本均为 20 条（与"桔皮书"一致）160 多款。这为承包商分析和比较不同合同条件文本（实质上反映的是不同承包方式）的区别提供了极大的便利。

（3）大多数条款相同

这一特点与结构体系统一的特点密切相关，亦可认为是其一个方面。为简明起见，以下用表格形式对三个合同条件文本进行粗略的比较，见表 1，表中括号中的数字表示条款的数目，"—"表示条的名称和条款数目与"新红皮书"完全相同。这样"红皮书"、"黄皮书"、"桔皮书"三个合同条件文本的大多数"条"的名称和条款的数目均相同（实际上大多数"款"的名称也相同，只是未在表中反映出来），可以明显反映出不同合同条件的根本区别。例如，在"新黄皮书"和"银皮书"的条件下，均有"设计"一条，说明由承包商负责设计，而在"新红皮书"的条件下，承包商则按图施工；"银皮书"第 3 条为"雇主的管理"，"新黄皮书"第 3 条则为"工程师"，说明在"新黄皮书"条件下，雇主是委托咨询公司为其管理工程，而在"银皮书"的条件下，则可能由雇主人员自行管理工程（实践中亦可能委托咨询公司管理工程）。

FIDIC 合同条件文本间的对比   表 1

编号	《施工合同条件》(新红皮书)	《设备与设计-建造合同》(新黄皮书)	《EPC/交钥匙项目合同条件》(银皮书)
1	一般规定（14）	—	—
2	雇主（5）	—	—
3	工程师（5）	—	雇主的管理（5）

续表

编号	《施工合同条件》 （新红皮书）	《设备与设计-建造合同》 （新黄皮书）	《EPC/交钥匙项目合同条件》 （银皮书）
4	承包商（24）	—	—
5	指定分包商（4）	设计（8）	设计（8）
6	职员和劳工（11）	—	—
7	永久设备、材料和工艺（8）	—	—
8	开工、延误和暂停（12）	—	—
9	竣工检验（4）	—	—
10	雇主的接收（4）	—	—
11	缺陷责任（11）	—	—
12	测量和估价（4）	竣工后检验（4）	竣工后检验（4）
13	变更和调整（8）	—	—
14	合同价格和支付（15）	—	—
15	雇主提出终止（5）	—	—
16	承包商提出暂停和终止（4）	—	—
17	风险和责任（6）	—	—
18	保险（4）	—	—
19	不可抗力（7）	—	—
20	索赔、争端和仲裁（8）	—	—

三、专用 FIDIC 合同版本

1. FIDIC 和谐版本及其特点

多年来，诸如世界银行、亚洲开发银行、非洲开发银行等国际多边开发银行在其贷款的国际项目的招标中，多采用 FIDIC 编制的合同条件范本，在 2005 年 5 月之前，这些国际多边开发银行的工程招标文件范本中大都采用 FIDIC1987 年出版的红皮书第四版，在以前使用 FIDIC 合同条件时，多边开发银行的通常做法是，针对各银行贷款项目的特点以及各银行的具体条件，在 FIDIC 原合同条件的基础上，引入一些补充的合同条款，同时对不适用的条款进行修改或删除，这种条款的补充以及修改无形中增大了招标文件编制中的工作量，同时也造成了各个国际多边开发银行的合同版本之间存在差异，这样就降低了招标过程中的效率，而且增加了标准招标文件范本中的不确定因素，容易在用户之间产生争议。在多年的实践中，多边开发银行认为，虽然工程合同条件的标准化具有很大优点，但上述问题的确也影响到实际工作的效率。1999 年，FIDIC 出版了一套新版合同条件，各个多边开发银行决定，在将 FIDIC 新版合同条件引入招标文件范本之前，通过对 FIDIC 新版本合同的修改，形成一个完全适用于各个多边开发银行贷款项目的标准合同条件版本。于是，在各个多边开发银行与 FIDIC 共同努力之下，一个供各个多边开发银行贷款项目专用的 FIDIC 新版施工合同条件在 2005 年 5 月发布，这一版本被称为"多边开发银行和谐施工合同"（MDB Harmonized Construction Contract）。世界银行已在其最新发布的招标文件范本中引入了这一多边开发银行专用的 FIDIC 施工合同条件，在 2006 年

3月，FIDIC又对该范本进行了一些修订，发布了第二版，该版本在最新的国际多边开发银行合同范本中对1999年版本进行了很多修改，但FIDIC声明，其1999年版本仍应该在非多边开发银行贷款项目中应用，2006年的版本仅供多边开发银行贷款项目使用。目前，MDB版合同的参与银行有：世界银行、亚洲开发银行、非洲发展银行、黑海贸易和发展银行、加勒比发展银行、欧洲复兴和开发银行、美洲洲际发展银行、伊斯兰发展银行、北欧发展银行等。

FIDIC和谐合同范本的编制主要是以其1999年出版的施工合同条件（新红皮书）为基本框架编写而成的，整个合同条件也分为20条，因此与1999年新红皮书类似，也体现了以下基础特点：用于雇主负责设计的施工项目；由监理工程师来为雇主管理合同的实施；合同价格的性质总体上为单价合同；合同风险分担总体对承包商有利，可以被认为是"亲承包商"。

和谐版本同时又具备自身的特点，主要体现在下列各方面：

（1）合同条件的编排结构更合理，更结构化

在和谐版本中，淡化了原来的"投标书附录"（Appendix to Tender）中的内容，而将大部分内容纳入了"专用条件"（Particular Conditions）中，同时将"专用条件"分为A部分与B部分。其中A部分为合同数据表（Contract Data），列明的是涉及通用条件相应条款中需具体的各类数据资料、如雇主的名称、工程师的名称、合同适用的具体法律名称、履约保函的额度等，而B部分为在通用条件基础上补充的"具体规定"（Specific Provisions），这样编排更能方便用户，增大了"专用条件"的实用性。

（2）措辞以及相关规定更符合多边开发银行贷款项目的做法

和谐版本中修改了原来的一些措辞，同时增加了银行体贴贷款项目中常用的词。如：将原"投标书附录"的定义删除，并化之以"合同数据"（Contract Data）的定义，增加了"银行"（Bank）、"借款人"（Borrower）等新定义。鉴于FIDIC在以前的合同版本中与世界银行习惯用法不太一致，如FIDIC在表示投标书这一概念时，用的是英文"Tender"，而有些多边开发银行习惯使用"Bid"，因此，FIDIC在和谐版本的第1.2款中规定，和谐版本中所出现的Tender（投标书）与Bid（投标书）为同义词。Tender（投标人）与Bidder（投标人）为同义词，Tender Documents（投标文件）与Bidding Documents（招标文件）为同义词。在规定争端解决机制时，FIDIC以前使用的是DAB（争端裁决委员会），而多边开发银行习惯用DRB（争端审议委员会），在和谐版本中，统一用DB（Dispute Board）表示争端委员会。这些关于措辞的规定或统一避免了多边开发银行在使用FIDIC合同条件时所带来的措辞不一致问题。关于雇主的资金安排问题，和谐版本也进行了适用于贷款项目的特别规定，即：如果银行向雇主发出通知暂停发放该工程款的某部分或全部，雇主应该在收到通知7天内转告给承包商，并附上相关细节，包括通知的日期，并送复印件通知工程师。如果雇主在收到此通知超出60天后才能用合适货币继续支付承包商，则需要向承包商出具相关证据证明此被拖延的支付是有保证的（第2.4款）。另外，和谐版本中还鼓励承包商尽量雇用当地分包商（第4.4款），项目中所有材料、设备的采购也必须从开发银行规定的合格来源国采购（第4.1款），明确规定承包商为项目进口的专有施工设备应当免税（第14.1款）。这些规定了反映了多边开发银行贷款项目的习惯做法，也反映了贷款项目的某种政策指向。

(3) 程序上更严密，更有操作性

在1999年FIDIC合同条件中，虽然有些地方对承包商可以索赔利润作出了规定，但没有规定利润时，利润按"费用"的5%来计算，1999年合同条件中，对合同价格在执行过程中发生变化情况，FIDIC对是否调整履约保函的额度没有明确的规定，这在实践中容易带来问题，和谐版本中，对此类情况进行了补充规定，即若合同执行过程中的变更导致合同中采用一种货币支付的那部分合同价格增加或降低了25%，则履约保函的额度应作相应调整。另外，和谐版本进一步规定，若承包商对更换监理工程师提出反对意见，只要有证据，雇主应予以公平合理地考虑，上述和谐版本中的补充规定，无疑大大增加了实践中操作的可行性。

2. FIDIC《设计-建造-运行》（DBO）合同

FIDIC于2008年9月在加拿大魁北克省举行的2008年会期间推出被国际工程界冠之为"金皮书"的DBO合同（Conditions of Contract for Design, Build and Operate Projects）（First Edition，2008）。

《设计-建造-运行》（DBO）合同承包方式是将设计、建造、设施长期运行（和维护）整合到一个合同中授予一个承包商（一般是具有设计、建造、运行要求的专业及技能的联营体或联合体）。首先，合同安排的形式可以基于"新建（或绿地）"模式（DBO），或者是基于"非新建（或褐地）"模式（ODB）。两种方式十分相同，可是合同安排和程序却十分不同。现在的DBO合同基于"新建（或绿地）"模式来编制DBO合同文件，对"非新建（或褐地）"模式条款所必须的变化在FIDIC"金皮书"《DBO合同指南》（下称《指南》）中作出说明；其次，现在DBO合同作出了20年运营期的规定，如果要求运营的时间短的话，《指南》中有进一步说明。

由于缺少标准格式合同，DBO合同多半是根据FIDIC黄皮书或橙皮书作大量修改或定制。虽然黄皮书或橙皮书（以及银皮书）充分涵盖了DBO合同的设计和施工方面，但FIDIC没有一个文件涉及与该类合同所包含的长期运营相关的风险和责任。所以，DBO合同的重心是在"运营"这个环节，取向是鼓励承包商设计运营一肩挑。

DBO模式是承包商设计并建设一个公共设施或基础设施，并且运营该设施，满足在工程使用期间公共部门的运营要求，承包商负责设施的维修保养，以及更换在合同期内已经超过其使用期的资产。该合同期满后，资产所有权移交回公共部门。与传统的设计-施工方式相比，DBO模式的主要特征是：承包商不仅承担设施的设计施工，在移交给雇主之前的一段时间内，还要负责其所建设施的运营。

DBO架构下，融资是由公共部门负责，所以DBO的承包商没有融资风险；DBO合同下，项目所有权始终归公共部门所有。承包商收回成本的唯一途径就是公共部门的付款，当然以其提供必须符合公共部门预先设定的产量及规范为前提。

DBO合同最大优势是优化项目的全寿命周期成本。从时间角度看，DBO合同可以减少不必要的延误，使施工的周期更为合理；从质量角度看，DBO合同可以保证项目质量长期的可靠性；从财务角度看，DBO合同下仅需要承担简单的责任而同时拥有长期的承诺保障。因此，DBO合同对于工程项目，特别是大型工程项目，可以简化项目程序、保证质量、优化全寿命周期成本，具有广阔的应用前景。对雇主而言，不仅可以优化全寿命周期成本，还可以向雇主提供可靠的有效率的技术创新。

2008年第一版DBO新合同文件编排遵循了先前FIDIC文件20条的传统编排及布局，DBO合同采取了同银皮书类似的结构，即雇主、承包商和雇主代表作为主要当事人，同样，合同中也包含了"次要当事人"：银行、保险经纪人、争议裁决委员会等。DBO合同针对1999版的合同对部分条款及条款布局进行了调整，部分原因是DBO合同的性质及内容，部分原因是对1999版文件结构的改善。虽然，新文件遵循了同样传统方式，尝试着继续提供已被全世界范围内的雇主和金融机构认同的公平和平衡的FIDIC合同文本，但是工作小组基于全世界范围用户的反馈，在新版DBO合同引入了许多改善之处。DBO新合同没有盲目地遵循1999版文件。新合同遵循1999版合同的哲学体系及编制体系，吸收了符合当今市场新的及现代的理念，其中改进最多的是处理及解决争议的条款，目的是避免争议而不是仅仅处理争议。同时，引入了新的条款来处理潜在争议。

四、FIDIC合同条件应用方式

FIDIC合同条件是在总结了各个国家、各个地区的雇主、咨询工程师和承包商各方经验基础上编制出来的，也是在长期的国际工程实践中形成并逐渐发展成熟起来的，是目前国际上广泛采用的高水平的、规范的合同条件。这些条件具有国际性、通用性和权威性。其合同条款公正合理，职责分明，程序严谨，易于操作。考虑到工程项目的一次性、唯一性等特点，FIDIC合同条件分成了"通用条件"（General Conditions）和"专用条件"（Conditions of Particular Application）两部分。通用条件适用于某一类工程。如红皮书适用于整个土木工程（包括工业厂房、公路、桥梁、水利、港口、铁路、房屋建筑等）。专用条件则针对一个具体的工程项目，是在考虑项目所在国法律法规不同、项目特点和雇主要求不同的基础上，对通用条件进行的具体化的修改和补充。

FIDIC合同条件的应用方式通常有如下几种：

（1）国际金融组织贷款和一些国际项目直接采用在世界各地，凡世界银行、亚洲开发银行、非洲开发银行贷款的工程项目以及一些国家和地区的工程招标文件中，大部分全文采用FIDIC合同条件。在我国，凡亚洲开发银行贷款项目，全文采用FIDIC红皮书。凡世界银行贷款项目，在执行世界银行有关合同原则的基础上，执行我国财政部在世界银行批准和指导下编制的有关合同条件。

（2）合同管理中对比分析使用

许多国家在学习、借鉴FIDIC合同条件的基础上，编制了一系列适合本国国情的标准合同条件。这些合同条件的项目和内容与FIDIC合同条件大同小异。主要差异体现在处理问题的程序规定上以及风险分担规定上。FIDIC合同条件的各项程序是相当严谨的，处理雇主和承包商风险、权利及义务也比较公正。因此，雇主、咨询工程师、承包商通常都会将FIDIC合同条件作为一把尺子，与工作中遇到的其他合同条件相对比，进行合同分析和风险研究，制定相应的合同管理措施，防止合同管理上出现漏洞。

（3）在合同谈判中使用

FIDIC合同条件的国际性、通用性和权威性使合同双方在谈判中可以以"国际惯例"为理由要求对方对其合同条款的不合理、不完善之处作出修改或补充，以维护双方的合法权益。这种方式在国际工程项目合同谈判中普遍使用。

(4) 部分选择使用

即使不全文采用 FIDIC 合同条件，在编制招标文件、分包合同条件时，仍可以部分选择其中的某些条款、某些规定、某些程序甚至某些思路，使所编制的文件更完善、更严谨。在项目实施过程中，也可以借鉴 FIDIC 合同条件的思路和程序来解决和处理有关问题。

需要说明的是，FIDIC 在编制各类合同条件的同时，还编制了相应的"应用指南"。在"应用指南"中，除了介绍招标程序、合同各方及工程师职责外，还对合同每一条款进行了详细解释和说明，这对使用者是很有帮助的。另外，每份合同条件的前面均列有有关措词的定义和释义。这些定义和释义非常重要，它们不仅适合于合同条件，也适合于其全部合同文件。

Ⅲ FIDIC 施工合同（新红皮书）的主要内容

《土木工程施工合同条件》，又称为 FIDIC "红皮书"，是进行土木建筑类工程项目建设，由雇主通过竞争性招标选择承包商承包，并委托监理工程师执行监督管理的标准化合同文件范本。为了区别于旧版的红皮书，习惯将应用最为广泛的 1999 年施工合同条件称为新红皮书。新红皮书涉及的合同文件包括：合同协议书、中标函、投标函及投标函附录、补充文件、合同条件、规范、图纸、资历表、合同协议书或中标函中列出的其他文件（如果有）。其中"合同条件"又分为通用条件和专用条件两部分。通用条件是 FIDIC 合同条件的第一部分，具有广泛适用性，可以直接放入工程项目的招标文件中。专用条件是根据工程项目的专业特点及工程所在地的政治、经济、法律、自然条件等特点，针对通用条件中条款的规定加以具体说明。专用条件可以对通用条件中的规定进行完善、修订、删减和增补。专用条件中条款的序号与通用条件中的相关条款序号对应，共同构成对某一问题的约定责任。本书的第二部分对通用条件进行了详细的阐述和说明。

新红皮书的通用条件共 20 条 163 款。概括了工程项目施工阶段雇主、承包商双方的主要权利和义务，工程师的主要职责与权利，各种可能预见事件发生的责任界限，正常履行合同过程中各方应遵守的工程程序，以及因意外事件而使合同被迫终止时各方应遵守的工作准则。

新红皮书通用条件的主要内容为：

1. 一般规定（General Provisions）

本条共有 14 个子款，包括：本合同条件中关键术语的规定、合同条件的组成及优先顺序、文件的提供照管及版权、保密规定和权益转让、合同语言、法律、联合承包等。具体内容有：

1.1 定义；1.2 解释；1.3 通信交流；1.4 法律和语言；1.5 文件优先次序；1.6 合同协议书；1.7 权益转让；1.8 文件的照管和提供；1.9 延误的图纸或指示；1.10 雇主使用承包商文件；1.11 承包商使用雇主文件；1.12 保密事项；1.13 遵守法律；1.14 共同的和各自的责任。

2. 雇主（The Employer）

本条共 5 款，规定了 FIDIC 施工合同中雇主的基本义务和权利，包括：雇主向承包商提供施工现场的义务、雇主向承包商提供的协助和配合义务、承包商对雇主资金安排的知情权、雇主的索赔权及应遵循的程序。具体内容有：

2.1 现场进入权；2.2 许可、执照或批准；2.3 雇主人员；2.4 雇主的资金安排；2.5 雇主的索赔。

3. 工程师（The Engineer）

本条共 5 款，规定了工程师的权力、义务和职责，包括工程师如何委托其权力给工程师助理、工程师如何下达指令、雇主更换工程师的限定、工程师进行确定时的程序。具体内容有：

3.1 工程师的任务和权力；3.2 由工程师付托；3.3 工程师的指示；3.4 工程师的替换；3.5 确定。

4. 承包商（The Contractor）

本条共 24 款，规定了 FIDIC 施工合同中承包商的基本义务和权利，包括：承包商的基本合同义务、履约保证的相关规定、承包商代表的要求、分包和权益转让的规定、承包商与其他人员的合作、现场放线的规定、承包商在现场管理中所承担的责任和享有的权利、进度报告的内容及提交程序等。具体内容有：

4.1 承包商的一般义务；4.2 履约担保；4.3 承包商代表；4.4 分包商；4.5 分包合同权益的转让；4.6 合作；4.7 放线；4.8 安全程序；4.9 质量保证；4.10 现场数据；4.11 中标合同金额的充分性；4.12 不可预见的物质条件；4.13 道路通行权和设施；4.14 避免干扰；4.15 进场通路；4.16 货物运输；4.17 承包商设备；4.18 环境保护；4.19 电、水和燃气；4.20 雇主设备和免费供应的材料；4.21 进度报告；4.22 现场保安；4.23 承包商的现场作业；4.24 化石。

5. 指定的分包商（Nominated Subcontractor）

本条共 4 款，规定了指定分包商的定义、承包商拒绝指定分包商的情形、承包商对指定分包商付款的注意事项。具体内容有：

5.1."指定的分包商"的定义；5.2 反对指定；5.3 对指定的分包商付款；5.4 付款证据。

6. 员工（Staff and Labour）

本条共 11 款，规定了承包商雇用职员和劳工时应注意的问题、承包商按要求为雇主方人员提供设施、对承包商遵守劳动法及工作时间的要求、承包商施工期间日常管理工作的要求、承包商人员的技术水平与职业道德要求等。具体内容有：

6.1 员工的雇用；6.2 工资标准和劳动条件；6.3 为雇主服务的人员；6.4 劳动法；6.5 工作时间；6.6 为员工提供设施；6.7 健康和安全；6.8 承包商的监督；6.9 承包商人员；6.10 承包商人员和设备的记录；6.11 无序行为。

7. 生产设备、材料和工艺（Plant, Materials and Workmanship）

本条共 8 款，内容包括承包商实施工程的相关规定、雇主人员的现场检查和检验、工程师对工程的拒收、不合格工程的返工、有关矿区使用费的规定等。具体内容有：

7.1 实施方法；7.2 样品；7.3 检验；7.4 试验；7.5 拒收；7.6 修补工作；7.7 生产设备和材料的所有权；7.8 土地（矿区）使用费。

8. 开工、延误和暂停（Commencement, Delays and Suspension）

本条共 12 款，规定了工程开工日期和竣工日期的确定方法、工程进度计划的编制要求、承包商的工期索赔和工程误期损害的补偿、暂停和复工的有关规定等。具体内容有：

8.1 工程的开工；8.2 竣工时间；8.3 进度计划；8.4 竣工时间的延长；8.5 当局造成的延误；8.6 工程进度；8.7 误期损害赔偿费；8.8 暂时停工；8.9 暂停的后果；8.10 暂停时对生产设备和材料的付款；8.11 拖长的暂停；8.12 复工。

9. 竣工试验（Tests on Completion）

本条共 4 款，规定了承包商在竣工试验中的义务、竣工试验延误时各方的责任、竣工试验未通过的处理方式等。具体内容有：

9.1 承包商的义务；9.2 延误的试验；9.3 重新试验；9.4 未能通过竣工试验。

10. 雇主的接收（Employer's Taking Over）

本条共 4 款，规定了雇主接收工程和单位工程的条件、承包商获得接收证书的程序、雇主接收部分工程的限制条件和处理方法、雇主对竣工试验干扰时应承担的责任等。具体内容有：

10.1 工程和单位工程的接收；10.2 部分工程的接收；10.3 对竣工试验的干扰；10.4 需要复原的地面。

11. 缺陷责任（Defect Liability）

本条共 11 款，规定了承包商在缺陷责任期限内的主要责任、修补缺陷费用的处理方法、延长缺陷责任期限的条件、签发履约证书的条件、履约证书颁发后承包商的工程等。具体内容有：

11.1 完成扫尾工作和修补缺陷；11.2 修补缺陷的费用；11.3 缺陷通知期限的延长；11.4 未能修补缺陷；11.5 移出有缺陷的工程；11.6 进一步试验；11.7 进入权；11.8 承包商调查；11.9 履约证书；11.10 未履行的义务；11.11 现场清理。

12. 测量和估价（Measurement and Evaluation）

本条共 4 款，规定了实际工程的测量方法和程序、承包商所完成工作的估价、有关工作的删减等。具体内容有：

12.1 需测量的工程；12.2 测量方法；12.3 估价；12.4 删减

13. 变更和调整（Variations and Adjustment）

本条共 8 款，规定了工程师的变更权、承包商的变更建议权、承包商对价值工程的运用、暂列金额的支付规定、法律改变对工程费用和工期的调整、物价波动对工程费用和工期的调整等。具体内容有：

13.1 变更权；13.2 价值工程；13.3 变更程序；13.4 以适用货币支付；13.5 暂列金额；13.6 计日工作；13.7 因法律改变的调整；13.8 因成本改变的调整。

14. 合同价格和付款（Contract Price and Payment）

本条共 15 款，规定了合同价格的确定和调整方法、预付款的支付和扣除、期中支付证书和最终支付证书的签发、材料和生产设备款的支付、付款时间和延误付款的处理、保留金的扣留和退还、支付货币的种类和比例等。具体内容有：

14.1 合同价格；14.2 预付款；14.3 期中付款证书的申请；14.4 付款计划表；14.5 拟用于工程的生产设备和材料；14.6 期中付款证书的颁发；14.7 付款；14.8 延误的付款；14.9 保留金的支付；14.10 竣工报表；14.11 最终付款证书的申请；14.12 结清证明；14.13 最终付款证书的颁发；14.14 雇主责任的终止；14.15 支付的货币。

15. 由雇主终止（Termination by Employer）

本条共 5 款，规定了导致雇主终止合同的承包商违约行为、雇主终止合同的程序、雇主终止合同后对承包商已完工作的估价和支付、雇主终止合同的权利等。具体内容有：

15.1 通知改正；15.2 由雇主终止；15.3 终止日期时的估价；15.4 终止后的付款；15.5 雇主终止的权利。

16. 由承包商暂停和终止（Suspension and Termination by Contractor）

本条共 4 款，规定了承包商可暂停工作或放缓进度的情形、导致承包商终止合同的雇主行为、承包商终止合同后应尽的义务、终止合同后雇主对承包商的付款等。具体内容有：

  16.1 承包商暂停工作的权利；16.2 由承包商终止；16.3 停止工作和承包商设备的撤离；16.4 终止时的付款。

17. 风险与职责（Risk and Responsibility）

  本条共 6 款，规定了雇主和承包商互为保障的权利、工程照管的责任、雇主风险及其后果的处理、工程知识产权和工业产权的保护、合同双方的赔偿责任等。具体内容有：

  17.1 保障；17.2 承包商对工程的照管；17.3 雇主的风险；17.4 雇主风险的后果；17.5 知识产权与工业产权；17.6 责任限度。

18. 保险（Insurance）

  本条共 4 款，规定了保险投保方投保的程序和要求、工程和承包商设备的保险要求、第三方人员和财产的保险要求、承包商人员的保险要求。具体内容有：

  18.1 有关保险的一般规定；18.2 工程和承包商设备的保险；18.3 人身伤害和财产损害保险；18.4 承包商人员的保险。

19. 不可抗力（Force Majeure）

  本条共 7 款，规定了不可抗力的概念、不可抗力发生后各方的责任、不可抗力导致终止合同的处理方法、法律因素导致合同解除的处理方法。具体内容有：

  19.1 不可抗力的定义；19.2 不可抗力的通知；19.3 将延误减至最小的义务；19.4 不可抗力的后果；19.5 不可抗力影响分包商；19.6 自主选择终止、付款和解除；19.7 根据法律解除履约。

20. 索赔、争端和仲裁（Claims，Disputers and Arbitration）

  本条共 8 款，规定了承包商索赔的程序、争端委员会的组成和运行机制、仲裁的前提、仲裁解决争端的规则和程序、解决争端的途径。具体内容有：

  20.1 承包商的索赔；20.2 争端裁决委员会的任命；20.3 对争端裁决委员会未能取得一致；20.4 取得争端裁决委员会的决定；20.5 友好解决；20.6 仲裁；20.7 未能遵守争端裁决委员会的决定；20.8 争端裁决委员会任命期满。

Ⅳ 国际其他施工合同文本

一、ICE 合同范本

英国建筑业编制工程合同范本的机构主要有两个：英国土木工程师学会（Institution of Civil Engineer，ICE）和英国合同审定联合会（Joint Contracts Tribunal，JCT）。ICE 创建于 1818 年，是英国代表土木工程师的学术中心、资质评定组织及专业代表机构，拥有会员 8 万多名，其中五分之一在英国以外的 140 多个国家和地区，具有较高的国际影响力，ICE 在土木工程建设合同方面具有高度的权威性，它编制的土木工程合同条件在土木工程中具有广泛的应用，是知名国际工程合同范本之一。

ICE 第一版施工合同条件出版于 1945 年，目前最新版本是 1999 年出版的第七版。多年来，ICE 编制出版的合同范本应用广泛，影响力最大的是适用于土木工程施工的《ICE 合同条件，工程计量模式》（ICE Conditions of Contract，Measurement Version，7th Edition）。早期的 FIDIC 合同条件主要是基于 ICE 合同条件的框架制定的，世界各国编制合同范本时也都参考借鉴了 ICE 合同条件的相关内容。

第七版《ICE 合同条件，工程计量模式》主要内容包括：工程师及工程师代表；转让与分包；合同文件；承包商的一般义务；保险；工艺与材料质量的检查；开工、延期与暂停；变更、增加与删除；材料及承包商设备的所有权；计量；证书与支付；争端的解决；特殊用途条款；投标书格式。此外，IEC 合同条件的最后附有投标书格式、投标书格式附件、协议书格式、履约保证等文件。

二、NEC（New Engineering Contract）合同范本

1993 年，ICE 研究制定了一套新型合同范本，称为"新合同条件"（New Engineering Contract，NEC），之后逐渐形成了一系列的合同范本。最新版的 NEC 系列合同范本是出版于 2005 年的第三版，简称 NEC3，其中包含 6 类合同文件：

（1）工程施工合同（Engineering and Construction Contract，ECC）：适用于雇主负责设计的施工合同，也适用于由承包商负责设计工作的合同。ECC 代表了 NEC 合同范本的核心思想，是整个 NEC 合同理论的基础。

（2）专业服务合同（Professional Service Contract，PSC）：适用于雇用专业咨询人员、项目经理、设计师、工程师等专业技术人员或机构。

（3）工程施工简明合同（Engineering and Construction Short Contract，ECSC）：适用于结构简单，风险较低，对项目管理要求不过高的工程。

（4）合同争议评判员合同（Adjudicator's Contract）：适用于雇主聘任合同争议评判员的合同。

(5) 定期服务合同（Term Service Contract）：适用于采购有固定期限的服务的合同。

(6) 框架合同（Framework Contract）：适用于雇主和承包商在完全确定工作内容前确定其工作关系的合同。

新合同范本 NEC 中 ECC 最具有代表性，ECC 合同虽然是标准合同，但它比较灵活，可以以不同的形式出现，其合同结构主要由核心条件、主要选项条件、次要选项条件、费用构成表和合同资料表等组成。具体内容可分为四部分：

1. ECC 核心条款

合同第一部分是 ECC 核心条款，是所有合同形式都必须有的条款，包括：总则、承包商的主要职责、工期、测试和缺陷、付款、补充事件、所有权、风险和保险、争端和合同终止。

2. ECC 主要选项

合同第二部分是 ECC 主要选项，不同选项对应不同的合同策略。雇主准备招标文件时，在不同项目风险分担和工程款支付方式下，可根据自身的管理能力和项目的具体情况，通过对主要选项的选择决定相应的合同模式。任何合同形式必须且只能选择一种主要选项，选定后会并入核心条款。主要选项有：

(1) 选项 A. 带分项工程表的标准合同（Priced Contract with Activity Schedule），适用于雇主能够给承包商确定工作范围的工程项目，其设计工作可能未全部完成，但需要雇主说明具体需求。此合同中每个分项工程都必须按照总价填写，承包商完成该分项工程即可得到付款，付款金额不会因工程量变化而改变。这种模式下，承包商要对分项工程表的准确性负责，承担较多风险。

(2) 选项 B. 带工程量清单的标准合同（Priced Contract with Bill of Quantities），适用于传统工程采购模式，雇主施工招标前已基本完成工程设计，合同双方将按照约定好的价格实施工程。此时合同形式为总价合同，承包商承担较多风险，雇主则需要对其提供的工程量清单的准确性负责。

(3) 选项 C. 带分项工程表的目标合同（Target Contract with Activity Schedule），适用于工作范围详细程度已足以让承包商提供报价的项目，采用成本加固定费用方式签订合同。承包商的投标报价即为目标成本，费用超支或节约时，雇主和承包商将会按照约定的方式进行分摊。此类合同形式下，合同双方均会致力于降低工程成本，而承包商要对分项工程表的准确性负责。

(4) 选项 D. 带工程量清单的目标合同（Target Contract with Bill of Quantities），适用于雇主和承包商有意愿通过利益共享机制进行合作的项目。此类合同形式下，由于项目可能未明确定义工作范围或预期设计变更的可能性较大，降低工程成本是双方共同目标，而雇主主要对工程量清单的准确性负责。

(5) 选项 E. 成本补偿合同（Cost Reimbursable Contract），适用于工期紧、质量要求较高的工程。在工作范围无法确定时，承包商要求按成本加固定费率获得管理费和酬金时，此类合同形式尤其适用。此类合同形式不利于节约工程成本，雇主承担较大的财务风险。

(6) 选项 F. 管理合同（Management Contract），适用于全部工程合同在管理承包商和工程承包商之间签订，设计、施工、安装工作全部分包的项目。管理承包商代表雇主进行工程管理,承包商获得实际成本另加一定比例费用的支付,雇主承担大部分财务风险,工程成本可能超支。

3. ECC 次要选项条款

合同第三部分是次要选项,ECC3 中共设计 18 个次要选项条款,雇主在准备合同文件时,可以根据具体情况,任意选择次要选项,也可以不选。次要选项包括:

X1. 为通胀引起调价(Price Adjustment for Inflation);X2. 法律的变化(Change in the Law);X3. 多种货币(Multiple Currencies);X4. 母公司担保(Parent Company Guaranties);X5. 区段竣工(Sectional Completion);X6. 提前竣工奖金(Bonus for Early Completion);X7. 延期损害赔偿(Delay Damages);X12. 伙伴合作协议(Partnering Agreement);X13. 履约保证(Performance Bond);X14. 支付承包商预付款(Advanced Payment to the Contractor);X15. 承包商在合理的技术和谨慎的限度下,为设计承担的责任(Limitation of the Contractor's Liability for His Design to Reasonable Skill and Care);X16. 保留金(Retention);X17. 缺陷履行的损害赔偿(Low Performance Damage);X18. 有限责任(Limitation of Liability);X20. 主要履行裁决人(Key Performance Indicators);Z. 附加合同条件(Additional Conditions of Contract)。

4. 费用构成表和合同资料表

三、JCT 合同范本

英国合同审定联合会 JCT 组建于 1931 年,其创始机构是英国皇家建筑师学会和全国建筑职业联合会。JCT 建立的主要目的是制定并修改标准化的建筑施工合同。JCT 合同体系有 1998 年版标准化格式合同和 2005 年版合同族,常用于房屋建筑项目中。2005 年版合同族中,每一合同类型均包括主合同和分包合同标准文本及其他跨域不同合同版本的标准文件。主要合同类型及其合同义件包括:

(1) 小型工程建筑合同(Minor Works Building Contract);
(2) 中型工程建筑合同(Intermediate Building Contract);
(3) 标准建筑合同(Standard Building Contract,分为有工程量清单、有估计工程量、无工程量清单三种);
(4) 设计建造合同(Design Build Contract);
(5) 大型工程合同(Major Project Construction Contract);
(6) JCT 高绩效伙伴合同(JCT-Constructing Excellence Contract);
(7) 施工管理专业合同(Construction Management Trade Contract);
(8) 管理建筑合同(Management Building Contract);
(9) 住宅许可工程建筑合同(Housing Grant Works Building Contract);
(10) 测量条件合同(Measured Term Contract);
(11) 成本加酬金建筑合同(Prime Cost Building Contract);
(12) 修复和维护合同(Repair and Maintenance Contract);
(13) 框架协议(Framework Agreement);
(14) 合同争议评判员协议(Adjudication Agreement)。

四、AIA 合同范本

美国建筑师协会（American Institute of Architects，AIA）成立于 1857 年，是美国主要的建筑师专业组织，其编制的一系列标准合同范本在美国建筑业及国际工程承包界具有较高的通用性和权威性。AIA 在 1911 年首次出版了"建筑施工通用条件"（General Conditions for Construction），随后进行多次修订和补充，已形成包括 90 多份独立文件的复杂体系。2007 年，AIA 对整个合同文件体系的编号系统和内容进行了较大规模的调整，根据文件性质不同分成六个系列：

A 系列：雇主与总承包商、CM 经理、供应商之间，总承包商与分包商之间的合同文件；施工合同通用条件以及与招标投标有关的文件；

B 系列：雇主与建筑师之间的合同文件；

C 系列：建筑师与专业咨询机构之间的合同文件；

D 系列：建筑师行业有关文件；

E 系列：电子文件协议附件；

G 系列：合同和办公管理中使用的文件。

AIA 合同范本的主要特点是为各种工程项目管理模式制定了不同的协议书，而同时把通用条件单独出版称为独立文件。AIA－A201－2007 是 AIA 系列合同条件中专用施工合同通用条件，共 12 条，主要内容包括：

1. 雇主

本条共 4 款，内容包括：雇主定义；雇主向承包商提供资料与服务的义务；雇主停工及自行施工的权利。

2. 承包商

本条共 17 款，内容包括：承包商的定义；承包商的一般义务；施工过程中承包商与雇主及其他承包商的协调关系；保护人员与财产义务。

3. 建筑师

本条共 2 款，内容包括：建筑师的角色及其权利义务。

4. 分包商

本条共 4 款，内容包括：对合同中分包商角色的定义；分包商的权利和义务。

5. 工程变更

本条共 4 款，内容包括：工程变更三种主要形式；变更命令；施工变更指示；次要工程变更的相关规定。

6. 工期

本条共 3 款，内容包括：合同工期的规定；工期延误及索赔等。

7. 支付与竣工

本条共 10 款，内容包括：支付的申请；支付证书的规定；支付的程序；实质性竣工与最终竣工的规定。

8. 保险与保函

本条共 4 款，内容包括：承包商的责任保险；雇主的责任保险；财产保险；履约担保与支付担保的规定。

9. 剥离检查与缺陷改正

　　本条共 3 款，内容包括：对工程剥离检查的规定；缺陷改正的要求；雇主接收不符合要求的工程。

10. 其他条款

　　本条共 7 款，内容包括：对合同适用法律的规定；继承人与受让人的角色；测试与检查；利息与法律时效等。

11. 合同终止和暂停

　　本条共 3 款，内容包括：承包商终止合同的权利和义务；雇主出于合理原因及其他原因终止合同的规定。

12. 索赔与争端的解决

　　本条共 4 款，内容包括：索赔的提出与索赔内容的规定；通过初始裁定解决争议的规定；调解和仲裁的相关规定。

第二部分　FIDIC施工合同条件解读与分析

1　Generally Provision（一般规定）

施工合同当事人应当在施工合同中明确一些主要内容，如工程范围、建设工期、合同价款、开工和竣工时间、资料交付时间、材料和设备供应、付款和结算、竣工验收、质量要求和保修范围、缺陷责任、变更和调整、风险和索赔以及其他注意事项等内容。FIDIC施工合同条件第1条［一般规定］的14个子款涵盖了以上贯穿整个施工合同的核心内容。

本章要求：熟悉本合同条件中关键术语的含义；
　　　　　　了解合同文件的组成；
　　　　　　了解合同双方沟通信息和文件颁发的规则；
　　　　　　了解合同语言和法律的规定，以及联合承包的规定。

1.1　Definitions（定义）

In the Conditions of Contract（"these Conditions"），which include Particular Conditions（专用条件）and these General Conditions（通用条件），the following words and expressions shall have the meanings stated. Words indicating persons or parties include corporations and other legal entities，except where the context requires otherwise.

定义，其目的是要清楚地规范事物的内涵与外延，特别是其外延。对名词的外延范围和边界解释有误，必然会导致合同理解的偏差。

FIDIC施工合同条件包括通用条件和专用条件两部分。通用条件适合整个土木工程，是对某一类工程都通用的条件，包括房屋建筑、工业厂房、公路、桥梁、水利、港口、铁路等类型的土木工程。专用条件是针对一个具体的工程项目，考虑到各个国家和地区的法律法规的不同、项目特点和雇主对合同实施要求的不同，对通用条件进行具体化、针对性地修改和补充。FIDIC施工合同条件的通用条件中共有58个定义，其术语可分为6大类，包括各种合同文件、项目参与各方、日期与竣工、款项与支付、工程和货物以及其他定义。这些定义基本覆盖了合同文件中的核心术语。专用条件中的条款序号和通用条件的相应条款互相对应，定义和用语也应与通用条件保持一致。

1.1.1　The Contract（合同）

1.1.1.1 "**Contract**" means the Contract Agreement（合同协议书），*the Letter of Acceptance*（中标函），*the Letter of Tender*（投标函），*these Conditions*（条件），*the Specification*（规范要求），*the Drawings*（图纸），*the Schedules*（资料表），*and the further documents*（*if any*）*which are listed in the Contract Agreement or in the Letter of Acceptance.*

本款说明了合同的主要组成要件。合同包括合同协议书、中标函、投标函、规范要求、图纸和资料等内容。此外，补充协议、来往信函、备忘录、会议纪要、合同协议书或者中标函中列明的其他文件也属于合同文件的范畴。合同规定属于合同组件的文件即为合同的一部分，该文件涵盖的内容就是合同涵盖的范围。一经列入合同的文件都具有法律效力。

1.1.1.2 "**Contract Agreement（合同协议书）**" *means the contract agreement（if any）referred to in Sub-Clause 1.6 [Contract Agreement].*

合同协议书是合同当事人为明确双方享受的权利和应尽的义务而达成的协议。合同协议书由合同双方按照相关法律法规订立，以双方共同遵守为前提，因此双方签订合同协议书时应遵循自愿、平等、公平、诚实、信用的原则。

FIDIC施工合同条件的合同协议书无需详尽列明每一项合同条款，但是应明确合同双方当事人、合同标的物、合作范围、合作期限、合同价款、工程款结算方式、合同组件及其解释程序、双方权利与义务及违约责任，以及其他的特定承诺项目等内容。除非另有协议说明，否则双方应在承包商收到中标函后28天内签订合同协议书（详细解释参见第1.6款［合同协议书］）。

FIDIC施工合同条件附录中列有合同协议书的推荐格式，供合同当事人选择使用。见例1.1。

【例1.1】CONTRACT AGREEMENT

This Agreement made the ＿＿＿＿ day of ＿＿＿＿ Between ＿＿＿＿ of ＿＿＿＿ (hereinafter called "the Employer") of the one part, and ＿＿＿＿ of ＿＿＿＿ (hereinafter called "the Contractor") of the other part.

Whereas the Employer desires that the Works known as ＿＿＿＿ should be executed by the Contractor, and has accepted a Tender by the Contractor for the execution and completion of these Works and the remedying of any defects therein,

The Employer and the Contractor agree as follows:

1. In this Agreement words and expressions shall have the same meanings as are respectively assigned to them in the Conditions of Contract hereinafter referred to.

2. The following documents shall be deemed to form and be read and construed as part of this Agreement:

(a) The Letter of Acceptance dated ＿＿＿＿
(b) The Letter of Tender dated ＿＿＿＿
(c) The Addenda nos ＿＿＿＿
(d) The Conditions of Contract
(e) The Specification
(f) The Drawings, and
(g) The completed Schedules.

3. In consideration of the payments to be made by the Employer to the Contractor as hereinafter mentioned, the Contractor hereby covenants with the Employer to execute and complete the Works and remedy any defects therein, in conformity with the provisions of the Contract.

4. The Employer hereby covenants to pay the Contractor, in consideration of the execution and completion of the Works and the remedying of defects therein, the Contract Price at the times and in the manner prescribed by the Contract.

In Witness whereof the parties hereto have caused this Agreement to be executed the day and year first before written in accordance with their respective laws.

SIGNED by：
for and on behalf of the Employer in the presence of

Witness：
Name：
Address：
Date：

SIGNED by：
for and on behalf of the Contractor in the presence of

Witness：
Name：
Address：
Date：

1.1.1.3 "***Letter of Acceptance（中标函）***" *means the letter of formal acceptance，signed by the Employer（雇主），of the Letter of Tender，including any annexed memoranda（备忘录）comprising agreements between and signed by both Parties. If there is no such letter of acceptance，the expression "Letter of Acceptance" means the Contract Agreement and the date of issuing or receiving the Letter of Acceptance means the date of signing the Contract Agreement.*

中标函是雇主对投标文件签署的正式接收函，包括其后所附的备忘录（由合同各方达成并签订的协议构成）。中标函表明雇主不仅正式接受了承包商的投标函且已签字确认，这些内容必须由双方签字认可，并作为备忘录附在中标函后。

FIDIC合同非常重视证据，要求合同文本和重要信函都必须由签署方签字认可。中标函不只是雇主作为招标人通知承包商中标的书面凭证，更在实际项目的招标投标中具有重要的法律意义。按照工程合同"要约承诺制"，投标函是要约，中标函是承诺。中标函发出后，意味着要约承诺的法律过程生效，即合同已经生效，因此无论合同协议书是否签订都不影响中标函承诺已经兑现的法律效力。且在中标函发出后，除不可抗力因素外，雇主不可改变中标结果（如宣布该标为废标），也不可随意宣布取消项目招标。如果雇主违反此类招标原则，应以适用定金罚则返还中标人提交的投标保证金，若给中标人造成了超过返还数额的损失，还应对该超过部分予以赔偿。同样，如果中标人主动放弃中标项目（比如声明或者以自己的行为表明不承担该招标项目），雇主对其已经提交的投标保证金有权不予以退还，若给雇主造成了超过投标保证金数额的损失，中标人还应对超过部分予以赔偿。

FIDIC合同中的中标函内容仅包含中标工程名称及中标金额等简要说明，通常只是雇主向中标人（承包商）告知其已中标的信函，就是很多人理解上的"一页纸"。相对于中标函，国内术语"中标通知书"则更详细，包括了中标工程名称、中标价格、工程范围、工期、开工及竣工日期、质量要求等内容。由于术语的措辞不同，国内使用FIDIC合同时需要在本条款内容里对中标通知书的定义加以解释说明。

如果在整个合同文件中没有出现"中标函"这个术语，则该"中标函"就可理解为"合同协议书"，中标函的签发和接收日期可理解为合同协议书的签署日期。例1.2、例1.3、例1.4分别列出了英文和中文的中标函式样。

【例1.2】LETTER OF ACCEPTANCE

Letter of Acceptance

[on letterhead paper of the Employer]
___(Date)___

To: ___(name and address of the Contractor)___ Subject: Notification of Award Contract No ___(number)___

This is to notify you that your Bid dated ___(date)___ for ___(execution of the name of the contract and identification number)___, as given in the Contract Data for the Accepted Contract Amount of the equivalent of ___(amount in numbers and words and name of currency)___, as corrected and modified in accordance with the Instructions to Bidders is hereby accepted by our Agency.

You are requested to furnish the Performance Security within 28 days in accordance with the Conditions of Contract, using for the Performance Security Form included in Section 9 (Contract Forms) of the Bidding Document.

Authorized Signature: _____
Name and Title of Signatory: _____
Name of Agency: _____
Attachment: Contract Agreement

【例1.3】中标函1

中标函

XXXX建设公司：

你方于X月X日（投标日期）所递交的XXXXXX工程项目施工投标文件已被我方接受，被确定为中标人。

中标价：XXXXXXX元。

工期：XX日历天。

工程质量：符合合格标准。

建造师：XXX（姓名）。

请你方在接到本通知书后的7日内到XXXX（指定地点）与我方签订施工合同，在此之前按招标文件第二章"投标人须知"第7.3款规定向我方提交履约担保。以及必须通过基本账户以银行转账的方式缴入差额履约担保（低价风险担保）金的现金部分￥XXXXXXX元整，并同时提供金额为￥XXXXXXX元的保函。超出七日未缴纳差额履约担保金，招标人将取消其中标资格，按规定另行确定中标人并没收其投标保证金。户名：XXXX，开户银行：XXXX支行，账号：XXXXXXXXXXXXXX（缴纳差额履约担保金之前到XX建设指挥部办理相关手续）。

特此通知。

招标人：XXXXXX（盖单位章）
XX年X月X日

【例1.4】中标函2

中标函

XXXXXX公司：

根据XXXXXX项目招标文件和你公司于XXXX年X月X日提交的投标文件，经评标委员会按照《中华人民共和国招标投标法》和招标文件确定的评标标准和方法，已完成评审和中标公示，确定你公司中标。请收到本通知书后XX天内，到我单位签订建设工程施工合同。

招标人：（盖章）   代理机构：（盖章）

法定代表人：（盖章）　　　　　　　　法定代表人：（盖章）

XXXX 年 X 月 XX 日

中标内容及条件

招标编号：XXXXX

工程名称	XXXXXX 项目	标段	第 X 标段
中标内容	XXXXXX		
工程规模	同中标内容	工程特征	施工
中标工期	XXX 日历天	质量目标	合格
中标价（大写）		XXXXXXXXX	
注册建造师	XXX	证书编号	XXXXXX
项目技术负责人	XXX	职称	工程师
招标代理机构	XXXXXX 公司	招标方式	公开
备 注	安全文明施工措施费	XXXXXX	
	建设劳保费	XXXXXX	
招标投标监管部门意见	经审查，该项招标活动符合法定的招标方式和程序，准予备案。 监管单位：　　　（盖章）　　经办人：　　　（签字） 　　　　　　　　　　　　　　　　　　　　XXXX 年 X 月 X 日		

1.1.1.4 "***Letter of Tender（投标函）***" *means the document entitled letter of tender, which was completed by the Contractor（承包商）and includes the signed offer to the Employer for the Works（工程）.*

　　投标函是承包商按照招标文件的条件和要求，向雇主提交的有关报价、质量目标等承诺和说明的函件，是承包商对招标文件相关要求所做的概括性说明和承诺。作为投标书的核心部分，投标函一般位于投标书的首要部分。

　　雇主一般会在招标文件中拟定投标函的格式，由承包商填写后作为承包商的正式报价函提交，因此承包商提交的投标函格式、内容必须符合招标文件的规定。投标函及其附件应装入单独信封，按招标要求密封提交，也可与其他已经密封的文件同时密封于更大的密封袋或密封箱中提交。

　　国内工程中，投标函又称为投标书、投标申请书、标书、标函等。作为响应招标的函件，承包商应尽量在招标文件规定格式的投标函中明确表达投标意图，如果不能表达投标意图，也可另附补充说明。文字应简明扼要，概念术语应准确清晰，避免产生歧义和误解。

FIDIC 施工合同条件附录中列有投标函推荐格式,供合同当事人选择使用。见例1.5。

【例 1.5】LETTER OF TENDER

  NAME OF CONTRACT: _____ (name of the contract)

  TO: _____ (name of agency of the employer)

  We have examined the Conditions of Contract, Specification, Drawings, Bill of Quantities, the other Schedules, the attached Appendix and Addenda Nos _____ for the execution of the above—named Works. We offer to execute and complete the Works and remedy any defects therein in conformity with this Tender which includes all these documents, for the sum of (in currencies of payment) _____ _____ Or such sum as may be determined in accordance with the Conditions of Contract.

  We accept your suggestions for the appointment of the DAB, as set out in Schedule _____

  [*We have completed the Schedule by adding our suggestions for the other Member of the DAB, but these suggestions are not conditions of this offer*]. *

  We agree to abide by this Tender until _____ and it shall remain binding upon us and may be accept at any time before that date. We acknowledge that the Appendix forms part of this Letter of Tender.

  If this offer is accepted, we will provide the specified Performance Security, commence the Works as soon as is reasonably practicable after the Commencement Date, and complete the Works in accordance with the above—named documents within the Time for Completion.

  Unless and until a formal Agreement is prepared and executed this Letter of Tender, together with your written acceptance thereof, shall constitute a binding contract between us.

  We understand that you are not bound to accept the lowest or any tender you may receive.

  Signature _____ in the capacity of _____

_____ duly authorised to sign tenders for and on behalf of _____

  Address: _____

  Date: _____

  * If the Tender does not accept, this paragraph may be deleted and replaced by:

  We do not accept your suggestions for the appointment of the DAB. We have included our suggestions in the Schedule, but these suggestions are not conditions of this offer. If these suggestions are not acceptable to you, we propose that the DAB be jointly appointed in accordance with Sub-Clause 20.2 of the Conditions of Contract.

1.1.1.5 "*Specification(规范要求)*" means the document entitled specification, as included in the Contract, and any additions and modifications to the specification in accordance with the Contract. Such document specifies the Works.

  规范是明文规定或约定俗成的标准,具有明晰性和合理性,是合同的一个重要组成部分。它的功能是从技术方面对雇主招标的项目进行详细的描述,提出执行过程中的技术标准、程序等。

  在 FIDIC 施工合同条件中,"规范"主要是雇主提供设计的"工料规范",其中既包括雇主要求承包商在履行施工合同中应遵守的质量、安全、工艺、操作、程序等规定,也包括按照合同对这些规定所作的任何补充和修改。相对于合同条件而言，技术条款规定承包商应遵守的工艺标准和技术要求，而合同条件是法律条款（商务条款），承包商同样应遵守合同条件中对技术条款的补充说明。

承包商在计算投标价格及采购材料、设备之前，均需了解规范中的技术要求，在施工过程中更需要仔细研究规范内容。雇主和工程师应熟悉规范，以此作为管理承包商现场工作的基础，保证项目达到既定的要求和目标。

1.1.1.6 "*Drawings (图纸)*" means the drawings of the Works, as included in the Contract, and any additional and modified drawings issued by (or on behalf of), the Employer in accordance with the Contract.

"图纸"是合同中规定的施工图纸，或在工程实施过程中雇主对施工图纸的修改和补充。图纸是合同文件的一个组成部分，本款并未明确该图纸是基本设计图纸还是施工详图，这取决于合同中对图纸深度的规定。

在FIDIC施工合同条件中，图纸由雇主提供，雇主对图纸的合法性负责。这可避免承包商和设计单位串通变更，使雇主增加投资，达到不当获利的目的。按照由雇主提供图纸的规定，雇主可以通过设计合同明确设计单位的设计责任，当承包商要求变更时必须拿出"设计图纸不合理"的依据，凭此依据，雇主可追究设计单位的设计责任，很自然地就形成了设计合同与施工合同之间的相互制约，大大减小了雇主被两方联合操纵的可能。承包商虽然没有权利更改图纸内容，但可从自身的施工经验和实际操作性出发，对图纸提出变更建议。

雇主提供的图纸必须足够详细，以便投标人在阅读技术条款、工程量清单之后能够准确地确定合同所包括的工作性质和范围。在招标投标阶段，国外一般很少能够提供整套的完整图纸，大多数情况下都需要承包商在中标后，随着施工过程的进行而要求雇主提供进一步的图纸。国内对图纸的设计规范中没有提供"工料规范"的要求，即没有明确某项工艺的具体做法或某种材料的具体要求，对于造价工程师来说很难按图纸的规定来确定价格，国内在签订合同时必须附加"施工期材料价格审核"。

1.1.1.7 "*Schedules (资料表)*" means the document(s) entitled schedules, completed by the Contractor and submitted with the Letter of Tender, as included in the Contract. Such document may include the Bill of Quantities (工程量表), data, lists, and schedules of rates and/or prices.

资料表是合同中各种以列表形式表示的文件，包括工程量表、数据表、单价分析表、计日工表、表册、费率等。招标文件通常包含这些文件的空白格式，由投标人在投标时填写并随投标函一起提交。合同中应详细定义资料表文件具体的涵盖范围。

1.1.1.8 "*Tender (投标书)*" means the Letter of Tender and all other documents which the Contractor submitted with the Letter of Tender, as included in the Contract.

投标书是投标人投标时随投标函一起，应提交给雇主的构成合同文件的全部文件的总称。投标书分为两部分，一是作为核心文件的投标函，二是投标人根据招标文件要求填写完成的各类资料表（如工程量表、计日工作计划表、单价表）以及投标保函等。

投标书由投标人或投标人代表签字认可，并对雇主和承包商双方都具有法律约束力。它代表投标人提交的投标文件是在充分领会招标文件、进行现场实地考察和调查的基础上编制的，表明投标人对招标文件提出的要求作出响应和承诺。投标书应密封后邮寄或派专人送达雇主。

在实际工程中，一套完整的投标文件，不仅包括上述构成合同一部分的投标书，还包括许多其他文件。这些文件可以看作投标书的辅助部分，通常包括雇主要求投标人提供的其他信息，如工程初步进度计划、施工方法总说明、分包计划、施工设备清单、关键职员名单、劳工组成、承包商现场组织机构图、施工场地安排等。但该辅助部分不一定构成合同文件，参见第1.1.1.1款［合同］及第1.1.1.2款［合同协议书］的规定。

1.1.1.9 "***Appendix to Tender（投标书附录）***" *means the completed pages entitled appendix to tender which are appended to and form part of the Letter of Tender.*

投标书附录是对合同条件规定的重要要求的具体化文件，表明投标人已认真阅读招标文件、理解招标文件要求，已根据招标文件的要求提出报价，承诺履行和承担招标文件要求的义务和责任。投标书附录一般以表格形式将合同条件中的核心内容简单列出，并给出在合同条件中相对应的条款号。

投标书附录一般附于投标函之后，也属于合同文件。雇主可以在招标时将某些要求写在投标书附录中，由此构成招标要求的一部分，投标人必须接受提出的这些要求，如有疑问可以在招标答疑中要求雇主澄清。一旦雇主澄清条款要求后，投标人必须进行实质性响应。投标人填报投标函附录时，可在满足招标文件实质性要求的基础上，提出比招标文件的要求更有利于雇主的承诺，这就要求投标人在投标时应仔细研究投标书附录的要求。FIDIC合同要求投标书附录页页签字，这些细节反映了合同的严密性。

FIDIC施工合同条件附录中列有投标书推荐格式，供合同当事人选择使用。见例1.6。

【例1.6】APPENDIX TO TENDER

Item	Sub-Clause	Data
Employer's name and address	1.1.2.2 & 1.3	
Contractor's name and address	1.1.2.3 & 1.3	
Engineer's name and address	1.1.2.4 & 1.3	
Time for Completion of the Works	1.1.3.3	days
Defects Notification Period	1.1.3.7	365 days
Electronic transmission systems	1.3	
Governing Law	1.4	
Ruling Language	1.4	
Language for communications	1.4	
Time for access to the Site	2.1	days after Commencement Date
Amount of Performance Security	4.2	% of the Accepted Contract

1 Generally Provision (一般规定)

	Amount, in the currencies and proportions in which the Contract Price is payable
Normal working hours	6.5 _____
Delay damages for the Works	8.7 _____ ‰ of the final Contract Price per day, in the currencies and proportions in which the Contract is payable
Maximum amount of delay damages	8.7 _____ ‰ of the final Contract Price
If there are Provisional Sums: Percentage for adjustment of Provisional Sums	13.5 (b) _____ %
Initials of signatory of Tender	_____
……	

1.1.1.10 "**Bill of Quantities（工程量表）**" and "**Day work Schedule**（计日工作计划表）" *mean the documents so named (if any) which are comprised in the Schedules.*

本款未给出工程量表和计日工作计划表的具体定义，只是说明它们都包含在"资料表"中。在某些具体工程中，可能没有计日工作计划表，所以本款对此定义的说明中有一个限定语"如果有的话"。

工程量表列出了为完成合同工程而必需的各分项工程的估算工程量，是为了方便统一管理，把要计算的各项工程量按类型分别列出（即手工预算的"列项"工作）形成的一张表格。它详细说明了各分部分项工程在合同要求下的细目数量，是承包商获得合同中关于工程量信息和有效而精确地编制投标书的依据。

计日工作计划表可理解为应对"清单外变更"的资料表文件。在某些具体工程中清单外的变更项有时没有相应的综合单价可参考，可根据计日工作计划表中的各项单价综合考虑合理消耗量，以单项工程量的形式来核算变更价款。计日工作计划表中的人工、机械都是综合单价，以此单价乘以相应工程量即为结算工程价。由于工程项目的复杂性，"清单外变更"的处理需考虑多种因素，但"计日工作计划表"及相应的合同规定为处理此类事件提供了解决方向。

工程量表及计日工作计划表格式如例1.7和例1.8所示。

【例1.7】BILL OF QUANTITIES

Bill of Quantity

Sr.	File No.:		Owner:		
	Description of work	QTY	UNIT	RATE	AMOUNT
1	Mobilisation				
1.1	Mob., Site office & Services				
2	Excavation & Back filling				
2.1	Excavation				

29

续表

File No.：		Owner：			
Sr.	Description of work	QTY	UNIT	RATE	AMOUNT
2.2	Back filling				
3	Sub-structure				
3.1	Villa				
3.2	Villa compound wall				
4	Super structure				
4.1	Villa GF slab				
4.2	Villa FF slab				

【例1.8】DAY WORK SCHEDULE

DAY WORK SCHEDULE　Rates： 　1. Labour					
Item no.	Description	Unit	Nominal quantity	Rate	Extended amount
D100	Ganger	hour	500		
D101	Labourer	hour	5000		
D102	Bricklayer	hour	500		
D103	Mason	hour	500		
D104	Carpenter	hour	500		
D105	Steelwork Erector	hour	500		
D106	—etc.—	hour			
D113	Driver for vehicle up to 10 tons	hour	1000		
D114	Operator for excavator, dragline, shovel, or crane	hour	500		
D115	Operator for tractor with dozer blade or ripper	hour	500		
D116	—etc.—	hour			
……	……	……	……		
	Subtotal				
D122	Allow percenta of Subtotal for Contractor's overhead, profit, etc., in accordance with paragraph 3 (b) above.				
	Total for Daywork：Labour ——————— (carried forward to Daywork Summary, p. ———————)				

1 Generally Provision (一般规定)

1.1.2 Parties and Persons (各方和人员)

这一部分定义的是合同的双方以及参与工程项目的其他重要角色。合同双方之间的相互信赖和守约，参与人员之间的合作与团队精神，是项目成功的重要保障。

1.1.2.1 "***Party (当事方 (一方))*** " *means the Employer or the Contractor, as the context requires.*

"当事方（一方）"指雇主或承包商，具体指代应根据合同上下文确定。在 FIDIC 施工合同条件中，只有雇主和承包商才是合同的双方，其他参与工程的人员或单位，均属于雇主一方或承包商一方。工程师也是雇主一方的人员（详细解释参见第 1.1.2.6 条 [雇主人员]）。

按照法律的要求，合同当事方只包含达成合同协议的签字方，一般只有两方。在某些工程中，也会出现三方、四方合同的情况。常见的三方合同是由雇主、承包商、分包商三方签订的，此类合同主要明确承包范围和义务、划分责任主体及工程价款和工程款支付。

1.1.2.2 "***Employer (雇主)*** " *means the person named as employer in the Appendix to Tender and the legal successors in title to this person.*

雇主是在投标书附录中称为"雇主"的当事人，以及如果雇主发生变动时有权继承原来雇主财产所有权的合法继承人。雇主既具有某项工程建设要求，又具有该项建设工程相应的建设资金和各种许可，在建设市场中发包工程建设的勘察、设计、施工任务，并最终得到建筑产品。

在国内工程建设中，雇主也有一些其他措辞和称呼，如招标及合同文件内的"甲方"、"雇主"、"发包方"或"建设单位"等。国内工程采用 FIDIC 合同时，可在合同中补充相关定义。

关于雇主人员在工程项目上的权利义务，FIDIC 合同的规定十分严密。雇主的大部分工作由工程师完成，雇主一般都不能越过工程师直接向承包商或分包商下发指令。雇主的责任与义务在 FIDIC 施工合同条件第 2 条 [雇主] 中有详细介绍。

1.1.2.3 "***Contractor (承包商)*** " *means the person(s) named as contractor in the Letter of Tender accepted by the Employer and the legal successors in title to this person(s).*

承包商是被雇主接受的、在投标函中被标明作为"承包商"的当事人，或者是该当事人财产所有权的合法继承人。承包商拥有一定数量的建设装备、流动资金、工程技术经济管理人员及一定数量的工人，取得建设行业相应资质证书和营业执照，能够按照雇主的要求提供不同形态的建筑产品并最终得到相应工程价款。

如果雇主将一个工程分为若干个独立的合同，并分别与几个承包商签订合同，凡直接与雇主签订承包合同的都称为承包商。承包商的名称和地址会在投标函附录中列出。

国内有"总承包商"、"施工单位"等措辞，必要时可在合同中补充定义。

承包商义务在 FIDIC 施工合同条件第 4.1 款 [承包商的一般义务] 中有详细说明。

1.1.2.4 "***Engineer (工程师)*** " *means the person appointed by the Employer to act as the Engineer for the purposes of the Contract and named in the Appendix to Tender, or other person appointed from time to time by the Employer and noted to the Contractor under Sub-Clause 3.4 [Replacement of the Engineer (工程师的替换)].*

工程师是由雇主任命并在投标书附录中指定为实施合同担任工程师的人员，或者根据第 3.4 款 [工程师的替换] 规定由雇主任命并通知承包商的其他人员。工程师主要从事普通工业与民用建筑物、构筑物建造施工的设计，组织并监督施工的工程技术工作。

工程师由雇主任命，既可以是雇主委派担任工程师的个人，也可以是由雇主委托的专业咨询机构。工程师在本款中被称为"人员（person）"，实际上此处的"person"既可以理解为自然人（human being），也可以理解为法人（corporation）。在多数情况下，工程师指的是专业咨询机构的人员，或是雇主所在机构中任命的职员。不管"工程师"所指是个人还是单位，其职责都是根据合同条款的有关规定，对实施合同所指项目进行合同管理、费用控制、进度跟踪和组织协调。

在 FIDIC 施工合同条件中，"工程师"为咨询工程师，不是独立的第三方，属于雇主人员，是雇主和承包商之间的中间人，同时也是双方的准仲裁员和雇主的代理人。其地位和作用很特殊，主要原因在于工程师经雇主授权负责管理合同。工程师有权根据合同条款作出对建设工程负责、对雇主负责的客观判断，对雇主和承包商发出指令从而约束双方，行使法律上准仲裁员的权利，甚至雇主也无法干涉咨询工程师的决定。一方面工程师监督管理承包商，宏观控制承包商在施工中履行合同的情况；另一方面在可能的情况下对雇主和承包商进行必要的调解。

无论是雇主、承包商还是工程师自己都应清楚地了解工程师的权力和职责范围，此项内容在第 3 条［工程师］中有详细介绍。

在国内工程环境下，"工程师"主要指监理公司，是独立的第三方，作为项目管理的枢纽，担当着组织、施工协调利益、解决纠纷的任务。

1.1.2.5 "Contractor's Representative (承包商代表)" *means the person named by the Contractor in the Contract or appointed from time to time by the Contractor under Sub-Clause 4.3〔Contractor's Representative〕, who acts on behalf of the Contractor.*

承包商代表是承包商在合同中指明的人员，或者承包商根据第 4.3 款［承包商代表］的规定任命的人员。在实践中，根据招标文件的要求，承包商在投标时需提供关键职员名单，并作为投标书的一部分提交给雇主。承包商代表作为其中最核心的人员，应当包括在该名单内。承包商通常在关键职员名单中除指明承包商代表外，同时提供两个甚至多个人员作为承包商代表的备选人，以防原指定人员因故不能出任该项目的承包商代表。

承包商代表在国内工程界习惯称为项目经理，实际上是承包商委派的施工项目经理。各国对于承包商代表资质要求不同，国际项目要求承包商代表具有国际（工程）项目经理资质证书（IPMP），而国内项目则以注册建造师作为承包商代表资质的认证。

1.1.2.6 "Employer's Personnel (雇主人员)" *means the Engineer, the assistants referred to in Sub-Clause 3.2〔Delegation by the Engineer（由工程师托付）〕and all other staff, labor and other employees of the Engineer and of the Employer; and any other personnel notified to the Contractor, by the Employer or the Engineer, as Employer's Personnel.*

雇主人员包括工程师，工程师的助理人员（详细解释参见第 3.2 款［由工程师付托］），工程师和雇主的所有其他职员、雇员和工人，工程师和雇主通知承包商雇佣的为雇主工作的任何其他人员。

FIDIC 合同条件明确将工程师列入雇主人员。雇主通常在聘请工程师前与其签订咨询委托合同，明确雇用工程师的条件，同时规定工程师的全部行为必须对雇主负责，雇主则为工程师所提供的服务支付酬金。

1.1.2.7 "*Contractor's Personnel（承包商人员）*" means the Contractor's Representative and all personnel whom the Contractor utilizes on Site（现场）, who may include the staff, labor and other employees of the Contractor and of each Subcontractor（分包商）; and any other personnel assisting the Contractor in the execution of the Works.

承包商人员包括承包商代表以及承包商聘用在现场工作的一切人员。"一切人员"包含下列各类人员：

（1）一般职员，通常分为承包商现场的技术人员、工程管理人员、财务管理人员，以及行政管理人员；

（2）工人，一般分为技术工人和普工；

（3）其他类型的雇员，如厨师、警卫及现场医疗护理人员等；

（4）分包商的一切人员；

（5）帮助承包商实施工程的一切人员，如大型施工设备的厂家派往项目现场帮助承包商培训设备操作工的技术人员等。

通常与承包商有雇佣关系的、且是为了该建设项目工程雇佣的个人或法人实体等，都可延伸定义为承包商人员。如派往施工现场帮助承包商培训设备操作工作的技术人员、聘请到现场咨询某个工程技术问题的专家等。

1.1.2.8 "*Subcontractor（分包商）*" means any person named in the Contract as a subcontractor, or any person appointed as a subcontractor, for a part of the Works; and the legal successors in title to each of these persons.

分包商是完成部分工程，在合同中指名为"分包商"或其后被任命为分包商的人员，以及这些人员各自财产所有权的合法继承人。分包商通常有两种类型：一类是在投标时承包商事先列明的分包商或其财产所有权的合法继承人；另一类是在工程实施过程中承包商随时任命的分包商或其财产所有权的合法继承人。后一类分包商的任命，需经工程师同意。

指定分包商是一类特殊的分包商，是雇主在招标文件中或在开工后指定的分包商。指定分包商应与承包商签订分包合同。雇主和工程师不直接管理分包商，当雇主和工程师对分包商的工作有要求时，一般都通过承包商下达。此项内容在第4.4款［分包商］和第5条［指定的分包商］中有说明。

1.1.2.9 "*DAB（争端裁决委员会）*" means the person or three persons so named in the Contract, or other person(s) appointed under Sub-Clause 20.2 [Appointment of the Dispute Adjudication Board（争端裁决委员会的任命）]or Sub-Clause 20.3 [Failure to Agree Dispute Adjudication Board（对争端裁决委员会未能取得一致）].

争端裁决委员会（Dispute Adjudication Board，DAB）是合同中指名为"DAB"的一名或三名人员，是处理合同当事人争端纠纷的临时性组织。通过DAB解决争端，是一种非法律途径的争端解决方式。

DAB一般在合同中指定（即在投标书附录中列出），也可以按照第20.2款［争端裁决委员会的委任］和第20.3款［未能同意争端裁决委员会的委任］的规定指定其他人员（一个或多个）。

争端裁决委员会的任务是针对在工程实施过程中合同双方发生的争端进行专家式的参考性裁决，属于调解性质。DAB方式解决争端有两个优势：一是组成DAB的成员为相关领域的专家，可以清楚地理解纠纷的过程及责任，具有权威性；二是DAB成员由合同双方指定，避免了裁决时对某一方的偏倚，具有公平性。

如果一方不同意调解，可按程序将争端提交仲裁。因此，DAB裁决没有最终的法律约束力。此项内容在第20款［索赔，争端与仲裁］中有说明。

FIDIC施工合同条件附录中列有争端裁决协议书的推荐格式，供合同当事人选择使用。见例1.9。

【例1.9】DISPUTE ADJUDICATION AGREEMENT

Name and details of Contract _____

Name and address of Employer _____

Name and address of Contractor _____

Name and address of Member _____

Whereas the Employer and the Contractor have entered into the Contract and desire jointly to appoint the Member to act as sole adjudicator who is also called the "DAB".

The Employer, Contractor and Member jointly agree as follows：

1. The conditions of this Dispute Adjudication Agreement comprise the "General Conditions of Dispute Adjudication Agreement", which is appended to the General Conditions of the "Conditions of Contract for Construction" First Edition 1999 published by the Fédération Internationale Des Ingénieurs Conseils (FIDIC), and the following provisions. In these provisions, which include amendments and additions to the General Conditions of Dispute Adjudication Agreement, words and expressions shall have the the same meanings as are assigned to them in the General Conditions of Dispute Adjudication Agreement.

2. [*Details of amendments to the General Conditions of Dispute adjudication Agreement, if any. For example*：

    In the procedural rules annexed to the General Conditions of Dispute Adjudication agreement, Rule _ is deleted and replaced by："..."]

3. In accordance with Clause 6 of the General Conditions of Dispute Adjudication Agreement, the Member shall be paid as follows：

    A retainer fee of _____ per calendar month,

    plus a daily fee of _____ per day.

4. In consideration of these fees and other payments to be made by the Employer and the Contractor in accordance with Clause 6 of the General Conditions of Dispute Adjudication Agreement, the Member, undertakes to act as the DAB (as adjudicator) in accordance with this Dispute Adjudication Agreement.

5. The Employer and the Contractor jointly and severally undertake to pay the Member, in consideration of the carrying out of these services, in accordance with Clause 6 of the General Conditions of Dispute Adjudication Agreement.

6. This Dispute Adjudication Agreement shall be governed by the law of _____

1.1.2.10 "FIDIC" *means the international federation of consulting Engineers* （国际咨询工程师联合会）.

FIDIC是国际咨询工程师联合会的法语（Fédération Internationale Des Ingénieurs Conseils）缩写，在我国翻译为菲迪克。FIDIC本意是指全球工程咨询行业权威性的国际非政府组织，但在习惯上有时也指 FIDIC 合同条款或 FIDIC 方法。详细说明参见第一部分对 FIDIC 的介绍。

1.1.3 Dates, Tests, Periods and Completion

这一部分主要是关于时间、工程检验和竣工方面的定义。在使用 FIDIC 合同条件的过程中，相关时间节点需要承包商注意。承包商对这些时间节点的把握，有利于工程的顺利开展。

施工合同中主要事项的典型顺序如图 1.1 所示。

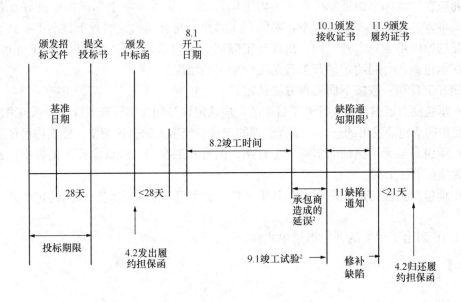

图 1.1　施工合同中主要事项的典型顺序

注：1. 竣工时间（在投标函附录中）用天数表示，加上根据第 8.4 款规定的任何延长期。
2. 为了表示事项的顺序，上图以承包商未能遵守第 8.2 款的规定为例。
3. 缺陷通知期限（在投标书附录中）用天数表示，加上根据第 11.3 款规定的任何延长期。

1.1.3.1 "*Base Date（基准日期）*" means the date 28 days prior to the latest date for of the Tender.

FIDIC 合同中，基准日期是提交投标书截止日期前 28 天的日期。这个日期与后期工程款额的调整有关。

将基准日期定义为投标截止前 28 天，原因如下：

（1）雇主的项目开发计划是从立项开始到工程交付使用之间的所有阶段的进度计划，包括由承包商实施的从招标投标开始到工程竣工这一阶段。把基准日期定为投标截止前 28 天，可使所有后续日期都与这个基准匹配。

（2）FIDIC 定义投标截止前 28 天为基准期，能限制雇主招标周期过短造成投标人投标困难，投标人无充裕时间消化招标要求。

基准日期之后的日期，应按日历日计，不考虑法定节假日和各种正常情况下可预见的特定气候等造成的延误。

1.1.3.2"Commencement Date（开工日期）" means the date notified under Sub-Clause 8.1 [Commencement of works].

开工日期是第 8.1 款［工程开工］中规定工程师通知承包商开工的日期。承包商在收到中标函后 42 天内，应开始施工，工期应从这天起开始计算。工程师应在不少于 7 天前向承包商发出"开工日期"的通知，通知书上写明的日期就是开工日期（详细规定参见第 8.1 款［工程的开工］）。

通常，开工日期会在中标函中直接定义。若承包商暂不具备开工条件，中标函一般规定承包商应在"收到书面通知后××天内进场"。雇主应尽量在中标函中安排好承包商进场的相关事宜。在工程实施过程中，实际开工时间常与合同约定的开工日期不一致。造成这种情况的原因可能有多种，如：出现开工障碍、预付款未到位、未办理施工许可证等。但也存在承包商比合同约定的开工日期提前施工的情况。

实际开工日期一般按下面三种方法认定：

（1）承包商有证据证明实际开工日期的，应认定该日期为实际开工日期。承包商的证据可以是雇主向承包商发出的通知、工程监理的记录、当事人的会议纪要、施工许可证等。

（2）承包商虽无证据证明实际开工日期，但有开工报告，应认定开工报告中记载的开工日期为实际开工日期。

（3）承包商无任何证据证明实际开工日期，亦无开工报告，应以合同约定的开工日期为准。

例 1.10 列出了中文的开工申请单式样。

【例 1.10】工程开工申请单

××××工程项目

承包单位＿＿＿＿＿＿＿＿＿＿＿＿　　　　　　合同号＿＿＿＿＿＿＿＿＿＿＿＿
监理单位＿＿＿＿＿＿＿＿＿＿＿＿　　　　　　编　号＿＿＿＿＿＿＿＿＿＿＿＿

工程开工申请单

A-8

致（总监理工程师）＿＿＿＿＿＿＿：
根据合同要求，我们已经做好＿＿＿工程开工前的一切准备工作，现要求该项工程正式开工，请予批准。
计划开工日期：＿＿＿＿＿＿＿
计划竣工日期：＿＿＿＿＿＿＿
本项工程现场负责人姓名：＿＿＿＿＿＿＿
附件：1. 施工组织设计报审表
　　　2. 施工技术方案报审表
　　　3. 施工放样报验单
　　　4. 建筑材料报验单
　　　5. 进场设备报验单
　　　6. 分项工程月进度计划
　　　……

承包人：　　　　年　　月　　日

1 Generally Provision（一般规定）

续表

道路、结构工程师意见	试验工程师意见	测量工程师意见

同意开工
/不同意开工
 	
签字：
      年 月 日
	同意开工
	/不同意开工
	
	签字：
	      年 月 日
		同意开工
		/不同意开工
		
		签字：
		      年 月 日

专业（驻地）监理工程师意见	总监理工程师意见

本项工程可以/不可以开工
 	
签字：
      年 月 日
	本项工程可以/不可以开工
	
	签字：
	      年 月 日

*1.1.3.3"**Time for Completion（竣工日期）**"means the time for completing the Works or a Section（单位工程）（as the case may be）under Sub-Clause 8.2［Time for Completion］, as stated in the Appendix to Tender（with any extension under Sub Clause 8.4-［Extension of Time for Completion（竣工时间的延长）］）, calculated from the Commencement Date.*

竣工日期是承包商完成合同规定承包范围内工程的日期，即合同工期的截止时间。竣工日期在投标书附录中写明，根据第8.2款［竣工时间］的规定，自开工日期算起至工程或单位工程竣工，也包括提出的任何延长期（详见第8.4款［竣工时间的延长］的规定）。

理解竣工时间时需注意如下几点：

（1）竣工时间指的是一个时间段，不是指一个时间点；

（2）开始计算竣工时间的日期为开工日期；

（3）竣工时间是根据第8.2款［竣工时间］完成工程的时间；

（4）竣工时间在投标书附录中规定；

（5）竣工时间可以指整个工程的竣工时间，也可以指某一区段的竣工时间，视具体情况而定；

（6）如果根据第8.4款［竣工时间的延长］，承包商获得了某一段工期的延长，则合同竣工时间为原竣工时间加上延长时间。

在实际工程中，如果竣工时间约定不清楚（如"工程应于XXXX年XX月XX日全部完工，竣工验收交付使用"），会导致合同双方就竣工时间产生争议。雇主认为"竣工"是指竣工验收，承包商则认为竣工应以是否完成合同约定工程范围为准。

工程实际竣工日期的确定有以下几种情况：

（1）工程正常通过竣工验收，承包商送交竣工验收报告的日期即为竣工日期；（2）工程按雇主要求修改后通过竣工验收的，实际竣工日期为承包商修改后提请雇主验收的日期；(3) 工程未经竣工验收，雇主擅自使用的，以转移占有工程之日为实际竣工日期；(4) 若因雇主原因，未在工程师收到承包商提交的竣工验收申请报告42天内完成竣工验收，或完成竣工验收后不予签发工程接收证书的，以提交竣工验收申请报告的日期为实际竣工日期。

1.1.3.4 "**Tests on Completion（竣工试验）**" *means the tests which are specified in the Contract or agreed by both Parties or instructed as a Variation（变更）, and which are carried out under Clause 9 [Tests on Completion] before the Works or a Section（as the case may be）are taken over by the Employer.*

竣工试验是雇主为了检验工程或单位工程的施工质量而在工程基本竣工时进行的检验。

理解竣工试验时需注意如下几点：

(1) 竣工试验在雇主接受工程或单位工程之前进行，承包商安排施工进度计划时应将竣工试验所需时间包含在竣工时间内；

(2) 竣工试验的内容和程序一般在规范等合同文件中规定；

(3) 如果合同没有规定，但经合同双方商定或雇主要求增加竣工试验的内容，则应按变更处理；

(4) 竣工试验应按照第9条 [竣工试验] 的规定进行。

1.1.3.5 "**Taking-Over Certificate（接收证书）**" *means a certificate issued under Clause 10 [Employer's Taking Over（雇主的接收）].*

接收证书是雇主在接收工程之后颁发给承包商的一个证书，以证明工程按照合同的要求已经实质性竣工。承包商收到接收证书表明工程进入缺陷通知期（详细解释参见第1.1.3.7款 [缺陷通知期]），承包商照管工程的责任随之转移给雇主，并可获得相应比例保留金的返还（详见第10条 [雇主的接收]、第14.9款 [保留金的支付] 及第17.2款 [承包商对工程的照管] 的规定），即接收证书是雇主和承包商之间的"物权移交"。从承包商收到接收证书之日起，除合同另有规定外，工程照管权（详细解释参见第17.2款 [承包商对工程的照管]）就完全移交给雇主。

接收证书的颁发，仅表明工程通过竣工试验达到了合同规定的"基本竣工"要求，而非承包商完成了合同规定的包括扫尾和清理施工现场的最终竣工要求。扫尾和清理施工现场等工作允许承包商在缺陷通知期内继续完成。

1.1.3.6 "**Tests after Completion（竣工后试验）**" *means the tests（if any）which are specked in the Contract and which are carried out in accordance with the provisions of the Particular Conditions after the Works or a Section（as the case may be）are taken over by the Employer.*

竣工后试验是合同中规定的，在工程或单位工程（视情况而定）被雇主接收后，根据专用条件的规定进行的试验（如果有）。竣工后试验必须在合同中有明文规定，否则认为无此类试验；如果合同中有竣工后试验的相关规定，应按照专用条件的规定来进行。试验应在工程或单位工程竣工后尽快进行。

竣工后试验相当于试生产、试运行，主要出现在有大量机电安装的机电工程中。土木工程项目中一般没有此类试验。

1 Generally Provision（一般规定）

1.1.3.7"Defects Notification Period（缺陷通知期限）"means the period for notifying defects in the Works or a Section（as the case may be）under Sub-Clause 11.1［Completion of Outstanding Work and Remedying Defects］, as stated in the Appendix to Tender（with any extension under Sub-Clause 11.3［Extension of Defects Notification Period］）, calculated from the date on which the Works or Section is completed as certified under Sub-Clause 10.1［Taking Over of the Works and Sections］.

缺陷通知期限是自工程接收证书中写明的竣工日期开始，至工程师颁发履约证书为止的日历天数。

工程通过竣工试验，雇主签发工程接收证书，仅表明工程已达到合同规定的"基本竣工"要求，但能否在动态运行环境下达到合同中规定的最终竣工要求暂不可知，因此需要设置缺陷通知期限以约束承包商在该段期限内对工程的施工质量负责。

理解缺陷通知期限时需注意如下几点：

（1）缺陷通知期限是从工程或单位工程的竣工日期起计，而竣工日期以接收证书写明的日期为准。"工程或单位工程"应是被证明完工的工程或单位工程，即雇主已经对该工程或单位工程接收，且向承包商颁发接收证书。

（2）缺陷通知期限是工程师通知承包商修复工程缺陷的期限，该期限的时间长度在投标书附录写明，且可按照第11.3款［缺陷通知期限的延长］的规定予以延期。

这与FIDIC施工合同（1987版）中的措辞"缺陷责任期"不同，也和我国建设工程中的"质量保修期"不同，如表1.1所示。

缺陷通知期、缺陷责任期与质量保修期的对比　　　　　　　　　表1.1

名称	出处	期限计算（均相同）	含义	修复范围	处理程序	质保金	应用范围	利弊
缺陷通知期	《FIDIC施工合同条件》	自工程接收证书中写明的竣工之日起，至工程师颁发履约证书为止的日历天数	分为合同工程的缺陷通知期和分阶段移交工程的缺陷通知期。主要工程及设备大多为一年，次要部位工程通常为半年，个别重要设备也可约定为一年半。缺陷修复不合格，可顺延期限	对期限内出现的所有缺陷都承担修复义务，不论该缺陷责任方是谁	先对缺陷进行处理，再确认责任方和明确费用	称"保留金"，担保用途广，不局限于质保。一般在工程接收证书签发后返一半，剩余的保留金作为质保金在缺陷通知期满后支付	国际工程FIDIC合同	（1）保留金在雇主颁发接收证书后至少可以收回一半，便于承包商尽早回收资金。（2）无论什么原因造成的缺陷都能及时处理。（3）期限内的非承包商责任的修理，承包商可要求雇主承担费用的基础上增加合理的利润。（4）缺陷通知期满后，雇主颁发履约证书后，承包商全部义务即告消失，降低了承包商风险

续表

名称	出处	期限计算（均相同）	含义	修复范围	处理程序	质保金	应用范围	利弊
缺陷责任期	《建设工程质量缺陷保证金管理暂时办法》2005年、《标准施工招标文件》2007年、FIDIC施工合同条件（1987版）	从实际竣工日期起计算	工程承包单位履行缺陷责任的期限。期限一般为6个月、12个月或24个月，最长不超过两年。缺陷修复不合格，可顺延期限	对期限内出现的所有缺陷都承担修复义务，不论该缺陷责任方是谁	先对缺陷进行处理，再确认责任方和明确费用	质量保证金的返还一般在缺陷责任期满后予以支付	国内合同	(1)缺陷责任期对质保金的返还有明确期限，期满可全部返还给承包商（除承包商未完成缺陷责任外），便于承包商尽早回收资金。(2)无论什么原因造成的缺陷都能及时处理。只是修理费用可能存在协商问题。(3)期限内的非承包商责任的修理，承包商可要求在雇主承担费用的基础上增加合理的利润。(4)承包商在缺陷期满后的缺陷修复义务消失，但仍应承担保修期内因自身原因造成的质量保修义务
质量保修期	《建设工程质量管理条例》2000年	从竣工验收合格之后即日起计算	工程承包单位对其完成的工程承诺的保修期限。最低保修期限为：(1)一般分项工程为设计文件规定的该工程的合理使用年限；(2)屋面防水工程、有防水要求的卫生间、房间和外墙面的防渗漏为五年；(3)供热与供冷系统，为2个采暖期、供冷期；(4)电气管线、给水排水管道、设备安装和装修工程为两年	仅对由承包商造成的质量问题或缺陷承担修复义务	先确认缺陷的责任，再决定是否要对缺陷进行处理	质量保证金的返还一般在缺陷责任期满后予以支付	国内合同	(1)因项目不同工程区质保期长短不一，特别是基础和结构工程质保期很长，易导致雇主借此长期扣留质保金。(2)因双方就确认责任方的问题上往往有纠纷难以划分，导致缺陷不能及时处理。(3)质量保修期期满后，保修义务消失

1.1.3.8 "*Performance Certificate（履约证书）*" means the certificate issued under Sub Clause 11.9 [*Performance Certificate*].

履约证书由雇主向承包商颁发，证明承包商已按合同规定完成全部施工工作（详见第 11.9 款［履约证书］的规定）。履约证书颁发后，承包商即可办理最终结算手续。

履约证书的作用有：

（1）证明施工合同已经被正式履行完毕。竣工验收、颁发接收证书等，均不代表工程师对工程的完全认可。只有收到履约证书，才证明承包商完全履行了合同。

（2）承包商可凭履约证书取回进场前向雇主提交的履约担保，同时宣告雇主和承包商之间的施工合同正式结束。

1.1.3.9 "*Day(日(天))*" means a calendar day（日历日）and "year" means 365 days.

"日历日"即自然日，是在同一时区从当日零点到次日零点之间的 24 小时。工程项目中，在计算有效天数时，接到信函的当天不予考虑（法律上不承认未满 24 小时的时间是一个日历日），应从次日开始计时。

"年"指 365 天。

1.1.4 Money and Payments（款项和付款）

款项和付款是工程师比较重要的日常事务。FIDIC 合同款项和付款相关章节中论述了单价合同的基本要义。

1.1.4.1 "*Accepted Contract Amount（中标合同金额）*" means the amount accepted in the Letter of Acceptance for the execution and completion of the Works and the remedying of any defects.

中标合同金额是雇主在中标函中接受的，为工程施工、竣工和修补任何缺陷而支付给承包商的价格。中标合同金额实际是承包商中标时的投标价格，该金额由两部分组成：一是承包商根据招标文件提供的工程量向雇主提交的工程报价（投标书中的总报价），另一部分是暂列金额（详细解释参见第 1.1.4.10 款［暂列金额］）。

如果在评标期间发现投标价格计算有误，雇主可对其进行修改，得到承包商（投标人）的确认后，该价格为有效投标价格。中标合同金额实际上是名义合同价格，实际合同价格只能在工程最终结算时确定。

1.1.4.2 "*Contract Price（合同价格）*" means the price defined in Sub-Clause 14.1 [*The Contract Price*], and includes adjustments in accordance with the Contract.

合同价格是按照第 14.1 款［合同价格］的规定确定的价格，包含根据合同进行的价格调整。作为工程全部完成后的"竣工结算价"，合同价格在工程实施过程中累计计价、根据合同要求调整得到，是一个"动态"价格。

合同价格与中标合同金额不同。中标合同金额是承包商中标时提出、经雇主接受的预期价款。合同价格是雇主用于支付承包商按照合同约定完成承包范围内全部工作的实际工程款，包括合同履行过程中按合同约定发生的价格变化。中标合同金额是固定的，但合同价格是变动的。中标函写明的合同价格并非承包商完成施工任务后得到的结算款额。实际工程中，最终结算的工程款可能受到合同的类型特点、发生应由雇主承担的责任事件、承包商延误工期或提前竣工等情况的影响。这些款额的调整都应包括在合同价格里。中标函内写明的合同价格会随着工程项目的进行而发生变化。承包商完成合同规定的全部任务后，累计获得的工程款总额也不一定等于中标函中原定合同价格与批准的变更和索赔补偿款额之和。

雇主应按合同规定的时间和方式向承包商支付合同价格。

1.1.4.3 "***Cost(成本(费用))***" means all expenditure reasonably incurred (or to be incurred) by the Contractor, whether on or off the Site, including overhead and similar charges, but does not include profit.

成本（费用）是承包商为完成合同规定的施工任务、在现场内外发生的或将要发生的全部合理开支，包括管理费和类似支出，但不包括利润。

1.1.4.4 "***Final Payment Certificate(最终付款证书)***" means the payment certificate issued under Sub-Clause 14.13 [Issue of Final Payment Certificate].

最终付款证书是支付证书的一种，是根据第14.13款［最终付款证书的签发］的规定由工程师签发的付款证书。最终付款证书的签发表明承包商收到合同规定的最后一笔工程款。

工程师在收到承包商按照第14.11款［最终付款证书的申请］和第14.12款［结清证明］规定提交的正式最终报表及结算清单后28天内，应向雇主递交一份最终付款证书。其中列明工程师认为按照合同规定雇主最终应支付给承包商的款额，以及雇主先前所有应支付和应得到的款额的收支差额。如果承包商未申请最终付款证书，工程师应要求承包商提出申请（详见第14.13款［最终付款证书的签发］的规定）。

1.1.4.5 "***Final Statement(最终报表)***" means the statement defined in Sub-Clause 14.11 [Application for Final Payment Certificate].

承包商向工程师提交工程最终结算申请书，要求工程师签发最终付款证书，经工程师同意后即成为最终报表。工程师据此最终报表向雇主签发最终付款证书后，承包商才可获得最终结算款。

第14.11款［申请最终付款证书］中明确规定了承包商可以申请最终付款证书的条件及需要提交的资料。

1.1.4.6 "***Foreign Currency(外币)***" means a currency in which part (or all) of the Contract Price is payable, but not the Local Currency(当地货币).

外币是可用于支付合同价格中全部或部分款项的、当地货币（详细解释参见第1.1.4.8款［当地货币］）以外的某种货币。外币是相对于当地货币而言的，随着工程项目的国际化，某些工程项目可能存在多币种支付的情况，此时应在合同专用条款中具体说明外币的种类及各种货币的支付比例和方式。

1.1.4.7 "***Interim Payment Certificate(期中付款证书)***" means a payment certificate issued under Clause 14 [Contract Price and Payment], other than the Final Payment Certificate.

期中付款证书是依据第14条［合同价格和付款］的规定由工程师签发的付款证书，但不包括最终付款证书。

FIDIC合同中有两类付款证书，一类是期中付款证书，另一类是最终付款证书（详细解释参见第1.1.4.4款［最终付款证书］）。期中付款证书是雇主对承包商报表中的所有工程相关费用（包括分包及设备相关款项）审核后，按月向承包商支付已完成工程量的付款

1 Generally Provision （一般规定）

证书，即根据工程师和承包商双方同意的工程量测量结果签发付款证书。雇主必须在工程师收到承包商的付款申请后56天内向承包商付款。如果付款延迟，承包商有权对未支付部分按合同约定的利率计算方式收取利息，若延迟时间超过合同规定的期限则承包商有权提出暂时停工。

期中付款证书是工程师审核承包商报表后颁发的，因此承包商申请期中付款证书时提交的资料应符合规定（详见第14.3款［期中付款证书的申请］的规定）。

1.1.4.8 "**Local Currency（当地货币）**" means the currency of the Country.

当地货币是工程所在国（详细解释参见第1.1.6.2款［工程所在国］）的货币。在国际工程中，用一定比例的当地币和外币支付合同款的情况十分普遍，支付比例以及兑换率在招标文件或合同文件中应明确规定。

1.1.4.9 "**Payment Certificate（付款证书）**" means a payment certificate issued under Clause 14［Contract Price and Payment］.

付款证书是按照第14条［合同价格和付款］的规定颁发的付款证书，包括期中付款证书和最终付款证书，详细解释参见第1.1.4.4款［最终付款证书］和第1.1.4.7款［期中付款证书］。

1.1.4.10 "**Provisional Sum（暂列金额）**" means a sum（if any）which is specified in the Contract as a provisional sum, for the execution of any part of the Works or for the supply of Plant（生产设备）, Materials（材料）or services under Sub-Clause 13.5［Provisional Sums］.

暂列金额是指招标人在工程量清单中暂定并包括在合同价款中的一笔款项，用于施工合同签订时还未确定或者不可预见的所需材料、设备、服务的采购，施工中可能发生的工程变更、合同约定调整因素出现时的工程价款调整以及发生的索赔、现场签证确认等的费用。参考第13.5款［暂列金额］的规定，暂列金额适用的范围"只应包括工程师已经指示的，与暂列金额有关的工作、供货或服务"，即暂列金额只能用于合同中"暂列金额"条款下写明的所有工作、供货、服务。

暂列金额由雇主或工程师支配，用于施工合同签订时尚未确定或者在施工过程中不可预见的所需材料、设备、服务的采购，或用于应对施工过程中可能发生的工程变更、合同约定调整因素出现时的工程价款调整以及发生的索赔、现场签证确认等。作为雇主的备用金，暂列金额可作为暂定工程、计日工、指定分包工程以及突发事件费用的开支。工程师有权依据工程进展的实际需要决定使用，且有权全部使用、部分使用，或者根本不予使用。

承包商得到暂列金额的支付需满足两个条件：一是工程师下达指令，要求承包商实施该项工作；二是实施的工作属于合同中规定暂列金额包含的工作范围。工程师有权要求承包商提交有关的报价单、收票、凭证、账目、收据等，证明承包商完成该项工作的实际费用。由于暂列金额是用于招标文件规定承包商必须完成的承包工作之外的费用，承包商报价时不得将承包范围内发生的间接费、利润、税金等计入其中。

暂定金额由工程师事先确定并填入招标文件中，额度一般用固定数表示，也可根据实际工程要求用投标价格的百分数表示，一般不超过估算总造价的20%。工程结算时，暂列金额应予核销，实际发生的暂定金额属于合同价格的一部分。

暂列金额主要涉及某些变更工作和指定分包商的工作，详见第13.5款［暂列金额］的规定。

1.1.4.11 "**Retention Money（保留金）**" *means the accumulated retention moneys which the Employer retains under Sub-Clause 14.3 [Application for Interim Payment Certificates（期中付款证书的申请）]and pays under Sub-Clause 14.9 [Payment of Retention Money（保留金的支付）].*

保留金是雇主根据第14.3款［期中付款证书的申请］的规定扣留的累计保留金，根据第14.9款［保留金的支付］的规定进行支付。

保留金与履约保函的性质类似，是履约担保（详细解释见第1.1.6.6款［履约担保］）的一种，目的是保证承包商在工程执行过程中恰当履约，否则雇主可以动用这笔款项，如：修复缺陷通知期内承包商本应修复的工程缺陷。保留金与履约保函共同构成对承包商的约束。

保留金总额一般为合同总价的2.5%～5%。采用月结算方式的工程，从第一个月起在给承包商的月进度付款中（不包括预付款和价格调整金额）扣留5%～10%，直至达到规定的保留金总额。如果在期中付款过程透支了工程款，雇主可从保留金中予以扣除。

关于保留金如何扣留和归还，详细规定见第14.3款［期中付款证书申请］和第14.9款［保留金的支付］。

1.1.4.12 "**Statement（报表）**" *means a statement submitted by the Contractor as part of an application, under Clause 14 [Contract Price and Payment], for a payment certificate（支付证书）.*

报表是承包商根据第14条［合同价格和付款］的规定，作为付款证书申请的组成部分，在申请工程款时提交的表格文件，其中包含完成工程量的合同价值以及其他相关情况等。报表包括期中报表（月报表）、竣工报表和最终报表（详见第14条［合同价格与付款］的规定）。

例1.11列出了中文的在建工程说明表式样。

【例1.11】Statement of Construction Project

在 建 工 程
STATEMENT OF CONSTRUCTION IN PROGRESS

For the year ended DEC. 31, XXXX　　　MONETARY UNIT: YUAN

单位：元

项目数	ITEMS	行次 LINE NO.	金额 AMOUNT	项目 EM	ITEMS	行次 EM LINE NO.	年初数 AT BEG. OF YEAR	年末数 AT END. OF YEAR
在建工程年初数	Construction in progress at beginning of year			1. 未完在建工程	Building work not yet completed			
加：本年投入在建工程支出	Add: Expenditures on construction in progress this year			[1]				

1 Generally Provision（一般规定）

续表

项目数	ITEMS	行次 LINE NO.	金额 AMOUNT	项目 EM	ITEMS	行次 EM LINE NO.	年初数 AT BEG. OF YEAR	年末数 AT END. OF YEAR
（1）购入工程用料	Construction materials purchased			[2]				
（2）购入需要安装设备	Equipment purchased that needs installation			[3]				
（3）购入不需要安装设备	Equipment purchased that does not need installation							
（4）建筑工程支出	Expenditures of building work			2. 未完安装工程	Installation work not yet completed			
（5）安装工程支出	Expenditures of installation work			[1]				
（6）预付工程价款	Prepayment to contractors			[2]				
（7）工程管理费	Construction administrative expenses			[3]				
				3. 待转已完工	Work completed not yet transferred			
本年支出合计：	TOTAL EXPENDITURE THIS YEAR			4. 待安装设备	Equipment to be installed			
减：本年已完工程转出数	Less：work completed and transferred out this year			5. 工程用料结存	Balance of construction materials			
本年其他转出数	Other amounts transferred out this year			6. 预付工程价款	Prepayment to contractors			
				7. 待摊工程管理费	Deferred construction administrative expenses			
本年转出数合计	TOTAL TRANSFERRED OUT THIS YEAR							
在建工程年末数	Construction in progress at end of year			合计	TOTAL			

1.1.5 Works and Goods（工程和货物）

本款定义了工程实施过程中投入的"硬件"，即材料、永久设备、施工机具等，以及完成的工程或单位工程。

1.1.5.1 "*Contractor's Equipment*（承包商设备）" *means all apparatus*（仪器），*machinery, vehicles and other things required for the execution and completion of the Works and the remedying of any defects. However, Contractor Equipment excludes Temporary Works*（临时工程），*Employer's Equipment*（雇主设备）（*if any*），*Plant, Materials and any other things intended to form or forming part of the Permanent Works*（永久工程）.

承包商设备是为实施和完成工程以及修补任何缺陷所需要的所有仪器、机械、车辆和其他物品，不包括临时工程、雇主设备及所有其他将构成或已构成永久工程的一部分的任何物品（生产设备、材料和其他任何物品）。

承包商设备的所有权属于承包商。这些设备是承包商为完成工程实体而使用的，在工程完工后需移出现场。在正常施工条件下，雇主对于承包商使用与不使用其设备不应进行干涉。

1.1.5.2 "*Goods*（货物）" *means Contractor's equipment, Materials, Plant and Temporary Works, or any of them as appropriate.*

货物指承包商设备、材料、生产设备和临时工程，也可以指其中之一。货物涵盖了一切工程建设过程中所需的物品。货物本身定义是中性的，无属性之分，与工程和其他不是"购买"而来的物品相区分。

1.1.5.3 "*Materials*（材料）" *means things of all kinds*（*other than Plant*）*intended to form or forming part of the Permanent Works, including the supply-only materials*（*if any*）*to be supplied by the Contractor under the Contract.*

材料是构成或将构成永久工程一部分的一切物品（工程设备除外），以及承包商根据合同规定有时需提供的"仅负责供应的材料"。对于"仅负责供应的材料"承包商只需按合同的要求供应，无需采购后再进行"加工"使其构成永久工程的一部分。

材料不包括临时工程（详见第1.1.5.7款［临时工程］的规定）所用的材料。

1.1.5.4 "*Permanent Works*（永久工程）" *means the permanent works to be executed by the Contractor under the Contract.*

永久工程由承包商按照合同规定实施，在竣工后移交给雇主，雇主拥有其所有权。永久工程一般使用年限在50年以上并且可保持其原基本性能，是为特定目的而设计建造供长期使用的建筑物、构筑物或设施。永久工程可能包括主体工程、附属工程、永久生活用房、永久给水排水系统、永久供电系统、永久供气系统、永久道路、铁路专用线、桥涵、码头等。

1.1.5.5 "*Plant*（生产设备）" *means the apparatus*（仪器），*machinery and vehicles intended to form or forming part of the Permanent Works.*

生产设备是构成或将构成永久工程一部分的机械、仪器和车辆。

本款中的"车辆"与工程中使用的车辆不同。本款中"车辆"是构成永久工程一部分的车辆，如：石油管线项目设计方案中采用水车给计量站供水，则承包商为此目的提供的水车就是生产设备；工程中使用的车辆一般属于施工机械，是承包商设备。

1.1.5.6 "*Section（单位工程）*" means a part of the Works specified in the Appendix to Tender as a Section (if any).

单位工程是 FIDIC 合同专用条件或投标书附录中专门定义的、能够单独接收使用的部分工程。与我国建设项目中的"单位工程"含义有所不同。

FIDIC 合同条件中的"section"为相对独立的永久工程的一部分，有时也将"section"翻译为"工程的一部分（部分工程）"或"（一个）区段"。实际工程中，工程是否划分单位工程，取决于雇主招标时的合同策略。雇主可通过项目结构分解，将项目分拆为若干个合同标段，通过分标和分合同委托施工任务，并通过施工合同实现对项目的目标控制。雇主对项目的分标方式，也是工程的承包方式。雇主招标时的"分标"策略决定了与雇主签约的承包商的数量和项目组织结构及管理模式，从根本上决定了合同各方面责任、权力和工作的划分。

我国建设项目中，单位工程是具有独立的设计文件、具备独立施工条件并能形成独立使用功能、但竣工后不能独立发挥生产能力或工程效益的工程，是构成单项工程的组成部分。如：公路工程划分标段，每个标段的路基工程、路面工程就是单位工程；建筑工程中办公楼是单项工程，其包含的土建工程、采暖工程、通风工程、照明工程以及热力设备及安装工程、电气设备及安装工程等都可称为单位工程。

1.1.5.7 "*Temporary Works（临时工程）*" means all temporary works of every kind (other than Contractor's Equipment) required on Site for the execution and completion of the Permanent Works and the remedying of any defects.

临时工程是为实施和完成永久工程以及修补任何缺陷在现场所需的各类临时性工程（承包商设备除外）。

临时工程与"临时建筑"相似，如：现场办公室、施工便道、便桥、水利工程中的围堰、人工砂石料系统、混凝土拌合系统、加工车间、实验室以及安全和照明设施等。工程竣工后，临时工程必须全部拆除，有时雇主会要求承包商保留一些临时工程，以便在工程运行中可以利用。

临时工程和临时设施不同。临时工程属于"工程"，目的是为了永久工程而修建，最后要拆除，它的全部价值将转移到工程造价中。临时设施是为完成合同约定的各项工作所服务的临时性生产和生活设施，它的价值通过折旧、摊销计入工程造价。

1.1.5.8 "*Works（工程）*" mean the Permanent Works and the Temporary Works, or either of them as appropriate.

"工程"可指永久工程和临时工程，也可根据情况指其中之一。详细解释参见第 1.1.5.4 款 [永久工程] 和第 1.1.5.7 款 [临时工程]。

1.1.6 Other Definitions

1.1.6.1 "*Contractor's Documents（承包商文件）*" means the calculations（计算书），computer programs and other software, drawings, manuals（手册），models and other documents of a technical nature（技术性文件）(if any) supplied by the Contractor under the Contract.

承包商文件是承包商根据合同提交的所有计算书、计算机程序和其他软件、图纸、手册、模型和其他技术性文件（如果有）。其中"其他技术文件"包括一些试验报告等。承包商文件一般不构成合同的一部分（详细解释参见第 1.1.1.1 款［合同］），此类文件只是根据合同要求由承包商向雇主提交的文件。在第 1.1.1.6 款［图纸］中，图纸是包含在合同中的工程图纸，以及由雇主或雇主代表按照合同要求发出的补充或修改图纸。本款涉及的"图纸"是承包商按照合同规定承担永久工程任何部分的设计工作情况下，由承包商按照规定语言及其他要求负责的承包商文件，详细解释参见第 4.1 款［承包商的一般义务］。

各国关于工程建设的相关法律法规中，通常也会对工程项目开工前承包商需要提供的文件作出规定，如我国的相关规定见例 1.12。

【例 1.12】我国工程建设相关法律法规规定，工程项目开工前承包商需提供的文件如下：
（1）总包单位的资质；（2）项目经理的法人委托书；（3）项目经理的资质；（4）项目技术负责人的资质；（5）专职安全员、专职质量检查员、材料取样员的资质；（6）施工组织设计，包括总进度计划；（7）施工安全用电方案；（8）安全保证体系；（9）质量保证体系；（10）质量计划；（11）选择的企业工程质量标准；（12）现场测量控制点的设置和保护；（13）劳务分包单位的资质（或挂靠的单位资质）；（14）特殊工种的上岗证（包括测量工、电工、电焊工、对焊工、吊车司机、塔吊司机等）；（15）项目的分部分项划分表；（16）建筑红线的测定成果表；（17）钢结构加工厂的资质；（18）外协部门的资质（材料化验室的资质、商品混凝土供应单位的资质），主材供应单位的资质；（19）雇主许可的施工总平面图的布置；（20）生产和生活设施的布置，场地的围护；（21）施工场地安全消防设施的布置；（22）施工人员进场安全交底；（23）进场材料的报验（包括水泥、砂、石、各类砖、管道、电缆、防水材料等）；（24）大型施工机械的安全检查证明、计量测量仪器仪表的校验证明；（25）建筑垃圾的处理方向，污水排放口设置等。

1.1.6.2 "Country（工程所在国）" means the country in which the Site (or most of it) is located, where the Permanent Works are to be executed.

工程所在国是实施永久工程的现场或工程的主要部分所位于的国家。某些管线项目、公路项目等"线性"工程可能跨越国境线，故工程所在国也指工程主要部分所在的国家。一般情况下，工程所在国通常为雇主的国家，但有时两者却不一致，如外资 BOT 或 BOO 项目。BOT 或 BOO 项目具体见例 1.13。

【例 1.13】
BOT（build-operate-transfer）即建设-运营-移交模式，是私营企业参与基础设施建设，向社会提供公共服务的一种方式。在 BOT 模式下，工程所在国政府（一般为当地政府）开放本国基础设施建设和运营市场，吸收国外资金、本国私人资金或其他来源资金，授予项目公司特权，由该公司负责融资和组织建设，建成后负责运营及偿还贷款，在特许期满时将工程移交给工程所在国政府。

BOO（Building-Owning-Operation）即建设-拥有-运营模式，是一种正在推行中的全新的市场化运行模式，即由企业投资并承担工程的设计、建设、运行、维护、培训等工作，硬件设备及软件系统的产权归属企业，而由政府部门负责宏观协调、创建环境、提出需求，政府部门每年只需向企业支付系统使用费即可拥有硬件设备和软件系统的使用权。

对于跨国工程，比如跨国大坝、跨国大桥等，这种工程必须严格区分其从属国的相互关系。

1.1.6.3 "Employer's Equipment（雇主设备）" means the apparatus, machinery and vehicles (if any) made available by the Employer for the use of the Contractor in the execution of the Works, as stated in the Specification; but does not include Plant which has not been taken over by the Employer.

雇主设备是雇主按照规范规定，向承包商提供的供其在施工期间使用的各类仪器、机械和车辆（如有时），不包括尚未被雇主接收的设备。雇主所提供的这些施工设备在规范中一般有具体规定，如设备类型、品牌、型号、燃料、负责人等。雇主设备一般有偿使用，具体应在规范或者其他合同文件中详细说明，以免造成误解。如果规范中没有提到雇主设备，雇主则无需向承包商提供任何施工机具。

1.1.6.4 "*Force Majeure （不可抗力）*" *is defined in Clause 19 [Force Majeure].*

不可抗力是合同双方在合同履行中出现的不能预见、不能避免、不能克服的客观情况，如恶劣天气、战争、动乱、罢工、地震、洪水、海啸、飓风等各种不可预见的破坏力大的因素（详见第19条［不可抗力］的规定）。

构成不可抗力具有不可预见的偶然性和不可控制的客观性等要件。一个事件或情况只有在同时满足下述四个条件时，才能称为不可抗力：（1）一方无法控制；（2）在签订合同前无法合理防范；（3）情况发生时，无法合理回避或克服；（4）该事件或情况不是由另一方的原因导致的。

不可抗力事件不可预见性、偶然性、客观性等特点决定了无法列举不可抗力的全部外延。因此，尽管不可抗力可以免责（详见第19条［不可抗力］），但是不可抗力的范围无法在合同中准确、详尽地界定。世界各国由于习惯和法律意识不同，对不可抗力的范围理解也不同。通常，自然现象（由自然原因引起的自然现象，如火灾、旱灾、地震、风灾、大雪、山崩等）及战争、严重的动乱等为不可抗力事件，各国的看法是一致的。对于除上述事件以外，如政府干预、不颁发许可证、罢工、市场行情的剧烈波动、政府禁令禁运、政府其他行为等人为障碍，是否属于不可抗力事件会引起争议。因此，合同当事人在签订合同时应具体约定不可抗力的范围。合同中对不可抗力事件范围的界定，应根据工程所在国的实际情况以及工程项目的特点来规定。

合同双方约定不可抗力范围相当于订立免责条款。订立此类免责条款的方法一般有三种：一是概括式，即在合同中只概括地规定不可抗力事件的含义，不具体列出可能发生的事件，若合同签订后客观情况发生了变化，双方对其含义产生争议，则由 DAB 或仲裁机构根据合同中规定的不可抗力含义来判断该客观情况是否构成不可抗力；二是列举式，即在合同中详尽列出属于不可抗力的事件，一旦发生了合同中所列明的事件而构成不可抗力，除合同列明的不可抗力事件外均不构成不可抗力；三是综合式，在合同中既概括不可抗力的具体含义，又列举属于不可抗力事件。

1.1.6.5 "*Laws （法律）*" *means all national (or state) legislation, statutes, ordinances and other laws, and regulations and by-laws of any legally constituted public authority.*

"法律"是工程所在国全国性（或州）的法律、条例、法令和其他法律，以及任何合法建立的公共当局制定的规则和细则等。法律的外延涉及国家法律、法规，地方细则以及规章等各种层次的法律性质的文件。具体工程合同的适用法律为其投标书附录中规定国家或地区的法律。

1.1.6.6 "*Performance Security （履约担保）*" *means the security (or securities, if any) under Sub-Clause 4.2 [Performance Security].*

履约担保是第4.2款［履约担保］规定的各项担保（如果有），即工程招标人（雇主）为防止承包商在合同执行过程中违约或不遵守合同规定，在招标文件中规定的要求承包商提交保证履行合同义务的担保。

在土木工程项目中，涉及的履约担保主要有投标履约担保和工程合同履约担保。工程投标履约担保是保证担保人（通常为担保公司）在投标人投标之前，向工程招标人（雇主）出具投标保函，保证中标人（承包商）与招标人签订合同并提供招标人所要求的履约保函。如果中标人违约，则保证担保人将在保额内赔付招标人的损失。投标担保的金额一般有所限定，如：我国招标投标相关法规中规定投标担保金额不得超过投标总价的2%、最高不得超过80万元人民币。

工程合同履约担保是保证担保人向雇主出具履约保函，保证承包商将在规定的日期内，以不超过双方议定的价格，遵守施工合同中规定的一切条款，按照约定的质量标准完成该工程项目。一旦承包商在施工过程中违约或因故无法完成合同，则保证担保人可向承包商提供资金或以其他资助形式使其有能力完成合同规定义务；也可安排新的承包商来接替原承包商，继续完成该工程项目；还可与雇主协商重新招标，由本次中标的承包商完成原合同中的剩余部分，由此产生的超出原合同造价的部分由保证担保人承担。如果承包商与雇主就上述解决方案不能达成协议，则保证担保人应在保额内赔付其损失。

履约担保一般有三种形式：银行保函、履约担保书和保留金。

银行保函是由商业银行开具的担保证明，通常为合同金额的10%左右，分为有条件的银行保函和无条件的银行保函：(1) 有条件的银行保函是承包商在没有实施合同或者未履行合同义务时，由雇主或工程师出具证明说明情况，并由担保人对已执行合同部分和未执行部分加以鉴定，确认后才能收兑银行保函，由雇主得到保函中的款项。建筑行业通常倾向于采用这种形式的保函。(2) 无条件的保函是承包商在没有实施合同或者未履行合同义务时，雇主不需要出具任何证明和理由，只要看到承包商违约，就可对银行保函进行收兑。

履约担保书是当承包商在履行合同中违约时，开出担保书的担保公司或者保险公司用该项保证金去完成施工任务或者向雇主支付该项保证金。工程采购项目履约担保采用履约担保书形式的，其金额一般为合同金额的30%～50%。

保留金是雇主根据合同规定，每次支付工程进度款时扣除一定数目的款项，作为承包商完成其修补缺陷义务的保证。保留金一般为每次工程进度款的10%，但总额一般应限制在合同价款的5%（通常最高不得超过10%）。

FIDIC施工合同条件对于履约担保的规定在第4.2款［履约担保］中有详细说明。

FIDIC施工合同条件附录中列有履约担保的推荐格式，供合同当事人选择使用。例1.14、例1.15分别列出了两种不同形式的履约担保的推荐格式。

【例1.14】履约担保函－担保保证范例格式

EXAMPLE FORM OF PERFORMANCE SECURITY -SURETY BOND

Brief description of Contract

Name and address of Beneficiary

(together with successors and assigns all as defined in the Contract as the Employer) . By this Bond, (name and address of contractor) (who is the contractor under such Contract) as Principal and (*name and address of guarantor*)

1 Generally Provision（一般规定）

as Guarantor are irrevocably held and firmly bound to the Beneficiary in the total amount of _____ (the "Bond Amount", say: _____) for the due performance of all such Principal's obligations and liabilities under the Contract. [Such Bond Amount shall be reduced by _____ % upon the issue of the taking-over certificate for the whole of the works under clause 10 of the conditions of the Contract.]⁽¹⁾

This Bond shall become effective on the Commencement Date defined in the Contract.

Upon Default by the Principal to perform any Contractual Obligation, or upon the occurrence of any of the events and circumstances listed in sub—clause 15.2 of the conditions of the Contract, the Guarantor shall satisfy and discharge the damages sustained by the Beneficiary due to such Default, event or circumstances.⁽²⁾ However, the total liability of the Guarantor shall not exceed the Bond Amount.

The obligations and liabilities of the Guarantor shall not be discharged by any allowance of time or other indulgence whatsoever by the Beneficiary to the Principal, or by any variation or suspension of the works to be executed under the Contract, or by any amendments to the Contract or to the constitution of the Principal or the Beneficiary, or by any other matters, whether with or without the knowledge or consent of the Guarantor.

Any claim under this Bond must be received by the Guarantor on or before (*the date six months after the expected of the Defects Notification Period for the Works*) _____ (the "Expiry Date"), when this Bond shall expire and shall be returned to the Guarantor.

The benefit of this Bond may be assigned subject to the provisions for assignment of the Contract and subject to the receipt by the Guarantor of evidence of full compliance with such provisions.

This Bond shall be governed by the law of the same country (or other jurisdiction) as that which governs the Contract. This Bond incorporates and shall be subject to the Uniform Rules for Contract Bonds, published as number 524 by the International Chamber of Commerce, and words used in this Bond shall bear the meanings set out in such Rules.

Wherefore this Bond has been issued by the Principal and the Guarantor on (*date*) _____

_____

Signature (s) for and on behalf of the Principal _____

_____

Signature (s) for and on behalf of the Guarantor _____

_____

(1) When writing the tender documents, the writer should ascertain whether to include the optional shown in parentheses [ ]

(2) insert: [and shall not be entitled to perform the Principal's obligations under the Contract.]

Or: [or at the option of the Guarantor (to be exercised in writing within 42 days of receiving the claim specifying such Default) perform the Principal's obligations under the Contract.]

【例1.15】保留金保函范例格式
EXAMPLE FORM OF RETENTION MONEY GUARANTEE

Brief description of Contract _____

Name and address of Beneficiary _____

(whom the Contract defines as the Employer.)

We have been informed that _____ (hereinafter called the "Principal") is your contractor under such Contract and wishes to receive early payment of [part of] the retention money, for which the

51

Contract requires him to obtain a guarantee.

At the request of the Principal, we (*name of bank*) ＿＿＿＿＿＿ hereby irrevocably undertake to pay you, the Beneficiary/Employer, any sum or sums not exceeding in total the amount of ＿＿＿＿＿＿ (the "guaranteed amount", say: ＿＿＿＿＿＿) upon receipt by us of your demand in writing and your written statement stating:

(a) that the Principal has failed to carry out his obligation(s) to rectify certain defect(s) for which he is responsible under the Contract, and

(b) the nature of such defect(s).

At any time, our liability under this guarantee shall not exceed the total amount of retention money released to the Principal by you, as evidenced by your notices issued under sub-clause 14.6 of the conditions of the Contract with a copy being passed to us.

Any demand for payment must contain your signature(s) which must be authenticated by your bankers or by a notary public. The authenticated demand and statement must be received by us at this office on or before (*the date 70 days after the expected expiry of the Defects Notification Period for the Works*) ＿＿＿＿＿＿ (the "expiry date"), when this guarantee shall expire and shall be returned to us.

We have been informed that the Beneficiary may require the Principal to extend this guarantee if the performance certificate under the Contract has not been issued by the date 28 days prior to such expiry date. We undertake to pay you such guaranteed amount upon receipt by us, within such period of 28 days, of your demand in writing and your written statement that the performance certificate has not been issued, for reasons attributable to the Principal, and that this guarantee has not been extended.

This guarantee shall be governed by the laws of ＿＿＿＿＿＿ and shall be subject to the Uniform Rules for Demand Guarantees, published as number 458 by the International Chamber of Commerce, except as stated above.

Date ＿＿＿＿＿＿　　　　　　Signature(s) ＿＿＿＿＿＿

1.1.6.7 "*Site (现场)*" *means the places where the Permanent Works are to be executed and to which Plant and Materials are to be delivered, and any other places as may be specified in the Contract as forming part of the Site.*

"现场"是将实施永久工程和运送生产设备与材料到达的地点，以及合同中可能指定为现场组成部分的任何其他场所。现场可包括：(1) 永久工程和临时工程用地；(2) 永久设备和材料的存放地，仓库等；(3) 办公和生活营地；(4) 合同明文规定的其他作为现场的用地。

1.1.6.8 "*Unforeseeable (不可预见)*" *means not reasonably foreseeable by an experienced contractor by the date for submission of the Tender.*

不可预见是一个有经验的承包商在提交投标书之前不能合理预见的情况。如果承包商想要证明某一事件是不可预见的，必须证明：

(1) 承包商不可能在提交投标书前预见该事件；

(2) 承包商没有预见到该事件的发生，并不是其主观上缺乏经验造成的；

(3) 承包商没有预见到该事件是合理的。

不可预见事件与不可抗力事件容易混淆（详细解释见第1.1.6.4款［不可抗力］和第19条［不可抗力］），两者的区别在于：不可预见事件主要包括一些不可预见的外部天然条件、人为条件、污染物等,比如自然灾害、战争、罢工和社会骚乱等,不包括不可预见的破坏力大的自然灾害等气候条件;不可抗力则包括恶劣天气、战争、动乱、罢工、地震、洪水、海啸、飓风等各种不可预见的破坏力大的因素。不可预见事件属于雇主风险(详见第 17.3 款[雇主的风险]的规定)所列第(h)项,而不可抗力所列(i)、(ii)、(iii)及(iv)项(详见第 19 条[不可抗力]的规定)与雇主风险所列第(a)、(b)、(c)及(d)项相重复,且不可抗力所列(v)项也属于雇主风险所列(h)项。

对于不可预见事件,如果承包商能证实该事件不是一个有经验的承包商在投标时可以合理预估的,则可按第 20.1 款[承包商的索赔]的规定向雇主提出索赔。

1.1.6.9 "*Variation (变更)*" *means any change to the Works, which is instructed or approved as a variation under Clause 13 [Variations and Adjustments].*

变更是根据第 13 条[变更和调整]的规定,经指示或批准作为变更的,对工程所做的任何更改,如合同中包括的任何工作内容的数量、质量或其他特性的改变,任何工作的删减以及工程实施顺序或时间安排的改变等。这种变动需根据工程师的指令或者先由承包商提出变更建议,工程师批准后方可实施。

第 13 条[变更和调整]中规定了变更后承包商享有的权利和义务以及雇主实现这些权利和义务的具体操作。

1.2　Interpretation(解释)

In the Contract, except where the context requires otherwise:
(a) words indicating one gender (性别) include all genders;
(b) words indicating the singular (单数) also include the plural (复数) and words indicating the plural also include the singular;
(c) provisions including the word "agree", "agreed" or "agreement" require the agreement to be recorded in writing, and
(d) "written" or "in writing" means hand-written, type-written, printed or electronically made, and resulting in a permanent record.

The marginal words (旁注) and other headings shall not be taken into consideration in the interpretation of these Conditions.

工程合同条款编制中涉及一些理解上容易产生偏差的词语,对此需要在合同中统一规定其含义。FIDIC 合同中词语含义在旁注和其他标题在本条件的解释中不应考虑,而应遵循:

(1)指代某一性别的词,包括所有性别,即阳性词也可以包括阴性词。如在工程合同中实际上无法区分所指对象、人员是男性还是女性,合同中的阳性词"他"包含对阴性词"她"的指代。

(2)单数形式词也有复数含义,反之亦然。

(3)各项包括"同意(商定)"、"达成(取得)一致"、或"协议"等词语的规定,都要求用书面形式。"书面"或"用书面"指手写、打字、印刷或电子制作,并形成永久性的记录。

"书面"文件是通过文字或书面材料成立意思表示的文件形式,包括法律文件、信函、电函和其他书面材料。书面形式具有意思表示准确、有据可查、便于预防纠纷的优点。根据现代各国的法律,书面形式是法律行为成立的基本形式,其中某些重要的法律行为必须以书面形式进行。"书面"文件的要求除文件形成格式"手写、打字、印刷、电子制作"外,应附加以文件有效性。文件有效性是"书面文件"成立的不可分割的定义部分。书面文件不只是书面形式,还应保证文件归属的责权各方表述的意见及签名齐全、合法。

书面文件又可分为一般书面文件和特殊书面文件。一般书面文件用文字来进行意思表示,如书面合同、授权委托书、信件、数据电文(包括电报、电传、传真、电子数据交换和电子邮件)及行为人协商同意的有关修改合同的文书、图表等。特殊书面文件为当事人的意思表示获得国家有关机关认可的文字记载形式,包括公证形式、鉴证形式、见证形式等。

"旁注和其他标题在本条件的解释中不应考虑"这一条体现出 FIDIC 合同的严密性,如:FIDIC 编著的各类官方指南,这些指南并不构成合同实体。

1.3 Communications(通信交流)

Wherever these Conditions provide for the giving or issuing of approvals(批准书), certificates(证明), consents(同意函), determinations(确定), notices(通知)and requests(请求), these communications shall be:

(a)in writing and delivered by hand(against receipt(取得对方收据)), sent by mail or courier, or transmitted using any of the agreed systems of electronic transmission as stated in the Appendix to Tender; and

(b)delivered, sent or transmitted to the address for the recipient's communications as stated in the Appendix to Tender. However:

(i)if the recipient(接收人)gives notice of another address, communications shall thereafter be delivered accordingly; and

(ii)if the recipient has not stated otherwise when requesting an approval or consent, it may be sent to the address from which the request was issued.

Approvals, certificates, consents and determinations shall not be unreasonably withheld or delayed. When a certificate is issued to a Party, the certifier(发证人)shall send a copy to the other Party. When a notice is issued to a Party, by the other Parry or the Engineer, a copy shall be sent to the Engineer or the other Party, as the case may be.

FIDIC 合同条件中多处提及发出或颁发批准、证书、同意、决定、通知和要求。此类通信信息都必须采用书面形式,派人面交并取得收据、或者邮寄、或由信使送达、或按投标函附录中所列通过经同意的电子传输系统传输,递交、邮寄或传递到投标函附录中规定的收件人地址。对任何批准、证书、同意及决定不得无故扣压或拖延。此项规定是为了确保工程实施过程中各方沟通顺畅。

FIDIC 合同条件中规定的有效送达有三种形式:面交有收据、邮寄、由信使送达,其他形式都不属于法定送达。如:采用一般快递公司递送时,获得快递公司的收件收据不算法定送达，只有快递公司将对方签收的签字收据复印给寄件方，才可视为寄件方获得了法定送达凭证，否则无法承认、确认文件送达的有效性。邮寄则不同，寄件方只要有发出挂号信的收据，且邮局无相应的退件证明，便可被确认为法定送达凭证。

例 1.16 列出了中文的文件收据示例。

【例 1.16】文件收据示例

收　条

今收到：　　　　　　　　　　　　　　　　　　　　　　　　年　　月　　日

序号	项目名称	单位	数量	备注
1				
2				
3				
4				
5				
6	合计			

接收单位电话：　　　　　　　　　　　　　设计单位电话：
接收单位签章：　　　　　　　　　　　　　设计单位签章：
接收单位经办人：　　　　　　　　　　　　设计单位经办人：

1.4　Law and Language（法律和语言）

The Contract shall be governed by the law of the country (or other jurisdiction) stated in the Appendix to Tender.

If there are versions of any part of the Contract which are written in more than one language, the version which is in the ruling language stated in the Appendix to Tender shall prevail.

The language for communications shall be that stated in the Appendix to Tender. If no language is stated there, the language for communications shall be the language in which the Contract (or most of it) is written.

合同应受投标函附录中规定的国家（或其他司法管辖区域）的法律制约。

如果合同的任何部分采用一种以上语言编写，构成不同版本，则以投标函附录中规定的主导语言编写的版本优先。

往来信函应使用投标函附录中规定的语言。如果投标函附录中没有规定，则往来信函应使用与编写合同（或大部分合同）相同的语言撰写。

1.5　Priority of Documents（文件的优先次序）

The documents forming the Contract are to be taken as mutually explanatory of one

another. For the purposes of interpretation, the priority of the documents shall be in accordance with the following sequence:
(a) the Contract Agreement (if any),
(b) the Letter of Acceptance,
(c) the Letter of Tender,
(d) the Particular Conditions (专用条件),
(e) these General Conditions (通用条件),
(f) the Specification,
(g) the Drawings, and
(h) the Schedules and any other documents forming part of the Contract.

If an ambiguity or discrepancy is found in the documents, the Engineer shall issue any necessary clarification or instruction.

合同文件有优先次序，构成合同的各个合同文件应互作说明、互为补充，这样便于解释合同文件的相关内容。合同文件优先顺序一般在合同通用条款中规定，也可根据项目的具体情况在专用条款内调整。如果合同文件相互之间出现矛盾，则应以文件签署日期在后的和内容重要的优先，即签署日期在后的和内容重要的文件应优先排列顺序。合同文件的优先顺序排列如下：

（1）合同协议书（如有时）；
（2）中标函；
（3）投标函；
（4）专用合同条件；
（5）通用合同条件；
（6）规范；
（7）图纸；
（8）资料表以及其他任何构成合同一部分的文件。

与 FIDIC 合同文件的规定相比，国内关于合同文件优先解释程序的执行惯例较为机械。如果合同文件之间有冲突，按合同组件次序来决定重要性和有效性。更为合理的解释方式应该依据以下原则：（1）以时间靠后的文件为准。任何文件的产生都需要过程，后序的文件通常会重新定义或补充定义前一文件的某些内容，所以时间靠后的文件优先解释更为合理。（2）以要求严格的文件为准。由于招标投标过程需要一系列文件支持，某些条款会在大体量的合同调整中被淡化，这种淡化通常是无意的或非针对性的，解释文件时优先采用较严格的文件更为合理。

FIDIC 合同组件中不包括招标文件，若需要将招标文件纳入合同，应在合同组件中明确，并给招标文件以合理的合同解释位次。招标文件中投标须知的引入是为了使承包商明确其对工程实体以及合同条款及要约承诺的影响，以避免合同组件前后冲突，引发不必要的争议。因此，投标须知一般位于图纸后、资料表以及其他文件前。如承包商在中标后，按照中标对应的投标承诺另外提交一份全新而完整的标书，并说明所有投标承诺以最后文件为准，可解决很多合同解释程序中发生的问题。

例 1.17、例 1.18 和例 1.19 给出了关于合同文件优先次序的三个实例。

1 Generally Provision（一般规定）

【例 1.17】

某一工程合同，规范中明确规定采料场的青苗补偿费由雇主承担，但合同特殊条款中又规定"承包商应负责采料场的使用费及相关的赔偿费"。工程实施过程中，当承包商向采料场所有者支付相应的赔偿费，然后将此费用按规范规定计入当月工程报表时，却遭到了工程师的拒绝。据此，承包商以索赔的形式提出补偿要求，但仍被工程师以合同优先顺序以及"相关的赔偿费"包括青苗赔偿为由予以拒绝。

【例 1.18】

某工程合同签订过程中，雇主与承包人合同谈判期间形成的备忘录中约定：全部施工用地补偿费已包含在承包人支付的土地租金中。招标文件、投标文件、合同条款均约定施工用地补偿费由承包人承担。工程开工后，产生了新的施工用地补偿，承包商认为备忘录虽然约定施工用地补偿费由承包人承担，但补偿范围未明确说明，而新增费用不在招标文件中列明的施工用地补偿费内容中，要求雇主承担该项费用。

合同备忘录的效力优先于招标文件、投标文件和合同条款。当合同备忘录中约定的内容不明确时，双方应依据招标文件或投标文件中的规定，无法达成一致意见时，可申请仲裁。

【例 1.19】

某工程的工程量清单中约定卫生间装修的马赛克采用白水泥勾缝，但在技术规范中写明此项工作使用普通硅酸盐水泥，施工图纸与确认的施工方案中均标注使用普通硅酸盐水泥。

工程实施过程中，雇主与承包商就勾缝材料的采用产生争议。雇主认为工程量清单中写明的勾缝材料是白水泥，且使用白水泥更为美观；承包商则认为图纸和技术规范中写明采用普通硅酸盐水泥，两种勾缝材料相比，普通硅酸盐水泥成本较低。

依据文件的优先次序，合同约定技术规范、施工图纸优先于工程量清单。故应采用承包商所主张的普通硅酸盐水泥。若雇主坚持要求使用白水泥，应在双方协商一致后进行变更，且由此产生的变更费用及承包商额外费用均由雇主承担。

1.6 Contract Agreement（合同协议书）

The Parties shall enter into a Contract Agreement within 28 days after the Contractor receives the Letter of Acceptance, unless they agree otherwise. The Contract Agreement shall bebased upon the form annexed to the Particular Conditions. The costs of stamp duties（印花税）and similar charges（if any）imposed by law in connection with entry into the Contract Agreement shall be borne by the Employer.

按 FIDIC 施工合同条件第 16.2 款［由承包商终止］规定，除非另有协议，合同双方应在承包商收到中标函后的 28 天内签订合同协议书。若 28 天内雇主没有签订合同协议书，承包商有权终止合同。

合同协议书将合同当事人、标的物、工期、合同价款、合同组件及解释程序等合同主架构搭起来，列明合同当事人及证明人以供签字确认。合同协议书是一份简化的合同，指向着对应的细节性合同组件。合同协议书中的内容必须清晰准确，如：当事人、标的物、工期、合同价款、合同组件、解释程序及其他特定承诺项，这些内容对应的指向须准确无误，并避免与合同其他部分冲突。

按照我国法律，施工合同是"要约承诺"式。中标通知书有效送达，合同即成立。是否签订合同协议书并不影响合同的有效性，但一个完整工程合同文本既需要有国家强制性的格式要求（如办理相关合同备案），也需要实现合同双方"合同条款再确认"的共同需求，这就需要合同双方有意识地进行合同协议书的签订。

雇主应承担法律要求的因签订合同协议书而产生的"印花税及类似费用（如果有）"。印花税是以经济活动中签立的各种合同、产权转移数据、营业账簿、权利许可证照等应税凭证文件为对象所征的税。印花税由纳税人按规定应税的比例和定额自行购买并粘贴印花税票，即完成纳税义务。

FIDIC 合同条件在附录中列有合同协议书的标准格式（见第 1.1.1.2 款［合同协议书］中例 1.1）。如果雇主对标准格式进行修改或补充，则应当对修改或补充后的合同协议书格式进行检查，确保与 FIDIC 合同条款规定的标准格式一致。最终的合同协议书以合同专用条件所附格式为依据。

此外，合同协议书中还可列入"合同协议书补遗书（Addendum）"文件，有时也称"备忘录（Memorandum）"。招标投标过程中，雇主自主或根据投标人的质询可能对招标文件进行补充和修改，或在合同双方签订协议书之前对合同文件中某些内容进行补充和修改。这些由雇主补充或修改的、合同双方协商一致同意补充和修改的意见，应以补遗书形式附在协议书后。补遗书是对原有文件的补充和修改，应注明补遗书中的内容是针对原有文件中哪项内容的补充和修改，其优先顺序仅次于合同协议书。

1.7 Assignment（权益转让）

Neither Party shall assign the whole or any part of the Contract or any benefit or interest in or under the Contract. However, either Party:

(a) may assign the whole or any part with the prior agreement of the other Party, at the sole discretion of such other Party, and

(b) may, as security in favour of a bank or financial institution, assign its right to any moneys due, or to become due, under the Contract.

合同权益转让是合同债权人将其权益转让给第三人享有，但不改变合同的内容。合同权益转让可分为部分转让和全部转让。部分转让时，受让的第三人加入合同关系，与原债权人共享债权，原债权人与受让部分合同权利的第三人或者分享合同债权，或者共享连带债权。如果转让合同无此约定，视为共享连带债权。合同权利全部转让给第三人时，该第三人即取代原债权人的地位而成为合同关系中的新债权人，原债权人脱离合同关系。

未经一方事先同意，另一方不得转让部分或整个合同，也不能转让根据合同应得的利益或权益。合同当事人可将其享有的按照合同到期或将到期的款项，以银行或金融机构为受益人，作为抵押转让出去。

国内工程中"转包"、"工程款专款专用"与 FIDIC 合同条件中的合同权益转让有关联。

(1) FIDIC 合同条款对权益转让的限制是禁止承包商将非雇主同意的全部或部分合同权益转让。全部转让是一种恶劣的合同行为，承包商的分包总会涉及权益转让问题。关于如何理解分包中的权益转让问题，FIDIC 合同条件中规定，非雇主同意的属于承包商的任何分包都不具有合同分包属性，承包商要为此类分包承担全部合同责任，从而避免了承包商以自己的专业分包来推卸合同责任的可能。

（2）承包商的应得款项主要是工程款。为避免承包商将工程款用于任何商业领域，使得雇主有面临工程款没有专用于工程而导致施工计划受阻的风险，FIDIC 合同条件中规定在银行账户之间划拨任何款项，都视为权益转让，现金支付也是权益转让。所有承包商应得款项的权益转让都必须经过雇主同意，并处于银行担保函约束之下，保证工程款专款专用的合同需要。

【例 1.20】

某工程雇主与承包商 A 签订了该工程的总承包合同。后经雇主同意，承包商 A 又将该工程的设计任务和施工任务分别委托给设计单位 B 和施工单位 C，并与他们分别签订了合同。合同签订后，设计单位 B 按时将设计文件和有关资料交付给施工单位 C，施工单位 C 也根据施工图纸进行施工。工程竣工后，雇主会同有关质量监督部门对工程进行验收，发现工程存在严重质量问题，经检查是由于设计不符合规范所致，原因是设计单位 B 设计前未对现场进行仔细勘察，导致设计不合理，给雇主造成重大损失。事后，雇主要求设计单位 B 和施工单位 C 承担相应的责任，而设计单位 B 以与雇主没有合同关系为由拒绝承担责任，施工单位 C 又以自己不是设计人为由推卸责任，雇主遂以设计单位 B 为被告向法院起诉。

1.8 Care and Supply of Documents（文件的保管和提供）

The Specification and Drawings shall be in the custody and care of the Employer. Unless otherwise stated in the Contract, two copies of the Contract and of each subsequent Drawing shall be supplied to the Contractor, who may make or request further copies at the cost of the Contractor.

Each of the Contractor's Documents shall be in the custody and care of the Contractor, unless and until taken over by the Employer. Unless otherwise stated in the Contract, the Contractor shall supply to the Engineer six copies of each of the Contractor's Documents.

The Contractor shall keep, on the Site, a copy of the Contract, publications named in the Specification, the Contractor's Documents (if any), the Drawings and Variations and other communications given under the Contract. The Employer's Personnel shall have the right of access to all these documents at all reasonable times.

If a Party becomes aware of an error or defect of a technical nature in a document which was prepared for use in executing the Works, the Party shall promptly give notice to the other Party of such error or defect.

本款规定了雇主和承包商对文件的保管事项以及各自所需要提供的文件。规范和图纸由雇主保护和保管，雇主应向承包商提供合同及每份后续图纸的两份复印件，承包商可自行复制或要求雇主为其提供更多的复印件，但费用自理（除非合同另有规定）。移交给雇主之前的承包商文件由承包商自己保护与保管，承包商应向工程师提供 6 份承包商文件复印件（除非合同另有规定）。承包商应在现场保留一份合同、规范中列出的所有文件、承包商文件、图纸、变更以及所有按照合同收发的往来信函。

FIDIC 合同中的规范主要是由雇主及设计师提供的工料规范。国家类规范具有公开性，不需要雇主保存和照管。合同份数和图纸份数可以在合同中约定。一般情况下，承包商至少需要 4 套图纸：施工现场一套，办公室一套，竣工图两套。图纸不足部分承包商可自费复印。

承包商文件由承包商保管的含义是：如果承包商文件丢失，工程师与雇主没有义务为其提供复印件。承包商需要有严密的资料保管制度，且需备份"合同指定的出版物及承包商文件"。承包商应备齐法定规范标准图集等文件，随时供工程师和雇主查阅。

如果合同当事人一方发现文件中有技术性错误或缺陷，应立即通知另一方。同时，提供文件的一方须对其文件内容负责，而另一方负有合作义务以降低错误造成的损失。如雇主提供的图纸存在错误，在使用该图纸编制计划和采购工程材料时，有经验的承包商可能会发现上述错误，在工程施工前要求雇主修改。要证明承包商明知错误却未立即报告雇主是一件困难的事，如果有足够证据能够证明承包商在知悉文件错误而未向雇主发出通知，雇主可以就由此造成的损失向承包商提出索赔，或者从承包商的索赔中扣减相应的损失。

雇主和承包商对各自的设计文件均保留版权和其他知识产权。通过签订合同，双方分别给予对方复印、使用及传输上述文件的许可。不经对方同意，任何一方均不得为第三方复印、使用或对外披露上述文件。

1.9 Delayed Drawings or Instructions（延误的图纸或指示）

The Contractor shall give notice to the Engineer whenever the Works are likely to be delayed or disrupted if any necessary drawing or instruction is not issued to the Contractor within a particular time, which shall be reasonable. The notice shall include details of the necessary drawing or instruction, details of why and by when it should be issued, and details of the nature and amount of the delay or disruption likely to be suffered if it is late.

If the Contractor suffers delay and/or incurs Cost as a result of a failure of the Engineer to issue the notified drawing or instruction within a time which is reasonable and is specified in the notice with supporting details, the Contractor shall give a further notice to the Engineer and shall be entitled subject to Sub-Clause 20.1 [Contractor's Claims] to:

(a) an extension of time for any such delay, if completion is or will be delayed, under Sub-Clause 8.4 [Extension of Time for Completion], and

(b) payment of any such Cost plus reasonable profit, which shall be included in the Contract Price.

After receiving this further notice, the Engineer shall proceed in accordance with Sub-Clause 3.5 [Determinations] to agree or determine these matters.

However, if and to the extent that the Engineer's failure was caused by any error or delay by the Contractor, including an error in, or delay in the submission of, any of the Contractor's Documents, the Contractor shall not be entitled to such extension of time,

Cost or profit.

如果承包商未能在合理的特定时间内收到工程建设必需的图纸或指示,以至于工程建设可能遭受延迟或中断,承包商应及时通知工程师。通知的内容应包括承包商所必需的图纸或指示的细节、承包商期望发出该图纸或指示的详尽理由和具体时间、若推迟发出该图纸或指示工程建设可能遭受的影响以及后果等。如果工程师在接到承包商合理的并附有详尽细节的通知后,仍未能在规定时间内向承包商发出图纸或指示,致使承包商遭受工期延误或费用损失,则承包商应再次向工程师发出通知,并有权根据第20.1款[承包商的索赔]的规定要求延长竣工时间(详细解释见第8.4款[竣工时间的延长]),并可要求将所遭受的费用损失和合理利润计入合同价格。工程师在收到该再次通知后,应按照第3.5款[确定]的规定尽快作出商定或确定。若工程师延迟发出图纸或指示是由于承包商的错误或拖延(包括承包商文件中的错误或提交拖延),则承包商无权要求竣工日期、费用和利润的增加。本款约定发生拖延图纸或指示的情况下,承包商可索赔利润。但利润往往是不在索赔之列的,所以双方经协商后可以在专用条款中删除此条,以招标条件的规定要求承包商来遵守。

FIDIC施工合同条件适用于"雇主提供设计的工程",所以图纸未按期发出首先是雇主责任。承包商可遵守相关程序的执行情况,要求雇主方承担责任。承包商应首先通知工程师,说明"图纸细节、要求的时间和理由、晚发的后果及性质"等,此后若工程师仍然未提供图纸,而承包商造成实质损失,承包商可"再"给工程师发文:"根据合同条款XX,要求给予工期与费用补偿"。

承包商要求工期和费用补偿有两个前提:工程师延迟发出图纸并非由于"承包商文件中的错误或提交拖延造成";工程师在第一次收到通知后未在规定时间发出图纸。其中,"承包商文件的错误或提交延迟",包括承包商文件表述性错误、未清楚表达所述,以及承包商未按规定流程准时提交文件等情况。

【例1.21】图纸滞后造成的索赔

某项道路工程,因要提高道路等级,故工程师建议把通道与涵洞进行归类、合并,则此图应由工程师设计交图。但实际出图时间比合同规定时间延误,所以承包商提出索赔要求。但是总的设计变更后,即使承包商索赔出一些费用,却为雇主节省了较多的工程款。

分析:(1)在要求的合理时间内发出了有关图纸、批示或给予批准;(2)承包商已向工程师发出书面通知,讲明工程进度等可能会受到阻延。除非工程师在合理时间内另行发出图纸、指示或批准,承包商则不索赔。

这种索赔的工程量及合同总价变更小于总合同价时,承包商只可索取增加工程成本,而无权索赔利润。若变更大于总合同价时,在合同价格中则要增加一笔款项。这一条款也要求工程师监理工程及实施变更必须早有计划及严密组织,若是因工程师拖延了承包商的施工进度,雇主就要多付出款项。

1.10 Employer's Use of Contractor's Documents(雇主使用承包商文件)

As between the Parties, the Contractor shall retain the copyright(版权)*and other intellectual property rights*(知识产权)*in the Contractor's Documents and other design docu-*

ments made by (or on behalf of) the Contractor.

The Contractor shall be deemed (by signing the Contract) to give to the Employer a non-terminable （无限期的）*transferable* （可转让的）*non-exclusive* （不排他的）*royalty-free* （免版税的）*licence to copy, use and communicate the Contractor's Documents, including making and using modifications of them. This licence shall:*

(a)apply throughout the actual or intended working life （寿命期）*(whichever is longer) of the relevant parts of the Works,*

(b)entitle any person in proper possession （正当占有）*of the relevant part of the Works to copy, use and communicate the Contractor's Documents for the purposes of completing, operating, maintaining, altering, adjusting, repairing and demolishing the Works, and*

(c)in the case of Contractor's Documents which are in the form of computer programs and other software, permit their use on any computer on the Site and other places as envisaged by the Contract, including replacements of any computers supplied by the Contractor.

The Contractor's Documents and other design documents made by (or on behalf of) the Contractor shall not, without the Contractor's consent, be used, copied or communicated to a third party by (or on behalf of) the Employer for purposes other than those permitted under this Sub-Clause.

由承包商或承包商授权人员编制的承包商文件及其他设计文件的版权和其他知识产权归承包商所有。承包商与雇主签署合同后，可视为承包商对雇主使用承包商文件给予了无期限、可转让、不排他、免版税的许可，允许雇主使用（如查阅、复制、传递等）承包商文件，并允许雇主对其进行修改和使用修改后的文件。雇主只能为本工程、本施工合同的目的才可使用承包商文件，未经承包商同意，雇主或其代表不能为了达到本款规定以外的其他目的使用、复制或与第三方交流承包商文件和其他设计文件。

一般来说，承包商给予雇主的使用许可应适用于工程相关部分的实际期限或预期寿命期中较长的期限。此项许可还应包括：(1)当具有工程相关部分正当占有权的任何人为了施工、运维、调整、修复或拆除该工程相关部分，承包商应允许该过程中承包商文件被复制、使用以及传递；(2)如果承包商文件的形式是计算机程序或其他软件，承包商应允许该形式下的承包商文件，在现场和合同中设想的其他场所的任何计算机上使用，包括对承包商提供的任何计算机进行替换。

承包商文件即工程上常说的"工程档案"。工程完工后，雇主要将工程的全部或部分权益让给他人，这种权益转让一般伴随着"工程资料"权益转让。如雇主出租办公楼，承租者可能要求雇主提供相关工程档案资料来了解承租楼房的工程情况，以便安排装修等事宜。一般来说，雇主在工程招标时会主动修改此项条款，以招标要求的形式直接要求投标人（承包商）放弃相关文件的版权及其他知识产权。投标人对此有疑义可走招标答疑程序，但如果雇主坚持此要求，投标人则要考虑实质性响应或放弃投标。由于工程项目单件性的特性，承包商放弃此项版权并不一定承担重大技术性损失，所以承包商一般都能接受此类要求。不排除承包商对自己的技术及文件有版权要求的情况，如承包商不愿意放弃此项版权，雇主在使用相关文件时需承担相关版权保护责任及版权使用费用。

1.11 Contractor's Use of Employer's Documents（承包商使用雇主文件）

As between the Parties, the Employer shall retain the copyright and other intellectual property rights in the Specification, the Drawings and other documents made by (or on behalf of) the Employer. The Contractor may, at his cost, copy, use, and obtain communication of these documents for the purposes of the Contract. They shall not, without the Employer's consent, be copied, used or communicated to a third party by the Contractor, except as necessary for the purposes of the Contract.

在合同双方之间，雇主应对规范、图纸和其他由雇主（或雇主授权的人员）编制的设计文件保留版权和其他知识产权。承包商可为合同目的，自费复印、使用及传输上述文件。除因履行合同而必需，不经雇主同意，承包商不得为第三方复印、使用或传输上述文件。

承包商使用雇主文件的版权规定很清楚，即除合同需要外，承包商不得复制、使用这些文件，或将其传送给第三方，即承包商可以使用和复制雇主的文件，但只能用于履行合同的目的。这既保障了承包商为实施工程而获得雇主方有关文件的权利，也保障了雇主对其文件享有的版权。

1.12 Confidential Details（保密事项）

The Contractor shall disclose all such confidential（机密的）and other information as the Engineer may reasonably require in order to verify the Contractor's compliance with the Contract.

在合理和工程需要的条件下，承包商应向工程师透露相关机密信息和其他信息，以便工程师查验承包商是否遵守合同规定。

在工程建设领域，有些承包商具有丰富工程经验，掌握了某些独特的可提高施工效率的施工技术和方法。为了保证其竞争力，投标时，这些承包商会将此类专门的施工技术和方法列为保密事项，以保护自己的利益。此类技术和方法也被称为"技术诀窍"，它不同于专利，不受法律保护，一旦公开，其他单位便可自由使用。

工程师有义务检查承包商是否遵守合同要求。即使承包商认为某些事项需要保密，但为了检查承包商的工作是否符合合同要求，工程师可合理要求承包商向工程师披露这些保密内容。工程师所获得的信息范围和文件复制要求应有所限制，且不允许为其他目的使用这些信息。

为保护承包商的利益，避免工程师提出过分的审查要求，工程师在行使审查权时，应确保其目的是核实承包商的工作是否符合合同，同时审查必须合法、合理。工程师也应从职业道德角度为承包商保密。

1.13 Compliance with Laws（遵守法律）

The Contractor shall, in performing the Contract, comply with applicable Laws. Unless otherwise sated in the Particular conditions:

(a) the Employer shall have obtained (or shall obtain) the planning（规划）, zoning（区域划定）or similar permission for the Permanent Works, and any other permissions described in the Specification as having been (or being) obtained by the Employer; and the Employer shall indemnify and hold the Contractor harmless against and from the consequences of any failure to do so; and

(b) the Contractor shall give all notices, pay all taxes, duties and fees, and obtain all permits, licences and approvals, as required by the Laws in relation to the execution and completion of the Works and the remedying of any defects; and the Contractor shall indemnify and hold the Employer harmless against and from the consequences of any failure to do so.

履行合同义务期间，承包商应遵守适用的法律。除非在专用条件中另有说明，雇主和承包商均应遵守相关适用法律、法规以及地方管辖区域的其他规定：

（1）雇主应已经或将要获得永久工程的规划、区域划定和其他类似许可，及规范中要求雇主应取得的其他许可；雇主应保障承包商不受其未得到上述许可的后果的侵害。雇主应获得的许可中，"类似许可证"应在专用条款中予以解释、澄清。

（2）承包商应取得法律中要求的与实施、完成工程和修补缺陷有关的各类许可和批准，并为实施、完成工程和修补缺陷发出通知、支付税款、关税和费用；承包商应保障雇主免遭因其未做到上述要求而造成的损失。承包商遵守适用法律应取得的各类许可中，某些许可可能在雇主招标前获得，但不要求承包商获得应由雇主获得的许可。

一方当事人应保障另一方免受其未能遵守此项要求而造成的损害。这项规定较严格，其涉及的金额可能远大于对费用和合理利润的索赔金额。因此，签订合同时双方应对涉及的责任进行明确规定。雇主负责获得永久工程涉及的规划和类似的许可，如雇主想获得其他许可，应在规范和雇主要求中明确规定，也应明确规定承包商应获得的所有其他的许可、批准等文件。但是如果相关适用法律（详细解释见第1.1.6.5款［法律］）发生变化，则承包商有权根据第13.7款［因法律改变的调整］的规定对工期和费用提出索赔。如果因行政当局造成工程延误或中断，承包商有权按照第8.5款［当局造成的延误］的规定提出工期延长。

1.14 Joint and Several Liability（共同的与各自的责任）

If the Contractor constitutes (under applicable Laws) a joint venture（合营企业，联营体）, consortium（联合企业，联合体）or other unincorporated grouping（未立案的组合，非法人组织）of two or more persons:

(a) these persons shall be deemed to be jointly and severally liable to the Employer

for the performance of the Contract;

　　(*b*)*these persons shall notify the Employer of their leader who shall have authority to bind the Contractor and each of these persons*;*and*

　　(*c*)*the Contractor shall not alter its composition or legal status without the prior consent of the Employer.*

　　如果承包商是由两个或两个以上遵照相关法律组成联营体、联合体或其他非法人组织的当事人，则：（1）这些当事人应在履行合同过程中对雇主负有共同的和各自的责任；（2）这些当事人应推选、指定其负责人并通知雇主，该负责人有权管理每个当事人及每位成员；（3）未经雇主同意，承包商不得改变其构成或法律地位。

　　国际工程承包中的联营体是两个或两个以上的公司根据适用的法律，组成一个投标单位来进行投标，并在中标后作为一个承包商来实施工程的单位。如果承包商是联营体或者是由两个或两个以上人员组成的其他组织，根据第 1.4 款［法律和语言］的规定，各当事人应就合同的履行向雇主承担连带责任。"连带责任"是依照法律规定或者当事人约定，两个或两个以上当事人对其共同债务全部承担或部分承担，并能因此引起其内部债务关系的一种民事责任。当责任人为多人时，每个人都负有清偿全部债务的责任，且保持各责任人之间的连带关系。

　　联营体既可以由一个国家内的两家或几家公司组成，也可由不同国家的公司联合组成。实际上，一般在投标阶段联营体各方需签订投标阶段的联合投标协议，中标后在原来协议的基础上签订新的联营体合同。联营体与合作体有所不同。合作体是由几家公司自愿结成合作伙伴，共同以合作体的名义与雇主签订工程承包意向合同（也称基本合同）。达成协议后，各公司再分别与雇主签订工程承包合同，并在合作体的统一计划、指挥和协调下完成承包任务。

　　承包商在决定以联营体或合作体形式参与投标之前，必须考虑这些要求。雇主也会在投标前或投标阶段，特别是在资格预审阶段检查联营体或合作体的承包资格。

思考题

　　1. 合同包括哪些文件？雇主的技术要求主要体现在哪些文件中？

　　2. FIDIC 施工合同条件和国内工程对"工程师"的定义有何不同？对工程项目的实施分别有什么优缺点？如何认识这种差异？

　　3. 简述雇主、工程师、承包商三者间的关系。

　　4. 简述 FIDIC 施工合同中主要事项的典型顺序。

　　5. 简述基准日期的定义。为什么需要指定基准日期？

　　6. 简述开工日期的认定和竣工时间的确定方法。

　　7. 简述竣工日期、接收证书、缺陷通知期三者间的联系。

　　8. 分别说明接收证书和履约证书的含义、作用以及颁发时间。

　　9. 简述中标合同金额与合同价格的费用组成以及两者的差异。

　　10. 工程师向雇主颁发期中付款证书和最终付款证书的期限分别是多少天？

　　11. 简述暂列金额的适用范围和作用。

12. 简述 FIDIC 施工合同条件中不可抗力和不可预见的联系和区别。
13. 简述履约担保的种类和形式。
14. 简述合同当事人在通信交流过程中的沟通途径以及有效送达形式。
15. 简述合同文件的优先次序以及解释方式。
16. 简述合同订立的原则、方式。
17. 简述合同转让的前提条件。
18. 承包商在什么条件下可以获得对延误图纸、指示造成损失的赔偿?
19. 分别说明雇主和承包商对文件的照管和提供职责。雇主在使用承包商文件时、承包商在使用雇主文件时分别有哪些注意事项?
20. 简述合同当事人在履行合同时的保障免责事项。
21. 简述联合承包的规定。

2 The Employer（雇主）

雇主是工程项目建设中最重要的角色，可以是个人、公司或政府部门及相关组织机构。作为施工合同当事人之一，雇主享有发布指示、任命工程师、指定分包商或供货商等权利，同时也承担提供现场占有权、按时支付工程款项、提供信息以及合作等义务。本条说明了雇主给予承包商现场进入权与占有权的相关规定，其核心是现场移交的注意事项与相关的索赔规定。

本章要求：了解雇主向承包商提供施工现场的义务；
　　　　　　了解雇主为承包商提供协助和配合等方面的义务；
　　　　　　了解承包商对雇主的项目资金安排的知情权；
　　　　　　了解雇主的索赔权以及遵循的程序。

2.1 Right of Access to the Site（现场进入权）

The Employer shall give the Contractor right of access to, and possession of（占用）, all parts of the Site within the time (or times) stated in the Appendix to Tender. The right and possession may not be exclusive to the Contractor. If, under the Contract, the Employer is required to give (to the Contractor) possession of any foundation, structure, plant or means of access, the Employer shall do so in the time and manner stated in the Specification. However, the Employer may withhold any such right or possession until the Performance Security has been received.

If no such time is stated in the Appendix to Tender, the Employer shall give the Contractor right of access to, and possession of, the Site within such times as may be required to enable the Contractor to proceed in accordance with the programme submitted under Sub-Clause 8.3 [Programme].

If the Contractor suffers delay and/or incurs Cost as a result of a failure by the Employer to give any such right or possession within such time, the Contractor shall give notice to the Engineer and shall be entitled subject to Sub-Clause 20.1 [Contractor's Claims] to:

(a) an extension of time for any such, delay, if completion is or will be delayed, under Sub-Clause 8.4 [Extension of Time for Completion], and

(b) payment of any such Cost plus reasonable profit, which shall be included in the Contract Price.

After receiving this notice, the Engineer shall proceed in accordance with Sub-Clause 3.5 [Determinations] to agree ordetermine these matters.

However, if and to the extent that the Employer'failure was caused by any error or delay by the Contractor, including an error in, or delay in the submission of, any of the Contractor's Documents, the Contractor shall not be entitled to such extension of time, Cost or profit.

  雇主应按投标函附录中规定的时间给予承包商进入和占用现场各部分的权利。根据合同要求，雇主需提供基础、结构、生产设备或进入手段等任何承包商可能用到现场各部分的占用权，并且应按规范要求在规定的时间内、以规定方式向承包商提供此现场进入权和占用权。承包商获得现场进入权和占用权的前提是，承包商已在规定时间内向雇主提交了履约担保。雇主如未收到履约担保，则有权暂时保留上述的现场进入权和占用权。

  如果投标书附录未规定承包商进入现场的时间，则雇主应在承包商依据第8.3款［进度计划］的规定，确定进行施工所需时间内给予承包商相应的现场进入权和占用权。如果雇主违反合同规定，未及时给予承包商现场进入和占用权，致使承包商遭受工期延误或费用损失，则承包商有权向工程师发出通知要求索赔（详见第20.1款［承包商的索赔］）。承包商提出的索赔可包括工期与费用，同时允许索赔合理利润。雇主应尽量避免此类错误的发生。工程师收到承包商的此类索赔通知后，应按照第3.5款［确定］的规定，对上述事项进行商定或确定。

  承包商对现场可能不享有专用权，即其他承包商或分包商同样享有现场进入权和占用权。如某工程项目中，土建施工与设备安装由不同的承包商承包，由于施工工序一般采用流水作业方式，承包商们可能同时使用施工现场，故现场的进入权和占用权并不由某一个承包商独享。

  由于进入权和占用权可能不由承包商独享，参考第4.6款［合作］的规定，承包商应按照合同规定或工程师的指示，为可能被雇佣在现场或其附近进行本合同未包括的任何工作人员（包括雇主人员、雇主雇用的其他承包商以及法定公共机构等），提供适当的工作环境和条件。如果承包商因工程师的指示，提供此工作环境和条件后增加了不可预见的费用，则该项指示构成变更（详见第13.1款［变更权］的规定），承包商可提出费用索赔。承包商应从招标文件提供的信息中查找有关其他承包商承包工程部分的实施计划，或向雇主要求此类实施计划的知情权。

  雇主必须按时向承包商提供现场及相关设施，否则需赔偿承包商由此遭受的损失；承包商在未及时获得现场及相关设施的使用权的情况下，提出索赔的前提是承包商已及时向工程师发出通知要求得到上述权利，且雇主拖延授权的原因并非出自承包商。

  例2.1、例2.2和例2.3分别列出了国内合同和国际合同中的"现场进入权"及限制条款。

【例2.1】某合同中的"进场条件和进场日期"条款

  承包商按专用条款约定的时间向发包人（雇主）提交施工用地的坐标位置、面积、占用时间、用途说明，并须单列要求雇主租地的坐标位置、面积、占用时间和用途说明。

  雇主根据批准的初步设计和条款约定由承包商提交的临时占地资料，与承包商约定进场条件，确定进场日期。雇主完成进场道路、用地许可、拆迁及补偿等工作，保证承包商能够按时进入现场开始准备工作。进场条件和进场日期在专用条款约定。

  因雇主原因造成承包商的进场时间延误，竣工日期顺延。雇主承担承包商因此发生的相关窝工费用。因承包商未能按时提交上述资料，导致条款约定的进场日期延误的，由此增加的费用或（和）竣工日期延误，由承包商负责。

【例 2.2】某国际工程合同中的"现场进入权"

Owner shall provide to the Contractor possession of the Site, with rights of access to and egress from the Site from the Commencement Date until Substantial Completion of the Facility. The Contractor acknowledges and agrees that it shall grant access and rights of temporary occupation to any third parties in relation to the Works as instructed by the Owner. During the Warranty Period the Owner shall grant to the Contractor rights of access and egress to and from the Facility and possession of such parts of the Facility as necessary to enable the Contractor to perform its obligations under the Contract.

【例 2.3】某国际工程合同中"现场进入权"的限制条款

The Contractor shall allow the Engineer and any person authorized by the Employer access to the Site and to any place where work in connection with the Contract is being carried out or is intended to be carried out.

2.2　Permits, Licences or Approvals（许可、执照或批准）

The Employer shall (where he is in a position to do so（按其所能）) provide reasonable assistance to the Contractor at the request of the Contractor：

(a) by obtaining copies of the Laws of the Country which are relevant to the Contract but are not readily available, and

(b) for（协助）the Contractor's applications for any permits, licencesor approvals required by the Laws of the Country：

　(i) which the Contractor is required to obtain under Sub-Clause 1.13［Compliance with Laws］,

　(ii) for the delivery of Goods, including clearance through customs（结关,清关,通关）, and

　(iii) for the export（出口）of Contractor's Equipment when it is removed from the Site.

承包商有权请求雇主提供工程所需的工程所在国的法律文本，以及承包商所需的许可、执照或批准。雇主应尽其所能提供合理协助，以便承包商取得或办理相关许可、执照或批准，包括第 1.13 款［遵守法律］中规定的承包商需要获取的各项许可、执照与批准，运输货物、出入关和设备离开现场时所需的许可。如果因雇主未能提供上述许可、执照或批准而致使承包商遭受损失，承包商有权向雇主提出索赔。

雇主需提供"合理的"协助，即雇主仅需在合理的范围内对承包商进行协助，而并不需要"全面、深入"地为承包商提供服务。承包商取得上述相关许可、执照或批准的途径并非只有通过雇主；承包商也可自行解决或者采取其他合法、合理、正当的方式获得。如果承包商向雇主提出的索赔超过了合理的限度，并对雇主造成损失，雇主也有权依据第 2.5 款［雇主的索赔］向承包商提出索赔。

实际工程中，由承包商协助雇主完成证照的申办更为普遍。

2.3 Employer's Personnel（雇主人员）

The Employer shall be responsible for ensuring that the Employer's Personnel and the Employer's other contractors on the Site：

(a) co-operate with the Contractor's efforts under Sub-Clause4.6 ［Co-operation］, and

(b) take actions similar to those which the Contractor is required to take under sub-paragraphs (a),(b) and (c) of Sub-Clause 4.8 ［Safety Procedures］and under Sub-Clause4.18 ［Protection of the Environment］.

雇主应保证在现场的雇主人员和承包商、各承包商之间紧密配合，相互合作。在现场的雇主人员和其他承包商应按照第4.6款［合作］的规定，配合承包商进行施工活动，推动项目建设正常、有序、安全地进行。同样，承包商也应为雇主人员、其他承包商、政府及相关机构人员在现场及现场附近的工作提供协助（详细解释参见第4.6款［合作］）。

根据第4.8款［安全程序］(a)、(b) 和 (c) 项的安全措施和第4.18款［环境保护］的环保措施规定，雇主及雇主人员、其他在现场出入的人员应遵守承包商的现场安全措施与环保措施相关规定和相关规章制度等。

2.4 Employer's Financial Arrangements（雇主的资金安排）

The Employer shall submit within 28 days after receiving any request from the Contractor, reasonable evidence that financial arrangements have been made and are being maintained which will enable the Employer to pay the Contract Price（as estimated at that time）in accordance with Clause 14 ［Contract Price and Payment］. If the Employer intends to make any material change（重大变更，实质性改变）to his financial arrangements, the Employer shall give notice to the Contractor with detailed particulars.

工程中，雇主拖欠承包商工程款的情况时有发生，对承包商会造成严重影响。工程项目通常涉及的资金数额较大，一旦雇主无法支付工程款，承包商会因此招致各种损失，如工期延迟、停工、资金链断裂、公司破产。本款规定了承包商对雇主资金安排的知情权，是对承包商权益的一种保护，旨在消除承包商履约时对雇主资金安排的顾虑，积极履行合同中规定的义务。

雇主应在收到此要求后28天内向承包商提供合理的证据，证明其工程款资金到位，且有能力按照第14条［合同价格和付款］的相关规定按时向承包商支付工程款。如果雇主对其资金安排作出实质性变更，则雇主应及时通知承包商并告知其详情。

雇主需提供的"合理证据"一般是银行开具的证明文件或类似说明。如果在合同中未明确规定此类证明文件或类似说明的性质或出处，在实际操作中容易存在较大的灵活操作空间，证明材料的真实性与有效性较难判断。当事人应在合同中对上述证明材料给予明确规定。

如果雇主未能遵守合同规定提供支付能力证明，承包商有权在按照第16.1款［承包商暂停工作的权利］的规定提前21天向雇主发出通知后，暂停或减缓施工进度。如果在承包商发出暂停工作通知后42天内，雇主仍未提供合理的支付能力证明，则承包商有权按照第16.2款［由承包商终止］的规定终止合同，此情况适用第16.3款［停止工作和承包商设备的撤离］和第16.4款［终止时的付款］中规定的程序（详细解释参见第16条［由承包商暂停和终止］）。

【例2.4】雇主开具的支付保函范例格式

合同简要介绍：

受益人名称和地址（合同定义为承包商的法人）：

我们已经得知（填入合同定义为"雇主"的法人，以下称为"委托人"）被要求开具银行保函。

应委托人的要求，我们（填入银行名称）在此不可撤回地承担在我方收到你方书面声明后，向你方——受益人/承包商支付总数不超过（填入"保函金额"，用文字表示）的一笔或多笔款项：

（a）对于按照合同应该支付的款额，委托人未能在合同规定的应支付此款额的期限满后14天内完全支付，及

（b）委托人未支付的数额。

任何支付要求必须附以一份关于委托人未完全支付的款额的［证明收款权力的文件列表］。要求支付的文件必须有你方签名，签名必须经你方银行或知名的公共机构证实。我方必须在此处，于（填入预计的工程缺陷责任期满后6个月的日期）或之前，收到你方经证实的要求和声明，在上述日期之后，本保函期满并应返还给我们。

除上文规定外，本保函受法律的约束，并受国际商会出版的编号为458的"即付保函的同意规则"的约束。

签名：
日期：

2.5 Employer's Claims（雇主的索赔）

If the Employer considers himself to be entitled to any payment under any Clause of these Conditions or otherwise in connection with the Contract, and/or to any extension of the Defects Notification Period, the Employer or the Engineer shall give notice and particulars（细节）to the Contractor. However, notice is not required for payments due under Sub-Clause 4.19［Electricity, Water and Gas］, under Sub-Clause 4.20［Employer's Equipment and Free-Issue Material］, or for other services requested by the Contractor.

The notice shall be given as soon as practicable after the Employer became aware of the event or circumstances giving rise to the claim. A notice relating to any extension of the Defects Notification Period shall be given before the expiry of such period.

The particulars shall specify the Clause or other basis of the claim, and shall include substantiation of the amount and/or extension to which the Employer considers himself to be entitled in connection with the Contract. The Engineer shall then proceed in accordance with Sub-Clause 3.5［Determinations］to agree or determine (i) the amount (if any) which the Employer is entitled to be paid by the Contractor, and/or (ii) the exten-

sion (if any) of the Defects Notification Period in accordance with Sub-Clause 11.3 [*Extension of Defects Notification Period*].

This amount may be included as a deduction in the Contract Price and Payment Certificates. The Employer shall only be entitled to set off against or make any deduction from an amount certified in a Payment Certificate, or to otherwise claim against the Contractor, in accordance with this Sub-Clause.

由于承包商的违约给雇主造成损失，雇主有权向承包商提出索赔。雇主提出索赔的内容包括款项和缺陷通知期限。当雇主认为根据合同规定其有权向承包商索赔某些款项或要求延长缺陷通知期时，雇主应在意识到引起索赔事件发生后，尽快向承包商发出通知，或由工程师向承包商发出通知，并附上详细说明书。通知所附的详细说明书应包括雇主索赔依据的条款和条目、索赔金额、延长缺陷通知期时间、相关的事实依据。此类通知发出后，工程师应按照第3.5款［确定］的规定确定承包商支付给雇主的赔偿额（如果有），以及缺陷通知期的延长时间（如果有）。上述赔偿款可从合同价格或付款证书中扣除，雇主仅有权按照相关规定从付款证书确认的金额中冲销或扣减该赔偿额，或者由承包商另行支付赔偿额，而无权向承包商提出其他支付要求。

对于承包商根据4.19款［电、水和燃气］或第4.20款［雇主设备和免费供应的材料］规定的到期应付款、或承包商要求的其他服务的应付款，雇主无需向承包商发出通知。即若由于雇主向承包商提供了水电、燃气、设备及服务等而承包商应向雇主支付款额，雇主或工程师不必发出上述通知。

【例2.5】索赔意向通知书

致：(被索赔单位名称)

根据《建设工程施工合同》XXXX条款的约定，由于发生了事件，且该事件的发生原因非我方原因所致。为此，我方向(被索赔单位名称)提出索赔要求。

附件：索赔事件资料

提出单位（盖章）：
负 责 人（签字）：
日　　　　期：

思考题

1. 分别说明承包商获得现场进入权与占用权以及由于权力被延误给予导致损失获得赔偿的前提条件。
2. 承包商在使用施工现场时应承担哪些责任？
3. 从现场、文件、人员三个角度出发，分别说明雇主向承包商提供协助和配合的具体义务。
4. 雇主应当如何证明其资金流转正常？
5. 简述承包商未获得雇主项目资金安排的知情权时享有的权利。
6. 简述雇主的索赔权以及遵循的程序。

3 The Engineer（工程师）

工程师，常被称为"咨询工程师（Consulting Engineer）"，是由雇主任命、帮助雇主进行工程项目相关管理工作的专业人员。工程师代表雇主管理工程，其能否充分发挥应有作用，是工程项目成败的关键之一。本条主要对工程师的职责和权力、工作方式、方法和内容以及工程师人选的替换进行了规定。

本章要求： 了解工程师的权力和职责范围；

了解工程师如何向其助手指派任务和托付权力；

了解工程师如何下达指令；

了解雇主替换工程师的规定；

了解工程师对事项进行确定的内容。

3.1 Engineer's Duties and Authority（工程师的任务和权力）

The Employer shall appoint the Engineer who shall carry out the duties assigned to him in the Contract. The Engineer's staff shall include suitably qualified engineers and other professionals who are competent to carry out these duties.

The Engineer shall have no authority（权限，授权）to amend the Contract.

The Engineer may exercise the authority attributable to the Engineer as specified（按照说明）in or necessarily to be implied（必然隐含）from the Contract. If the Engineer is required to obtain the approval of the Employer before exercising a specified authority, the requirements shall be as stated in theParticular Conditions. The Employer undertakes not to impose further constraints on the Engineer's authority, except as agreed with the Contractor.

However, whenever the Engineer exercises a specified authority for which the Employer's approval is required, then (for the purposes of the Contract) the Employer shall be deemed to have given approval.

Except as otherwise stated in these Conditions：

(a) whenever carrying out duties or exercising authority, specifiedin or implied by the Contract, the Engineer shall be deemed to act for the Employer；

(b) the Engineer has no authority to relieve either Party of any duties, obligations or responsibilities under the Contract； and

(c) any approval, check, certificate, consent, examination, inspection, instruction, notice, proposal, request, test, or similar act by the Engineer (including absence of disapproval（未表示不同意））shall not relieve the Contractor from any responsibility he has under the Contract, including responsibility for errors, omissions, discrepancies（误差）

and non-compliances（未遵办）。

工程师作为雇主人员，由雇主任命（详细解释参见第 1.1.2.4 款 [工程师]），是具有适当资质、能力的工程师（人员）和专业人员。工程师代表雇主管理工程，但本质上来说工程师只是雇主任命、委派、雇佣为项目提供专业工程管理服务的人员，工程师不是施工合同当事人，仅是合同当事人（雇主）的委托人。

工程师有向雇主建议的权力。对于合同中不合理或错误的条款，工程师可向雇主指出，并由雇主出面与承包商进行协商和谈判。除另有说明外，工程师无权解除雇主或承包商任一方合同规定的任何权利、义务或职责，且工程师的任何决定不应解除承包商根据合同规定应承担的，包括对错误、遗漏、误差和未遵办在内的任何职责。工程师受雇主委托监管承包商的合同行为，工程师的确认是对承包商合同行为的评定，此类评定不能改变合同赋予承包商的责任。

工程师可行使合同中明文规定或必然隐含的属于工程师的权力。除另有说明外，工程师履行或行使上述权力时，均视为代表雇主执行。雇主可通过专用条件规定工程师行使权力时须取得雇主的批准，这种情况一般出现在雇主具有良好的工程管理能力的情况下。工程师行使需要由雇主批准的规定权力时，为了合同的目的，应视为雇主已经予以批准。如果雇主想要进一步限制工程师行使权力，需征得承包商同意。这实质上消除了承包商对工程师行使权力的质疑权，同时保证承包商执行工程师的指令。对于承包商而言，无需为执行工程师的指令承担责任风险。实际工程中，常出现承包商执行工程师的某项指令后，雇主却提出此项指令不代表雇主意愿，以工程师越权为由解聘工程师并要求承包商无偿整改。将工程师的指令视为已取得雇主的批准，这使得承包商无需为工程师和雇主的决定分歧承担责任与风险。

3.2　Delegation by the Engineer（由工程师付托）

The Engineer may from time to time assign du ties and delegate authority to assistants, and may also revoke such assignmentor delegation. These assistants may include a resident engineer（驻地工程师）,*and/or independent inspectors*（独立检查员）*appointed to inspect and/or test items of Plant and/or Materials. The assignment, delegation or revocation shall be in writing and shall not take effect until copies have been received by both Parties. However, unless otherwise agreed by both Parties, the Engineer shall not delegate the authority to determine any matter in accordance with Sub-Clause 3.5 [Determinations].*

Assistants shall be suitably qualified persons, who are competent to carry out these duties and exercise this authority, and who are fluent in the language for communications defined in Sub-Clause 1.4 [Law and Language].

Each assistant, to whom duties have been assigned or authority has been delegated, shall only be authorised to issue instructions to the Contractor to the extent defined by the delegation. Any approval, check, certificate, consent, examination, inspection, instruction, notice, proposal, request, test, or similar act by an assistant, in accordance with the delegation, shall have the same effect as though the act had been an act of the Engineer. However:

(a) any failure to disapprove any work, Plant or Materials shall not constitute approval, and shall therefore not prejudice the right of the Engineer to reject the work, Plant or Materials;

(b) if the Contractor questions any determination or instruction of an assistant, the Contractor may refer the matter to the Engineer, who shall promptly confirm, reverse or vary the determination or instruction.

工程项目工期长、规模大、现场工作量繁重，施工过程中仅靠工程师一人难以完成合同指派的任务。因此工程师可委托其助手协助工作。工程师可随时向其助手指派任务和委托权力，也可撤销这种指派或委托。工程师助手的指派、委托或撤销应采用书面形式，并在双方收到抄送文本后方生效。工程师助手一般分为驻地工程师和独立检查人员（检验或试验各项工程设备、材料的检查人员），应具有相应的资质、能履行被委托的任务、行使相应权力、流利使用第1.4款［法律和语言］规定的交流语言。

工程师助手行使权利不可超出委托规定的范围。已被指派任务或托付权力的助手，应在被授权的委托范围内向承包商发出指示，此类指示的效力应视为等同于由工程师作出。工程师助手对任何工作、生产设备或材料未提出否定意见，不构成批准，工程师有拒绝承认上述事物的权利。承包商对工程师助手的确定或指示提出质疑，可告知工程师，工程师收到该项告知后应迅速对上述确定或指示进行确认、取消或变更。

工程师不应将确定任何事项的权利（详见第3.5款［确定］的规定）托付给他人。对于重大的或有重要影响的工作，如根据第3.5款［确定］的规定所需确定的任何事项，其成果对工程影响较大，此类工作一般不允许工程师委托工程师助手来执行，工程师若需委托，则应征得雇主和承包商双方的批准、认可、同意。

【例3.1】XX专业监理工程师授权书

根据项目监理机构组建报告和监理工作需要，我以XXXX项目总监理工程师的名义授权XXX同志为本项目XX专业监理工程师，按照委托监理合同和监理规划的要求，履行监理工程师的下列职责：

1. 负责编制本专业的监理实施细则；
2. 负责本专业监理工作的具体实施；
3. 组织、指导、检查和监督本专业监理员的工作，当人员需要调整时，向总监理工程师提出建议；
4. 审查承包单位提交的涉及本专业的计划、方案、申请、变更，并向总监理工程师提出报告；
5. 负责本专业检验批、分项工程验收及隐蔽工程验收；
6. 定期向总监理工程师提交本专业监理工作实施情况，对重大问题及时向总监理工程师汇报和请示；
7. 根据本专业监理工作实施情况做好监理日记；
8. 负责本专业监理资料的收集、汇总及整理，参与编写监理月报；
9. 核查进场材料、设备、构配件的原始凭证、检测报告等质量证明文件及其质量情况，根据实际情况认为有必要时对进场材料、设备、构配件进行平行检验，合格后予以签认；

10. 负责本专业的工程计量工作，审核工程计量有关数据和原始凭证。

……

总监理工程师：
日　　　　期：

3.3　Instructions of the Engineer（工程师的指示）

The Engineer may issue to the Contractor (at any time) instructions and additional or modified Drawings which may be necessary for the execution of the Works and the remedying of any defects, all in accordance with the Contract. The Contractor shall only take instructions from the Engineer, or from an assistant to whom the appropriate authority has been delegated under this Clause. If an instruction constitutes a Variation, Clause 13 [Variations and Adjustments] shall apply.

The Contractor shall comply with the instructions given by the Engineer or delegated assistant, on any matter related to the Contract. Whenever practicable, their instructions shall be given in writing. If the Engineer or a delegated assistant：

(a) gives an oral instruction,

(b) receives a written confirmation of the instruction, from (or on behalf of) the Contractor, within two working days after giving the instruction, and

(c) does not reply by issuing a written rejection and/or instruction within two working days after receiving the confirmation, then the confirmation shall constitute the written instruction of the Engineer or delegated assistant (as the case may be).

工程师可在任何时候，按合同规定向承包商发出指示和图纸（如实施工程和修补缺陷可能需要的附加或修正图纸）。承包商仅接受工程师或工程师助手（详细解释见第3.2款［由工程师付托］）的指示。如果该指示内容构成一项变更，则应参照第13条［变更和调整］的规定进行办理。

工程师或工程师助手发出的指示应采用书面形式。如果工程师或工程师助手给出口头指示，且在给出指示后两个工作日内收到承包商或承包商代表对该指示的书面确认回执，并在收到书面确认后两个工作日内未发出书面拒绝或其他指示，则视为上述口头指示已经成为工程师或工程师助手的书面指示。

"工程师可在任何时候按合同规定向承包商发出指示"，具体时间范围是合同有效期内，即中标通知书有效送达到履约证书有效送达。实际工程中，当工程建设进入尾声，承包商会逐步退场，工程师的服务也相应表现为某种形式的"退场"。此时承包商容易对工程师发出的指示或通知的效力产生质疑，特别是一些重大的变更及修补，承包商可能会以各种借口推托。但只要工程师的指示是在合同规定的时间范围内发出的，承包商应遵循。

工程师可在合同规定的范围内直接向承包商发出指令，一旦工程师的指令超出了合同的范围，应以"变更（详见第13条［变更和调整］的规定）"形式发出。承包商的合同范围外工作通常会增加工程量或资金，如果工程师下达的指示构成了实质性的变更，应遵循有关变更和调整的相关规定。承包商在执行工程师的指示前，也应仔细审阅指示，对于超出合同范围的工作应向工程师提出下达变更，减少风险。

【例 3.2】监理工程师通知单

　　致：

　　事由：

　　内容：

　　要求：以上问题限施工单位日内整改完毕，并自检合格后，书面反馈我部复查符合要求（方可继续施工）。

监理机构：

总/专业监理工程师：

日期：

3.4　Replacement of the Engineer（工程师的替换）

　　If the Employer intends to replace the Engineer, the Employer shall, not less than 42 days before the intended date of replacement, give notice to the Contractor of the name, address and relevant experience of the intended replacement Engineer. The Employer shall not replace the Engineer with a person against whom the Contractor raises reasonable objection by notice to the Employer, with supporting particulars.

　　工程师作为雇主人员，由雇主聘任并为雇主服务。雇主拥有替换工程师的权力，如果雇主对工程师的工作表现不满意，拟替换工程师，应于拟替换日期 42 天前向承包商发出通知，告知承包商新工程师的姓名、地址和相关工作经验。若承包商对此人选有异议，可提出合理的反对意见，并附详细的依据支持该反对意见，如承包商和新工程师人选存在纠纷无法合作等。若承包商提出的异议合理，雇主应改选拟替换工程师。

【例 3.3】总监理工程师变更申请书

　　致：XX 公司

　　应 XX 建设单位要求，现申请将总监理工程师由 XX 同志变更为 XX 同志。由 XX 同志负责 XX 工程项目的监理工作。

XX 工程监理有限公司

XXXX 年 XX 月 XX 日

3.5　Determinations（确定）

　　Whenever these Conditions provide that the Engineer shall proceed in accordance with this Sub-Clause 3.5 to agree or determine any matter, the Engineer shall consult with each Party in an endeavour to reach agreement. If agreement is not achieved, the

Engineer shall make a fair determination in accordance with the Contract, taking due regard of all relevant circumstances. The Engineer shall give notice to both Parties of each agreement or determination, with supporting particulars. Each Party shall give effect to each agreement or determination unless and until revised under Clause 20 [Claims, Disputes and Arbitration].

　　工程师承担工程中各项协调工作，担当组织、协调、解决纠纷等工作任务。当规定工程师需按本款对任何事项进行商定或确定时，工程师应在作出确定之前充分听取雇主与承包商双方的意见，尽量促成双方满意的协议。如果雇主与承包商产生分歧，工程师应综合考虑，依据合同规定作出公正的确定，并向双方都发出附有详细依据的通知。双方在收到通知后应当履行该确定事项的内容。如果某一方对工程师的确定持有不同意见，在收到上述确定通知后，该方可按照第20条[索赔、争端和仲裁]的规定申诉，但在申诉结果生效前，双方应当继续履行工程师的确定事项。

【例3.4】
　　由于某地连日暴雨，造成某房地产项目工地无法正常施工，以致工期延误。甲房地产开发公司（雇主）与乙工程建设公司（承包商）就工期延误的责任划分发生了争议，雇主主张是承包商对于恶劣天气准备不足而造成的工期延误。而承包商主张连日暴雨的影响已超出承包商的准备所能应对的程度，应属于自然灾害类的不可抗力影响，从而据此提出工期索赔。
　　双方争执十分激烈以致影响工程的正常施工。在此纠纷发生后，工程师积极听取双方的主张，依据工程实际调查情况与相关合同规定及案例，否决乙方不可抗力的主张，裁定工期索赔不成立。
　　此时承包商对工程师的确定不服，并提出申诉。
　　最终，工程师在综合考虑下作出了支持承包商的工期索赔的确定，化解了这一矛盾。
　　在此案例中，在申诉结果出来之前，承包商依据合同规定仍然要保持工程施工的正常进行，履行工程师目前的裁定，不可采取罢工等手段，这是违反合同义务的。

思考题

1. 简述工程师的职责和权力范围。
2. 雇主能否越过工程师直接向承包商下达指示，为什么？
3. 简述工程师助手的任命程序和权力范围。
4. 具体说明工程师如何向承包商下达指令以及指令的要求。
5. 简述雇主替换工程师的权力。
6. 简述工程师对事项进行确定的职责。

4 The Contractor（承包商）

作为工程项目施工过程的具体实施者，承包商在工程中具有十分关键的作用。承包商必须具备相应的施工资质、技术和管理能力，并严格执行、认真履行合同中规定的相应责任。

本章要求：了解承包商的基本责任；

了解履约担保的相关规定；

了解承包商代表的相关条款及对分包、转让、合作以及现场放线的规定；

了解现场作业、安全、质量保证、环保的有关规定；

了解现场数据、现场条件、道路通行权、运输、化石等方面承包商承担的责任与拥有的权力；

了解进度报告以及提交程序的内容。

4.1 Contractor's General Obligations（承包商的一般义务）

The Contractor shall design (to the extent specified in the Contract), execute and complete the Works in accordance with the Contract and with the Engineer's instructions, and shall remedy any defects in the Works.

The Contractor shall provide the Plant and Contractor's Documents specified in the Contract, and all Contractor's Personnel, Goods, consumables（消耗品）and other things and services, whether of a temporary or permanent nature, required in and for this design, execution, completion and remedying of defects.

The Contractor shall be responsible for the adequacy, stability and safety of all Site operations and of all methods of construction. Except to the extent specified in the Contract, the Contractor (i) shall be responsible for all Contractor's Documents, Temporary Works, and such design of each item of Plant and Materials as is required for the item to be in accordance with the Contract, and (ii) shall not otherwise be responsible for the design or specification of the Permanent Works.

The Contractor shall, whenever required by the Engineer, submit details of the arrangements and methods which the Contractor proposes to adopt for the execution of the Works. No significant alteration to these arrangements and methods shall be made without this having previously been notified to the Engineer.

If the Contract specifies that the Contractor shall design any part of the Permanent Works, then unless otherwise stated in the Particular Conditions：

(a) the Contractor shall submit to the Engineer the Contractor's Documents for this part in accordance with the procedures specified in the Contract；

(b) these Contractor's Documents shall be in accordance with the Specification and Drawings, shall be written in the language for communications defined in Sub-Clause 1.4 [Law and Language], and shall include additional information required by the Engineer to add to the Drawings for co-ordination of each Party's designs;

(c) the Contractor shall be responsible for this part and it shall, when the Works are completed, be fit for such purposes for which the part is intended as are specified in the Contract; and

(d) prior to the commencement of the Tests on Completion, the Contractor shall submit to the Engineer the "as-built" documents (竣工文件) and operation and maintenance manuals in accordance with the Specification and in sufficient detail for the Employer to operate, maintain, dismantle, reassemble, adjust and repair this part of the Works. Such part shall not be considered to be completed for the purposes of taking-over under Sub-Clause 10.1 [Taking Over of the Works and Sections] until these documents and manuals have been submitted to the Engineer.

承包商应按照合同要求和工程师的指示，完成合同中规定的由承包商负责的部分或全部工程。在实施和完成施工义务的同时，修补工程中的任何缺陷，并按照规定提供相应的生产设备、承包商文件、承包商人员、货物、消耗品、其他物品和服务等。承包商应对所有现场作业、施工方法以及全部工程的完备性、稳定性、安全性承担责任。工程师可随时要求承包商提供施工方法和施工安排等，如果承包商随后需要修改，应事先通知工程师。

承包商应对所有承包商文件、临时工程及按照合同要求的每项生产设备、材料的设计承担责任，但不对永久工程的设计或规范负责，除非合同另有规定。如果合同要求承包商负责设计某部分永久工程，承包商应按照规定程序向工程师提交符合规范和图纸要求，并用合同规定的语言书写的承包商文件，同时还应包括工程师为协调各方所需附加的资料。承包商应对该设计部分负责，工程竣工时应使该部分设计符合合同规定。竣工试验开始前，承包商应按照规范要求向工程师提交竣工文件和操作维护手册，此类资料应详尽，以便雇主使用。如果承包商未提交此类竣工文件和操作维护手册，该部分工程不能视为完工和验收。

承包商的任何义务都与费用相对应。按照FIDIC合同条件，承包商义务主要有：(1)完成项目本体；(2)完成项目本体需要进行的各项措施；(3)对完成的项目本体及完成项目所采用的措施承担责任（包括合同内的设计责任）。上述承包商义务在清单计价中对应的费用为：(1)工程本体相关费用，由分项工程综合单价费用构成；(2)完成工程实体相关的措施费用，包括人员货物的组织及各种非工程实体的临时性措施工程（比如脚手架等），即清单中的措施费用（包括开办费用）；(3)为工程实体的完备性承担责任（主要指修补缺陷）以及为工程实体的稳定性负责（主要指为工程质量负责）而产生的费用，如维护工程的工作效能所导致的费用。如果合同规定承包商承担部分工程设计责任，相应地也要承担设计费。由于工程项目具有单件性，因此每个项目中承包商要承担的义务不完全相同。只有承包商合同义务与发生的费用一一对应，才能够体现合理的工程造价。

实施、完成工程项目并修补工程中的任何缺陷，是承包商最基本、最重要的义务。围绕该义务，承包商应承担的主要责任如下：

(1) 对现场施工作业、施工方法负责。
1) 提供相关生产设备、消耗品、货物等物品；2) 提供临时或永久性的工作人员；3) 提供合同规定的相关服务。
(2) 对全部工程施工质量负责。
1) 保证工程实体按规范要求、合同要求实施，其完备性符合合同要求；2) 保证工程实体能达到所要求的使用目的；3) 保证工程实体能达到所要求的使用年限。
(3) 对全部承包商文件、临时工程及合同规定的生产设备和材料的设计负责。
1) 提供相关施工方法及施工安排的文件；2) 提供临时工程并保证其符合相关施工及安全规定；3) 提供合同要求的生产设备、材料的设计。
(4) 对合同规定的部分工程的设计负责，并为该部分工程的图纸、施工质量、竣工文件、操作维护手册等负责。

4.2 Performance Security（履约担保）

The Contractor shall obtain (at his cost) a Performance Security for proper performance, in the amount and currencies stated in the Appendix to Tender. If an amount is not stated in the Appendix to Tender, this Sub-Clause shall not apply.

The Contractor shall deliver the Performance Security to the Employer within 28 days after receiving the Letter of Acceptance, and shall send a copy to the Engineer. The Performance Security shall be issued by an entity and from within a country (or other jurisdiction) approved by the Employer, and shall be in the form annexed to the Particular Conditions or in another form approved by the Employer.

The Contractor shall ensure that the Performance Security is valid and enforceable until the Contractor has executed and completed the Works and remedied any defects. If the terms of the Performance Security specify its expiry date, and the Contractor has not become entitled to receive the Performance Certificate by the date 28 days prior to the expiry date, the Contractor shall extend the validity of the Performance Security until the Works have been completed and any defects have been remedied.

The Employer shall not make a claim under the Performance, Security, except for amounts to which the Employer is entitled under the Contract in the event of:

(a) failure by the Contractor to extend the validity of the Performance Security as described in the preceding paragraph, in which event the Employer may claim the full amount of the Performance Security,

(b) failure by the Contractor to pay the Employer an amount due, as either agreed by the Contractor or determined under Sub-Clause 2.5 [Employer's Claims] or Clause 20 [Claims, Disputes and Arbitration], within 42 days after this agreement or determination,

(c) failure by the Contractor to remedy a default within 42 days after receiving the Employer's notice requiring the default to be remedied, or

(d) circumstances which entitle the Employer to termination under Sub-Clause 15.2 [Termination by Employer], irrespective of whether notice of termination has been given.

The Employer shall indemnify and hold the Contractor harmless against and from all damages, losses and expenses (including legal fees and expenses) resulting from a claim under the Performance Security to the extent to which the Employer was not entitled to make the claim.

The Employer shall return the Performance Security to the Contractor within 21 days after receiving a copy of the Performance Certificate.

国际工程中，雇主常要求承包商提供履约担保，以保证承包商按照合同履行义务和职责。承包商应按投标书附录规定的金额（如果投标书附录中未提出保证金额则本款规定不适用）和币种提供履约担保。承包商应在收到中标函 28 天内，向雇主提交履约担保，并抄送给工程师一份副本。开具履约担保的机构应是雇主批准、认可的国家（或其他司法管辖区）内的实体机构，且开具的履约担保应采用专用条件所附的范例格式，或雇主批准、认可的其他格式。承包商应保证在工程全部竣工和修复缺陷前，履约担保一直有效，且可被执行。如果履约担保的条款规定了其有效期，若承包商在有效期期满前 28 天无法获得履约证书，则应将履约担保的有效期延长，至工程完工和缺陷修复。

雇主根据合同规定及履约担保提出索赔有以下几种情况：（1）承包商未按上述规定延长履约担保有效期，雇主可没收该履约担保的全部金额；（2）在合同双方商定或由工程师作出确定后 42 天内，承包商未支付其已同意支付或由工程师决定（详细解释参见第 2.5 款 [雇主的索赔] 或第 20 条 [索赔、争端和仲裁]）的索赔款；（3）在收到雇主发出的补救违约通知后 42 天内，承包商仍未对其违约行为进行纠正补救；（4）雇主根据第 15.2 款 [由雇主终止] 的规定有权终止合同的情况。

如果雇主在无权提出履约担保的情况下向承包商索赔，则由此使承包商招致的一切损失由雇主承担，包括损害赔偿费、法律方面的费用和开支等。雇主应在收到工程师签发的履约证书 21 天内将履约担保退还给承包商。

履约担保的条款内容在国际上并无统一格式，FIDIC 施工合同条件附录中列有履约担保的推荐格式，供合同当事人选择使用。见例 1.14 和例 1.15。在实际操作中，雇主通常会根据实际需要将担保条件设置得更严格，以获取更大的保证能力。常见的设置条件有：

（1）接保即付，即取消对雇主提供承包商违约说明的要求。通常要求银行只要接到雇主通知立即支付担保金额。

（2）承包商关于雇主保函的任何质疑，均不应获得银行任何形式的支持。

（3）合同中的任何行为及不合法规定，均不能解除担保义务。

4.3 Contractor's Representative（承包商代表）

The Contractor shall appoint the Contractor's Representative and shall give him all authority necessary to act on the Contractor's behalf under the Contract.

Unless the Contractor's Representative is named in the Contract, the Contractor shall, prior to the Commencement Date, submit to the Engineer for consent the name and particulars of the person the Contractor proposes to appoint as Contractor's Representative. If consent is withheld or subsequently revoked, or if the appointed person fails to act as Contractor's Representative, the Contractor shall similarly submit the name and particulars of another suitable person for such appointment.

The Contractor shall not, without the prior consent of the Engineer, revoke the appointment of the Contractor's Representative or appoint a replacement.

The whole time of the Contractor's Representative shall be given to directing the Contractor's performance of the Contract. If the Contractor's Representative is to be temporarily absent from the Site during the execution of the Works, a suitable replacement person shall be appointed, subject to the Engineer's prior consent, and the Engineer shall be notified accordingly.

The Contractor's Representative shall, on behalf of the Contractor, receive instructions under Sub-Clause 3.3 [Instructions of the Engineer].

The Contractor's Representative may delegate any powers（职权）, functions（任务）and authority（权力）to any competent person, and may at any time revoke the delegation. Any delegation or revocation shall not take effect until the Engineer has received prior notice signed by the Contractor's Representative, naming the person and specifying the powers, functions and authority being delegated or revoked.

The Contractor's Representative and all these persons shall be fluent in the language for communications defined in Sub-Clause 1.4 [Law and Language].

承包商代表作为承包商实际驻场的管理人员，应被赋予按合同所需要的、代表承包商工作时的一切权力。除非合同中写明承包商代表的姓名，否则承包商应在开工日期前将拟任承包商代表的人员姓名、详细资料提交给工程师并征得同意。如果该承包商代表未经过工程师同意或承包商撤销该人员的任命，则该人员不能担任承包商代表。未经工程师同意，承包商不得私自更换承包商代表。承包商代表应将其全部时间用于现场工作。工程施工期间，若承包商代表需临时离开现场，承包商应指派他人代其履行有关职责，该指派人员同样也需征得工程师的同意。

承包商代表应代承包商接受工程师的各项指令（详细解释参见第3.3款［工程师的指示］）。承包商代表可将其权力和职责委托给任何有能力的下属，也可随时撤销委托，此类委托和撤销委托必须通知工程师，并写明被委托的具体职权、任务和权力，征得工程师同意后方可生效。承包商代表及其委托人员应具有流利使用合同规定语言（详细解释参见第1.4款［法律和语言］）的能力。

承包商代表履行职责时应与工程师密切配合，保证工程项目的顺利完成。

4.4 Subcontractors（分包商）

The contractor shall not subcontract the whole of the works.
The Contractor shall be responsible for the acts or defaults of any Subcontractor, his

agents or employees, as if they were the acts or defaults of the Contractor. Unless otherwise stated in the Particular Conditions:

(a) the Contractor shall not be required to obtain consent to suppliers of Materials (材料), or to a subcontract for which the Subcontractor is named in the Contract;

(b) the prior consent of the Engineer shall be obtained to other proposed Subcontractors;

(c) the Contractor shall give the Engineer not less than 28 days' notice of the intended date of the commencement of each Subcontractor's work, and of the commencement of such work on the Site; and

(d) each subcontract shall include provisions which would entitle the Employer to require the subcontract to be assigned to the Employer under Sub-Clause 4.5 [Assignment of Benefit of Subcontract] (if or when applicable) or in the event of termination under Sub-Clause 15.2 [Termination by Employer].

承包商不得将整个工程分包出去。承包商应对任何分包商、分包商代理人及分包商雇员的行为或违约负责。除非专用条件中另有规定，承包商在选择材料供货商及指定分包商时无需经工程师同意，其他分包商则需经工程师同意。承包商应至少提前28天通知工程师分包商所承担工作的拟定开工日期和该工作在现场的开工日期。承包商与分包商签订分包合同时，分包合同中应加入有关规定，使分包合同能在特定情况（详细解释参见第4.5款［分包合同权益的转让］和第15.2款［由雇主终止］）下被转让给雇主。

工程中承包商常需要分包商共同协作完成任务。分包商工作的质量直接影响整个工程的实施，在选择分包商时，承包商应遵守工程所在地的法律，在符合主合同（雇主与承包商签订的施工合同）要求的同时，注重考察其综合能力，包括报价的合理性、技术力量、财务力量、信誉等。

在分包工作实施的过程中，承包商必须遵守分包合同的规定，履行其在分包合同中的义务和职责。由于分包商与雇主无直接合同关系，分包商无需接受工程师或工程师助理的指令，如果分包商擅自接受该指令，则承包商可不为其行为带来的后果负责。承包商应委派专人与分包商进行工作对接，监督和管理分包商的工作，使分包工作按时、保质地进行。

4.5 Assignment of Benefit of Subcontract（分包合同权益的转让）

If a Subcontractor's obligations extend beyond the expiry date of the relevant Defects Notification Period and the Engineer, prior to this date, instructs the Contractor to assign the benefit of such obligations to the Employer, then the Contractor shall do so. Unless otherwise stated in the assignment, the Contractor shall have no liability to (不承担责任) the Employer for the work carried out by the Subcontractor after the assignment takes effect.

缺陷通知期限通常为工程竣工后一年。如果在缺陷通知期（详细解释参见第1.1.3.7款［缺陷通知期限］）期满之日，分包商的义务还未结束，则工程师可在该日期之前指示承包商将此类义务的权益转让给雇主，承包商应照办。参见第 4.4 款 [分包商] 中 (d) 项的规定，分包合同应包括上述权益转让规定，因此当承包商安排权益转让事宜时，分包商应遵守分包合同的规定配合权益转让。如在转让中没有其他说明，则在权益转让后，承包商不再对分包商实施的工作向雇主负责。

　　工程师只有在主合同中涉及分包工程的缺陷责任通知期期满之前通知承包商，承包商才有义务安排上述转让事宜。分包合同权益的转让通常比较复杂，雇主对于超出主承包商合同期限的分包商，可单独发包并管理。

　　有时在承包商的缺陷通知期结束后，分包商的缺陷通知期却未结束，如：提供机电设备的分包商（供货商）按分包合同或适用法律向承包商提供一年以上的维修保证。此时如果分包商提供的设备出现问题，由于承包商的合同义务完全结束，雇主无法要求承包商负责，且由于雇主与分包商无直接合同关系，雇主也无法直接要求分包商负责。在这种情况下，工程师提出分包权益转让时，承包商应当按照要求安排转让事宜。

4.6　Co-operation（合作）

The Contractor shall, as specified in the Contract or as instructed by the Engineer, allow appropriate opportunities for carrying out work to:

(a) the Employer's Personnel,

(b) any other contractors employed by the Employer, and

(c) the personnel of any legally constituted public authorities,

who may be employed in the execution on or near the Site of any work not included in the Contract.

Any such instruction shall constitute a Variation if and to the extent that it causes the Contractor to incur Unforeseeable Cost. Services for these personnel and other contractors may include the use of Contractor's Equipment, Temporary Works or access arrangements which are the responsibility of the Contractor.

If, under the Contract, the Employer is required to give to the Contractor possession of any foundation, structure, plant or means of access in accordance with Contractor's Documents, the Contractor shall submit such documents to the Engineer in the time and manner stated in the Specification.

　　对于某些工程，尤其是大型项目和改建项目，施工现场通常不由承包商独享，会出现多方同时施工的情形（详细解释参见第 2.1 款 [进入现场的权利]）。承包商应依据合同的规定或工程师的指示，为可能被雇佣在现场或现场附近从事本合同未包括工作的人员（包括雇主人员、其他承包商及其人员、某些公共当局的工作人员）提供适当的工作条件。承包商提供"适当的工作条件"是为上述人员和其他承包商提供服务，包括使用承包商设备、临时工程以及提供进场安排。如果由于提供上述便利导致承包商增加不可预见的费用，工程师的该项指示应构成变更。

　　如果工程师的指示超出合同中规定的任务范围，即构成变更的情况，承包商应主动要求工程师按变更程序处理。此类为雇主及其人员或其他承包商提供服务而造成的任何工期延误，或者为法定的公共机构提供服务导致工期延误或中断，均构成工期延长条件（详细解释参见第 8.4 款［竣工时间的延长］和第 8.5 款［当局造成的延误］），承包商有权提出延长竣工时间。

4.7　Setting Out（放线）

　　The Contractor shall set out the Works in relation to original points（原始基准点），*lines*（基准线）*and levels of reference*（基准标高）*specified in the Contract or notified by the Engineer. The Contractor shall be responsible for the correct positioning of all parts of the Works, and shall rectify any error in the positions, levels, dimensions or alignment of the Works.*

　　The Employer shall be responsible for any errors in these specified or notified items of reference, but the Contractor shall use reasonable efforts to verify their accuracy before they are used.

　　If the Contractor suffers delay and/or incurs Cost from executing work which was necessitated by an error in these items of reference, and an experienced contractor could not reasonably have discovered such error and avoided this delay and/or Cost, the Contractor shall give notice to the Engineer and shall be entitled subject to Sub-Clause 20.1 ［Contractor's Claims］to：

　　(a) an extension of time for any such delay, if completion is or will be delayed, under Sub-Clause 8.4 ［Extension of Time for Completion］, and

　　(b) payment of any such Cost plus reasonable profit, which shall be included in the Contract Price.

　　After receiving this notice, the Engineer shall proceed in accordance with Sub-Clause 3.5 ［Determinations］to agree or determine (i) whether and (if so) to what extent the error could not reasonably have been discovered, and (ii) the matters described in sub-paragraphs (a) and (b) above related to this extent.

　　承包商现场开工的首要工作是测量放线，确定整个工程的位置。放线所需的原始数据一般在合同中规定或由工程师向承包商发出。承包商应按照合同规定或工程师通知的原始基准点、基准线和基准标高对工程放线，负责对工程的所有部分正确定位，并纠正在工程的位置、标高、尺寸或定线中的任何错误。

　　若承包商在放线过程中出现差错，未能准确按照给定的数据完成放线工作，由此产生的问题应由承包商来负责。若雇主提供的原始数据出现问题，造成了放线工作差错，雇主应承担相应负责，承包商有权索赔。雇主需为提供错误的数据负责，但承包商有核实雇主方提供的数据的准确性的义务，在使用原始数据前应"作出合理的努力"来核实数据的准确性。

　　雇主提供的数据出现错误时，满足以下三个条件，承包商才有权根据第 20.1 款［承包商的索赔］的规定要求工期和费用索赔：

　　（1）证明雇主的错误数据导致承包商延误了工期和（或）产生了额外费用；

4 The Contractor（承包商）

（2）证明此类错误是作为有经验的承包商也无法合理发现的错误，即承包商在"作出合理的努力"之后仍然没有发现该错误；

（3）按照第 20.1 款［承包商的索赔］规定的程序及时向工程师发出通知提出索赔。

在收到上述通知后，工程师应按照第 3.5 款［确定］的规定，组织合同双方协商或由工程师直接确定"该错误是否能被合理发现或达到不能被合理发现的程度"。如果错误达到不能被合理发现的程度，工程师还应根据规定确定承包商应获得的工期、费用补偿。

对于此类索赔，承包商在使用雇主给予的数据之前本有义务对数据进行检查，指出其中的问题。承包商应建立内部文件审核系统，对提交给雇主的文件以及从雇主处接收的文件审核并记录，以便在索赔发生争议时出示"作出合理的努力核实数据"的证据。

4.8 Safety Procedures（安全程序）

The Contractor shall：
(a) comply with all applicable safety regulations，
(b) take care for the safety of all persons entitled to be on the Site，
(c) use reasonable efforts to keep the Site and Works clear of unnecessary obstruction so as to avoid danger to these persons，
(d) provide fencing，lighting，guarding and watching of the Works until completion and taking over under Clause 10［Employer's Taking Over］，and
(e) provide any Temporary Works（including roadways，footways，guards and fences）which may be necessary，because of the execution of the Works，for the use and protection of the public and of owners and occupiers of adjacent land.

工程施工现场属于比较危险的作业区域，强调安全问题不仅仅是对现场人员人身安全的保护。做好现场安全工作的前提是承包商拥有良好的现场组织管理能力。

承包商应遵守以下安全规定：

（1）承包商应遵守所有适用的安全规章；

（2）承包商应照管好有权进入现场的所有人员的安全；

（3）承包商应保持现场有序，避免出现障碍物，对上述人员的安全造成威胁；

（4）在工程竣工雇主验收工程（详细解释参见第 10 条［雇主的接收］的规定）前，承包商应在现场设置围栏、照明、保安等；

（5）为避免工程实施过程对公众及毗邻财产所有者或用户的安全产生影响，承包商应提供必要的临时工程（包括道路、人行路、防护设施等）。

安全工作的好坏会极大地影响承包商的社会形象与业内声誉。

各国对安全施工的法律要求各不相同，工程安全程序的规定应根据实际情况，在合同中写明。若承包商不独自占用现场，也应在合同中写明其在现场的安全责任。

4.9 Quality Assurance（质量保证）

The Contractor shall institute a quality assurance system to demonstrate compliance with the requirements of the Contract. The system shall be in accordance with the details stated in the Contract. The Engineer shall be entitled to audit any aspect of the system.

Details of all procedures and compliance documents shall be submitted to the Engineer for information before each design and execution stage is commenced. When any document of a technical nature is issued to the Engineer, evidence of the prior approval by the Contractor himself shall be apparent on the document itself.

Compliance with the quality assurance system shall not relieve the Contractor of any of his duties, obligations or responsibilities under the Contract.

承包商应建立质量保证体系，表明其遵守合同的各项要求。该体系应符合合同的详细规定。承包商应在每一设计和实施阶段开始前，向工程师提交所有具体工作的执行程序和执行文件供其参阅。在向工程师提交任何技术性文件时，文件上应有经承包商自己事先批准认可的标识。在执行质量保证体系时，不应解除承包商在合同中的任何义务和责任，即承包商对合同义务的履行不会受到该质量保证体系的影响。

工程师凭借合同文件的相关规定来监督、管理承包商的施工活动。对于工程实体的施工质量，工程师依据规范和图纸等技术性文件，来判断承包商是否按照合同规定履行施工义务。工程师通常要求承包商根据合同中对施工质量的要求，编制承包商内部实施工程的质量保证程序文件，由承包商人员遵照执行。

目前国际上具备较高管理水平的企业一般执行 ISO 9001 标准。承包商应尽可能在工程项目的管理中按照 ISO 9001 标准实施施工活动，并努力获得 IOS 9000 质量体系认证。

4.10　Site Data（现场数据）

The Employer shall have made available to the Contractor for his information, prior to the Base Date, all relevant data in the Employer's possession on sub-surface and hydrological conditions at the Site, including environmental aspects. The Employer shall similarly make available to the Contractor all such data which come into the Employer's possession after the Base Date. The Contractor shall be responsible for interpreting all such data.

To the extent which was practicable (taking account of cost and time), the Contractor shall be deemed to have obtained all necessary information as to risks, contingencies (偶发事件) and other circumstances which may influence or affect the Tender or Works. To the same extent, the Contractor shall be deemed to have inspected and examined the Site, its surroundings, the above data and other available information, and to have been satisfied before submitting the Tender as to all relevant matters, including (without limitation):

（a）the form and nature of the Site, including sub-surface conditions,

（b）the hydrological（水文的）and climatic conditions,

（c）the extent and nature of the work and Goods necessary for the execution and completion of the Works and the remedying of any defects,

(d) the Laws, procedures and labour practices (劳务惯例) of the Country, and

(e) the contractor's requirements for access, accommodation, facilities, personnel, power (电力), transport, water and other services.

雇主应在基准日期前将其已获得的施工现场地下、水文条件及环境方面的所有相关数据，及基准日期后获得的所有此类资料，提供给承包商；承包商应对工程项目现场及其周围环境进行调查，同时对雇主提供的有关数据和资料进行详细查阅和核实。

在费用和时间允许的情况下，承包商应在投标前调查清楚可能对投标书或工程实施产生影响的有关风险、偶发性事件和其他情况。承包商应掌握的资料包括：(1) 现场地形条件和地质条件；(2) 水文气候条件；(3) 工程范围以及为完成相应工作任务（包括实施、完成工程和修补任何缺陷）所需要的各类物资；(4) 工程所在国的法律、法规以及劳务惯例；(5) 承包商对各项施工条件的需求，包括现场交通条件、人员和食宿安排、水电以及其他有关设施。上述承包商需要了解的内容，包括了现场地表情况、进入现场后的施工开展条件，以及承包商依据雇主提供的地下管线图、原地形地貌图、地质勘探资料及现场实地勘察资料等文件而应得到的对地下情况的合理判断。承包商应当明了其在现场实施合同义务所可能产生的问题与费用，并对相关义务费用包干。

合同中常以签证方式来确定承包商已经履行"地下障碍物清除"、"现场必要的清理及平整"等工作的合同义务。由于现场条件对工程费用影响较大，如果承包商在投标时将此类风险费用预估过高则其报价会失去竞争力；如果承包商报价过低，则在工程实施过程发生此类风险的情况下，可能产生亏损。因此，承包商应认真研究雇主提供的有关现场条件的各项资料和数据，利用现场踏勘和标前会议等机会要求雇主澄清相关事项，采取相应措施规避或降低风险。

4.11 Sufficiency of the Accepted Contract（中标合同金额的充分性）

The Contractor shall be deemed to:

(a) have satisfied himself as to the correctness and sufficiency of the Accepted Contract Amount, and

(b) have based the Accepted Contract Amount on the data, interpretations, necessary information, inspections, examinations and satisfaction as to all relevant matters referred to in Sub-Clause 4.10 [Site Data].

Unless otherwise stated in the Contract, the Accepted Contract Amount covers all the Contractor's obligations under the Contract (including those under Provisional Sums, if any) and all things necessary for the proper execution and completion of the Works and the remedying of any defects.

承包商应被认为已确信中标合同金额的正确性和充分性，已将中标合同金额建立在清楚了解现场情况、地质条件等数据（详细解释参见第4.10款[现场数据]）的基础上。除非合同另有规定，中标合同金额应被视为承包商承诺此报价涵盖了其完成合同规定的一切工作的费用，包括根据暂列金额应承担的义务（如果有），以及为正确实施、完成工程和修补缺陷所需的全部费用。

本款的规定可杜绝承包商以漏项为由，在合同执行过程中以其投标价格未包括合同中的某些内容为由，向雇主提出索赔。

4.12 Unforeseeable Physical Conditions（不可预见的物质条件）

In this Sub-Clause, "physical conditions" means natural physical conditions and man-made and other physical obstructions and pollutants, which the Contractor encounters at the Site when executing the Works, including sub-surface and hydrological conditions but excluding climatic conditions.

If the Contractor encounters adverse physical conditions which he considers to have been Unforeseeable, the Contractor shall give notice to the Engineer as soon as practicable.

This notice shall describe the physical conditions, so that they can be inspected by the Engineer, and shall set out the reasons why the Contractor considers them to be Unforeseeable. The Contractor shall continue executing the Works, using such proper and reasonable measures as are appropriate for the physical conditions, and shall comply with any instructions which the Engineer may give. If an instruction constitutes a Variation, Clause 13 [Variations and Adjustments] shall apply.

If and to the extent that the Contractor encounters physical conditions which are Unforeseeable, gives such a notice, and suffers delay and/or incurs Cost due to these conditions, the Contractor shall be entitled subject to Sub-Clause 20.1 [Contractor's Claims] to:

(a) an extension of time for any such delay, if completion is or will be delayed, under Sub-Clause 8.4 [Extension of Time for Completion], and

(b) payment of any such Cost, which shall be included in the Contract Price.

After receiving such notice and inspecting and/or investigating these physical conditions, the Engineer shall proceed in accordance with Sub-Clause 3.5 [Determinations] to agree or determine (i) whether and (if so) to what extent these physical conditions were Unforeseeable, and (ii) the matters described in sub-paragraphs (a) and (b) above related to this extent.

However, before additional Cost is finally agreed or determined under sub-paragraph (ii), the Engineer may also review whether other physical conditions in similar parts of the Works (if any) were more favourable than could reasonably have been foreseen when the Contractor submitted the Tender. If and to the extent that these more favourable conditions were encountered, the Engineer may proceed in accordance with Sub-Clause 3.5 [Determinations] to agree or determine the reductions in Cost which were due to these conditions, which may be included (as deductions) in the Contract Price and Payment Certificates. However, the net effect of all adjustments under sub-paragraph (b) and all these reductions, for all the physical conditions encountered in similar parts of the Works, shall not result in a net reduction in the Contract Price.

The Engineer may take account of any evidence of the physical conditions foreseen by the Contractor when submitting the Tender, which may be made available by the Contractor, but shall not be bound by any such evidence.

"物质条件"是承包商在现场施工时遇到的自然物质条件、人为的或其他物质障碍及污染物，包括水文条件和地表以下的条件，但不包括气候条件。如果承包商在现场施工时遇到其认为不可预见的不利物质条件，应尽快通知工程师，并在通知中说明该物质条件的情况以及承包商认为其不可预见的理由，以便工程师进行检验。如果承包商遇到不可预见的物质条件并向工程师发出通知，因此类物质条件导致承包商延误工期和增加费用，承包商有权根据第 20.1 款［承包商的索赔］的规定要求工期延长和费用补偿。

承包商应当对上述不可预见的物质条件采取必要的合理措施，在该合理措施下继续施工，并遵循工程师可能发出的任何指示；如果指示构成变更，则应按照第 13 条［变更和调整］中的规定处理。工程师在收到承包商此类通知并对该物质条件进行检验和研究后，根据第 3.5 款［确定］的规定来决定承包商是否满足理赔条件，即上述不可预见的物质条件是否达到不可预见的程度，以及就该不可预见的物质条件向承包商赔付的费用额度和延长的工期时间。

工程师在决定对承包商工期和费用进行补偿前，应判断实际施工条件是否比承包商在投标时预见的更为有利；如果是的话，工程师可以扣减相应的费用，但扣减的费用不得超过索赔费用。如果承包商提供了其在投标阶段所预见的物质条件的证据，则工程师可予以考虑，但不受其约束。

工程实际进行中，通常会出现与承包商提交的投标文件、雇主发出的招标文件、承包商的现场勘察所预见的物质条件不同的情况。此类不可预见的物质条件出现后通常会对承包商造成工期延误或费用损失。承包商可据此提出索赔，其前提条件有：
（1）承包商遇见了他认为不可预见的不利物质条件；
（2）承包商将此情况及时通知工程师，并且提出充分理由；
（3）该情况对承包商有不利影响。

不可预见的物质条件的"不可预见程度"，往往容易产生争议。工程师对此的判断与确定，是承包商是否能成功索赔的关键，也是容易产生争议的焦点。如：在地下清障时，旧建筑的基础由于较易在以往图纸资料中被发现，属于"可预见"的情况，一般不会成为索赔依据；而地层中的孤石由于无法在已有的地下图纸中反映，可成为承包商索赔的依据。

【例 4.1】某雇主通过公开招标与某承包商签订了一份框架结构高层写字楼的施工合同。该写字楼采用钻孔灌注桩基础。承包商按期开始施工，其施工进度计划也已得到工程师批准。但在土方开挖过程中，由于现场附近的一条主干道修路，车辆都集中到工地边上的一条路上行驶，交通堵塞造成挖土机和运土汽车均达不到投标计算时的工效，每天只能完成计划挖运土方量的一半，施工受交通影响很大。由于土方开挖工效降低，机械费相应增加，施工进度计划也远远落后于原计划。

承包商按照合同中规定的程序和时间提出索赔，索赔要求顺延工期 10 天和补偿增加的机械费、管理费和利润损失。承包商认为工地边上的这条路并不是主要交通道路，交通堵塞对施工的影响属于不可预见。工程师对此以承包商无索赔权予以了反驳，认为交通情况不属于不可预见的物质条件，承包商在投标报价时应对包括交通情况在内的现场及现场周围环境进行详尽调查（详细解释参见第 4.10 款［现场数据]),承包商也应被视为已将其影响考虑在投标报价内(详细解释参见第 4.11 款[中标合同金额的充分性])。

4.13 Rights of Way and Facilities (道路通行权和设施)

The Contractor shall bear all costs and charges for special and/or temporary rights-of-way which he may require, including those for access to the Site. The Contractor shall also obtain, at his risk and cost, any additional facilities outside the Site which he may require for the purposes of the Works.

承包商应为其所需的专用或临时道路(包括进场道路的通行权)承担全部费用和开支。承包商还应自担风险和费用,获得现场以外实施工程所需的任何附加设施。

为方便承包商设备和人员往来现场,承包商需为工程项目的实施提供方便的交通道路。如果项目现场靠近公共道路,则承包商可方便使用此类道路。如果现场处于较偏僻的地方,则承包商可能需要设置一些特别的或临时道路。承包商可根据施工所需,自费获得现场外任何附加设施的使用权。但使用这些附加设施需得到工程师的同意(详细解释参见第 4.23 款[承包商的现场作业])。同时,在雇主或其人员的要求下,承包商应对其所用的进场通路进行必要的维护(详细解释参见第 4.15 款[进场通路])。

4.14 Avoidance of Interference (避免干扰)

The Contractor shall not interfere unnecessarily or improperly with:
(a) the convenience of the public, or
(b) the access to and use and occupation of all roads and footpaths, irrespective of whether they are public or in the possession of the Employer or of others.

The Contractor shall indemnify and hold the Employer harmless against and from all damages, losses and expenses (including legal fees and expenses) resulting from any such unnecessary or improper interference.

承包商应避免工程的实施对公众便利,对所有道路和人行道的进入、使用和占用产生不必要或不当的干扰。这些道路无论是公共道路还是雇主或他人的私家道路,承包商都应避免对其产生干扰。如果工程施工不得已进入、使用和占用上述道路,应控制在必要和恰当的范围内。

因承包商不必要和不恰当的干扰他人导致任何赔偿或损失,承包商应自行承担一切后果,并保障雇主免受由此导致的任何影响,如各类赔偿费、法律方面的费用等。

由于工程施工活动可能在市区或其他人口稠密的区域,工程实施过程中可能对环境带来不利影响,如噪声、污染、占用道路、车辆设备堵塞交通等。各国的法律对施工造成的各类影响规定不同。除了占用交通道路之外,承包商还应根据工程所在国的法律法规要求,注意尘土、噪声等影响,并采取相应的措施加以防范。如:土方开挖时勤洒水,避免尘土飞扬;特殊时期须停止有噪声的施工作业等。

4.15 Access Route（进场通路）

The Contractor shall be deemed to have been satisfied as to the suitability and availability of access routes to the Site. The Contractor shall use reasonable efforts to prevent any road or bridge from being damaged by the Contractor's traffic or by the Contractor's Personnel. These efforts shall include the proper use of appropriate vehicles and routes.

Except as otherwise stated in these Conditions：

(a) the Contractor shall (as between the Parties) be responsible for any maintenance which may be required for his use of access routes；

(b) the Contractor shall provide all necessary signs or directions along access routes, and shall obtain any permission which may be required from the relevant authorities for his use of routes, signs and directions；

(c) the Employer shall not be responsible for any claims which may arise from the use or otherwise of any access route，

(d) the Employer does not guarantee the suitability or availability of particular access routes, and

(e) Costs due to non-suitability or non-availability, for the use required by the Contractor, of access routes shall be borne by the Contractor.

承包商应对进入现场的通路路线及其适宜性清楚了解，同时应选用适当的运输工具和路线，避免车辆来回通行的过程中对道路或桥梁产生损害。除非合同中另有规定，承包商应对其使用的通路自行进行必要的维护或维修，并在征得政府主管部门同意的情况下，沿进场通路设置警示牌和路标。雇主无需对因使用有关进场通路引起的索赔负责，也无需保证进场通路的适宜性。如果现有进场通路无法满足承包商对可用性、适宜性的要求，则承包商应自行承担费用设置必要的进场通路。

进场通路由承包商确保、维护与负责，雇主不需承担责任。与 FIDIC 合同条件中的规定不同，国内工程中一般由雇主提供"三通一平"的条件。承包商应在投标阶段进行仔细的现场考察，详细了解施工过程中必须使用的通道和路线的状况，估计所需的工程量（如果有），并在投标报价中予以考虑。

4.16 Transport of Goods（货物运输）

Unless otherwise stated in the Particular Conditions：

(a) the Contractor shall give the Engineer not less than 21 days' notice of the date on which any Plant or a major item of other Goods will be delivered to the Site；

(b) the Contractor shall be responsible for packing, loading, transporting, receiving, unloading, storing and protecting all Goods, and other things required for the Works; and

(c) the Contractor shall indemnity and hold the Employer harmless against and from all damages, losses and expenses (including legal fees and expenses) resulting from the transport of Goods, and shall negotiate and pay all claims rising from their transport.

工程施工过程中，始终伴随着货物的运输。除非专用条件中另有规定，承包商应提前21天通知工程师其所需的任何生产设备或每项其他主要货物的进场日期，承包商应负责工程需要的所有货物和其他物品的包装、装货、运输、接收、卸货、存储和保护。如果货物的装运导致其他方提出索赔，承包商应保障雇主免受此类索赔产生的损失和损害（包括法律费用和开支），并自行与索赔方谈判协商，支付有关索赔款。

4.17　Contractor's Equipment（承包商设备）

The Contractor shall be responsible for all Contractor's Equipment. When brought on to the Site, Contractor's Equipment shall be deemed to be exclusively intended for the execution of the Works. The Contractor shall not remove from the Site any major items of Contractor's Equipment without the consent of the Engineer. However, consent shall not be required for vehicles transporting Goods or Contractor's Personnel off Site.

承包商应对一切承包商设备负责。承包商设备（详细解释参见第1.1.5.1款［承包商设备］）运至现场后，该类设备被视为专用于工程的施工。未经工程师同意，承包商不得从现场运走任何主要的承包商设备。但运送货物或载承包商人员离场的车辆无需经过工程师同意。

一般情况下，施工机械设备的进出场费要比日常运行费高很多。承包商在其设备进场后，不会愿意付出更多费用将工程设备重复进场。如果承包商作出如此不合情理的设备调配安排，则承包商可能存在设备或者其他方面的问题。雇主一般不会接受承包商设备在工程实施阶段随意进、退场。此外，大型工程设备的购置费较高，将此类设备留置在工程现场，对于雇主来说可成为承包商的另一种"履约担保"，以保证承包商按合同规定完成合同义务。一旦承包商不按规定履约或出现经济危机，雇主有权对上述承包商设备进行处置，以收回因承包商的某些行为使雇主遭受的损失（详细解释参见第15.2款［由雇主终止］）。

4.18　Protection of the Environment（环境保护）

The Contractor shall take all reasonable steps to protect the environment (both on and off the Site) and to limit damage and nuisance to people and property resulting from pollution, noise and other results of his operations.

The Contractor shall ensure that emissions, surface discharges and effluent from the Contractor's activities shall not exceed the values（数值）indicated in the Specification, and shall not exceed the values prescribed by applicable Laws.

承包商应采取一切适当的措施，保护施工现场内外的环境，避免因施工作业产生污染、噪声和其他对公众和财产造成损害和妨害的影响。承包商应确保因施工作业产生的气体排放、地面排水及排污等不超过规范中和适用法律中规定的界限。施工过程中现场内外的环境保护责任应全部由承包商来承担,并应避免由于环保而发生的纠纷干扰到雇主,如有此种情况发生,则承包商应承担由此造成的一切损失。

环境的保护日益受到世界各国的重视,工程施工过程易造成环境污染。FIDIC合同条件此款专门规定环境保护的有关事项。

4.19　Electricity, Water and Gas（电、水和燃气）

The Contractor shall, except as stated below, be responsible for the provision of all power（电力）, water and other services he may require.

The Contractor shall be entitled to use for the purposes of the Works such supplies of electricity, water, gas and other services as may be available on the Site and of which details and prices are given in the Specification. The Contractor shall, at his risk and cost, provide any apparatus（仪器）necessary for his use of these services and for measuring the quantities consumed.

The quantities consumed and the amounts due (at these prices) for such services shall be agreed or determined by the Engineer in accordance with Sub-Clause 2.5 [Employer's Claims] and Sub-Clause 3.5 [Determinations]. The Contractor shall pay these amounts to the Employer.

除明文规定外,承包商应负责供应其所需的所有电、水、燃气和其他服务。但如果现场已有这些设施和服务,则承民包商无需再自行提供。承包商有权使用现场已有的电、水、燃气和其他服务,并按规范中规定的价格和条件向雇主支付相关费用。承包商应自担风险,提供计量仪器来计量其使用这类设施和服务的消耗量。上述设施和服务的消耗量以及应支付给雇主的使用费,由工程师根据第2.5款[雇主的索赔]和第3.5款[确定]进行确认,且承包商应无条件向雇主支付此类费用。

合同双方在付款相关条款内应明确此类设施和服务的计量方式和支付事宜,以避免双方就此类问题产生争议。如果承包商自行负责申报工程用电、水和燃气,则相应的风险由承包商自行承担。

4.20　Employer's Equipment and Free-Issue Material（雇主设备和免费供应的材料）

The Employer shall make the Employer's Equipment (if any) available for the use of the Contractor in the execution of the Works in accordance with the details, arrangements and prices stated in the Specification. Unless otherwise stated in the Specification:

(a) the Employer shall be responsible for the Employer's Equipment, except that

(b) the Contractor shall be responsible for each item of Employer's Equipment whilst any of the Contractor's Personnel is operating it, driving it, directing it or in possession or control of it.

The appropriate quantities and the amounts due (*at such stated prices*) for the use of Employer's Equipment shall be agreed or determined by the Engineer in accordance with Sub-Clause 2.5 [*Employer's Claims*] and Sub-Clause 3.5 [*Determinations*]. The Contractor shall pay these amounts to the Employer.

The Employer shall supply, free of charge, the "free-issue materials" (*if any*) in accordance with the details stated in the Specification. The Employer shall, at his risk and cost, provide these materials at the time and place specified in the Contract. The Contractor shall then visually inspect them, and shall promptly give notice to the Engineer of any shortage, defect or default in these materials. Unless otherwise agreed by both Parties, the Employer shall immediately rectify the notified shortage, defect or default.

After this visual inspection, the free-issue materials shall come under the care, custody and control of the Contractor. The Contractor's obligations of inspection, care, custody and control shall not relieve the Employer of liability for any shortage, defect or default not apparent from a visual inspection.

雇主应在需要时向承包商提供相关设备（称为"雇主设备"），按规范中的具体规定和收费标准供承包商在工程施工中使用，并对此类雇主设备负责。但在承包商人员操作、指挥、占用或控制上述雇主设备时，由承包商对其承担责任。承包商应遵循合同中规定的使用细节、安排，向雇主支付按合同规定应支付的价格。承包商使用雇主设备的适当数量和应付金额，工程师应按照第2.5款［雇主的索赔］和第3.5款［确定］的要求确定。

如果合同中规定雇主向承包商提供免费材料，雇主还应按照规范要求的细节，向承包商免费提供"免费供应的材料"。雇主自担风险和费用，将该类材料运送至指定地点。承包商在接收此类材料时应进行目视检查，如发现数量不足、质量缺陷等问题，应及时通知工程师。工程师在收到通知后应立即将数量补足或更换缺陷材料。承包商经检查对此类材料进行接收，应负责此类材料的后续看管。如果材料的数量不足和质量缺陷等问题让承包商无法目测发现，即使此类材料已移交给承包商，雇主仍应为之负责。

合同中会规定由雇主向承包商提供一定的施工设备和工程材料供其使用。此类雇主设备一般为有偿提供，材料则为无偿提供。雇主向承包商有偿提供此类施工设备，可认为向承包商出租该施工设备。规范中一般会具体规定此类设备的使用条件，如雇主收费标准、设备类型和使用状况、技术方法、操作员和燃料供应、设备维修等事项。雇主出租该施工设备的条件应优于市场租赁条件。

4.21 Progress Reports（进度报告）

Unless otherwise stated in the Particular Conditions, monthly progress reports shall be prepared by the Contractor and submitted to the Engineer in six copies. The first report shall cover the period up to the end of the first calendar month following the Commencement Date. Reports shall be submitted monthly thereafter, each within 7 days after the last day of the period to which it relates.

Reporting shall continue until the Contractor has completed all work which is known to be outstanding at the completion date stated in the Taking-Over Certificate for the Works.

Each report shall include:

(a) charts and detailed descriptions of progress, including each stage-of design (if any), Contractor's Documents, procurement, manufacture, delivery to Site, construction, erection and testing; and including these stages for work by each nominated Subcontractor (as defined in Clause 5 [Nominated Subcontractors]);

(b) photographs showing the status of manufacture and of progress on the Site;

(c) for the manufacture of each main item of Plant and Materials, the name of the manufacturer, manufacture location, percentage progress, and the actual or expected dates of:

 (i) commencement of manufacture,
 (ii) Contractor's inspections, and
 (iii) Test, and
 (iv) shipment and arrival at the Site;

(d) the details described in Sub-Clause 6.10 [Records of Contractor's Personnel and Equipment];

(e) copies of quality assurance documents, test results and certificates of Materials;

(f) List of notices given under Sub-Clause 2.5 [Employer's Claims] and notices given under Sub-Clause 20.1 [Contractor's Claims];

(g) safety statistics, including details of any hazardous incidents and activities relating to environmental aspects and public relations; and

(h) comparisons of actual and planned progress, with details of any events or circumstances which may jeopardize the completion in accordance with the Contract, and the measures being (or to be) adopted to overcome delays.

进度报告是一项实体性文件，并且应该在每月开始后的7天，即在5个工作日递交。为满足这项要求，承包商必须记录和收集每月的信息，包括分包商的信息等。为监督项目的实施，承包商可能已将大部分信息作为其内部程序和档案的一部分记录下来，所以，必须以符合本款要求及满足承包商内部程序的方式为目的进行记录。对承包商而言，收集和协调来自分包商的信息可能会出现问题。

除本款规定的进度报告内容之外，某项施工合同还要求承包商在月进度报告中列入该月出现的质量事故的次数以及补救措施，即：该月内雇主/工程师发现承包商工作质量问题而下达的整改通知，英文为 Nonperformance Report（违规报告）。

进度报告实际上是承包商每月所做的一次工作总结，记入重要的事件和资料。如果不按时提交，工程师可以拒绝承包商的期中支付证书的申请。详细解释参见第 14.3 款 [期中付款证书的申请]。

【例4.2】国内某工程进度报告范例

为了保证XX项目的顺利进行，在确保工程质量、安全的前提下，保证施工进度按照计划执行至关重要。目前，项目施工共有五大板块，1号楼、7号楼、3号楼的地下车库、3号楼、景观桥，现根据现场的实际观察结果作出报告，以便为施工进度的统计、分析、安排提供有用的信息。汇报如下：

一、1号楼：

(1) 墙体抹灰

计划进度：7月26日～8月25日完成11到20层抹灰工程

实际进度：3、4、5、6、8、10、11、12、13层已经抹完，2、9、14、15、17、18、19、层正在进行，完成度75%。注：每层施工人数，2人，完成时间，20天左右可完成一层

结论：实际施工进度将滞后于计划进度。

(2) 外装工程——保温层施工

计划进度：8月5日～8月25日完成保温施工

实际进度：k1～k3、a27～v24面外墙正在施工，其他外墙面未施工。

结论：实际施工进度将滞后于计划进度。

二、7号楼：

(1) 外墙饰面——涂料施工

计划进度：7月26日～8月24日完成外墙饰面中涂料施工部分

实际进度：v1～v31面外墙正在做涂料、a5～d26面外墙正在做、h31～v31面外墙已经做完、v1～a5面外墙正在做喷涂，完成度70%

结论：实际施工进度将滞后于计划进度。

(2) 首层地面

1) 防潮及保温层施工

计划进度：7月26日～8月9日完成防潮及保温施工

实际进度：除去部分地面堆积施工材料影响施工，其他已完成，完成度95%

2) 地面面层施工

计划进度：8月12日～8月13日完成地面施工

实际进度：除去部分地面堆积施工材料影响施工，其他已完成，完成度95%

结论：实际施工进度滞后于计划进度。

(3) 砌体工程——首层墙体砌筑

计划进度：8月16日～8月20日完成首层墙体砌筑

实际进度：已经开始砌筑填充墙，预计可完成进度计划

结论：实际施工进度有望同步于计划进度。

(注：卫生间排水支管从24层安装到了13层，水电安装从8月12日因故停工至今。)

三、3号楼的地下车库

(1) 第一流水段

1) 防水工程——底板防水施工

计划进度：7月26日～8月2日完成底板防水施工

实际进度：已完成

2) 结构工程——底板结构施工

计划进度：8月2日～8月25日完成底板结构施工

实际进度：正在布置地梁和筏板的钢筋，实际完成度为30%

结论：实际施工进度将滞后于计划进度。

(2) 第二流水段

1）结构工程——底板结构施工
计划进度：7月26日～8月4日完成底板结构施工
实际进度：已完成
2）结构工程——墙体、顶板结构施工
计划进度：8月8日～8月17日完成墙体、顶板施工
实际进度：已完成
结论：实际施工进度同步于计划进度。
（3）第三流水段：结构工程——顶板、墙体施工
计划进度：7月26日～8月1日完成顶板、墙体施工
实际进度：已浇筑、正在养护，完成度90%
结论：实际施工进度滞后于计划进度。
（4）第四流水段
1）结构工程——底板结构施工
计划进度：8月10日～8月19日完成底板结构施工
实际进度：已完成
2）结构工程——顶板、墙体、混凝土施工
计划进度：8月23日～8月25日完成顶板、墙体、混凝土施工
实际进度：正在做墙体置模，完成度30%
结论：实际施工进度滞后于计划进度。
四、3号楼
结构施工（标高～1.950～0.000）——夹层施工
计划进度：8月2日～8月11日完成夹层施工
实际进度：已完成
结论：实际施工进度同步于计划进度。
五、景观桥
桥体装饰
1）桥路面装饰
计划进度：7月26日～8月4日完成桥路面装饰
实际进度：基本已完成，除与地下车库交接处因施工牵绊未完成部分
2）桥侧面装饰
计划进度：7月26日～8月4日完成桥侧面装饰
实际进度：正在做石材干挂，北面完成80%、南面完成20%
3）桥栏杆、路灯安装
计划进度：8月5日～8月10日完成桥栏杆、路灯安装
实际进度：桥面路灯部分管线已埋置，其他部分未曾动工，完成度30%
结论：实际施工进度滞后于计划进度。

4.22 Security of the Site（现场保安）

Unless otherwise stated in the Particular Conditions：
(a) the Contractor shall be responsible for keeping unauthorized persons off the Site, and

(b) authorised persons shall be limited to the Contractor's Personnel and the Employer's Personnel; and to any other personnel notified to the Contractor, by the Employer or the Engineer, as authorised personnel of the Employer's other contractors on the Site.

有权进入现场的人仅限于合同相关人员,未经授权的人不得进入现场。

承包商负有保证现场安全的义务,并且可要求未授权人员离开现场。当有一个以上的承包商在现场施工时,专用条款和规范中应详细规定现场保安程序。如果现场是一块较大场地或现有施工现场的一个部分,或者项目涉及了雇主认为特别敏感的或保密事项,那么专用条款应规定控制进入现场通道的附加要求。

承包商负责现场保安的责任必须与其他条款同时考虑,如第4.6款与其他承包商合作的规定、第4.8款关于现场围栏和其他临时工程的规定、第17.2款关于承包商负责照管工程以及第18条保险要求。

4.23 Contractor's Operations on Site(承包商的现场作业)

The Contractor shall confine his operations to the Site, and to any additional areas which may be obtained by the Contractor and agreed by the Engineer as working areas. The Contractor shall take all necessary precautions to keep Contractor's Equipment and Contractor's Personnel within the Site and these additional areas, and to keep them off adjacent land.

During the execution of the Works, the Contractor shall keep the Site free from all unnecessary obstruction, and shall store or dispose of any Contractor's Equipment or surplus materials. The Contractor shall clear away and remove from the Site any wreckage, rubbish and Temporary Works which are no longer required.

Upon the issue of a Taking-Over Certificate, the Contractor shall clear away and remove, from that part of the Site and Works to which the Taking-Over Certificate refers, all Contractor's Equipment, surplus material, wreckage, rubbish and Temporary Works. The Contractor shall leave that part of the Site and the Works in a clean and safe condition. However, the Contractor may retain on Site, during the Defects Notification Period, such Goods as are required for the Contractor to fulfil obligations under the Contract.

承包商只能在"工程师同意的作为工作区域"的地方或现场实施工程,此要求适用于分包商及职员、承担设计任务的咨询工程师等。这项要求可能不适用于构成工程一部分的生产设备中的机械和电气设备的制造。承包商和工程师应讨论现场外工程的范围以及通知和检查要求。

承包商人员不应进入相邻现场的要求与第4.14款[避免干扰]规定的不得干扰公共的便利,以及第4.8款[安全程序](e)项规定的提供保护雇主和占有相邻现场的要求相关联。应保持现场整洁和清理其他障碍物的要求也与第4.8款的安全规定有关。竣工时应清理现场的要求应与第10条[雇主的接收]和第11条[缺陷责任]一起理解。第11.7款[进入权]赋予了承包商在缺陷通知期限内进入现场的权力,本款最后一句话也赋予了其可在现场保有货物、设备材料和临时工程的权力,以便承包商能够履行其义务,但应确定其使用的现场区域。

【例4.3】某国际工程合同中"现场工作区的增加"的条款

The Contractor may submit a proposal for adding to the Working Areas to the Owner for acceptance. A reason for not accepting is that:

(1) the proposed addition is not necessary for Providing the Works, or

(2) the proposed area will be used for work not in this contract.

4.24 Fossils（化石）

All fossils, coins, articles of value or antiquity, and structures and other remains or items of geological or archaeological interest found on the Site shall be placed under the care and authority of the Employer. The Contractor shall take reasonable precautions to prevent Contractor's Personnel or other persons from removing or damaging any of these findings.

The Contractor shall, upon discovery of any such finding, promptly give notice to the Engineer, who shall issue instructions for dealing with it. If the Contractor suffers delay and/or incurs Cost from complying with the instructions, the Contractor shall give a further notice to the Engineer and shall be entitled subject to Sub-Clause 20.1 [Contractor's Claims] to:

(a) an extension of time for any such delay, if completion is or will be delayed, under Sub-Clause 8.4 [Extension of Time for Completion], and

(b) payment of any such Cost, which shall be included in the Contract Price.

After receiving this further notice, the Engineer shall proceed in accordance with Sub-Clause 3.5 [Determinations] to agree or determine these matters.

FIDIC此款规定的关键问题在于化石与文物的所有权。应用此款规定时应与工程所在国关于化石和文物的相关法律法规相对应。在西方国家里，一般这种雇主土地上得到的"化石与文物"，其所有权属于雇主。由于某些"化石与文物"有着极大的经济价值，所以在相关事项发生后，雇主很看重"化石与文物"的保护与照管。我国法律法规中规定"化石与文物"为国家所有，要求在发现化石与文物时应通知相关政府部门，所以发现化石与文物事项首先就成了"不可抗力"，雇主和承包商应各自承担相关损失。本款要求雇主单独承担相关费用就显然不合理，此项规定对国内工程应删除。

【例4.4】

某地铁工程施工现场在施工过程中发现了古代墓葬群，是具有考古价值的文物。承包商在发现此墓葬群后立刻通知监理工程师，并根据国家相关法规通知相关政府部门，由相关政府部门派出考古队伍对现场进行了调查与发掘。因此，承包商不得不停工等待考古结束，耽误了施工进度。

由于属于"不可抗力"，承包商据此提出了工期索赔，要求工期延长，在将索赔通知发给工程师后，经由雇主和工程师的商定，同意承包商索赔要求，给予工期延长。

思考题

1. 具体说明承包商的一般义务。
2. 承包商的主要责任有哪些？其中最基本、最重要的责任是什么？
3. 当由承包商负责工程设计时承包商应承担哪些责任？
4. 雇主对承包商的制约有哪几种形式？履约担保的提交要求有哪些？在什么情况下雇主可以根据履约担保提出索赔？
5. 简述承包商代表的任命要求及权力范围。
6. 简述承包商在选择分包商时应遵循的要求。
7. 作为承包商或分包商，是否必须同意分包合同权益的转让？分别说明理由。
8. 当多方共同使用现场时承包商应如何配合？若因此遭受损失承包商应如何应对？
9. 简述合同双方就放线工作的责任划分。若放线错误，承包商在何种条件下可以提出索赔？对此，工程师如何裁定承包商具有该索赔权？
10. 简述质量保证体系的作用和意义。
11. 承包商在提交投标书之前应掌握施工现场的哪些数据？
12. 具体说明中标合同金额的充分性的含义。
13. 简要说明"不可预见的物质条件"的含义及其判定依据。
14. 若因不可预见的物质条件导致承包商工期延误和增加费用，承包商可获得赔偿的前提条件是什么？
15. 分别说明承包商在安全施工、文明施工、绿色施工三个方面应承担的责任。
16. FIDIC施工合同条件中对进场通路、电、水、燃气的规定与国内工程的"三通一平"有何区别？
17. 简述雇主向承包商提供雇主设备的有偿性。
18. 简述进度报告的内容及提交程序。
19. 简述承包商作业的区域范围。
20. 在施工过程中发现化石时承包商应承担什么责任？

5 Normited Subcontractors（指定的分包商）

在大型工程中，由于部分工程的复杂性与专业性，承包商常在工程师同意下雇用分包商来承担相应工程，如钢构、幕墙、智能化等。分包是相对于总承包而言的，只能将一项或若干项具体的工程施工分包给其他人，但不可将合同的责任和义务分包出去。承包商不能期望通过分包，逃避自己在合同中的法律和经济责任，仍需对其分包商在设计、工程质量和进度等方面的工作负全面责任，而分包商在现场则要接受承包商的统筹安排和调度，只对承包商承担分包合同内规定的责任并履行相关义务。

在分包商的选择方面，雇主拥有指定权，这一权力加强了雇主对于相关专业性较强或比较重要的部分的施工过程的掌控，一定程度上保证了施工质量及雇主的其他特殊需求。FIDIC 合同也对指定的分包商作出了专门的规定。

本章要求：了解"指定分包商"的定义；

了解反对指定的内容；

了解指定分包商的付款以及付款证据的内容。

5.1 Definition of "nominated Subcontractor"（"指定的分包商"的定义）

In the Contract, "nominated Subcontractor" means a Subcontractor:

(a) who is stated in the Contract as being a nominated Subcontractor, or

(b) whom the Engineer, under Clause 13 [Variations and Adjustment], instructs the Contractor to employ as a Subcontractor.

指定的分包商，可以是雇主和承包商在签订合同时商定好的，也可以在签订主合同后，由工程师指令承包商去雇用某专业公司作为指定分包商来承担某部分工作，但这样做，需要按第 13 条 [变更和调整] 的有关规定作为变更的内容来处理。详细内容参见第 13.5 款 [暂定金额]。第 1.1.2.8 款 [分包商] 定义的分包商包括为实施部分工程的目的而任命的分包商，也包括第 1.1.5.3 款 [材料] 定义的提供构成永久性工程一部分的"材料"的人员。按照 FIDIC 合同规定，指定的材料供应商也可定义为指定分包商，并适用于本条规定。

5.2 Objection to Nomination（反对指定）

The Contractor shall not be under any obligation to employ a nominated Subcontractor against whom the Contractor raises reasonable objection by notice to the Engineer as soon as practicable, with supporting particulars. An objection shall be deemed reasonable if it arises from (among other things) any of the following matters, unless the Employer agrees to indemnify the Contractor against and from the consequences of the matter:

(a) there are reasons to believe that the Subcontractor does not have sufficient competence, resources or financial strength;

(b) the subcontract does not specify that the nominated Subcontractor shall indemnify the Contractor against and from any negligence or misuse of Goods by the nominated Subcontractor, his agents and employees; or

(c) the subcontract does not specify that, for the subcontracted work (including design, if any), the nominated Subcontractor shall:

(i) undertake to the Contractor such obligations and liabilities as will enable the Contractor to discharge his obligations and liabilities under the Contract, and

(ii) indemnify the Contractor against and from all obligations and liabilities arising under or in connection with the Contract and from the consequences of any failure by the Subcontractor to perform these obligations or to fulfill these liabilities.

承包商并不是无条件接受雇主指定的分包商。若分包商未能履行其分包合同中规定的义务，不仅会给承包商而且也会给雇主带来严重的损失。分包商的违约可能影响到工程有关部分的衔接，导致整个工程进度拖延及其他分包商的索赔。

承包商与分包商的责任关系比较复杂，"各负其责"的合同条款在工程实施过程中较难实现，为了避免出现责任纠纷，FIDIC合同条款中规定，承包商承担任何分包商的一切责任，彻底消除"承包商与分包商各负其责"的情况。承包商虽然出于合同目的承担了所有分包商的责任，但也拥有拒绝指定分包商的权利。

只要承包商提出合理的拒绝理由，雇主不能强迫承包商接受其指定的分包商。承包商反对的理由不限于本款第（a）至（c）项的规定，但必须是"合理的"。如果承包商怀疑分包商的表现，不希望雇用指定分包商，而雇主却坚持，施工中就有可能出现问题。若雇主要打消承包商的疑虑，可以参照本款，在保证承包商不承担由于雇用该分包商产生的一切后果的责任的前提下，促使承包商接受指定分包商。如在分包合同中规定分包商接受总承包商合同中的专用合同条件，要求提供各类银行保函并扣押保留金，购买相应的分包保险等。

【例5.1】某工程项目承包商反对指定分包的处理

在某工程项目中，雇主指定了钢结构工程的分包商，而承包商对此分包商调查后，发现该分包商的资质与工程项目履历不能够承担此项目的钢结构工程分包，如果采用其分包，势必会对工程产生不利影响。

承包商在分包合同确定前及时通知工程师，向其提交了反对指定并附具体证明材料。

情况一：经协商与确定，采纳承包商的反对，承包商可以不雇用此分包商。

情况二：雇主坚持指定该分包商，并通过与承包商的协商，免除了承包商对此分包商的义务和责任，承包商同意在此前提下雇用该分包商。

5.3 Payments to nominated Subcontractor （对指定的分包商付款）

The Contractor shall pay to the nominated Subcontractor the amounts which the Engineer certifies to be due in accordance with the subcontract. These amounts plus other charges shall be included in the Contract Price in accordance with sub-paragraph (b) of Sub-Clause 13.5 [Pro-

visional Sums], *except as stated in Sub-Clause 5.4* [*Evidence of Payments*].

根据本款规定，指定分包商的付款是由总承包商来负责的，而款项的具体金额则由工程师来确定。本款中的"其他收费"指的是承包商因负责管理指定分包商而向雇主收取的管理费和利润，为指定分包合同额的一个百分数，一般在有关数据表或投标函附录中规定。通常，指定分包商承担的工作从主合同中的暂定金额中支付。参见第13.5款［暂定金额］。

除非合同中另有明确规定，分包商不能就付款、索赔和工期等问题直接与雇主交涉，甚至无权就此直接向雇主提交通知，一切与雇主的往来均需通过承包商。雇主只负责按照总承包合同支付承包商的工程款并赔偿其可能的经济损失，分包商按分包合同再从承包商处取得其应得部分。若承包商无力偿还债务，分包商同样将蒙受损失。因此，分包商的利益通常与承包商利益密切相关。

【例5.2】某公路项目分包合同纠纷

某公路项目，分包合同在工程施工的条款方面与总承包商合同的条件相同，并在序言部分写明："整个分包合同受总承包合同的制约，总承包合同中对总承包商的约束性条款，同样也适用于分包商"，但在付款方面又与总承包商合同有些差异。

在项目实施过程中，分包商认为应按分包合同进行付款，总承包商则坚持应与总承包合同相同，双方形成争端，并且寻求工程师的裁决。

工程师认为分包商在签约时已经注意到总承包合同的支付条件，并指出在双方的分包合同中又明确规定分包合同受总承包合同的制约，据此分包合同就变成总承包合同的子合同，分包商要求按与总承包合同不同的方式付款并无充分的合同条款作为支持。

5.4 Evidence of Payments（付款证据）

Before issuing a Payment Certificate which includes an amount payable to a nominated Subcontractor, the Engineer may request the Contractor to supply reasonable evidence that the nominated Subcontractor has received all amounts due in accordance with previous Payment Certificates, less applicable deductions for retention or otherwise. Unless the Contractor：

(a) submits this reasonable evidence to the Engineer, or

(b) (i) satisfies the Engineer in writing that the Contractor is reasonably entitled to withhold or refuse to pay these amounts, and

(ii) submits to the Engineer reasonable evidence that the nominated Subcontractor has been notified of the Contractor's entitlement, then the Employer may (at his sole discretion) pay, direct to the nominated Subcontractor, part or all of such amounts previously certified (less applicable deductions) as are due to the nominated Subcontractor and for which the Contractor has failed to submit the evidence described in sub-paragraphs (a) or (b) above. The Contractor shall then repay, to the Employer, the amount which the nominated Subcontractor was directly paid by the Employer.

工程师有权检查承包商是否已将工程款转付给指定的分包商，在某些情况下，也可以直接向分包商付款。将指定分包商的款项支付给承包商后,应从承包商处收回任何支付给指定分包商的款项。

向指定分包商直接付款前,工程师应根据(b)(i)项规定的程序检查工程款项未支付给指定分包商的理由。任何随后从承包商付款中扣减工程款的行为,均需遵守第2.5款[雇主的索赔]的程序。在采取直接向指定分包商付款时也应考虑合同的有关规定。

雇主向分包商直接付款,使得分包商的权益得到了保障。若合同中没有这种直接付款的条款,雇主又直接向分包商付款,则可能使承包商拒绝承担施工合同中的某些义务,并造成承包商要求雇主再次就分包商的工作直接向其付款,导致雇主向承包商与分包商进行双重付款的被动局面。因此,若雇主不能就此事先与承包商达成协议,则工程师通常建议雇主在向分包商直接付款前,应首先获得分包商的赔偿保障,即当这种直接付款出现问题时,分包商应保证退回全部款项,通常是采用分包商自费向雇主提供银行保函的形式。但是,对于雇主使用暂定金额这笔预列费用,并在其金额限制下直接支付给分包商的情况,承包商无权根据合同其他条款进行索赔或要求双重付款。

【例5.3】某港口项目,由于总承包商与分包商发生持续争执,双方互不相让,总承包商拒绝在问题解决之前向分包商支付,导致施工进度有所放慢。

雇主出于同情心,同时为了保证项目的顺利实施,在分包商的一再要求下,直接支付给了分包商。总承包商这时提出根据合同的规定,自己应该就分包工程得到雇主的支付。雇主认为已对此直接向分包商付款,若再向总承包商付款,就形成了双重付款。双方为此形成争端,寻求仲裁。

裁决是合同中并没有赋予雇主对分包商直接付款的权利,因此雇主应只向总承包商付款。至于总承包商拒绝向分包商付款而可能引发工程在实施中出现的问题,或拖延工期,雇主则可以根据合同有关条款对总承包商进行制裁,包括使用罚款措施。

【例5.4】付款证书的格式

工程款支付证书

工程名称:

致:＿＿(承包商名称)＿＿

根据施工合同的规定,经审核承包商的付款申请和报表,并扣除有关款项,同意本期支付工程款共(大写)＿＿＿＿＿(小写:＿＿＿＿＿)

请按合同规定及时付款。

其中:

1. 承包商申报款为:

2. 经审核承包商应得款为:

3. 本期应扣款为:

4. 本期应付款为:

附件:

1. 承包商的工程付款申请表及附件;

2. 项目监理机构审查记录。

项目监理机构:＿＿＿＿＿＿＿

总监理工程师:＿＿＿＿＿＿＿

日　　　期:＿＿＿＿＿＿＿

5 Normited Subcontractors（指定的分包商）

思考题

1. 简述指定的分包商的定义。
2. 承包商如何反对指定分包？
3. 分包商能否就付款、索赔和工期等问题直接与雇主交涉，为什么？
4. 向指定分包商付款前，工程师应做好哪些准备？
5. 简述雇主在向分包商付款前的注意事项。

6　Staff and Labour（员工）

承包商需要雇用员工和劳务来完成工程任务，合同的执行也是由这些人员来实际落实，因此，对于承包商雇用的员工及劳务人员，必须有确定的要求与规定。本合同条件第4.1款［承包商的一般义务］规定了雇主要求承包商提供"所有承包商人员"的信息，在本条中专门规定了对招募、雇用承包商职员和劳务的要求，并规定了管理和记录其人员信息的特别要求。本条中发生的费用基本都在综合单价或项目管理费中。

本章要求：了解承包商雇用员工的相关事项以及员工的工资标准和劳动条件等；

了解对承包商遵守劳动法以及工作时间的要求；

了解承包商为员工提供设施以及健康和安全保障的要求；

了解对承包商的监督和承包商人员与设备的记录的要求；

了解对承包商人员的要求以及日常管理方面的规定。

6.1　Engagement of Staff and Labour（员工的雇用）

Except as otherwise stated in the Specification, the Contractor shall make arrangements for the engagement of all staff and labour, local or otherwise, and for their payment, housing, feeding and transport.

为了执行项目，承包商需要雇用员工与劳务人员，本款规定：

（1）承包商应自行安排雇用当地或异地的职员和劳工，支付他们的工资，并安排他们的食宿和交通；

（2）如果在规范中有其他规定，则应按照规范的规定执行。

有时可能会出现由于地区法令等原因强制要求承包商雇用本地劳工或其他雇用政策的情况，承包商应遵从。此种法令要求，不论是否已经在招标文件中说明，都会以"对现场的了解"而视为承包商的责任。

6.2　Rates of Wages and Conditions of Labour（工资标准和劳动条件）

The Contractor shall pay rates of wages, and observe conditions of labour, which are not lower than those established for the trade or industry where the work is carried out. If no established rates or conditions are applicable, the Contractor shall pay rates of wages and observe conditions which are not lower than the general level of wages and conditions observed locally by employers whose trade or industry is similar to that of the Contractor.

合同条件的专用条款中可规定工资标准和劳动条件应符合当地规定的附加要求。根据第1.13款［遵守法律］和第6.4款［劳动法］的规定，承包商应遵守有关工资和劳动条件的当地法律和规定。

6.3 Persons in the Service of Employer（为雇主服务的人员）

The Contractor shall not recruit, or attempt to recruit, staff and labour from amongst the Employer's Personnel.

雇主人员通常比承包商更了解当地的情况，承包商需要这种人才，但聘用雇主人员会对雇主造成损害，不仅可能会影响雇主的工作、泄露保密事项，而且承包商与雇主人员若发生直接利益关系，这对于项目会造成很大的损害。

如果在承包商雇用之前雇主人员已经离职，则不适用本款规定。但如果承包商或分包商意图说服雇主人员离开雇主，则构成了违约行为。

6.4 Labour Laws（劳动法）

The Contractor shall comply with all the relevant labour Laws applicable to the Contractor's Personnel, including Laws relating to their employment, health, safety, welfare, immigration and emigration, and shall allow them all their legal rights.

The Contractor shall require his employees to obey all applicable Laws, including those concerning safety at work.

劳动法保障了劳动提供者的基本权益。

一般来说，与工程雇用职员和劳工相关比较密切的内容涉及以下几方面：

（1）雇用程序和解雇程序；
（2）最低工资；
（3）福利条件，如劳保用品的发放等；
（4）办理社会保险或雇主责任险；
（5）病休与带薪休假；
（6）工作时间以及加班费支付问题等。

6.5 Working hours（工作时间）

No work shall be carried out on the Site on locally recognized days of rest, or outside the normal working hours stated in the Appendix to Tender, unless:

(a) otherwise stated in the Contract,
(b) the Engineer gives consent, or
(c) the work is unavoidable, or necessary for the protection of life or property or for the safety of the Works, in which case the Contractor shall immediately advise the Engineer.

保障员工工作时间之外的休息时间以及正常的节假日，是基于安全或其他当地要求而作出的规定。实际工程中，如果需要加快进度避免工期延误，可在征得工程师同意后，安排正常工作时间以外的工作,应参照第 8.6 款 [工程进度] 中的规定来进行。第 8.6 款规定使得雇主可以就任何额外的监理费用向承包商提出索赔,作为工程师同意在正常工作时间之外工作的一个条件,工程师可以作出与第 8.6 款规定类似的指示。

国内工程采用 FIDIC 合同订立施工承包合同时,一般会加一条"承包商工作时间视为已考虑了地方政府的规定。由承包商安排的加班及其他工作时间所产生的费用及相关事项,均由承包商自行承担。承包商应保证雇主不受此类事项的干扰"。此条可解除雇主的相关责任。

【例 6.1】某工程由于雇主方的原因,要求承包商提前完成工程并交付使用,缩短了合同的计划工期。承包商为达成提前交工的目标,在征得工程师同意的前提下,不得不延长工作时间并在法定休息日安排加班赶工,由此产生了额外的赶工费用支出。承包商据此提出索赔,与雇主和承包商双方协商后,承包商获得了该项费用的索赔。

6.6 Facilities for Staff and Labour(为员工提供设施)

Except as otherwise stated in the Specification, the Contractor shall provide and maintain all necessary accommodation and welfare facilities for the Contractor's Personnel. The Contractor shall also provide facilities for the Employer's Personnel as stated in the Specification.

The Contractor shall not permit any of the Contractor's Personnel to maintain any temporary or permanent living quarters within the structures forming part of the Permanent Works.

承包商有责任为承包商和雇主等现场工作人员提供必要的工作和生活设施。由于现场人员大部分是承包商人员,因此应由承包商提供此类设施。

本款规定承包商不得提供施工现场的任何场所为其员工的居住场所。新浇筑的混凝土、新砌体、新装修等会对人体造成损害,施工场地也没有充分的生活类的安全保障,不具有居住的安全条件。此类场所的居住行为极难被政府相关部门监管,可能成为各种违法犯罪的庇护场所。若承包商人员在这些场所滞留,可能给工程交工带来问题。因此工程现场相关区域不允许居住。

6.7 Health and Safety(健康和安全)

The Contractor shall at all times take all reasonable precautions to maintain the health and safety of the Contractor's Personnel. In collaboration with local health authorities, the Contractor shall ensure that medical staff, first aid facilities, sick bay and ambulance service are available at all times at the Site and at any accommodation for Contractor's and Employer's Personnel, and that suitable arrangements are made for all necessary welfare and hygiene requirements and for the prevention of epidemics.

The Contractor shall appoint an accident prevention officer at the Site, responsible for maintaining safety and protection against accidents. This person shall be qualified for this responsibility, and shall have the authority to issue instructions and take protective measures to prevent accidents. Throughout the execution of the Works, the Contractor shall provide whatever is required by this person to exercise this responsibility and authority.

The Contractor shall send, to the Engineer, details of any accident as soon as practicable after its occurrence. The Contractor shall maintain records and make reports concerning health, safety and welfare of persons, and damage to property, as the Engineer may reasonably require.

健康和安全是工程施工中的最重要的问题，承包商应采取一切合理措施保护其雇员的健康和安全。安全事故不仅会给承包商造成直接经济损失，而且会延误工程的工期。流行性疾病也是承包商应关注的问题之一。

作为一个成熟的管理者，即使合同中没有严格规定相关安全与健康注意事项，项目经理也应关注并保障施工现场人员的安全与健康。应工程师要求，承包商须保留有关安全与健康事项的记录，这些记录将构成第 4.21 款（g）项的下月进度报告安全统计数字基础。

本款的规定与国际劳工组织的 167 号公约是一致的，将劳工的健康和安全统一起来。

6.8 Contractor's Superintendence(承包商的监督)

Throughout the execution of the Works, and as long thereafter as is necessary to fulfill the Contractor's Obligations, the Contractor shall provide all necessary superintendence to plan. arrange, direct, manage, inspect and test the work. Superintendence shall be given by a sufficient number of persons having adequate knowledge of the language for communications (defined in Sub-Clause 1.4 [Law and Language]) and of the operations to be carried out (including the methods and techniques required, the hazards likely to be encountered and methods of preventing accidents), for the satisfactory and safe execution of the Works.

工程进行过程中，承包商应对工程的计划、管理、检查、检验等进行必要的监督。承包商的监督可由安排在现场各个方面的不同层次的管理人员来完成。

6.9 Contractor's in Personnel（承包商人员）

The Contractor's Personnel shall be appropriately qualified, skilled and experienced in their respective trades or occupations. The Engineer may require the Contractor to remove (or cause to be removed) any person employed on the Site or Works, including the Contractor's Representative if applicable, who:
(a) persists in any misconduct or lack of care,
(b) carries out duties incompetently or negligently,
(c) fails to conform with any provisions of the Contract, or
(d) persists in any conduct which is prejudicial to safety, health, or the protection

of the environment.

If appropriate, the Contractor shall then appoint (or cause to be appointed) a suitable replacement person.

FIDIC 合同在本款中对承包商人员的资格作出了要求,合格的承包商人员应当在技术水平和职业道德两方面都达到本款中规定的要求,符合要求的高素质的承包商人员是项目顺利实施的保障,若人员达不到要求,项目则无法进行。工程师对不合格的承包商人员甚至承包商代表(项目经理)拥有撤换的权力,但此项权力不可滥用。

【例 6.2】在某工程项目中,承包商的质检部门人员经常拖延检验进度,并且工作不认真,发生过多次漏检、错检,甚至编造检验报告的问题,对工程进度与质量带来重大风险。为了消除此项风险,工程师要求承包商代表撤换此人员,并列出了确切证据。经协商,承包商代表同意撤换此人员,并指定了合适的替代人员,消除了此项风险,保证了本项目的正常开展。

6.10 Records of Contractor's Personnel and Equipment(承包商人员和设备的记录)

The Contractor shall submit, to the Engineer, details showing the number of each class of Contractor's Personnel and of each type of Contractor's Equipment on the Site. Details shall be submitted each calendar month, in a form approved by the Engineer, until the Contractor has completed all work which is known to be outstanding at the completion date stated in the Taking-Over Certificate for the Works.

为便于雇主了解项目现场的施工状况,尤其是施工进度,本款规定,承包商应按照工程师认可的方式,每月提交详细的人员考勤与设备数量的详细记录,直到承包商完成工程接收证书中规定的竣工日期时的全部未完成工作为止。

有关设备的报告应包含在第 4.21 款(d)项规定的月进度报告中。对于大型和复杂的项目而言,须在专用条款中要求提供项目特定部分所使用的设备的数量。根据第 20.1 款[承包商的索赔]递交的同期记录也应与此记录保持一致。

6.11 Disorderly Conduct(无序行为)

The Contractor shall at all times take all reasonable precautions to prevent any unlawful, riotous or disorderly conduct by or amongst the Contractor's Personnel, and to preserve peace and protection of persons and property on and near the Site.

由于国际工程项目的复杂性,项目执行期间可能会出现一些影响安定的现象,如罢工、骚乱等。这些事件不仅会影响工程项目的进程,危及现场及邻近人员和财产安全,对承包商的形象也会造成负面影响。承包商应通过工程所在当地政府、工会等机构及时掌握相关动态,采取措施预防此类事件的发生。

如果承包商未能采取措施预防上述事件发生,可能导致第 18.3 款[人身伤害和财产损害险]规定的保险索赔,或者第 17.1 款[保障]规定的保障索赔以及第 4.14 款[避免干扰]下的索赔。也可能影响在其他条款下的雇主责任,但第 19.1 款[不可抗力的定义]

(iii) 项规定的不可抗力和第 17.3 款［雇主的风险］(c) 项规定的雇主风险责任除外。

思考题

1. 承包商在雇用员工和劳务人员时应遵守哪些规定？
2. 简述员工的工资标准、劳动条件、工作时间的相关要求。
3. 如果承包商招收雇主人员可能产生什么后果？如果承包商试图招收雇主人员应满足什么前提条件？
4. 简述承包商为员工提供设施以及健康和安全保障的要求。
5. 简述承包商的监督职责。
6. 简述对承包商人员和日常管理方面的要求。

7 Plant, Materials and Workmanship
（生产设备、材料和工艺）

工程质量管理和控制是工程项目管理的核心内容之一。质量管理可分为承包商主动的内部质量控制和雇主对工程质量的实时监管与验收，这两方面质量管理配合良好的前提下能够实现高效可靠的质量控制，保障工程项目合格完成。本条给出了设备材料验收与工艺检验的有关规定。

本章要求：了解承包商实施工程各个环节的总体要求；
了解材料质量控制的方法；
了解雇主现场检验的内容和程序以及承包商配合的义务；
了解工程师拒收与不合格工程返工的条件及注意事项。

7.1 Manner of Execution （实施方法）

The Contractor shall carry out the manufacture of Plant, the production and manufacture of Materials, and all other execution of the Works:

(a) in the manner (if any) specified in the Contract,

(b) in a proper workmanlike and careful manner, in accordance with recognised good practice, and

(c) with properly equipped facilities and non-hazardous Materials, except as otherwise specified in the Contract.

（a）项中规定，承包商应以合同中规定的方法进行施工。国内工程对"施工组织设计"中的施工方案要求很严，对于各类型工程，基本都有相关的国家、地方或企业的施工规范，其内容细致详实，因此国内工程符合（a）项的情况较多。

（b）项是对合同中没有规定的情况，要求按照公认的良好惯例进行工程施工，保证施工质量。

（c）项是对施工装备与材料的安全性要求。

7.2 Samples （样品）

The Contractor shall submit the following samples of Materials, and relevant information, to the Engineer for consent prior to using the Materials in or for the works:

(a) manufacturer's standard samples of Materials and samples specified in the Contract, all at the Contractor's cost, and

(b) additional samples instructed by the Engineer as a Variation.

Each sample shall be labeled as to origin and intended use in the Works.

承包商在工程材料用于工程项目前,应向工程师提交材料样品及相关资料,以征得工程师的同意。

工程材料的好坏直接影响工程质量,在质量管理和控制中通常以检验样品的方式对材料的各项性能指标进行检测。为了避免重复工作,承包商可在一些大宗材料(如水泥)的采购前,先联系厂家获取材料的技术数据,与工程需要的材料的技术数据进行比较,判断其是否符合工程要求,并且在购买前应将该数据提交给工程师,在获得工程师的批准后再进行采购。工程师在收到此类数据后应尽快作出采购与否的决定,如若拖延并造成损失,承包商可依据第1.3款[通信联络]的规定发起索赔。

FIDIC合同在招标投标时有工料规范,其中已明确相关工料标准,施工过程中要求承包商提供样品,主要明确外观等细节标准。这些工料新标准的确立对投标报价不能造成实质性影响,相关分项工程的综合单价也不会因样品申报而调整。

某些项目招投标阶段的许多内容,特别是外观及效果类设计,雇主与设计方基本都没有详细论证,相关标准难以确定。在清单计价模式下,施工期要审核材料价并调整计入合同价格,需依靠综合单价分析表来完成。由于综合单价分析表完全由投标人编制,分析表的合同义务涵盖面的解释权完全在承包商,因此施工期材料审核制不适用于单价合同。

承包商申报使用材料样品的时间可提前至招标投标阶段,以承包商申报的样品来确立产品标准。工程上申报的样品,除承包商申报样品外,设计师也会被要求提供设计封样,此时,样品应直接归入"工料规范"内。承包商实际使用的材料,经设计师及雇主相关人员直接确认后(设计合同会规定相应的设计师配合),工程师认同承包商的材料样品已达到"工料规范"的要求。

【例7.1】

某宾馆大楼的装饰装修和设备安装工程,经公开招标投标确定由某建筑装修工程公司和设备安装公司承包工程施工,并签订了施工承包合同。合同价为2600万元,工期230天。合同规定:雇主与承包商"每提前或延误工期一天,按合同价的万分之二进行奖罚","石材及主要设备由雇主提供,其他材料由承包方采购"。

承包商与石材厂商签订了石材购销合同;雇主经与设计方商定,对主要装饰石料制定了材质、颜色和样品。施工进行到22天时,由于设计变更,造成工程停工9天,承包商8天内提出了索赔意向通知;施工进行到36天时,因雇主方挑选确定石材,使部分工程停工累计达16天(位于关键路线上),承包商10天内提出了索赔意向通知;施工进行到52天,雇主方挑选确定的石材送达现场,进场验收时发现该批石材大部分不符合质量要求,工程师通知承包商该批石材不得使用。承包商要求将不符合要求的石材退换,因此延误工期5天。石材厂商要求承包商支付退货运费,承包商拒绝。工程结算时,承包商因此向雇主方要求索赔;施工进行到73天时,该地受罕见暴风雨袭击,施工无法进行,延误工期2天,施工方5天内提出了索赔意向通知;施工进行到237天时,施工方因人员调配原因,延误工期三天;最后,工程在252天后竣工。

7.3 Inspection(检验)

The Employer's Personnel shall at all reasonable times
(a) have full access to all parts of the Site and to all places from which natural Materials are being obtained, and

(b) during production, manufacture and construction (at the Site and elsewhere), be entitled to examine, inspect, measure and test the materials and workmanship, and to check the progress of manufacture of Plant and production and manufacture of Materials.

The Contractor shall give the Employer's Personnel full opportunity to carry out these activities, including providing access, facilities, permissions and safety equipment. No such activity shall relieve the Contractor from any obligation or responsibility.

The Contractor shall give notice to the Engineer whenever any work is ready and before it is covered up, put out of sight, or packaged for storage or transport. The Engineer shall then either carry out the examination, inspection, measurement or testing without unreasonable delay, or promptly give notice to the Contractor that the Engineer does not require to do so. If the Contractor fails to give the notice, he shall, if and when required by the Engineer, uncover the work and thereafter reinstate and make good, all at the Contractor's cost.

为实行有效的质量管理，本款规定，雇主方人员有进入现场或有关场所检查工程的权力，且承包商有义务协助此类检查。承包商的任何义务与责任不因检查而发生变化。承包商在任何已完工程被隐蔽之前，应向工程师发出通知，以便工程师进行检查、测量和检验。

FIDIC合同条件对于隐蔽工程的规定与国内相关规范相同。工程师未在隐蔽工程验收单上签字，此隐蔽工程视为不合格，必须使用一切必须、正当的检查检验手段来重新鉴定其质量状况。工程师在认为检验与检查结果不能证实工程可靠性的情况下，有权要求承包商返工。

7.4 Testing（试验）

This Sub-Clause shall apply to all tests specified in the Contract, other than the Tests after Completion (if any).

The Contractor shall provide all apparatus, assistance, documents and other information, electricity, equipment, fuel, consumables, instruments, labour, materials, and suitably qualifiedand experienced staff, as are necessary to carry out the specified tests efficiently. The Contractor shall agree, with the Engineer, the time and place for the specified testing of any Plant, Materials and other parts of the Works.

The Engineer may, under Clause 13 [Variations and Adjustments], vary the location or details of specified tests, or instruct the Contractor to carry out additional tests. If these varied or additional tests show that the tested Plant, Materials or workmanship is not in accordance with the Contract, the cost of carrying out this Variation shall be borne by the Contractor, notwithstanding other provisions of the Contract.

The Engineer shall give the Contractor not less than 24 hours' notice of the Engineer's intention to attend the tests. If the Engineer does not attend at the time and place agreed, the Contractor may proceed with the tests, unless otherwise instructed by the Engineer, and the tests shall then be deemed to have been made in the Engineer's presence.

If the Contractor suffers delay and/or incurs Cost from complying with these instructions or as a result of a delay for which the Employer is responsible, the Contractor shall give notice to the Engineer and shall be entitled subject to Sub-Clause 20.1 [Contractor's Claims] to:

(a) an extension of time for any such delay, if completion is or will be delayed, under Sub-Clause 8.4 [Extension of Time for Completion], and

(b) payment of any such Cost plus reasonable profit, which shall be included in the Contract Price.

After receiving this notice, the Engineer shall proceed in accordance with Sub-Clause 3.5 [Determinations] to agree or determine these matters.

The Contractor shall promptly forward to the Engineer duly certified reports of the tests. When the specified tests have been passed, the Engineer shall endorse the Contractor's test certificate, or issue a certificate to him, to that effect. If the Engineer has not attended the tests, he shall be deemed to have accepted the readings as accurate.

本款规定了合同中指明的试验程序，以及按照第13条［变更和调整］的指示进行的额外试验程序。竣工验收在第9条［竣工试验］中进行了规定，也可参见第7.4款的评述。

根据第7.3款［检验］的规定，承包商需发出工程已经完成的通知。工程师应至少提前24小时向承包商表明参加试验的意图，并与承包商商定试验的时间和地点。若工程师打算改变特定细节，需要根据第13条［变更和调整］的规定签发变更令。如果工程师未能参加试验，且没有发出适当的指示，承包商可进行试验工作，且应视为该项试验是在工程师在场的情况下进行的，工程师也应将试验结果看作是准确的并应予以接受。

试验结束后，承包商需向工程师递交被证实的试验报告，若试验通过，工程师应颁发有关证书。若工程或部分工程未能通过试验，工程师可根据第7.5款［拒收］的规定对该项试验予以拒绝，且应给出拒绝的原因。承包商必须修复该项物件并保证符合合同规定。雇主可根据第9.4款［未能通过竣工试验］的规定同意接受该项物件。

7.5 Rejection（拒收）

If, as a result of an examination, inspection, measurement or testing, any Plant, Materials or workmanship is found to be defective or otherwise not in accordance with the Contract, the Engineer may reject the Plant, Materials or workmanship by giving notice to the Contractor, with reasons. The Contractor shall then promptly make good the defect and ensure that the rejected item complies with the Contract.

If the Engineer requires this Plant, Materials or workmanship to be retested, the tests shall be repeated under the same terms and conditions. If the rejection and retesting cause the Employer to incur additional costs, the Contractor shall subject to Sub-Clause 2.5 [Employer's Claims] pay these costs to the Employer.

若检验、检查、测量的结果表明工程中任何设备、材料或工艺存在缺陷或不符合合同要求,工程师可通知承包商,并说明理由,拒绝接收该设备、材料或工艺。在拒收后,承包商应立即修复缺陷,并确保达标。

工程师有重新进行检验的权力,承包商应予以配合,重新检验的要求应与初次检验一致。由于拒收或重新检验给雇主带来的费用增加,雇主有权依照第2.5款[雇主的索赔]的规定发起索赔。

【例7.2】某工程的某现浇混凝土构件出现了较为严重的裂缝与蜂窝麻面,经检验,不符合规范要求。因此,工程师拒收,并要求承包商立即整改。通过整改,该构件达到规范要求,从而避免了质量问题的发生。

7.6 Remedial Work（修补工作）

Not withstanding any previous test or certification, the Engineer may instruct the Contractor to:

(a) remove from the Site and replace any Plant or Materials which is not in accordance with the Contract,

(b) remove and re-execute any other work which is not in accordance with the Contract, and

(c) execute any work which is urgently required for the safety of the Works, whether because of an accident, unforeseeable event or otherwise.

The Contractor shall comply with the instruction within a reasonable time, which shall be the time (if any) specified in the instruction, or immediately if urgency is specified under-sub-paragraph (c).

If the Contractor fails to comply with the instruction, the Employer shall be entitled to employ and pay other persons to carry out the work. Except to the extent that the Contractor would have been entitled to payment for the work, the Contractor shall subject to Sub-Clause 2.5 [Employer's Claims] pay to the Employer all costs arising from this failure.

对于承包商已完成的工作,即使已经进行了检验或给予了认可,但若该项工作不符合合同,工程师有权命令承包商移除该项工作并予以修复。这体现了 FIDIC 合同条件的一个原则:即工程师的认可和批准不解除承包商的任何合同义务,承包商的合同义务就是提供给雇主一个符合合同规定的工程。

发生了事故、不可预见事件或其他事件而必须实施保护工程安全的紧急工作时,承包商应当配合工程师尽快完成该项工作,若承包商拒绝执行,雇主有权雇佣他人完成该项工作。若该项工作属于承包商合同义务内工作,雇主有权对此项花费向承包商提出索赔。

7.7 Ownership of Plant and Materials（生产设备和材料的所有权）

Each item of Plant and Materials shall, to the extent consistent with the Laws of the Country, become the property of the Employer at whichever is the earlier of the following times, free from liens and other encumbrances:

(a) when it is delivered to the Site;

(b) when the Contractor is entitled to payment of the value of the Plant and Materials under Sub-Clause 8.10 [Payment for Plant and Materials in Event of Suspension].

工程的建设周期一般比较长，承包商采购的永久设备和材料较多，在国际工程中，常规定这些设备和材料在安装或消耗到工程上之前，其所有权归雇主所有。

本款中提到的抵押权在国内发生的可能性较低。目前我国银行抵押贷款的审批相对较慢，同时对于生产材料等易运输的物品，银行将其作为抵押物的可能性也较小。由于金融体制不够灵活，将工程材料设备抵押的情况不易出现。对于一些大型工程，承包商利用生产资料抵押以快速套现的情况有可能发生。此时，本款雇主的保护性规定的用处有所体现。

7.8 Royalties（土地（矿区）使用费）

Unless otherwise stated in the Specification, the Contractor shall pay all royalties, rents and other payments for:

(a) natural Materials obtained from outside the Site, and

(b) the disposal of material from demolitions and excavations and of other surplus material (whether natural or man-made), except to the extent that disposal areas within the Site are specified in the Contract.

工程施工过程中，通常需要从现场内外取用一些天然材料。施工过程结束后，遗留的废弃物也需要处置。

若规范中没有另行规定，承包商应自行支付从现场外取得的天然材料的一切费用。施工中开挖和超出的废弃物或者剩余材料的处理费，也由承包商自行负担。如果在现场内指定了废弃物处理区，承包商可免费在此区域内处置其废弃物。

思考题

1. 简述承包商实施工程各个环节的总体要求。
2. 试说明对材料质量控制的方法。
3. 简述雇主现场检验的内容和程序。
4. 简述合同规定的试验内容和程序。
5. 分别说明承包商配合现场检验和试验的义务。
6. 简述工程师拒收与不合格工程返工的条件及注意事项。

8 Commencement, Delays and Suspension（开工、延误和暂停）

进度管理是项目管理的主要内容之一，无论是雇主，还是承包商，通常将工期、费用和质量三个指标作为判断项目是否成功的标准。从工程实施进程来看，与工期管理密切关联的内容有：开工、进度、竣工、缺陷通知期以及工程延期。FIDIC 施工合同通用条件从第 8 条到 11 条是对工期管理的内容。本条基本上覆盖的是开工、进度、暂停、工期延长等方面的内容。

本章要求：熟悉本合同条件中的关键术语的含义；
了解工程开工、施工及竣工时间的确定；
了解承包商索赔工期的权利和条件；
了解雇主对承包商延误工期的管理方法以及收取延期赔偿费的规定；
了解工程暂停的条件以及暂停的后果。

8.1 Commencement of Works（工程的开工）

The Engineer shall give the Contractor not less than 7 days' notice of the Commencement Date. Unless otherwise stated in the Particular Conditions, the Commencement Date shall be within 42 days after the Contractor receives the Letter of Acceptance.

The Contractor shall commence the execution of the Works as soon as is reasonably practicable after the Commencement Date, and shall then proceed with the Works with due expedition and without delay.

工程师应在不少于 7 天前向承包商发出开工日期的通知。除非专用条件中另有说明，开工日期应在承包商收到中标函后 42 天内。承包商应在开工日期后，在合理可能的情况下尽早开始工程的实施，随后应以正当速度，不拖延地进行工程。

合同的起点开始于中标通知书，或者 FIDIC 施工合同条件第 1.6 款［合同协议书］定义的合同协议书中规定的时间，有关的保函和保险的安排必须在发出中标通知书之前完成。如果雇主决定发出拟使合同成立的信函，则应在意向书中明确写明它不是中标通知书，这一点十分重要。

开工日期是工期的计算起点，用以确定工程的实际竣工时间，其法律意义涉及竣工结算及利息的起算时间、计算违约金的数额以及风险转移等问题。开工日期指雇主和承包商在协议中约定的承包商开始施工的日期，即承包商同意施工的"竣工时间"的开始。在施工开始之前，商定日历天数可以避免潜在的争议。决定开工日期后，工程师应计算竣工的日历天数。投标书附录中给出了竣工时间的天数，这个天数可指整个工程也可指工程的任何区段。"天"被定义为日历日，而不是工作日，所以天数包括周末和节假日。

根据本款的要求，工程师决定开工日期：
（1）除专用条款另有规定外，开工日期应在承包商收到中标通知书后42天内。
（2）工程师应至少提前7天向承包商发出开工日期的通知。

对施工合同而言，一个项目可能跨越几年的时间。7天的通知期限很短，因此，承包商必须在收到中标通知书后立即开始准备工作。FIDIC施工合同条件第2.1款［现场进入权］要求雇主在投标附录规定的自开工日期之日起的一定天数内向承包商交付进入和占用现场部分的权利。无论何种原因，如果工程师不能达到规定天数的要求，或者雇主不能交付现场占有权，雇主和承包商应就合同条款的变更达成一致。工程师没有权利签发改变这项要求指示的权力。

本款要求承包商应在开工日期后，在合理可能的情况下"尽早"开始工程的实施，随后应"以正当速度，不拖延地"进行工程。对正当速度和不拖延的解释将根据具体情况而定，但是，该项要求承包商即使出现问题时，也应继续施工。

【例8.1】在实际工程中开工日期存在争议的两种常见情况如下：

第一种是施工许可证取得时间晚于合同约定的开工日期。在雇主未办理施工许可证情况下，承包商又先于合同签订而开工，双方就开工日期产生争议，雇主主张以合同约定为开工日期，承包商则主张以施工许可证取得之日作为工期起算点。国内建筑工程在开工之前，建设单位应当按照国家规定向工程所在地县级以上人民政府建设行政主管部门申请施工许可证，虽然前期因为尚未取得施工许可证是违规的，但是这是监管部门的行政管理范围，并不影响承包商作为开工日期。因此，施工许可证与实际开工日期无关，一旦承包商按照合同开工，实际施工的时间即为此开工日期。

第二种是雇主提供的开工条件时间晚于合同约定的开工日期。当合同约定开工日期时间晚于开工日期的施工条件之后，双方就开工日期产生争议，雇主主张以合同约定为开工日期，承包商主张以实际进场施工日期为开工日期，最终法院认为以现场实际具备开工条件的日期作为开工日期，不是合同约定日期。

8.2　Time for Completion（竣工时间）

The Contractor shall complete the whole of the Works, and each Section (if any), within the Time for Completion for the Works or Section (as the case may be), including:

(a) achieving the passing of the Tests on Completion, and

(b) completing all work which is stated in the Contract as being required for the Works or Section to be considered to be completed for the purposes of taking over under Sub-Clause 10.1 [Taking Over of the Works and Sections].

本款主要说明承包商应在竣工时间内完成其承担的所有工作，这与竣工后工程各项权利的移交直接相关。划分清楚责任主体，如工程出现缺陷可以要求承包商返工或者重做等，到将来工程移交，工程权利转移，这中间发生任何事都会对工程产生深远影响，因此合同对此进行详细规定，符合工程的实际需要。

在竣工时间期满之前，承包商负有义务完成第10.1款［工程和单位工程的接收］中的接收要求，包括通过第9条［竣工试验］规定的竣工验收要求的所有工程。如果要求在全部工程竣工时间之前完成单位工程，投标书附录中必须描述这些单位工程，以及每一区段的竣工时间和误期违约赔偿金。

FIDIC 施工合同条件第 10.1 款［工程和单位工程的接收］中虽提及了本款，但对此并没有什么帮助。除实际施工和试验外，专用条款中可以规定更为详细的必须完成的工程清单。

【例 8.2】

在国内工程实际中，由于工程建设过程受到多种因素的影响，致使工程不能按期竣工，对于竣工时间到底是以完工日期、提交竣工报告还是工程验收合格之日为准需要特别说明。在工程实际中，竣工时间约定不清楚，比如"工程应于××××年××月××日全部完工，并竣工验收交付使用"，有可能导致双方对竣工时间产生争议，雇主认为"竣工"是指竣工验收，承包商则认为竣工应该以是否完成合同约定的工程范围为准。根据《最高人民法院关于审理建设工程施工合同纠纷案件适用法律问题的解释》其中第十四条规定：当事人对建设工程实际竣工日期有争议的，按照以下情形分别处理：(1) 建设工程经竣工验收合格的，以竣工验收合格之日为竣工日期；(2) 承包人已经提交竣工验收报告，发包人拖延验收的，以承包人提交验收报告之日为竣工日期；(3) 建设工程未经竣工验收，发包人擅自使用的，以转移占有建设工程之日为竣工日期。

【例 8.3】

某采用 FIDIC 施工合同条件的工程中，约定的工程竣工时间为 5 月 1 日，承包商在 4 月 15 日就完成了施工，并提前通知了工程师，要求在该日期进行竣工检验。但由于外部配合条件不具备竣工检验的要求，直到 5 月 15 日工程师才发出竣工检验的通知。经过 3 天试验后表明质量合格，到 5 月 18 日有关各方在验收记录上签字。工程师颁发工程接收证书中注明的竣工日期应为 4 月 15 日。

8.3　Programme（进度计划）

The Contractor shall submit a detailed time programme to the Engineer within 28 days after receiving the notice under Sub-Clause 8.1 [Commencement of Works]. The Contractor shall also submit a revised programme whenever the previous programme is inconsistent with actual progress or with the Contractor's obligations. Each programme shall include:

(a) the order in which the Contractor, intends to carry out the Works, including the anticipated timing of each stage of design (if any), Contractor's Documents, procurement, manufacture of Plant, delivery to Site, construction, erection and testing,

(b) each of these stages for work by each nominated Subcontractor (as defined in Clause 5 [Nominated Subcontractors]),

(c) the sequence and timing of inspections and tests specified in the Contract, and

(d) a supporting report which includes:

(i) a general description of the methods which the Contractor intends to adopt, and of the major stages, in the execution of the Works, and

(ii) details showing the Contractor's reasonable estimate of the number of each class of Contractor's Personnel and of each type of Contractor's Equipment, required on the

8　Commencement, Delays and Suspension（开工、延误和暂停）

Site for each major stage.

Unless the Engineer, within 21 days after receiving a programme, gives notice to the Contractor stating the extent to which it does not comply with the Contract, the Contractor shall proceed in accordance with the programme, subject to his other obligations under the Contract. The Employer's Personnel shall be entitled to rely upon the programme when planning their activities.

The Contractor shall promptly give notice to the Engineer of specific probable future events or circumstances which may adversely affect the work, increase the Contract Price or delay the execution, of the Works. The Engineer may require the Contractor to submit an estimate of the anticipated effect of the future event or circumstances, and/or a proposal under sub-Clause 13.3 [Variation Procedure].

If, at any time, the Engineer gives notice to the Contractor that a programme fails (to the extent stated) to comply with the Contract or to be consistent with actual progress and the Contractor's stated intentions, the Contractor shall submit a revised programme to the Engineer in accordance with this Sub-Clause.

承包商在收到开工日期通知后28天内应向工程师递交一份详细的进度计划。承包商可以在投标阶段准备其进度计划，并可在谈判过程中或在收到中标通知书和签署合同协议书的过程中计划工程。但是承包商绝不能到收到开工日期通知，并开始计算工期的实际日历天数时，才开始准备最终进度计划。详细的计划也可以包括一年中某些时段可能减少的工程内容。

本款规定了进度计划应包括信息的详细要求，这些要求在专用条款和规范中可以补充说明或详细规定。在决定计划的格式和应包括的内容时，承包商应牢记进度计划将被用来阐明任何延误情形是否将造成竣工时间的延误。一般而言，进度计划必须包括：

（1）承包商计划实施工程的工作顺序；

（2）从设计、采购、制造、施工和试验，包括指定分包商从事工程的每一阶段的预计时间；

（3）每个指定分包商工作的各个阶段；

（4）合同中规定的检查和检验的顺序和时间；

（5）承包商拟采用的施工方法和施工阶段；

（6）对各阶段现场所需的承包商人员和设备的数量的合理估算和说明。

进度报告要求的信息非常广泛，承包商应周密地计划其工程的实施。如果工程师对信息格式或所使用的特定电脑软件有额外要求时，为便于承包商在投标时计算其费用，应在专用条款、规范或雇主要求中规定这些要求。所要求的信息是以"承包商的计划"和"预计的时间"的方式规定，此项规定十分重要。如果有些情况改变了承包商的计划和预计时间，如果修改后的计划能满足竣工时间的要求，这时承包商可以修改其计划。

承包商不能期望或要求工程师批准甚至同意其进度计划。如工程师声明计划与合同不符，工程师应在收到进度计划后21天内通知承包商进行修改。承包商应根据该进度计划，按照合同项下的其他义务进行工作。计划中的任何意图或要求都不能改变合同项下承包商应承担的义务。

FIDIC 施工合同条件第 4.21 款［进度报告］项下承包商的月进度报告列明了需要提供的计划信息和支持文件，需使用相同的格式或者电脑软件编制计划和各种不同的报告。

如果实际进度落后于计划，与进度不符，或计划与合同不符，工程师可要求承包商采取行动，即：

（1）根据本款第一项或最后一项递交修改后的计划；或者

（2）根据第 8.6 款［工程进度］递交修改后的计划和支持文件，表明承包商如何加快进度。

本款规定雇主人员在安排他们的活动时应依据进度计划而定，因此，如果出现变化，应立即通知工程师，以便工程师及雇员调整计划。如果承包商的工作比计划提前，考虑到将来可能发生的延误，工程师可以他没有准备妥当图纸或提供适当监督为由予以拒绝。使用"提前开工"和"推迟开工"型的计划是非常有用的（承包商考虑到工期紧张，经工程师同意后可以"提前开工"，但如果承包商工程进度比计划提前，工程师考虑到后面可能发生的延误等情况，要求承包商"延迟开工"），或者承包商应与工程师商定比原计划提前的工程计划。月进度报告中可标明任何此类比计划提前的工程。

当承包商预料到可能对工程造成不利影响、增加合同价格、或延误工程施工的事件或情况时，承包商应及时将向工程师发出通知。承包商通知的要求涵盖了对承包商活动有不利影响的任何事情，而不仅仅是那些影响计划或者承包商打算递交索赔的事情。除第20.1 款［承包商的索赔］项下要求的索赔通知外，在这两个条款项下也要求对延误或者影响价格的事项发出通知。

对于本款的所有通知，要求必须"立即"发出，比第 20.1 款［承包商的索赔］中要求的"不迟于 28 天"的时间短很多。但是，该项通知似乎与其他条款项下潜在的延误通知一样具有相同的作用，如 FIDIC 施工合同条件第 1.9 款［延误的图纸或指示］规定的延误图纸或指示通知。

实际上，本款的通知是一项"早期预警通知"，它给予了工程师机会，以便在承包商遭受延误或额外费用之前采取措施解决这些问题。本款虽没有要求承包商与工程师开会讨论有关问题和可能的解决方案，但是使得工程师能够要求承包商递交估价和建议。为更好地管理工程项目，工程师一般会与承包商开会讨论潜在的问题和最佳解决方案。

【例 8.4】

在我国的一个外资项目中，雇主与承包商协商采取加速措施，将工程提前 3 个月，双方签署了加速协议，由雇主支付一笔赶工费用。但加速协议过于简单，未详细分清双方责任，特别是雇主的合作责任。协议中没有承包商权益保护条款（例如，承包商应雇主要求加速，只要采取了加速措施，即使没有效果，也应获得最低补偿），也没有赶工费支付时间的规定。承包商采取了加速措施，由于气候、雇主的干扰、承包商责任等原因使总工期未能提前，结果承包商未能获得任何补偿。

8.4 Extension of Time for Completion （竣工时间的延长）

The Contractor shall be entitled subject to Sub-Clause 20.1 [Contractor's Claims] to an extension of the Time for Completion if and to the extent that completion for the pur-

8 Commencement, Delays and Suspension（开工、延误和暂停）

poses of Sub-Clause 10.1 [Taking Over of the Works and Sections] is or will be delayed by any of the following causes：

(a) a Variation (unless an adjustment to the Time for Completion has been agreed under Sub-Clause 13.3 [Variation Procedure]) or other substantial change in the quantity of an item of work included in the Contract,

(b) a cause of delay giving an entitlement to extension of time under a Sub-Clause of these Conditions,

(c) exceptionally adverse climatic conditions,

(d) Unforeseeable shortages in the availability of personnel or Goods caused by epidemic or governmental actions, or

(e) any delay, impediment or prevention caused by or attributable to the Employer, the Employer's Personnel, or the Employer's other contractors on the Site.

If the Contractor considers himself to be entitled to an extension of the Time for Completion, the Contractor shall give notice to the Engineer in accordance with Sub-Clause 20.1 [Contractor's Claims]. When determining each extension of time under Sub-Clause 20.1, the Engineer shall review previous determinations and may increase, but shall not decrease, the total extension of time.

大部分国际工程合同都赋予承包商在某些情况下索赔工期的权利。这些情况包括两个方面：一方面是由于雇主方的过错导致工期的延误；另一方面是外部情况导致工期延误。这种规定主要来自于工程建设的独特性质以及风险分担理论。但在某个合同中规定在哪些具体情况下允许承包商索赔工期，则取决于雇主的工程采购策略和项目的具体特点。从本款的规定以及 FIDIC 施工合同条件的其他相关条款来看，FIDIC 合同条件允许承包商索赔工期的规定还是比较宽松的。如承包商认为他有权提出延长竣工时间，承包商应根据第 20.1 款 ［承包商的索赔］的规定向工程师发出通知。工程师每次按照第 20.1 款规定决定延长的时间时，应审查以前做的决定，可以增加但不能减少总的延长时间。

本款列举了承包商有权要求竣工时间延长的情形。对工程造成延误或妨碍的事件本身是不允许的，但如果承包商声称由于本款所述原因，第 10.1 款 ［工程和单位工程的接收］规定的竣工时间受到了实际延误，承包商可按第 20.1 款 ［承包商的索赔］的规定向工程师发出通知，要求延长竣工时间。当确定延长竣工时间及延长时间时，工程师应根据第 3.5 款 ［决定］的规定，表示同意或作出决定。

虽然根据第 1.3 款 ［通信交流］规定不得"无故扣压或拖延"，但第 3.5 款 ［确定］中并没有规定工程师决定延长工期的时间期限。为了使承包商能够修正其计划并满足竣工日期要求，或者使承包商能够加快工作并在以前合同中规定的竣工日期内完成工程，工程师应尽快做出延长工期的决定。如果工程师的决定出现延误，承包商可就没有必要的赶工费用或者额外费用或者因延迟决定而造成的延误提出索赔。

承包商仅有权就解除第 8.7 款 ［误期损害赔偿费］项下的误期损害赔偿费责任的工期延长提出索赔，但不包括额外付款。除了本款的有关规定外。如果与其他条款出现交叉，通常承包商可根据有关条款就额外付款提出索赔。

有关事项列举如下：

(1) 变更。第13条[变更和调整]赋予了工程师签发变更工程指示的权力，并且工程师可在签发指示前要求承包商递交建议书，如果工程师没有要求承包商递交建议书，承包商应根据第8.3款[进度计划]尽快发出通知，如果承包商认为变更可能延误竣工时间，那么他应根据第20.1款[承包商的索赔]发出通知前28天内提出索赔，如果工程数量发生实际变化，且根据第12条[测量和估价]中的规定可以计量，承包商也可就工期延长提出索赔。

(2) 其他条款。有关承包商有权提出工期延长索赔的其他条款如下：第1.9款[延误的图纸和指示]、第2.1款[现场进入权]、第4.7款[放线]、第4.12款[不可预见的物质条件]、第4.24款[化石]、第7.4款[试验]、第10.3款[对竣工验收的干扰]、第13.7款[因法律改变的调整]、第16.1款[承包商暂停工作的权利]、第17.4款[雇主风险的后果]、第19.4款[不可抗力的后果]。

(3) 气候条件。为证明工期延误是正当的，承包商必须声明气候条件是异常不利的，并实际延误了工程的竣工。承包商也有必要提交过去五年中正常气候状况的记录。雇主也许已经获得此类记录并根据第4.10款[现场数据]在投标阶段准备妥当，或者承包商可根据第4.10款（b）项获得已有的此类信息。为了记录实际情形，承包商有必要自项目开始时准备一些必要的仪器，如测量降雨的计量仪器，或者一些能够自动记录不利天气出现时或正常工作时间外出现不利天气的仪器，因气候条件而提出的索赔只涉及额外时间，不涉及费用；特殊情况不包括在第4.12款[不可预见的物质条件]中规定的不可预见的物质条件范围之内。

(4) 人员或货物的短缺。根据第1.1.6.8款[不可预见]规定，短缺是一个有经验的承包商无法预见的，并且是由于流行病或政府行为造成的，政府的行为不限于项目所在国政府。

(5) 雇主原因。如果因雇主原因造成了延误，作为合同另一方的承包商有权要求补偿。第（e）项赋予了承包商就工期延长提出索赔的权利，但是许多情形也在第17.3款[雇主的风险]和17.4款[雇主风险的后果]中有所体现，雇主在现场的其他承包商的情况应与第4.6款[合作]一起理解，第4.6款仅提出费用的支付，而不涉及时间的延误。

【例8.5】

某河道改道工程某标段内，项目开工于2015年10月份，预计在2016年10月初竣工，在主体完工90%（包括筑堤及水工建筑）后，此时坡面尚未种植植被，堤顶尚未做路面固化。2016年7月20日北京遭遇大到暴雨的异常天气，内河暴涨，为保证人民群众的财产安全，北京开闸将河水引入河道，致使堤面亏空，坡面土流失，最终承包商与雇主协调延长工期并给予一定的补偿。此案例中由于异常不利天气导致工期延误，虽然没有在合同中共同商定不利气候，但还是获得工期延长与补偿，其一是因为雇主开闸，致使承包商损失，给予一定的补偿和工期延误是合情合理的，其二是因为此次暴雨雨量大，时间长，双方默认此次异常天气。

8.5 Delays Caused by Authorities（当局造成的延误）

If the following conditions apply, namely:

(a) the Contractor has diligently followed the procedures laid down by the relevant legally constituted public authorities in the Country,

(b) these authorities delay or disrupt the Contractor's work, and

(c) the delay or disruption was Unforeseeable, then this delay or disruption will be considered as a cause of delay under sub-paragraph (b) of Sub-Clause 8.4 [Extension of Time for Completion].

对于任何合同来说，合同双方应各自承担由自己一方的错误造成的损失，而第三方对合同实施造成的影响则属于风险分担问题。但公共当局的行为延误了工程实施，该由哪方负责？

本款规定：

(1) 承包商已经积极遵守了施工所在国的合法当局制定的程序；

(2) 这些当局延误或打扰了承包商的工作；

(3) 延误或打扰是承包商无法提前预见的。

如果上述三个条件都满足，则此类延误或打扰可作为承包商提出工期索赔的原因。

从本款看，虽然合法当局的打扰可以作为承包商索赔工期的一个原因，但同时提出了三个前提条件，只有承包商提出证据，证明自己的做法符合这三个条件，才能获得索赔工期的权利。

工程的实施受公共当局的规则、政策影响的可能性较大。如：环境保护部门在非常时期对于施工噪声的限制，自由贸易区对经过其土地附近的管线工程的种种限制等都可以归于这一类情况。

本款赋予了承包商一项按照第8.4款（b）项提出工期延误索赔的附加权利，并未要求工程师遵守第3.5款［确定］中的程序，但为了对延期作出决定，要求工程师遵守第20.1款［承包商的索赔］中规定的程序。

按照有关法律法规，"工程所在国依法成立的有关公共当局"的准确含义可能是一个引起争议的潜在来源。公营机构私有化的趋势可能降低该条款的使用范围。

8.6 Rate of Progress（工程进度）

If, at any time:

(a) actual progress is too slow to complete within the Time for Completion, and/or

(b) progress has fallen (or will fall) behind the current programme under Sub-Clause 8.3 [Programme], other than as a result of a cause listed in Sub-Clause 8.4 [Extension of Time for Completion], then the Engineer may instruct the Contractor to submit, under Sub-Clause 8.3 [Programme], a revised programme and supporting report describing the revised methods which the Contractor proposes to adopt in order to expedite progress and complete within the Time for Completion.

Unless the Engineer notifies otherwise, the Contractor shall adopt these revised methods, which may require increases in the working hours and/or in the numbers of Contractor's Personnel and/or Goods, at the risk and cost of the Contractor. If these revised methods cause the Employer to incur additional costs, the Contractor shall subject to Sub-Clause 2.5 [Employer's Claims] pay these costs to the Employer, in addition to delay damages (if any) under Sub-Clause 8.7 below.

工程师受聘于雇主来管理工程，工程进度也是工程师管理的重要内容之一。

本款的规定为工程师提供了管理承包商的施工进度的合同依据。其核心内容是在两种情况下工程师可以要求承包商赶工，并且由承包商承担自己的赶工费和雇主方为赶工付出的额外费用（为配合承包商加班，雇主人员一般也加班，导致雇主比正常情况施工多付加班费等）。

如果实际进度过于缓慢以致无法按竣工时间完工，实际进度已经（或将要）落后于计划进度，工程师可指示承包商提交一份修订的进度计划以及证明文件，详细说明承包商为加快施工并在竣工时间内完工拟采取的修正方法，承包商提交工程师认可后方可执行。如果加快进度的措施导致雇主增加额外费用，雇主可根据第3.5款［确定］规定的程序作出决定。

本款规定仅适用于第8.4款［竣工时间的延长］没有包括的原因所造成的延误。延误是否由第8.4款项下的事件造成，取决于工程师根据第3.5款所作出的决定或者由争议裁决委员会随后作出的决定。如果承包商决定按照第20.4款［取得争端裁决委员会的决定］的规定将争议提交争端裁决委员会，则应首先根据20.1款［承包商的索赔］的规定发出通知，并根据其他条款规定对赶工费用、雇主费用和误期损害赔偿费提出偿付索赔。

如果承包商发生了该款项下的赶工费用，并且争议裁决委员会随后决定承包商有权要求工期延长，则存在一项潜在的索赔费用的诱因。

8.7 Delay Damages（误期损害赔偿费）

If the Contractor fails to comply with Sub-Clause 8.2 [Time for Completion], the Contractor shall subject to Sub-Clause 2.5 [Employer's Claims] pay delay damages to the Employer for this default. These delay damages shall be the sum stated in the Appendix to Tender, which shall be paid for every day which shall elapse between the relevant Time for Completion and the date stated in the Taking-Over Certificate. However, the total amount due under this Sub-Clause shall not exceed the maximum amount of delay damages (if any) stated in the Appendix to Tender.

These delay damages shall be the only damages due from the Contractor for such default, other than in the event of termination under Sub-Clause 15.2 [Termination by Employer] prior to completion of the Works. These damages shall not relieve the Contractor from his obligation to complete the Works, or from any other duties, obligations or responsibilities which he may have under the Contract.

按期完工是承包商的合同义务。本款规定承包商未能按期完工应向雇主支付误期损害赔偿，同时规定了支付赔偿费的标准以及拖期天数的计算方法和误期损害赔偿费的最高限额。

"误期损害赔偿费"理念在国际工程中被广泛接受,并被认为是一种合理而有效的约束机制。有些国家的法律规定,"赔偿费"与"罚款"的概念是不同的,前者的额度是获得赔偿一方因对方违约而损失的额度,而后者则带有惩罚性质,通常大于实际损失。由于在工程合同中,误期损害赔偿费标准是在签订合同前由雇主方确定下来的,只是在招标时对拖期损失的一种合理预见,因此,与实际的误期损失可能不一致。但如果误期损害赔偿费标准明显高于雇主的损失太多,或被认为带有惩罚性质,则有可能被法律认定此规定没有效力。

投标附录必须规定,如果工程未能按工期完工,承包商应向雇主支付的误期损害赔偿的日赔偿金额和最高赔偿限额。上述金额以最终合同价格百分比的形式予以规定。根据第14.1款[合同价格]规定,在考虑所有计量的重新调整、变更合同规定的其他情形后,该项金额为最终金额。因此,直到双方就最终付款证书达成一致,才能最终决定误期损害赔偿费的金额。

按照"损害"的一般定义,误期损害赔偿费金额应是对雇主遭受实际损失的合理估价。如果合同赋予了雇主扣除"违约金"的权力,则应在专用条款和投标书附录中对于本款相关的规定进行修订。

8.8 Suspension of Work (暂时停工)

The Engineer may at any time instruct the Contractor to suspend progress of part or all of the Works. During such suspension, the Contractor shall protect, store and secure such part or the Works against any deterioration, loss or damage.

The Engineer may also notify the cause for the suspension. If and to the extent that the cause is notified and is the responsibility of the Contractor, the following Sub-Clauses 8.9, 8.10 and 8.11 shall not apply.

工程执行过程中常常出现不能持续实施工程的情况,本款规定了工程师下达暂停工作的指示的权利以及承包商在暂停期间的义务。

工程师可随时指示承包商暂停部分或全部工程。暂停期间,承包商应保护、保管以及保障该部分或全部工程免于遭受任何损失、损蚀或损害。比如某工地因施工现场管理混乱,工人未按要求佩戴安全帽被工程师责令停工整改,在停工期间承包商不能停止对混凝土的养护工作及撤走工地看管人员。

本款中,工程师没有义务给出暂停的原因,但"可以"通知暂停的原因。很明显,工程师的合理做法是告诉承包商暂停的原因以及暂停的可能内容,以便承包商决定如何履行其"保护、保管和保证"那部分工程的义务。

第8.9款[暂停的后果]、第8.10款[暂停时对生产设备和材料的付款]、第8.11款[拖长的暂停]这三个条款中规定了承包商获得补偿的权利。

例8.6和例8.7列出了两种不同形式的工程暂停指令。

第二部分　FIDIC 施工合同条件解读与分析

【例 8.6】

_____工程项目

承包单位_____　　合同号_____
监理单位_____　　编　号_____

工程暂时停工指令

致（承包商）_____ 　　由于 _____的原因。根据合同有关条款，现通知你截止于___年___月___日___时起对_____工程暂停施工，没有收到我或者我的授权人签发的复工指令不得复工。 　　驻地监理工程师：　　　　　　　　　　　　　　　　　　　　年　　月　　日 　　总监理工程师：　　　　　　　　　　　　　　　　　　　　　年　　月　　日
承包商签收： 　　　　　　　　　　　　　　　　　　　　　　承包商：　　　　　年　　月　　日

【例 8.7】

××××××××工程
工程暂时停工令

承包单位：_____　　合同号：_____
监理单位：_____　　编　号：_____

停工依据：
停工范围：
停工原因：
停工日期：　　　　　　　　　　　　　　　　　　　　　　　　　年　　月　　日

停工后应做如下处理：

监理工程师签字：

年　月　日

承包商签收：

年　月　日

8.9　Consequences of Suspension（暂停的后果）

If the Contractor suffers delay and/or incurs Cost from complying with the Engineer's instructions under Sub-Clause 8.8 [Suspension of Work] and/or from resuming the work, the Contractor shall give notice to the Engineer and shall be entitled subject to Sub-Clause 20.1 [Contractor's Claims] to：

(a) an extension of time for any such delay, if completion is or will be delayed, under Sub-Clause 8.4 [Extension of Time for Completion], and

(b) Payment of any such Cost, which shall be included in the Contract Price.

After receiving this notice, the Engineer shall proceed in accordance with Sub-Clause 3.5 [Determinations] to agree or determine these matters.

The Contractor shall not be entitled to an extension of time for, or to payment of the Cost incurred in, making good the consequences of the Contractor's faulty design, workmanship or materials, or of the Contractor's failure to protect, store or secure in accordance with Sub-Clause 8.8 [Suspension of Work].

本款明确规定了承包商的索赔权利，核心问题的计算依据。

暂停期间承包商的费用问题通常涉及承包商的项目现场人员和现场施工设备的闲置费、总部和现场管理费等。计算的标准通常是依据承包商投标报价，有时需要承包商对某些内容进行价格分解。由于停工期间，设备和人员只是闲置，因此，雇主一般不会同意按工作时的费率来支付闲置费，这需要承包商将暂停期间各项开支，做好记录，作为索赔费用的依据。在实践中，有些项目，为了避免麻烦和争执，在合同谈判阶段，雇主和承包商可能就施工设备和人员闲置费等相关费用商定一个补偿标准，在实际发生暂停时执行。

承包商导致暂停期间，相关费用由承包商自己承担，雇主不予补偿，因此承包商应注意自己在暂停期间的行为，履行好自己一方的义务。这是索赔成功的保证。

如果承包商因遵守工程师在第8.8款［暂时停工］中规定发出的指令，和（或）因为复工而遭受延误和（或）招致增加费用，承包商应向工程师发出通知，有权根据第20.1款［承包商的索赔］的规定要求：

（1）根据第8.4款［竣工时间的延长］的规定，如竣工时间已经或将要受到延误，对任何此类延误给予工期延长；

（2）支付计入合同价格的任何此类费用和合理利润。

工程师收到此项通知后，应按照第3.5款［确定］的规定，对这些事项表示同意或者作出决定。

如果工程暂停是由于承包商修复有缺陷的设计、工艺或材料引起的，或由于承包商未能按照第8.8款［暂时停工］的规定保护、保管或保证安全引起的，则承包商无权获得延期和增加费用。

为了对费用和工期延误提出索赔，承包商必须根据第20.1款［承包商的索赔］规定发出例行的通知。本款也包括复工的费用，如重新动员的费用。

8.10 Payment for Plant and Materials in Event of Suspension（暂停时对生产设备和材料的付款）

The Contractor shall be entitled to payment of the value (as at the date of suspension) of Plant and/or Materials which have not been delivered to Site, if:

(a) the work on Plant or delivery of Plant and/or Materials has been suspended for more than 28 days, and

(b) the Contractor has marked the Plant and/or Materials as the Employer's property in accordance with the Engineer's instructions.

由于暂停一般是无计划的，所以按计划进行的一系列资金事项必然受到影响。如，暂停导致承包商已付款的设备材料交付延期，则雇主至少要保证部分付款，以免发生更多的附加费用。所以本款规定虽然与暂停密切相关，但其本质属于付款内容。

在下述情况下，承包商有权得到尚未运到现场的生产设备和（或）材料（按暂时开始的日期时）价值的付款：

（1）生产设备的生产和生产设备和（或）材料的交付被暂停达28天以上；

（2）承包商已根据工程师的指示，标明上述生产设备和（或）材料为主的财产。

如果承包商要求支付尚未运抵的生产设备和（或）材料的价格，应通知工程师并获得工程师的确认，无论该项付款是第14.3款［期中付款证书的申请］项下的月付款证书中的一项还是作为第20.1款［承包商的索赔］项下的一项索赔。

本款主要说明如果有关生产设备工作、材料等运送被暂停28天，并且承包商根据工程师的指示已将这些设备材料记为雇主财产，则承包商有权获得未被运到现场的生产设备的支付，付款应为该生产设备在停工开始日期时的价值。如某工地因某些原因停工，停工前承包商向厂家订购一批雇主的生产设备并且将其登记为雇主财产，在停工满28天后雇主向支付购买设备部分款项，为保障雇主财产一般向承包商支付30%到50%的设备款，保承包商有充足的资金准备复工。此笔费用实际功用应该是"安抚承包商及承包商的供应"，以规避承包商及承包商的供应商可能发生的更大索赔。

8.11 Prolonged Suspension（拖长的暂停）

If the suspension under Sub-Clause 8.8 [Suspension of Work] has continued for more than 84 days, the Contractor may request the Engineer's permission to proceed. If the Engineer does not give permission within 28 days after being requested to do so, the Contractor may, by giving notice to the Engineer, treat the suspension as an omission under Clause 13 [Variations and Adjustments] of the affected part of the Works. If the suspension affects the whole of the Works, the Contractor may give notice of termination under Sub-Clause 16.2 [Termination by Contractor].

上述条款规定，如果暂停工程，承包商可索赔费用和工期，但如果工期暂停时间太长，建设投资成本将会增大。FIDIC 合同条件规定暂停在 28 天到 84 天之内，如果工程暂停已持续 84 天以上，承包商可要求工程师同意继续施工。若接到请求后的 28 天工程师未给予许可，则承包商可通知工程师将把暂停影响到的工程视为删减。如果此类暂停影响到了整个工程，承包商可终止合同。

如果没有取消暂停，并且承包商选择将暂停部分工程作第 13.1 款［变更权］（d）项下的删减工程时，则应通过协议或根据第 12.4 款［删减］确定工程价值，根据第 13.1 款（d）项删减工程的规定，已删减工程不能由他人实施。如果暂停了整个工程，并且承包商决定根据第 16.2 款（f）项规定发出终止合同通知，则应根据第 19.6 款［自主选择终止、付款和解除］进行支付。至于因不可抗力而终止合同，应增加利润的损失，其他损失或第 16.4 款［终止时的付款］（c）项下的损害费用。对于雇主而言，这种代价当然很昂贵，因此应避免拖长暂停，并且不能用于其他目的，或者将其作为对付承包商的一种方式。

8.12 Resumption of Work（复工）

After the permission or instruction to proceed is given, the Contractor and the Engineer shall jointly examine the Works and the Plant and Materials affected by the suspension. The Contractor shall make good any deterioration or defect in or loss other Works or Plant or Materials, which has occurred during the suspension.

本款主要说明复工事项的复杂性。复工前首先需要解决停工的索赔事项、复工所必需的重新开工动员及停工造成的工程缺陷修复。本款中并未说明由哪方负责修复费用，此项内容可以参考第 8.9 款［暂停的后果］。从造价角度说，暂停施工时间过长，雇主需与承包商进行"简化结算"，而复工工程费用要与前面的"简化结算"相接，又要对复工后新的动员费与修复费进行计算。

承包商在暂停施工原因消失、具备复工条件时提出复工申请的，工程师应审查承包商报送的工程复工报审表及有关材料，若符合要求，应及时签署审查意见，并报雇主批准后签发工程复工令。在发出复工令后，承包商和工程师应共同检查受暂停影响的工程、生产设备和材料。承包商负责修复在暂停期间发生的工程、生产设备或材料中的任何变质、缺陷或损失。

如果承包商和工程师未能就他们共同检查的结果达成一致,工程师可以签发指示,承包商可以选择按照第 20.1 款［承包商的索赔］和其他条款的规定发出通知。如果双方就修复费用的支付存在争议,也应遵从同样的程序。在工程暂停期间应在现场保存合同保险文件,并应根据第 18.1 款［有关保险的一般要求］的规定通知保险人有关暂停事宜。

例 8.8 列出了工程复工指令的中文格式。

【例 8.8】

×××××××改建工程

承包单位：＿＿＿＿＿＿＿＿＿＿　　　合同号：＿＿＿＿＿＿＿＿＿＿
监理单位：＿＿＿＿＿＿＿＿＿＿　　　编　号：＿＿＿＿＿＿＿＿＿＿

工程复工指令

复工依据：		
复工范围：		
复工原因： 　　指令停工整改已落实,＿＿＿＿＿＿＿＿＿＿已符合设计及规范要求。		
复工日期：　　　　　　　　　　　　　　　　　　　　年　月　日　时		
复工后应做如下工作： 　　复工后项目部要更加严格按照合同和规范要求加强技术、质量的管理力度,并加强对施工人员质量意识的教育。		
总（驻地）监理工程师审批意见： 签名：　　　　日期：　　（公章）	现场监理签名、日期	承包商收到日期、签名

注　本表由现场监理填报、总（驻地）监理审批后,送承包商签收。

思考题

1. 简述开工日期的定义。如何理解开工日期是"承包商同意施工的'竣工时间'的开始"？
2. 影响承包商开工的因素可能有哪些？

3. 承包商在竣工时间内应履行哪些义务？
4. 简述如何确定开工、施工及竣工时间。
5. 进度计划是否属于合同文件？具体包含哪些内容？
6. 如何修订进度计划？
7. 简述承包商索赔工期的权利和条件。
8. 简述误期损害赔偿费的定义。
9. 简述承包商可因"公共当局的行为延误工程实施"提出索赔的条件。由于公共当局产生的工期延误属于雇主风险还是承包商应承担的风险？承包商能否索赔费用？
10. 在什么情况下工程师可以要求承包商赶工？
11. 简述误期损害赔偿费的定义。承包商是否有权就"误期损害"提出工期索赔？
12. 简述雇主对承包商延误工期的管理方法。
13. 分别说明工程师下达暂停工作的指示的权利以及承包商在暂停期间的义务。
14. 简述工程暂停的可能原因。
15. 就暂时停工，承包商享有哪些权利？如果复工时间遭到拖延，承包商享有哪些权利？
16. 合同双方在复工前、复工后分别需要承担哪些责任？

9 Tests On Completion（竣工试验）

工程竣工试验是体现工程已经基本完成的一个里程碑，也是雇主控制质量的一个十分关键的手段。对于竣工试验，合同规定的内容通常包括：进行竣工试验的前提条件；双方各自的义务；试验过程中出了问题怎么办（如试验被延误，试验结果不合格）等。本条规定了承包商在竣工试验时的义务、开始试验的条件、试验结果评定时应考虑的特殊情况等。在考虑竣工试验结果时需注意，雇主预先使用工程对工程的性能或其他特性造成的影响。

本章要求：熟悉本合同条件中的关键术语的含义；
了解承包商在竣工试验过程中的义务；
了解如果试验被延误，延误试验的一方的责任和对方的权利；
了解竣工试验不能通过情况下的处理方式。

9.1 Contractor's Obligations（承包商的义务）

The Contractor shall carry out the Tests on Completion in accordance with this Clause and Sub-Clause 7.4 [Testing], after providing the documents in accordance with sub-paragraph (d) of Sub-Clause 4.1 [Contractors General Obligations].

The Contractor shall give to the Engineer not less than 21 days' notice of the date after which the Contractor will be ready to carry out each of the Tests on Completion. Unless otherwise agreed, Tests on Completion shall be carried out within 14 days after this date, on such day or days as the Engineer shall instruct.

In considering the results of the Tests on Completion, the Engineer shall make allowances for the effect of any use of the Works by the Employer on the performance or other characteristics of the Works. As soon as the Works, or a Section, have passed any Tests on Completion, the Contractor shall submit a certified report of the results of these Tests to the Engineer.

第8.2款［竣工时间］中要求在颁发接收证书之前，工程或单位工程应按第10.1条［工程和单位工程的接收］的规定通过竣工验收。只有承包商向工程师提交了FIDIC合同条件第4.1款［承包商的一般义务］（d）项列明的文件，才能按照本款和第7.4款［试验］规定的要求进行竣工验收。这项要求是指承包商负责设计的永久工程任何一部分的竣工图纸以及操作和维护手册。在竣工后要求进行试验的项目通常是承包商设计的并需要满足性能规范的生产设备。

FIDIC合同要求承包商向工程师提交有关文件，而合同并未要求工程师批准此类文件。第4.1款（d）项要求此类文件应"足够详细，使雇主能够操作、维护、拆卸、再组装、调整和修复该部分工程"。因此，雇主可要求工程师确认承包商递交的文件是可接受的。

　　承包商在准备妥当进行竣工验收时，必须提前21天将其可以进行竣工试验的日期通知工程师，以便工程师有时间安排专业工程师参加，也便于雇主进行适当安排。雇主也可要求将来负责维护工程的人员观察试验。竣工试验必须在承包商向工程师发出此项通知日期后的14天内进行。本款未规定某一特定项目完成时是否应立即进行竣工试验，也未规定在颁发接收证书之前是否必须立即进行全部竣工验收。何时进行竣工验收将取决于工程的具体情况和规范的具体要求。

　　试验的顺序是试运行前的试验、试运行试验、投产试验以及在投产运行期间进行的性能试验。性能试验应表明"工程是否符合雇主要求规定的标准以及担保清单"。竣工试验只是中期试验，目的是检查雇主可否按照第10条［雇主的接收］的规定接收和占有工程。在按照第12条［测量和估价］进行竣工后验收时和按照第19条［不可抗力］规定颁发履约证书之前、缺陷通知期限结束时，应检查工程是否符合雇主的要求和担保清单。

　　若试验通过，则承包商应向工程师提交一份有关此试验结果的报告；若工程或单位工程的试验未能通过，工程师可拒收，并责令承包商自费修复缺陷。工程师或承包商可要求按相同的条款和条件进行重新试验。

9.2　Delayed Tests（延误的试验）

　　If the Tests on Completion are being unduly delayed by the Employer, Sub-Clause 7.［Testing］(fifth paragraph) and/or Sub-Clause 10.3［interference with Tests or Completion］shall be applicable.

　　If the Tests on Completion are being unduly delayed by the Contractor, the Engineer may by notice require the Contractor to carry out the Tests within 21 days after receiving the notice. The Contractorshall carry out the Tests on such day or days within that period as the Contractor may fix and of which he shall give notice to the Engineer.

　　If the Contractors fails to carry out the Tests on Completion within the period of 21 days, the Employer's Personnel may proceed with the Tests at the risk and cost of the Contractor. The Tests on Completion shall then be deemed to have been carried out in the presence of the Contractor and the results of the Tests shall be accepted as accurate.

　　本款规定了延误试验的两种情况及其处理方法。

　　如果雇主无故延误竣工试验，承包商可按照第7.4款［试验］的规定向工程师发出通知，并可按照第20.1款［承包商的索赔］的规定提出工期延长和额外费用补偿。如果竣工试验延误了14天以上，根据第10.3款［对竣工试验的干扰］的规定，应视为雇主在竣工验收完成之日接收了工程，承包商在缺陷通知期限期满之前，应尽快进行有关验收。第10.3款［对竣工试验的干扰］规定了工程师颁发接收证书和有关索赔的程序。

　　雇主有强制试验权，如果承包商延误了试验，工程师可要求承包商在收到通知后21天内进行竣工试验。若承包商在收到通知后21天内仍不进行试验，雇主有权独立进行试验，且试验风险和费用均由承包商承担。此竣工试验应被视为是在承包商在场的情况下进行的，且试验结果应被认为是准确的。

9.3　Retesting（重新试验）

　　If the Works, or a Section, fail to pass the Tests on Completion, Sub-Clause 7.5 [Rejection] shall apply, and the Engineer or the Contractor may require the failed Tests, and Tests on Completion on any related work, to be repeated under the same terms and conditions.

　　如果工程或单位工程未能通过竣工验收，应适用 FIDIC 施工合同条件第 7.5 款 [拒收] 的规定。第 7.5 款 [拒收] 规定工程师可拒收"生产设备、材料或工艺"，承包商必须修复这些缺陷。工程师也可要求进行重新试验，并由承包商承担可能由此造成的额外费用。

【例 9.1】

　　某在建大厦，某一部分工程未通过竣工验收，承包商积极开展修复缺陷工作，工程师对已修复缺陷工程质量有怀疑，指示承包商取样重新试验，试验结果表明该部分的施工质量虽达到行业规范的要求，但未达到合同约定标准，工程师判定：（1）承包商重新修复该处缺陷；（2）重新修复缺陷承包商损伤的工期和费用均不给予补偿；（3）如承包商再次修复，仍未能达到合同标准，将降低该部分项目合同单价。

9.4　Failure to Pass Tests on Completion（未能通过竣工试验）

　　If the Works, or a Section, fail to pass the Tests on Completion repeated under Sub-Clause 9.3 (Retesting), the Engineer shall be entitled to:

　　(a) order further repetition of Tests on Completion under Sub-Clause 9.3;

　　(b) if the failure deprives the Employer of substantially the whole benefit of the Works or Section, reject the Works or Section (as the case may be), in which event the Employer shall have the same remedies as are provided in sub-paragraph (c) of Sub-Clause 11.4 [Failure to Remedy Defects]; or

　　(c) issue a Taking-Over Certificate, if the Employer so requests.

　　In the event of sub-paragraph (c), the Contractor shall proceed in accordance with all other obligations under the Contract, and the Contract Price shall be reduced by such amount as shall be appropriate to cover the reduced value to the Employer as a result of this failure. Unless the relevant reduction for this failure is stated (or its method of calculation is defined) in the Contract, the Employer may require the reduction to be (i) agreed by both Parties (in full satisfaction of this failure only) and paid before this Taking-Over Certificate is issued, or (ii) determined and paid under Sub-Clause 2.5 [Employer's Claims] and Sub-Clause 3.5 [Determinations].

　　本款规定了未能通过竣工验收的"工程或区段"的相关事项，并给出了工程未能通过再次竣工试验的处理方法。

　　如果工程或单位工程按相同的条款或条件进行重新试验后仍未通过，则：

(1) 工程师有权指示再一次进行重新试验;

(2) 如果不合格的工程或单位工程基本无法达到使用或营利的目的,雇主可拒收此工程或单位工程,并从承包商处得到相应的补偿;

(3) 若雇主提出要求,可在扣减一定的合同价格之后颁发接收证书。

如果工程的某个特定部分,或者生产设备某个部件未能通过验收,那么工程的全部或单位工程就没有通过验收。如果工程师随后根据本款第(a)项的规定决定重新进行竣工试验,这些试验只涉及技术方面,也许能够或者不能解决任何问题。如果某一项验收还没有通过再次验收,尽管已根据第 7.5 款 [拒收] 进行了修复,承包商也可在选择本款第(b)和(c)项之前考虑其他技术替代方案。第 7.6 款 [修补工作] 使得工程师有权指示承包商将生产设备或材料移出现场或进行更换,或拆除并重新实施其他工程。如果承包商未能执行该项指示,雇主有权安排他人实施该项目工程并可根据第 2.5 款 [雇主的索赔] 规定索赔费用。

本款第(b)项规定了工程未能通过竣工试验被雇主拒收的情况下,根据第 11.4 款 [未能修补缺陷] 第(c)项的规定,雇主可以终止全部或部分合同,并且可以收回第 11.4 款第(c)项定义的全部费用。雇主和承包商应就接收未能通过验收的工程达成一致,并作为一项变更由双方签字确认,明确规定接收工程的条款。

【例 9.2】

某承包商为雇主修建我国境内的一座工业厂房。合同签订后,承包商完成了工程施工任务。雇主认为工程质量不符合合同约定,存在多处漏雨现象,迟迟不能通过验收。但是在工程完工后,雇主的机械设备就已经搬进了厂房(并投入使用)。

承包商委托律师向人民法院提起诉讼,要求雇主向承包商支付工程款,并支付逾期付款利息。雇主认为,合同约定在验收合格后才可支付工程款,由于该工程没有通过验收,因此付款条件尚不具备。同时雇主提出,承包商拖延工期,根据合同约定应当向雇主支付违约金 15 万元。

根据《最高人民法院关于审理建设工程施工合同纠纷若干问题的意见》,工程未经竣工验收,就擅自使用的,又以使用部分质量不符合约定为由主张权利的不予支持。建设工程未经竣工验收,发包人擅自使用的,以转移占有之日为竣工之日。最终,两级法院依法判令雇主支付工程款及逾期付款利息。对于雇主要求承包商承担违约金的请求,因雇主没有提出反诉,未被法院支持。

思考题

1. 简述竣工试验的含义、目的、作用。
2. 简述承包商在竣工试验过程中的义务。
3. 简述延误试验的情况及其处理方法。
4. 简述竣工试验不能通过情况下的处理方式。

10 Employer's Taking Over（雇主的接收）

本条规定了雇主接收工程应遵守的程序。工程实施过程中，当工程实施到达验收阶段时，虽然工程验收无需投入大量的工作，但责任重大，备受项目各方重视。合同中应清晰规定出验收程序，以便接收工作顺利完成。

本章要求：熟悉本合同条件中关键术语的含义；

了解雇主接收工程和单位工程的前提条件以及承包商获得接收证书的程序；

了解雇主接收部分工程的限制条件和处理方法；

了解雇主阻碍承包商按时进行竣工试验的后果责任。

10.1 Taking Over of the Works and Sections（工程和单位工程的接收）

Except as stated in Sub-Clause 9.4〔Failure to Pass Tests on Completion〕, the works shall be taken over by the Employer when (i) the Works have been completed in accordance with the Contract, including the matters described in Sub-Clause 8.2〔Time for Completion〕and except as allowed in sub-paragraph (a) below, and (ii) a Taking-Over Certificate for the Works has been issued, or is deemed to have been issued in accordance with this Sub-Clause.

The Contractor may apply by notice to the Engineer for a Taking-Over Certificate not earlier than 14 days before the Works will, in the Contractor's opinion, be complete and ready for taking over. If the Works are divided into Sections, the Contractor may similarly apply for a Taking-Over Certificate for each Section.

The Engineer shall, within 28 days after receiving the Contractor's application：

(a) issue the Taking-Over Certificate to the Contractor, stating the date on which the Works or Section were completed in accordance with the Contract, except for any minor outstanding work and defects which will not substantially affect the use of the Works or Section for their intended purpose (either until or whilst this work is completed and these defects are remedied); or

(b) reject the application, giving reasons and specifying the work required to be done by the Contractor to enable the Taking-Over Certificate to be issued. The Contractor shall then complete this work before issuing a further notice under this Sub-Clause.

If the Engineer fails either to issue the Taking-Over Certificate or to reject the Contractor's application within the period of 28 days, and if the Works or Section (as the case may be) are substantially in accordance with the Contract, the Taking-Over Certificate shall be deemed to have been issued on the last day of that period.

本款规定了除第9.4款［未能通过竣工试验］中所述情况外雇主应接收工程的两种情况；第一种是除本款第（a）项允许的情况外，工程已按合同规定的要求竣工，此项要求包括第8.2款［竣工时间］规定的事项；第二种是工程师已按照本款的规定颁发工程接收证书，或被视为已颁发，此时雇主应接收工程。

若工程的情况符合本款规定，雇主应安排工程的接收事宜。需注意，工程通过竣工试验达到了合同规定的"基本竣工"要求后，承包商应在其认为可进行移交工作前14天以书面形式向工程师申请颁发接收证书。"基本竣工"是指工程已通过竣工试验，能够按照预定目标交给雇主占用或使用，而非完成了合同规定的包括扫尾、清理施工现场及不影响工程使用的某些次要部位缺陷修复工作后的最终竣工。

本款第（a）项规定，工程师向承包商颁发接收证书时，注明的工程或单位工程不包括"任何对工程或单位工程预期使用功能没有实质影响的少量收尾工作和缺陷（直到或当收尾工作和缺陷修补完成时）"。此规定较明确，如果没有实质影响工程预期的使用功能，一些未完工程或缺陷对接收证书的颁发不造成延误。某一特定项目是否"实质影响"工程的使用由工程师决定，但是，强调工程的使用有助于更清晰地界定雇主何时可接收工程。根据第11.1款［完成扫尾工作和修补缺陷］（a）项的规定，承包商应在缺陷通知期限内根据工程师的指示完成这些少量收尾工作。此规定有助于准确判定承包商是否按合同规定的工期完成了施工义务，也有利于雇主尽早使用或占有工程，及时发挥工程效益。

如工程师在承包商提出接收证书申请后28天内不予答复，且工程或单位工程基本符合合同的规定，则应视为在第28天当天接收证书已经签发。在这种情况下，工程竣工的日期，即缺陷通知期的开始日期并未明确，因为签发证书的日期不一定同于工程竣工日期，竣工日期通常早于接收证书的签发日期。在正常情况下，工程师签发接收证书中会注明工程的竣工日期。

如工程师拒绝了承包商提出的颁发接收证书申请，必须给出拒绝的原因，并指明承包商仍须完成的工程，以便能够签发接收证书。承包商需完成相应工程并向工程师发出另外的通知。

工程竣工证书的颁发日期是承包商在84天内签发竣工报表的起始时间，根据FIDIC施工合同条件第14.10款［竣工报表］规定，竣工报表应包括任何进一步索赔的估计金额。

工程的验收程序大致可描述为：（1）准备好竣工试验；（2）申请竣工试验；（3）提交竣工材料；（4）开始竣工试验；（5）通过竣工试验；（6）申请接收证书；（7）签发接收证书；（8）雇主接收工程。

10.2　Taking Over of parts of the Works（部分工程的接收）

The Engineer may, at the sole discretion of the Employer, issue a Taking-Over Certificate for any part of the Permanent Works.

The Employer shall not use any part of the Works (other than as a temporary measure which is either specified in the Contract or agreed by both Parties) unless and until the Engineer has issued a Taking-Over Certificate for this part. However, if the Employer does use any part of the Works before the Taking-Over Certificate is issued:

(a) the part which is used shall be deemed to have been taken over as from the date on which it is used,

(b) the Contractor shall cease to be liable for the care of such part as from this date, when responsibility shall pass to the Employer, and

(c) if requested by the Contractor, the Engineer shall issue a Taking-Over Certificate for this part.

After the Engineer has issued a Taking-Over Certificate for a part of the Works, the Contractor shall be given the earliest opportunity to take such steps as may be necessary to carry out any outstanding Tests on Completion. The Contractor shall carry out these Tests on Completion as soon as practicable before the expiry date of the relevant Defects Notification Period.

If the Contractor incurs Cost as a result of the Employer taking over and/or using a part of the Works, other than such use as is specified in the Contract or agreed by the Contractor, the Contractor shall (i) give notice to the Engineer and (ii) be entitled subject to Sub-Clause 20.1 [Contractor's Claims] to payment of any such Cost plus reasonable profit, which shall be included in the Contract Price. After receiving this notice, the Engineer shall proceed in accordance with Sub-Clause 3.5 [Determinations] to agree or determine this Cost and profit.

If a Taking-Over Certificate has been issued for a part of the Works (other than a Section), the delay damages thereafter for completion of the remainder of the Works shall be reduced. Similarly, the delay damages for the remainder of the Section (if any) in which this part is included shall also be reduced. For any period of delay after the date stated in this Taking-Over Certificate, the proportional reduction in these delay damages shall be calculated as the proportion which the value of the part so certified bears to the value of the Works or Section (as the case may be) as a whole. The Engineer shall proceed in accordance with Sub-Clause 3.5 [Determinations] to agree or determine these proportions. The provisions of this paragraph shall only apply to the daily rate of delay damages under Sub-Clause 8.7 [Delay Damages], and shall not affect the maximum amount of these damages.

第10.1款［工程和单位工程］和第10.3款［对竣工试验的干扰］规定了投标书附录规定的全部工程和单位工程的接收事宜。本款规定了没有规定作为单位工程的部分工程的接收事项，明确划分雇主和承包商的责任，尤其是一些未颁发接收证书但是雇主已经使用的情况下责任主体的确定。

本款的规定给予了雇主随时可以接收承包商已经完成的任一部分工程的权利。"部分（Part）"指合同中某单位工程中的一个部分，雇主可自主决定使用和要求工程师颁发部分工程的接收证书，且雇主有权决定在其他工程未完之前接收某部分工程。如果雇主在颁发证书前已使用了任何部分工程，则：

(1) 从开始使用日期起,该部分应视为已被雇主接收;
(2) 该部分由雇主负责保管;
(3) 承包商提出要求,工程师应颁发该部分接收证书。

本款中规定雇主在接收之前使用工程,即认为雇主接收了该部分工程,同时要求工程师给予承包商机会进行该部分的竣工试验,承包商应在该部分工程的缺陷通知期内完成试验。FIDIC 施工合同条件第 9.1 款[承包商的义务]和第 9.4 款[未能通过竣工试验]对竣工试验中发现该部分工程不合格的情况已作出说明。

如果雇主使用部分工程只是一项临时措施,而合同中对此进行了规定或者双方当事人对此达成一致,就不需要颁发接收证书。一般合同中并不考虑接收部分工程,部分工程的接收也会引起竣工验收等问题的出现。应尽快进行此类竣工试验,并与工程其他部分的验收协调进行。

若因雇主使用和(或)接收部分工程导致承包商增加费用,承包商可以发出通知,根据第 20.1 款[承包商的索赔]和第 3.5 款[确定]的规定提出索赔。承包商有权向雇主索赔相应的费用和合理的利润。本款没有提及延长工期的索赔权,因接收部分工程造成了其他部分工程的延误,承包商可依据其他条款,如第 8.4 款[竣工时间的延长]第(e)项规定,将此类延误归因于雇主,从而要求工期延长。

【例 10.1】

上海某城市广场项目,承包商按雇主要求,在项目主体结构完成 2/3 时,建成项目售楼处。由于承包商疏忽,未要求工程师颁发接收证书,售楼处建成后雇主便自行装修并派遣人员入驻。因装修不当致使大厅墙面开裂,抹灰层大面积脱落,雇主以土建工程质量存在问题为由要求承包商进行修复。

分析:承包商未及时向工程师申请颁发接收证书而雇主已经装修和派人进场,此时应视为雇主已接收该部分工程。此后出现的人为的质量问题应由雇主负责,如果有合理依据能够证明质量问题的产生是由于承包商造成的,承包商仍需承担维修责任。

10.3　Interference with Tests on Completion(对竣工试验的干扰)

If the Contractor is prevented, for more than 14 days, from carrying out the Tests on Completion by a cause for which the Employer is responsible, the Employer shall be deemed to have taken over the Works or Section (as the case may be) on the date when the Tests on Completion would otherwise have been completed.

The Engineer shall then issue a Taking-Over Certificate accordingly, and the Contractor shall carry out the Tests on Completion as soon as practicable, before the expiry date of the Defects Notification Period. The Engineer shall require the Tests on Completion to be carried out by giving 14 days' notice and in accordance with the relevant provisions of the Contract.

If the Contractor suffers delay and/or incurs Cost as a result of this delay in carrying out the Tests on Completion, the Contractor shall give notice to the Engineer and shall be entitled subject to Sub-Clause 20.1 [Contractor's Claims] to:

(a) an extension of time for any such delay, if completion is or will be delayed,

under Sub-Clause 8.4 [Extension of Time for Completion], and

(b) payment of any such Cost plus reasonable profit, which shall be included in the Contract Price.

After receiving this notice, the Engineer shall proceed in accordance with Sub-Clause 3.5 [Determinations] to agree or determine these matters.

因雇主原因妨碍承包商进行竣工试验，给承包商造成经济损失，雇主应向承包商赔偿或支付任何有关费用以及合理的利润，并将之加入合同价格。雇主对竣工试验的干扰，一般表现为增加竣工试验内容。

雇主原因妨碍承包商进行竣工试验达 14 天以上，将视为雇主已在原定竣工试验之日接收了工程或单位工程，工程师应颁发接收证书。承包商应按照本款的规定向工程师发出通知，索赔损失的工期、费用和利润，并按照第 20.1 款［承包商的索赔］和第 3.5 款［确定］的程序办理索赔事宜。

竣工时间延误的原因有多方面（如第 8.4 款［竣工时间的延长］中列出的原因），且可能是由于多种交叉事件导致的。承包商索赔时，应注意造成延误的关键原因及其责任方。

影响竣工验收的原因消除后，工程师可向承包商发出通知，给出 14 天期限以进行试验，承包商应在缺陷通知期内在条件允许下尽快完成竣工试验。FIDIC 施工合同条件第 7.4 款［试验］规定了承包商在此情况下应遵循的竣工试验程序。

如果在缺陷通知期限期满后，造成延误的因素仍未消失，工程师采取任何下一步行动前，应首先由雇主和承包商双方达成一致意见。此类情形超出了合同的规定，也超出了工程师的权力范围。

10.4 Surfaces Requiring Reinstatement（需要复原的地面）

Except as otherwise stated in a Taking-Over Certificate, a certificate for a Section or part of the Works shall not be deemed to certify completion of any ground or other surfaces requiring reinstatement.

承包商完成了全部工程或者直至缺陷通知期限期满之后，才有可能进行实际的最终复原工作。复原工程的完成是缺陷通知期限内应实施的"少量未完工程"，或者作为第 11.10 款［未履行的义务］中的一项未履行的义务。

除非接收证书中另有说明，接收证书不应视为包括复原工程。即使工程师签发了接收证书，也不代表任何需要复原地面的复原工作也同时完成，接收证书中若未标明，复原地面工作则属于扫尾工作，承包商可在缺陷通知期内完成。在本款中，只是针对单位工程和部分工程的接收证书作出此类规定，而未提到整个工程接收证书的签发是否代表承包商已完成地面复原工作。颁发接收证书时，雇主可能会认为，如果颁发的是整个工程的接收证书，即使该证书上没有注明地表复原工作已经完成，也应认为已经完成；而承包商会认为，无论是单位工程、部分工程，还是整个工程，所签发的接收证书一般仅仅证明工程"基本"竣工，而非全部工程竣工。签订合同时，可在专用条件中加以说明，以免产生误解和纠纷。

【例 10.2】

关于会所西侧门厅地面破坏后恢复方案

由于幼儿园地源热泵中央空调水管主管道预留施工，需破坏会所西侧门厅混凝土钢筋地面，故破坏后恢复方案如下：

1. 把回填土分层夯实；
2. 钢筋网片焊接牢固；
3. 混凝土浇筑恢复至与原地面一致平整。

××建筑有限公司
××××年××月××日

思考题

1. 简述雇主接收工程和单位工程的前提条件。
2. 简述承包商获得接收证书的程序。
3. 雇主使用部分工程的前提是什么？
4. 简述雇主在颁发接受证书前使用工程的处理方法。
5. 简述雇主阻碍承包商按时进行竣工试验的可能原因和后果责任。
6. 复原工作是否影响接收证书的颁发？为什么？

11 Defects Liability（缺陷责任）

雇主接收工程之后，工程实施进入最后阶段。工程完成后，承包商在一定时期内仍需对其实施的工程质量和缺陷负责，FIDIC 施工合同条件中将这一时间段称之为"缺陷责任期限"。本条规定了承包商在缺陷责任期限中的责任以及工程最终验收的标志。

本章要求：了解承包商在缺陷责任期限的主要责任；

　　　　　　了解延长缺陷责任期限的情况；

　　　　　　了解履约证书签发的条件；

　　　　　　了解承包商收到履约证书后应注意的事项。

11.1 Completion of Outstanding Work and Remedying Defects（完成扫尾工作和修补缺陷）

In order that the Works and Contractor's Documents, and each Section, shall be in the condition required by the Contract (fair wear and tear excepted) by the expiry date of the relevant Defects Notification Period or as soon as practicable thereafter, the Contractor shall：

(a) complete any work which is outstanding on the date stated in a Taking-Over Certificate, within such reasonable time as is instructed by the Engineer, and

(b) execute all work required to remedy defects or damage, as may be notified by (or on behalf of) the Employer on or before the expiry date of the Defects Notification Period for the Works or Section (as the case may be).

If a defect appears or damage occurs, the Contractor shall be notified accordingly, by (or on behalf of) the Employer.

在缺陷责任期限内，雇主应占有和使用工程，并负责日常维护工作。发现工程的任何缺陷或其他问题，雇主或雇主人员应立刻通知承包商缺陷工程内容，并将通知抄送给工程师，以便工程师能够根据合同规定采取必要的措施。工程师在缺陷责任期限内仍具有一定的权力和责任，但无权发出任何变更指示。根据第 13.1 款 [变更权] 规定，工程师的变更指示只能在颁发接收证书之前签发。

通常在雇主接收工程时，承包商可留存一些不影响工程功能的扫尾工作，承包商除了有在缺陷责任期限内修复缺陷的责任外，还必须在工程师通知的合理时间内完成扫尾工作。扫尾工作的范围以及修复缺陷应达到合同中规定的标准。

缺陷责任期限结束时，工程除正常"损耗"外，必须符合合同要求。因雇主使用工程原因所引起的工程的任何问题，雇主应承担责任。如果由于各种原因雇主不能在接收工程之后立即全部占有和使用项目，雇主将可能失去整个缺陷责任期限内的相关利益。

FIDIC 合同条件下，投标书附录中规定了缺陷责任期限的时间一般为 365 天，雇主可以在招标文件中修改缺陷责任期限。通常，365 天的缺陷责任期限对土木工程项目较适用，而电气、机械和建筑服务工程的缺陷责任期可能会超过 365 天。如，空调等设备的性能试验只能在制冷、制热期进行，若将该项验收规定为竣工后检验，并可对设备进行调整，则缺陷责任期限应包括设备调整后的一个制冷、制热周期，此类情况下缺陷责任期限应为 730 天。

【例 11.1】

某房地产开发公司与某建筑公司签订施工合同，修建某小区，建成后，经验收质量合格，验收一个月后，开发商发现房屋楼顶漏水，遂要求建筑公司负责无偿修理，并要求赔偿，建筑公司以施工合同中并未规定缺陷通知期限，以工程已经验收合格为由，拒绝无偿修理要求。开发商遂向法院提起诉讼。法院判定承包商对工程质量负有责任，一般保修期限为 3 年。

11.2　Cost of Remedying Defects（修补缺陷的费用）

All work referred to in sub-paragraph (b) of Sub-Clause 11.1 [Completion of Outstanding Work and Remedying Defects] shall be executed at the risk and cost of the Contractor, if and to the extent that the work is attributable to:

(a) any design for which the Contractor is responsible,

(b) Plant, Materials or workmanship not being in accordance with the Contract, or

(c) failure by the Contractor to comply with any other obligation.

If and to the extent that such work is attributable to any other cause, the Contractor shall be notified promptly by (or on behalf of) the Employer, and Sub-Clause 13.3 [Variation Procedure] shall apply.

工程师可根据第 11.1 款（b）项的规定通知承包商完成修补缺陷或损害工作。修复缺陷的工作分为两类：一类是由于承包商负责的原因造成的；另一类是其他原因造成的。对于前一类情况，承包商应承担维修费用及维修过程中的风险。承包商合同外的缺陷修补应按工程变更处理，变更的索赔费用应包括缺陷修补责任所需的费用。对于后一类情况，则由雇主负担一切费用和风险。如果维修工作不是由于承包商负责的原因造成的，雇主应立即通知承包商，并根据第 13.3 款［变更程序］的规定以工程师签发变更令的形式向承包商支付修复费用。

在缺陷责任期限内，工程师无权要求承包商进行日常的维护工作以及修复由雇主人员造成的损坏部分。本款第（a）至（c）项列举了应由承包商自费修复工程项目的类型，除此之外，雇主应支付其他修复工程的任何费用。第（c）项包含了更广泛的事项，雇主有必要规定和证明承包商未能遵守合同的责任。

在缺陷责任期限内，承包商可能留有少量的人员，负责与雇主的联络和沟通。如果出现缺陷或发生损害，雇主应立即通知承包商，承包商应按相关规定处理。工程发生质量等问题的原因有时较复杂，本款规定雇主在得知工程发生问题便可通知承包商，而不是判断出该问题应由承包商负责再向承包商发出通知。因此，本款的规定对承包商较为不利。实际工程中，若缺陷责任期内工程出现问题，雇主立即通知承包商查看问题并修复。在不影响修复的情况下，由雇主方和承包商组成事故原因调查小组联合调查，并依据调查结果来判断责任方。如果双方无法达成一致意见，可按合同中的争端解决程序来处理。

11.3　Extension of Defects Notification Period（缺陷责任期限的延长）

The Employer shall be entitled subject to Sub-Clause 2.5 [Employer's Claims] to an extension of the Defects Notification Period for the Works or a Section if and to the extent that the Works, Section or a major item of Plant (as the case may be, and after taking over) cannot be used for the purposes for which they are intended by reason of a defect or damage. However, a Defects Notification Period shall not be extended by more than two years.

If delivery and/or erection of Plant and/or Materials was suspended under Sub-Clause 8.8 [Suspension of Work] or Sub-Clause 16.1 [Contractor's Entitlement to Suspend Work], the

Contractor's obligations under this Clause shall not apply to any defects or damage occurring more than two years after the Defects Notification Period for the Plant and/or Materials would otherwise have expired.

在缺陷责任期限内工程发生了质量问题，将会导致工程或单位工程无法按既定目的使用。本款给出了此类情况下工程缺陷责任期限能否予以延长的原则性规定：如果缺陷是承包商负责的原因导致的，雇主有权延长缺陷责任期限，同时规定最多延长 2 年，即缺陷责任期限最多为 3 年。为确定是否有权延长缺陷责任期限，雇主必须证明某项缺陷或损害致使整个工程、某单位工程或某项主要生产设备不能达到既定的使用功能。如果雇主在缺陷责任期限期满之前发现相关情况，并认为有权延长缺陷责任期限，应根据第 2.5 款 [雇主的索赔] 的规定立刻通知承包商，并告知工程师。工程师可根据第 3.5 款 [确定] 的规定作出决定。

本款第二项规定内容涉及工程暂停情况下永久设备和材料推迟交付和（或）安装的情况，"该永久设备和（或）材料的缺陷责任期限本应届满 2 年后"，承包商不再有任何修复义务。此规定隐含着，这类因暂停而被推迟安装的永久设备和材料有独立的缺陷责任期限，但事实上，通常情况下，此类永久设备和材料是没有独立的缺陷责任期限的（大型相对独立的永久设备除外）。

如果承包商延误了第 8.8 款 [暂停施工] 或第 16.1 款 [承包商暂停工作的权利] 条件下的交付、生产设备的安装和材料，那么应相应延长缺陷责任期限中的日历天数。但根据第 11.3 款 [缺陷责任期限的延长] 的规定，承包商负责修复缺陷或损坏的义务并不适用于生产设备和材料在缺陷责任期限原期满日期两年后发生的任何缺陷或损害。这项限制一般优先于合同条款中的其他要求，特别是生产设备和材料方面出现的问题。

11.4　Failure to Remedy Defects（未能修补缺陷）

If the Contractor fails to remedy any defect or damage within a reasonable time, a date may be fixed by (or on behalf of) the Employer, on or by which the defect or dam-

age is to be remedied. The Contractor shall be given reasonable notice of this date.

If the Contractor fails to remedy the defect or damage by this notified date and this remedial work was to be executed at the cost of the Contractor under Sub-Clause 11.2 [Cost of Remedying Defects], the Employer may (at his option):

(a) carry out the work himself or by others, in a reasonable manner and at the Contractor's cost, but the Contractor shall have no responsibility for this work; and the Contractor shall subject to Sub-Clause 2.5 [Employer's Claims] pay to the Employer the costs reasonably incurred by the Employer in remedying the defect or damage;

(b) require the Engineer to agree or determine a reasonable reduction in the Contract Price in accordance with Sub-Clause 3.5 [Determinations]; or

(c) if the defect or damage deprives the Employer of substantially the whole benefit of the Works or any major part of the Works, terminate the Contract as a whole, or in respect of such major part which cannot be put to the intended use. Without prejudice to any other rights, under the Contract or otherwise, the Employer shall then be entitled to recover all sums paid for the Works or for such part (as the case may be), plus financing costs and the cost of dismantling the same, clearing the Site and returning Plant and Materials to the Contractor.

针对承包商不履行在缺陷责任期限的修复义务，本款规定了相应的处理方法。雇主在采用本款规定的三种处理方法之前，必须确保：

(1) 提前通知承包商，其完成修复工作的合理截止日期。

(2) 造成缺陷或损害的原因在于承包商。

虽然在第 11.2 款 [修复缺陷的费用] 中规定，如果所要修复缺陷不是承包商原因造成的，承包商的修复工作可按变更处理。但本款并未规定，如果承包商不修复非承包商原因造成的缺陷，应如何处理。一般而言，即使缺陷不是由承包商原因造成的，承包商也有义务修复缺陷，并按变更得到补偿。

缺陷修复前，雇主应与工程师和承包商协商，就缺陷修复问题达成一致，并向承包商发出通知。雇主可以：

(1) 作出其他施工安排，并根据第 2.5 款 [雇主的索赔] 向承包商索赔有关费用。或

(2) 根据第 3.5 款 [确定] 的程序接收含有缺陷的工程，并可减少合同价格。或

(3) 终止整个合同或有关部分工程的合同。此情况应适用第 15 条 [由雇主终止] 的终止程序和本款第 (c) 项规定的附加要求。

本款第 (c) 项是在 FIDIC 合同中特殊的雇主索赔事项，即因承包商导致的缺陷或损害使得雇主无法享用全部工程或部分工程所带来的全部利益时，雇主可向承包商索赔一切由此产生的费用。

11.5 Removal of Defective Work（移出有缺陷的工程）

If the defect or damage cannot be remedied expeditiously on the Site and the Employer gives consent, the Contractor may remove from the Site for the purposes of repair such items of Plant as are defective or damaged. This consent may require the Contractor to increase the amount of the Performance Security by the full replacement cost of these items, or to provide other appropriate security.

　　某些工程缺陷可能在现场无法修复或维修代价太大，如工程中安装的一些大型永久设备等。本款的规定主要是针对在现场不便修复而需要移出现场进行维修的永久设备等。

　　某永久设备在移出现场进行修复之前，需获得雇主的同意。雇主需了解修复该项设备所需的时间以及在缺少此生产设备时，如何保证工程处于可使用的状态。由于此类永久设备移出现场，雇主将无法控制承包商对设备的处置，故雇主可要求承包商追加担保额度或提供其他担保。若雇主对承包商比较信赖，可能对承包商免于此类要求。承包商的信誉在此情况下会给承包商带来一定的"收益"，这也是"信用价值"的体现。

　　本款规定的情形可能导致承包商需要根据第11.3款［缺陷责任期限限的延长］延长缺陷责任期限。

【例11.2】

　　某项目按施工合同承包商需要为雇主安装某大型机电设备，在安装后发现某部件由于厂家在运输过程中机械损伤，需要将整个零件移出现场，运回厂家更换，承包商告知雇主损害程度及维修更换时间，经过雇主同意后，将其返厂维修。

11.6　Further Tests（进一步试验）

　　If the work of remedying of any defect or damage may affect the performance of the Works, the Engineer may require the repetition of any of the tests described in the Contract. The requirement shall be made by notice within 28 days after the defect or damage is remedied.

　　These tests shall be carried out in accordance with the terms applicable to the previous tests, except that they shall be carried out at the risk and cost of the Party liable, under Sub-Clause 11.2 [Cost of Remedying Defects], for the cost of the remedial work.

　　对于有缺陷的工程部分，尤其是缺陷与永久设备相关时，修复后要进一步试验才能知道其性能能否达到要求。本款明确规定了进一步试验的工作。

　　如果工程师通知，承包商有义务进行此类试验。缺陷应由承包商负责时，若承包商不进行此类试验，会导致雇主用第9.2款［延误的试验］等相关条款来保护自己；缺陷不应由承包商负责时，雇主可采用第11.3款［缺陷责任期限的延长］来延长缺陷责任期限。

　　此类试验按照合同中试验适用条件进行，但是此类试验的风险和费用由责任方承担，并承担修补工作的费用。

11.7　Right of Access（进入权）

　　Until the Performance Certificate has been issued, the Contractor shall have such right of access to the Works as is reasonably required in order to comply with this Clause, except as may be inconsistent with Employer's reasonable security restrictions.

在雇主已经使用工程的情况下,在缺陷责任期限内承包商有权进入工程,进行缺陷修补工作,但是雇主出于安全考虑,可对承包商的进入权采用合理的限制。

本款的规定既考虑了承包商维修工程的合理之需,又考虑了雇主基于项目的保密性的安保需求。

11.8 Contractor to Search(承包商调查)

The Contractor shall, if required by the Engineer, search for the cause of any defect, under the direction of the Engineer. Unless the defect is to be remedied at the cost of the Contractor under Sub-Clause 11.2 [Cost of Remedying Defects], the Cost of the search plus reasonable profit shall be agreed or determined by the Engineer in accordance with Sub-Clause 3.5 [Determinations] and shall be included in the Contract Price.

承包商是工程的具体建造者,对工程较为了解,如果工程出现了问题,雇主常希望由承包商调查事故原因。

只要工程师要求,承包商有义务调查质量事故的起因。由于调查的结果可能关系到双方的责任问题,因此,承包商调查应在工程师指导以及监督下进行,以保证过程的客观性。承包商在不涉及第20.1款[承包商的索赔]发出通知的情况下有权索赔额外费用,但双方经常会对该项费用产生争议,解决争议应遵守第20.1款规定的程序。

雇主通知承包商有关工程缺陷后,工程师应进行有关问题的技术评估。如果缺陷是由承包商造成的,则此类调查费用由承包商承担,否则雇主应向承包商支付调查费用。调查某些工程缺陷时,单方给出的试验调查报告的说服性与合法性较难保证,通常会委托多方试验以明确划分责任,此类费用应由导致缺陷的一方承担。

【例11.3】
某雇主开发商拟建10栋商品房,根据工程地质勘察资料和设计要求,采用振动沉管灌注桩,桩尖深入沙夹卵石层500毫米以上,按地勘报告桩长应在9~10米以上。该工程振动沉管灌注桩施工完后,由某工程质量检测机构采用低应变动测方式对该批桩进行桩身完整性检测,并出具了相应的检测报告。承包商按规定进行主体施工,个别栋号在施工进行到3层左右时,主体结构倾斜,产生大量的裂缝,承包商和雇主分别从外地请了两家检测机构对部分桩进行了抽检。经现场对部分桩进行了高、低应变检测,发现该工程振动沉管灌注桩存在非常严重的质量问题,有的桩身未能进入持力层,有的桩身严重缩颈,有的桩甚至是断桩,最终承包商结算承包商和雇主委托检测单位的相关费用。

11.9 Performance Certificate(履约证书)

Performance of the Contractor's obligations shall not be considered to have been completed until the Engineer has issued the Performance Certificate to the Contractor, stating the date on which the Contractor completed his obligations under the Contract.

The Engineer shall issue the Performance Certificate within 28 days after the latest of the expiry dates of the Defects Notification Periods, or as soon thereafter as the Contractor has supplied all the Contractor's Documents and completed and tested all the

Works, including remedying any defects. A copy of the Performance Certificate shall be issued to the Employer.

Only the Performance Certificate shall be deemed to constitute acceptance of the Works.

本款规定了承包商获得履约证书的前提条件，可分两类情况：

（1）如果承包商在缺陷责任期限内完成了扫尾工作，且没有发生工程缺陷，或发生了缺陷，但承包商及时在缺陷责任期限内完成修复工作，则工程师应在缺陷责任期限期满后的 28 天内向承包商签发履约证书；

（2）如果缺陷责任期限期满时，承包商还有未完成工作，如提交文件、修复缺陷等，工程师应在此类工作完成之后尽快给承包商签发履约证书。

在第二种情况下，FIDIC 合同并没有给出工程师必须签发履约证书的时间限制，只是规定"尽快"，容易导致合同双方理解上的差异，双方可在专用条件中给出具体的时间（如 7 天或 14 天），这个时间一般不会超过承包商完成所有剩余工作后的 28 天。

工程实施过程中，工程师通常会拖延签发履约证书的时间。由于履约证书签发的问题涉及承包商的利益，如保留金和履约保函的退还等，如果发生拖延签发的情况，承包商的利益就会受损。尽管承包商可根据第 1.3 款［通信与联络］的规定来保护其权益，但该款的约束力不大。双方在订立合同时，承包商可提出在专用条件中对此类情况增加条款，如：如果在整个工程达到上述履约证书签发的条件后，工程师无故拖延签发履约证书，则应视为在本应签发履约证书的截止日已经签发。

履约证书是承包商已按合同规定完成全部施工义务的证明，证书颁发后工程师就无权再指示承包商进行任何工作，承包商即可办理最终结算手续。工程在缺陷责任期限内通过竣工试验后，工程师应在期满后的 28 天内，向雇主要求签发解除承包商承担工程缺陷责任的证书，并将副本送给承包商。收到履约证书意味着承包商应在 56 天内提交包括所有未完成工程的最终付款证书时间的开始。

11.10 Unfulfilled Obligations（未履行的义务）

After the Performance Certificate has been issued, each Party shall remain liable for the fulfillment of any obligation which remains unperformed at that time. For the purposes of determining the nature and extent of unperformed obligations, the Contract shall be deemed to remain in force.

履约证书的颁发，仅代表承包商与合同有关的义务已经完成，而合同尚未终止，双方的合同义务此时只限于财务和管理方面以及一些特别的法律意义上的义务。

第 11.9 款［履约证书］要求履约证书应注明承包商完成合同义务的日期。这与本条款提及的"未履行义务"不同，直到颁发履约证书时有些义务可能还尚未被履行，如：第 11.11 款［现场清理］项下的现场清理工作和第 10.4 款［需要复原的地面］项下的地面复原工作、第 14.11 款［最终付款证书的申请］项下的最终付款证书的申请、在颁发履约证书时尚未通知的由承包商负责的任何潜在缺陷的调查和修复等。

在 FIDIC 合同条件中，并没有规定合同的有效期，只是规定了"竣工时间"和"缺陷责任期限"。本款的规定意味着只要有关合同的任何事宜在双方之间还没有解决，仍应根据施工合同的规定来处理。

11.11 Clearance of Site（现场清理）

Upon receiving the Performance Certificate, the Contractor shall remove any remaining Contractor's Equipment, surplus material, wreckage, rubbish and Temporary Works from the Site.

If all these items have not been removed within 28 days after the Employer receives a copy of the Performance Certificate, the Employer may sell or otherwise dispose of any remaining items. The Employer shall be entitled to be paid the costs incurred in connection with, or attributable to, such sale or disposal and restoring the Site.

Any balance of the moneys from the sale shall be paid to the Contractor. If these moneys are less than the Employer's costs, the Contractor shall pay the outstanding balance to the Employer.

承包商在缺陷责任期限内可能要做一些扫尾工作和修复工作，在现场留存适当的设备或材料。签发履约证书时，承包商若未能及时运走在现场留存的一些施工机具或清理一些剩余物品，占用了雇主的现场空间，对此情况本款规定：

（1）在收到履约证书之时，承包商应立即将留在现场的承包商的设备、剩余材料、残物、垃圾或临时工程等运走；

（2）如果承包商在收到履约证书后28天内上述物品仍没有清理，雇主可对留下的任何物品予以出售或另作处理；

（3）雇主为上述工作付出的费用应由承包商支付，可从出售承包商物品的收入中扣取，多退少补。

本款规定实际上是要求承包商在收到履约证书后28天内清理好现场，而工程师是在缺陷责任期限28天后才颁布履约证书，因此承包商有足够时间将有价值的施工设备运走，工程现场剩下的多是已损坏、价值不高或运费大于其价值的施工设备，此类设备产权仍属于承包商，本款规定履约证书颁发后承包商不清理的相关物品，雇主有权在期限之后自行处理，解决了承包商丢弃的施工设备问题。

【例11.4】某工程地质勘查报告标明，其附属机房的地基下方存在软弱淤泥层，下部为岩石持力层，弱淤泥层最深的地方7米，最浅的地方5米。主体工程竣工，经过验收合格后即投入使用。工程使用初期正值雨季，连续16天下雨后，雇主发现机房地基下陷，墙体出现开裂、墙角裂开、墙壁开裂、通道变形、天花板松脱、漏水、发霉等工程缺陷，严重影响了生产经营。雇主认为承包商为赶工期，地基处理不完全是造成工程质量问题的主要原因；而承包商则认为工程已经通过竣工验收，说明工程质量合格。在协商达不成一致意见后，雇主对承包商提起仲裁，要求承包商赔偿工程质量问题所导致的各项损失。

雇主提请的仲裁要求为：承包商在60天内自担费用修补好工程缺陷，否则需向雇主支付工程缺陷的修复费用，预计为100万元，以及修复期间造成雇主的经济损失（包括主机房停工造成的各项损失，估算约200万元）。经仲裁机构调查裁决，要求承包商在60天内修补好工程缺陷，并自担修补费用；否则需向雇主支付工程缺陷的修复费用 100 万元，费用从雇主未支付给承包商的工程款中扣减。修复期间造成雇主的经济损失最终由估价机构估算为 125 万元，由承包商负责赔偿。

思考题

1. 分别说明雇主、承包商、工程师在缺陷通知期限内的主要责任。
2. 在何种情况下合同当事人应承担什么责任？
3. 简述延长缺陷责任期限的条件。
4. 简述承包商不履行在缺陷责任期限的修复义务时的处理办法及前提。
5. 雇主可如何控制承包商对存在缺陷或损害的设备的处置？
6. 简述工程的缺陷或损害可能影响工程性能的处理办法。
7. 简述履约证书签发的前提和程序。
8. 履约证书的颁发是否意味着合同的终止，为什么？
9. 简述承包商收到履约证书后的义务和注意事项。

12　Measurement and Evaluation（测量和估价）

工程测量工作是工程建设中重要的技术基础工作之一，测量结果不仅为施工和运营提供重要的资料和技术依据，而且关系到雇主和承包商后期的工程款项结算，因此工程测量工作各参与方及其人员必须做好原始记录，明确各方职责，严格遵守测量工作程序，保证测量数据准确、可靠。

本章要求：了解实际工程的测量程序和方法；
　　　　　　　了解对工程进行估价的价款事项；
　　　　　　　了解采用新费率或价格的条件；
　　　　　　　了解工程的删减对合同价格的影响。

12.1　Works to be Measured（需测量的工程）

The Works shall be measured, and valued for payment（为了付款）, *in accordance with this Clause.*

Whenever the Engineer requires any part of the Works to be measured, reasonable notice shall be given to the Contractor's Representative, who shall：

(a) promptly either attend or send another qualified representative to assist the Engineer in making the measurement, and

(b) supply any particulars（具体资料）*requested by the Engineer.*

If the Contractor fails to attend or send a representative, the measurement made by (or on behalf of) the Engineer shall be accepted as accurate.

Except as otherwise stated in the Contract, wherever any Permanent Worksare to be measured from records, these shall be prepared by the Engineer. The Contractor shall, as and when requested, attend to examine and agree the records with the Engineer, and shall sign the same when agreed. If the Contractor does not attend, the records shall be accepted as accurate.

If the Contractor examines and disagrees the records, and/or does not sign them as agreed, then the Contractor shall give notice to the Engineer of the respects in which the records are asserted to be inaccurate. After receiving this notice, the Engineer shall review the records and either confirm or vary them. If the Contractor does not so give notice to the Engineer within 14 days after being requested to examine the records, they shall be accepted as accurate.

为了付款，应对工程进行测量和估价。根据合同的要求，工程师应通过测量来核实工程的工程量并确定工程的价值，以此来支付承包商应得到的款项。工程量表中的工程量是在编制招标文件时，根据图纸和规范估算的工作量，不能作为在履行合同规定义务过程中承包商应完成的实际工程量。本款首句强调了在实施合同中所完成的实际工作量要通过测量来核实，工程结算付款前须对完成工程进行实际测量。

FIDIC合同采用工程量清单计价模式，由招标代理机构或工程师对图纸和规范分析后，将整个项目分解成若干细目，经过计算标明每个施工工序的估算工程量，作为招标文件的工程量清单。投标人在编写投标文件时填上对应的单价，并计算出总价作为签约合同金额，承包商应对其所报的单价负责。

最终的合同款项由承包商完成的实际工程量决定。付款时，工程师有权对工程的任何部分进行测量，若工程师发出通知，承包商应按照本款的规定进行配合。对于工程师的测量，承包商应派出专人协助工程师完成"测量工程的任何部分"的测量，提供有关"测量工程的任何部分"的具体资料供工程师查阅。若承包商不参加测量工作，或未派代表参加，则由工程师进行的或由工程师批准的测量应被视为对工程该测量部分的正确测量，承包商应予以认可。

FIDIC施工合同条件适用于由雇主提供设计的工程，意味着雇主设计是合同的一个部分，承包商无权单方面修改作为合同组件的工程图纸。任何不合规范或图纸的工程实物，即使其偏差合理，也会被直接定性为"不符合合同要求"的工程缺陷，这种"超"图纸的偏差会被定性为"不合格产品"而被要求返工。

本款制定了工程测量的工作程序。工程师应提前准备好对任何永久工程进行测量时所需的记录和图纸。承包商应按照要求参与工程测量，且被要求进行记录内容审查时到场，就记录内容与工程师达成一致后，在上述文件上签字。由于测量工作的内容记录、任何在现场记录的数据和由现场数据构成的资料是后期估价、索赔等的重要资料来源，因此这些资料都必须由工程师和承包商双方或双方代表签字确认。如果承包商缺席此类记录及图纸的审查和承认工作，或在审查上述记录和图纸之后，承包商不同意或不签字认同但未在14天内向工程师提出申诉，则应视为这些记录和图纸正确无误。承包商也可对测量结果提出申诉，接到申诉后工程师应复查该记录和图纸，就有争议的内容进行确认或修改。

依据不同的工程情况，本款的应用情况主要有：

（1）按照完全标准的FIDIC施工合同条件施工的工程。即承包商完全按照雇主提供的图纸施工，没有提出任何修改意见和雇主变更，也没有任何签证类、索赔类的费用发生。合同顺利履行完毕后，清单所列费用与施工过程实际费用逐项一一对应，此时对实际工程进行测量即为测量图纸。

（2）按照相对完整的FIDIC施工合同条件规定施工的工程。即在工程施工过程中发生了图纸变更以及其他各种签证。图纸变更归于图纸，核算办法同（1）项是测量图纸，而签证部分则存在现场实测程序。这实际是常见的"图纸＋签证"确定工程造价的方法。

（3）以扩大初步设计图招标投标，单价包干工程。在施工图未出全，确定的承包商已进场施工的情况下，到中期付款时就须以新出施工图为依据"测量"工程，以使每次的工程付款都代表工程实际状况。此时的"测量"会得出新出的施工图，相对于招标投标的扩大初步设计图通过"实测"的新出施工图更能体现工程实际情况。新施工图有时会产生一些扩大初步设计图投标清单中没有的"项"，这种情况应以图纸为基本的"测量工程"手段重新测量和计算工程量。

【例 12.1】

在某国际公路工程项目中,雇主和承包商签订合同时规定,公路两边(除沼泽地以外)均需开挖排水沟。承包商和工程师现场代表商定的排水沟计量方法是以标准断面乘以完成的长度,并以此作为期中付款证书的计价依据。由于历次期中付款证书均在无争议的情况下获得工程师的批准,承包商便忽略了规范中规定的"原始记录需由工程师现场代表签署确认"这一要求。当工程师在合同结束后审查最终报表时,发现工程的造价远远超出了工程预算,因而不得不对已完成工程数量逐一复查。在复查过程中,工程师发现边沟数量的计算表上无工程师代表签字,因此拒绝承认最终报表中的数量。此时,原任现场工程师代表已离开了工程师所在的咨询公司,而承包商又不能出示工程师代表签字的原始记录,只好寄希望于现场抽样测量。但由于当地已经连下了几个月雨,未经铺砌的排水沟大部分已被淤积或冲毁,其他部分也已面目全非,因此承包商无法在现场抽样测量中找到对自己有利的依据。即便是按合同规定的争端解决程序提交工程师作出决定也只会无益,而承包商出于种种考虑又不愿意因此而提请仲裁,最终只得以不菲的代价换取了一个沉痛的教训。

12.2 Method of Measurement(测量办法)

Except as otherwise stated in the Contract and notwithstanding local practice:

(a) measurement shall be made of the net actual quantity(实际净数量)*of each item of the Permanent Works, and*

(b) the method of measurement shall be in accordance with the Bill of Quantities or other applicable Schedules.

测量方法,即"工程量计算规则"通常 FIDIC 合同招标投标时会专门列出由专业协会推荐的标准工程量计算规则,但也允许工程师根据实际情况来调整相应计算规则。FIDIC 合同可使用自定义工程量计算规则,给合同操作带来了便利,同时也存在投标各方难以统一的问题。针对投标各方对于合同条款理解的偏差问题,可在招标投标过程中召开澄清会议来详细解释。

不同国家和地区的工程量计量方法不完全相同。除非合同中另有规定,否则无论当地有怎样的计量习惯都应遵守以下两点:(1)采用实际净数量作为"永久工程的任何部分"的测量内容;(2)采用工程量表或其他适用资料表作为"永久工程的任何部分"的测量方法。实际净数量是由 FIDIC 合同规定的工程量计算规则确定的实际测量数量,如模板的数量就是与已完工的混凝土表面接触的净面积。

国际工程中,工程计量通常采用永久工程的净用量,不计诸如钢筋搭接或易损材料的损耗等,超量部分承包商应在投标报价时的单价构成中考虑。如:按照操作规程的要求,混凝土灌注桩工程必须超灌以保证桩头混凝土质量,这种工程规律及国家规范要求的"超灌"不是合同要求的净数量,而是承包商的措施要求,因此在计量时不考虑超灌产生的混凝土数量,超灌产生的费用由承包商投标时在综合单价内考虑。又如:基坑土方开挖时,放坡是否应计算、基坑计算范围应以大底板边为界还是以地下室结构外边为界等问题,可根据具体工程合同自定义工程量计算规则而定,通常根据需要选择便于计算的规则为依据。

在测量实际净数量的基础上,测量方法有现场测量(如土石方工程)、按施工图纸测算（如混凝土和钢筋工程）、仪表测量（如灌浆工程）、按单据计算、按工程师批准计量等方式。

12.3 Evaluation（估价）

Except as otherwise stated in the Contract, the Engineer shall proceed in accordance with Sub-Clause 3.5 [Determinations]to agree or determine the Contract Price by evaluating each item of work, applying the measurement agreed or determined in accordance with the above Sub-Clauses 12.1 and 12.2 and the appropriate rate or price for the item.

For each item of work, the appropriate rate or price for the item shall be the rate or price specified（明确规定）for such item in the Contract or, if there is no such item, specified for similar work. However, a new rate or price shall be appropriate for an item of work if:

(a)(i) the measured quantity of the item is changed by more than 10% from the quantity of this item in the Bill of Quantities or other Schedule,

(ii) This change in quantity multiplied by such specified rate for this item exceeds 0.01% of the Accepted Contract Amount,

(iii) this change in quantity directly changes the Cost per unit quantity（单位成本）of this item by more than 1%, and

(iv) this item is not specified in the Contract as a "fixed rate（固定费率）item";

or

(b)(i) the work is instructed under Clause 13 [Variations and Adjustments],

(ii) no rate or price is specified in the Contract for this item, and

(iii) no specified rate or price is appropriate because the item of work is not of similar character, or is not executed under similar conditions, as any item in Contract.

Each new rate or price shall be derived from any relevant rates or prices in the Contract, with reasonable adjustments to take account of the matters described in sub-paragraph (a) and/or (b), as applicable. If no rates or prices are relevant for the derivation of a new rate or price, it shall be derived from the reasonable Cost of executing the work, together with reasonable profit, taking account of any other relevant matters.

Until such time as an appropriate rate or price is agreed or determined, the Engineer shall determine a provisional rate or price for the purposes of Interim Payment Certificates.

对于每项工作而言，测量得到的工程量与相应费率或价格的乘积即为该项工作的估价。第12.1款［需测量的工程］规定了测量工程的工作程序，第12.2款［测量方法］规定了测量工程的方法定义，可见测量工程是估价的基准资料来源。在测量工作的基础上，本款对估价原则进行了规定：

（1）每项工作内容适用的费率或价格，都应是合同对此类工作内容规定或者合同规定之外类似工作内容的费率或价格。

(2) 在下列情况中，有关工作内容宜采用新的费率或价格：

1) 该项工作测出的数量变化超过工程量表或其他资料表中所列数量的 10% 以上。在此基础上，此数量变化与该项工作上述规定的费率的乘积超过中标合同金额的 0.01%，直接改变该项工作的单位成本超过 1%，且合同中未规定该项工作是固定费率项目；

2) 如果某项工作是根据第 13 条［变更与调整］的规定指示进行的工作，合同中没有规定其费率或价格，也没有适用的可参照的费率或价格。

(3) 对于一项工作而言，考虑到第（2）条有关事项，工程量表中虽然列有同类工作的费率或价格，但对具体变更工作而言已不适用，则应在原单价和价格的基础上制定合理的新单价或价格。若发生变更的工作内容在工程量表中没有同类工作的费率和价格，则应遵循与合同单价水平相一致的原则，将实际实施该项工作的合理成本、合理利润和其他相关事项作为基础，以确定新的费率或价格。

(4) 在适宜费率或价格商定之前，某项工作内容用于期中付款证书的费用或价格由工程师临时确定。

按照 FIDIC 合同，数量关系发生变化或者工作内容发生变化的工作，有三种费率或价格的确定方式：一是按合同规定的费率或价格（原费率或价格）根据同类工作的费率或价格计算变更工程费用；二是重新制定新的费率或价格；三是根据实际工程合理成本、利润，在原费率和价格的基础上确定新费率或价格。

通过本款（a）和（b）两项条件可发现，（b）项包括了"rate（费率）"、"price（价格）"两项可调整项目。而（a）项判定数量变化以及由其引起的合同价格变化是否超出限定，其中提到的可调整项目只有"rate（费率）"，这与 FIDIC 合同条件下"量价分离"和"量变价不变"的主张有关，"量"是指咨询工程师在工程量清单中填写的估算工程量，"价"是指投标人在工程量清单中填入的单价。FIDIC 合同条款对于费率和价格的调整存在不少限制。就本款（a）项而言，并不是存在工程量变化就能调整费率，而是要达到"10% 数量变化"，也并不是实现了"10% 数量变化"就能调整费率，还需满足 0.01% 总额变化和 1% 单位成本变化两个条件，如果合同中规定该项工作费率固定，即使满足前面数量、总额、单位成本变化，费率仍然不可调整，有此限制的费率可调的工作范围就大大减少。

12.4 Omissions（删减）

Whenever the omission of any work forms part（or all）of a Variation, the value of which has not been agreed, if:

(a) the Contractor will incur（or has incurred）cost which, if the work had not been omitted, would have been deemed to be covered by a sum forming part of the Accepted Contract Amount;

(b) the omission of the work will result（or has resulted）in this sum not forming part of the Contract Price; and

(c) this cost is not deemed to be included in the evaluation of any substituted work, then the Contractor shall give notice to the Engineer accordingly, with supporting parti-

culars. Upon receiving this notice, the Engineer shall proceed in accordance with Sub-Clause 3.5 [Determinations] to agree or determine this cost, which shall be included in the Contract Price.

删减工作内容是一种常见的工程变更形式。工程师发布删减工作的变更指示后，承包商不再实施部分工作，导致承包商无法获得被删减工作产生费用的款项，承包商由此损失该部分工作的间接费、利润、税金等利益。引起工作删减的原因可能来自工程项目不同参与方或客观因素，常见情形大致可分为设计优化、施工条件改变和不可抗力等。工作的删减会改变雇主与承包商之间订立合同的初始状态，符合下列三个条件时承包商可向工程师发出通知提出费用索赔，并提供具体的证明材料。

(1) 删减的工作使承包商发生的费用未包含在中标合同金额中；
(2) 删减的工作未被包括在合同价格中；
(3) 所删减工作的价值，即产生的费用，未包含在任何替代工作的估价中。

承包商能否获得删减工作的利润补偿，还需考虑删减工作发生后承包商实际的利润损失和报价行为的合理性。当由于雇主原因导致工作内容删减时，如果承包商损失的利益包含在其他应支付或已支付的项目中，或者雇主提出用其他替代工作补偿承包商因删减工作导致的利益损失，则承包商实际上并不存在利益损失，故不能获取删减工作的利润补偿。当采用不平衡报价策略进行投标时，承包商在维持总报价保持竞争力的前提下，调整某些工程量清单项目的综合单价以降低风险、争取在结算时获取更高利益；但对于雇主来说，若不能准确识别承包商的不平衡报价行为，且在此情况下发生删减工作，按照原报价向承包商进行利润补偿，则将导致低价中标、高价结算，造成经济损失。因此，在承包商采取不平衡报价方法参与投标的情况下，删减工作的利润补偿应进行适当调整。对于报价远高于正常水平的工作内容，其利润补偿应依据正常水平报价进行计算；对于报价低于正常水平但仍有利润的工作内容，其利润补偿应依据原报价进行计算；对于报价低到不计利润时，其利润补偿不成立。

【例 12.2】

雇主和承包商签订的合同内容主要包括科研楼和职工宿舍的土建、水电及消防工程。在双方签订工程承包合同之后，承包商按合同约定的开工日期如期进场。工程开工后，雇主欲对科研楼进行二次装饰，故将楼地面找平层、天棚粉刷和楼梯栏杆等工作内容删减，但同时将科研楼二次装饰的工作继续分配给了该承包商。承包商就工作删减提出利润补偿要求，但雇主不同意，双方由此产生分歧。

在该案例中，承包商投标报价不存在不平衡报价行为，完成楼地面找平层、天棚粉刷和楼梯栏杆等工作本可获得相应的报酬，同时由于雇主在施工中提出新的施工要求，修改了原定项目计划导致工作删减，承包商理应得到相应利润补偿。但是，雇主提出将二次装修任务作为替代工作，弥补了承包商由于删减工作产生的利益损失。故该承包商不满足删减工作的利润补偿条件，雇主也无需向其进行利润补偿。

【例 12.3】

在某隧道工程项目中，雇主和承包商签订合同时，约定工作面为三类围岩，需进行喷混凝土、打系统锚杆、加钢筋网等支护工作。但承包商在施工后期发现，隧道其中一段工作面为一类围岩。鉴于一类围岩不需要进行支护，雇主提出将该隧道区段工作面围岩的支护工作删减。由此承包商提出该部分工作的利润补偿，雇主以其未完成实质性工作为由拒绝补偿。

在上述案例中，由于雇主对围岩性质勘察不准确，导致施工后期删减喷混凝土、打系统锚杆和加钢筋网等工作内容。即使是经验丰富的承包商，也无法预见围岩性质的差异。因此由于工作内容的删减致使承包商在即将或已经投入的工作器具、材料中遭受损失，且雇主并未分配其他工作来代替删减工作，导致承包商的利益损失无法在替代工作或其他项目上得到补偿。综上，承包商符合删减工作利润补偿条件。

思考题

1. 简述工程测量的意义、程序和方法。
2. 实际工程的测量工作可能如何进行？
3. 简述估价原则。
4. 如何确定数量关系发生变化或者工作内容发生变化的工作的费率或价格？采用新费率或价格的条件有哪些？
5. 简述工程的删减对合同价格的影响。
6. 简述承包商可就工作删减提出索赔的条件。

13 Variations and Adjustment（变更和调整）

随着工程实施，受设计方案、施工计划和外部条件的干扰，通常需要对工程的部分工作内容、施工方法、工作计划进行修改，从而形成变更和调整。变更和调整的方式可以是工程师发出变更指示或承包商提交建议书。本节主要规定了变更权，变更的范围、内容、程序和调整计算方法等内容。

本章要求：熟悉本合同条款中的关键术语的含义；
了解工程师变更工程的权利范围；
了解承包商提出变更建议的权利以及获得批准后应履行的义务和应获得的收益；
了解工程变更的程序；
了解变更价款货币比例的确定方式；
了解暂定金额使用范围和支付范围以及计日工作实施程序和支付方法；
了解因立法变动和物价波动原因产生的费用和工期的调整。

13.1 Right to Vary（变更权）

Variations may be initiated by the Engineer at any time prior to issuing the Taking-Over Certificate for the Works, either by an instruction or by a request for the Contractor to submit a proposal.

The Contractor shall execute and be bound by（受约束，遵守）*each Variation, unless the Contractor promptly gives notice to the Engineer stating* (*with supporting particulars*) *that the Contractor cannot readily obtain the Goods required for the Variation. Upon receiving this notice, the Engineer shall cancel, confirm or vary the instruction.*

Each Variation may include：

(a) changes to the quantities of any item of work included in the Contract (however, such changes do not necessarily constitute a Variation),

(b) changes to the quality and other characteristics of any item of work,

(c) changes to the levels, positions and/or dimensions of any part of the Works,

(d) omission of any work unless it is to be carried out by others,

(e) any additional work, Plant, Materials or services necessary for the Permanent Works, including any associated Tests on Completion, boreholes（钻孔）*and other testing and exploratory work, or*

(f) changes to the sequence or timing of the execution of the Works.

The Contractor shall not make any alteration and/or modification of the Permanent Works, unless and until the Engineer instructs or approves a Variation.

在颁发工程接收证书前的任何时间，如果工程师认为有必要对工程或其中任何部分的形式、质量或数量作出任何变更，有权指示承包商或要求承包商提交建议书进行变更。变更内容包括：

(1) 增加或减少合同中所包括的任何工作内容的数量（工作内容的数量变化并不一定是变更）；

(2) 改变任何工作内容的质量、类型或者其他性质；

(3) 改变工程任何部分的标高、基线、位置和尺寸；

(4) 删减任何合同约定的工作内容，但不允许用变更指令的方式删减工作并将已删减的工作交由其他承包商实施；

(5) 工程竣工所必需的任何种类的附加工作、生产设备、材料或服务，包括任何有关的竣工试验、钻孔、其他试验和勘探工作等；

(6) 改变工程任何部分所规定的施工顺序或时间安排。

FIDIC合同对变更权利作出了明确规定，赋予了工程师变更工程的权利。当雇主通过工程师或工程师自身决定对工程图纸或合同文件规定的工作内容进行更改时，工程师有权变更，且有权指示承包商进行变更，此类变更也可称为指令变更。指令变更是工程师在雇主授权范围内根据施工现场的实际情况，在确实需要进行工程变更时有权发布变更指令。指令内容包括详细的变更内容、变更工程量、变更项目的施工技术要求和有关部门文件图纸，以及变更处理的原则。

FIDIC合同未赋予承包商变更工程的权利，承包商对工程的变更必须经过工程师的批准和指示。承包商可以提交变更建议书，但建议书本身不构成变更，只有被工程师批准后才视为变更，或对建议书内容进行部分变更。在无工程师指示或同意变更的授权时，承包商不得擅自对永久工程进行任何改动，即承包商在未收到工程师的变更指令时，无权对永久工程做任何改变或修改，也即承包商对雇主提供的图纸无权进行改变或修改。这也是可用测量图纸的方法进行很多测量工作的重要原因（详细解释参见第12.1款［需测量的工程］）。

FIDIC合同条款中变更权具有两个特点，一是具有一定强制性，二是工程师的变更指示是工程变更有效成立的前提。在接到工程师的变更指示后，承包商如果难以获得工作变更所需要的货物，应及时通知工程师并附上具体的证明材料。工程师可以取消原变更指示、修改原指示内容或确认情况后仍坚持原变更指令。此规定要求承包商无条件执行变更，除非确实"没有适用的货物"支持变更，体现了变更权的强制性。

理解上述合同变更工程的范围和情况时需注意如下几点：

(1) 变更内容包括合同中任何工作的工程量变化，但工作内容的数量变化不一定是变更。如：工程师要求增加管线上的安全阀，用于工程的安全阀数量会增加，此为变更；在地基开挖中，实际开挖量超过工程量表中的数量，此类工程量变化不能算变更。在特殊情况下，工作量改变可能是由于承包商违约所致，引起的费用须由承包商承担，这种工程量改变也不是变更。工程实施过程中，实际测量的工程量与招标文件工程量表中的工程量不一致时，不一定进行变更，在确定第12.3款［估价］是否适用时，应考虑工作的数量变动幅度及其对合同价格带来的影响。

(2) 雇主有权将合同规定的相应工作内容交由相应的承包商，但已经发包给其他承包商或分包给其他分包商的工作内容，不构成对承包商的变更指令。

（3）改变工程任何部分所规定的施工顺序或时间安排构成变更，间接说明雇主对合同中施工顺序和时间安排的规定负有责任。

【例 13.1】雇主和承包商签订某桥梁工程项目施工承包合同，该桥梁基础为扩大基础，上部结构为预应力混凝土 T 梁。开工前，承包商提交了详细的施工组织设计并得到工程师批准。但在进行基础开挖时，承包商发现地基实际土质条件与雇主提供的勘察设计资料不符，不能满足承载力要求。承包商应按照规定及时通知工程师，要求雇主对工程地质重新勘察并对设计进行变更，按变更后的设计图纸进行施工，并及时申报变更费用。工程师收到承包商的变更建议书后，应对现场情况予以确认，并批准变更。

13.2 Value Engineering（价值工程）

The Contractor may, at any time, submit to the Engineer a written proposal（书面建议）which（in the Contractor's opinion）will, if adopted,（i）accelerate completion,（ii）reduce the cost to the Employer of executing, maintaining or operating the Works,（iii）improve the efficiency or value to the Employer of the completed Works, or（iv）otherwise（另外，别的方式）be of benefit to the Employer.

The proposal shall be prepared at the cost of the Contractor（承包商自费）and shall include the items listed in Sub-Clause 13.3 [Variation Procedure].

If a proposal, which is approved by the Engineer, includes a change in the design of part of the Permanent Works, then unless otherwise agreed by both Parties：

（a）the Contractor shall design this part,

（b）sub-paragraphs（a）to（d）of Sub-Clause 4.1 [Contractor's General Obligations] shall apply, and

（c）if this change results in a reduction in the contract value of this part, the Engineer shall proceed in accordance with Sub-Clause 3.5 [Determinations] to agree or determine a fee, which shall be included in the Contract Price. This fee shall be half（50%）of the difference between the following amounts：

（i）such reduction in contract value, resulting from the change, excluding adjustments under Sub-Clause 13.7 [Adjustments for Changes in Legislation] and Sub-Clause 13.8 [Adjustments for Changes in Cost], and

（ii）the reduction（if any）in the value to the Employer of the varied works, taking account of any reductions in quality, anticipated life or operational efficiencies.

However, if amount（i）is less than amount（ii）, there shall not be a fee.

价值工程（Vault Engineering），也称价值分析（Vault Analysis），现代管理学对其的定义是"通过对产品功能的分析，正确处理功能（function）与成本（cost）之间的关系来节约资源、降低产品成本的一种有效方法"，即研究如何以最低寿命周期成本，来实现对象（产品、作业或服务等）的必要功能，常用公式 $V=F/C$ 反映价值工程的方法和原理。

承包商作为工程建设的具体执行方，对工程建设中的具体情况较为了解，且通常有类似项目的承包经验以及丰富的施工经验,可能有一些加快施工进度、提高施工效率、降低施工成本的方法。实际工程中,为了鼓励承包商借助自身经验,提出有利于工程建设的建议,本款规定承包商可随时向工程师提交有关加快施工进度、降低工程成本、提高竣工工程价值或给雇主带来其他利益的建议,经工程师认可后将予以采纳。

  承包商可向雇主或工程师提交建议书,建议对工程进行改变或修改(详细解释参见第13.1款[变更权])。但这份建议书本身不构成变更,只有被工程师批准后才视为变更,或对建议书内容进行部分变更。此类建议书由承包商自费完成编制,且应符合第13.3款[变更程序]中的规定,包括"变更工作的实施方法与计划、工程总体进度计划因变更必须进行调整的建议以及承包商对变更的费用估计"等书面内容。如果没有对实际工程建设的质量、进度、造价等方面进行深入的价值工程分析,承包商需承担编制变更建议书后不被工程师认可、批准的风险,同时承担建议书获得批准后与变更工程设计有关事务的一切连带责任。这要求承包商必须具备发现价值的能力以及把握价值的能力,才能向雇主提出合理化建议以实现项目价值的最大化,实现雇主及自身的利益最大化。

  除非双方另有协议,否则一旦工程师批准了建议书的实施内容,允许承包商对永久工程设计进行部分修改,承包商就应负责变更工程设计有关事务,并按照第4.1款[承包商的一般义务]中的相关规定承担连带责任。如果由于承包商提出的设计和施工方案优化建议给项目带来很大的收益,使合同双方都从中获益,承包商可以得到一定的报酬作为奖励,其额度为变更工程所节省费用的一半。此类"报酬"是由于工程变更引起合同价值中该变更工作的价值相应减少,工程师应按照第3.5款[确定]的规定,商定应包括在合同价格里的费用,对承包商减少的合同价款进行一定补偿。节省费用的计算公式为降低的合同价值减去因变更引起工程质量、预期寿命、运营效率等方面给雇主带来的潜在损失,但合同价值的减少不包括因第13.7款[因法律改变的调整]和第13.8款[因成本改变的调整]的规定作出的调整,并且如果合同价值的减少量小于雇主潜在损失,则承包商不能获得此类报酬。

  与第13.1款[变更权]不同,本款鼓励承包商主动提出优化工程建设、降低施工成本的建议。在实际操作中,承包商有时为避免潜在亏损而提出工程变更建议,工程师一般会拒绝此类变更建议,但有时为保障工程顺利进行,在基本不损害工程价值的基础上也会接受承包商的此类建议。

13.3 Variation Procedure(变更程序)

  If the Engineer requests a proposal, prior to instructing a Variation(在发出变更指示之前),*the Contractor shall respond in writing as soon as practicable, either by giving reasons why he cannot comply*(*if this is the case*) *or by submitting*:

  (*a*)*a description of the proposed work to be performed and a programme for its execution,*

  (*b*)*the Contractor's proposal for any necessary modifications to the programme according to Sub-Clause 8.3*[*Programme*]*and to the Time for Completion , and*

  (*c*)*the Contractor's proposal for evaluation of the Variation.*

The Engineer shall, as soon as practicable after receiving such proposal (under Sub-Clause 13.2 [Value Engineering]or otherwise), respond with approval, disapproval or comments. The Contractor shall not delay any work whilst awaiting a response.

Each instruction to execute a Variation, with any requirements for the recording of Costs, shall be issued by the Engineer to the Contractor, who shall acknowledge receipt.

Each Variation shall be evaluated in accordance with Clause 12 [Measurement and Evaluation], unless the Engineer instructs or approves otherwise in accordance with this Clause.

本款对变更执行程序进行了规定：

（1）若工程师在正式发出变更令前要求承包商编制建议书，承包商应尽快书面答复是否能提交建议书。承包商如提交建议书，应提交变更工作的实施方法与计划、工程总体进度计划因变更必须进行调整的建议以及承包商对变更的费用估计等资料，如无法提交建议书则应说明理由。

（2）工程师在收到承包商的建议书后应尽快给予批准、不批准或提出意见的确切回应，承包商在等待答复期间不应延误任何工作。

（3）工程师发出变更指令后，承包商应在收到该指令后及时回函说明，并按照要求执行每项变更和记录各项支出费用。

（4）每项变更按第12条［测量与估价］的规定，以单价合同方式进行估价支付，除非工程师根据本款另有指示或批准。

承包商提出变更建议，可能面临三种可能：一是工程师认为变更建议不合理或部分内容不合理，予以拒绝或向承包商提出修改建议；二是工程师认为变更建议合理但变更价值大于预估收益或短时间内无法判断更改的设计对整个工程的影响，不允许变更；三是工程师认为建议合理且变更能带来大收益或变更代价可接受，则允许变更，此时承包商不仅耗费了编制建议书的精力和财力，还需要承担后续设计等工作。可以看出，变更可实施性、变更成本、变更影响等因素，都可能使工程师对承包商提出的变更建议予以拒绝。因此，承包商在提出变更建议书时，应充分遵循提高经济效益、保证工程质量、控制工程造价等原则。

13.4　Payment in Applicable Currencies（以适用货币支付）

If the Contract provides for payment of the Contract Price in more than one currency, then whenever an adjustment is agreed, approved or determined as stated above, the amount payable（支付款项）in each of the applicable currencies（适用货币）shall be specified. For this purpose, reference shall be made to the actual or expected currency proportions of the Cost of the varied work, and to the proportions of various currencies specified for payment of the Contract Price.

国际工程项目中，支付工程款可能涉及一种以上货币，一般分为外币、当地币两部分。合同款可以按照合同中规定的货币比例进行支付。对于因发生变更而调整合同价格的工作内容，在确定变更前应确定支付调整款额适用的货币，并参考完成变更工作所需要的货币比例以及合同规定的支付合同价格使用的货币比例。

外币支付易受到国家金融政策和国际汇率变化的影响。工程中有时会发生施工合同用外币支付而雇主要求变更工作以当地币支付的情况，考虑到当地币支付上的便利，承包商可能会接受雇主以当地币支付变更项目。这种适用货币的变化属于合同变更，应有经双方确认的书面文件来支持，以免在结算时引发对适用货币的争议。

对于施工合同中以多种货币支付的情况，一旦发生变更导致清单费用变化，应按照合同规定将合同、工程实体、主清单、变更清单等相关项目对应起来。对应工程的同时，应支付的币种也应该对应合同中规定的币种。如果出现合同无法对应币种的新清单项目，则应考虑按合同中规定的各币种所占比例分配适用变更工作的币种比例。

FIDIC施工合同中未明确说明是否由工程师来确定变更款额的具体货币比例。但本款指出的货币比例确定方法与变更价款数额的确定方法一致，为"商定、批准或确定"，即由工程师与承包商协商确定，或者由承包商提出货币比例后工程师批准确定，当双方意见不一致时由工程师暂定，后续可按争端程序来解决。

13.5　Provisional Sums（暂列金额）

Each Provisional Sum shall only be used, in whole or in part, in accordance with the Engineer's instructions, and the Contract Price shall be adjusted accordingly. The total sum paid to the Contractor shall include only such amounts, for the work, supplies or services to which the Provisional Sum relates, as the Engineer shall have instructed. For each Provisional Sum, the Engineer may instruct：

（a）work to be executed（including Plant, Materials or services to be supplied）by the Contractor and valued under Sub-Clause 13.3［Variation Procedure］; and/or

（b）Plant, Materials or services to be purchased by the Contractor, from a nominated Subcontractor（as defined in Clause 5［Nominated Subcontractors］）or otherwise; and for which there shall be included in the Contract Price：

（i）the actual amounts paid（or due to be paid（应付））by the Contractor, and

（ii）a sum for overhead charges（管理费）and profit, calculated as a percentage of these actual amounts by applying the relevant percentage rate（if any）stated in the appropriate Schedule. If there is no such rate, the percentage rate stated in the Appendix to Tender shall be applied.

The Contractor shall, when required by the Engineer, produce quotations（报价单）, invoices（发票）, vouchers（凭证）and accounts（账单）or receipts in substantiation（收据）.

暂列金额是雇主金额，只有工程师才有权决定是否动用、动用数额（详细解释参见第1.1.4.10款［暂列金额］）。暂列金额有可能动用或不动用，由于它属于合同中工程量表的一部分，动用的金额即为合同价格组成部分。

动用暂列金额向承包商支付款项必须满足两个条件：一是该款项所支付的工作是工程师下达指令要求承包商执行的，二是该项工作属于以暂列金额支付的工作范围。工程师可以动用暂列金额来指示承包商实施某项工作，并按第13.3款［变更程序］来估价。工程师也可以动用暂列金额来指示承包商从指定分包商处或其他渠道获得永久设备、材料或服务，在这种情况下承包商可获得两笔款项：承包商为该项工作实际已付或应付的费用，且能出示相应报价单、发票、凭证及账单或收据等证明材料；以及承包商实施该项工作的管理费和利润。其中，该项工作的管理费和利润可以按照有关明细表中规定的百分比收取，如果明细表中无相关规定则采用投标书附录中规定的百分比。

暂列金额作为雇主的备用金，通常包含两类费用：一是招标时雇主在资料表中列明的具体工作和估算金额，二是作为一笔应急费用用于支付不可预见工作产生的费用。通常，合同出现此类费用的原因可能是以下几个方面：（1）工程建设过程中可能发生由雇主负责的应急费用或不可预见费用，如计日工涉及的费用；（2）招标时雇主暂不能确定投标人在工程某些部分给出的固定单价的深度；（3）招标时雇主不能确定某项工作是否包含在合同中；（4）雇主希望由指定分包商实施某项工作。雇主在合同中规定的暂列金额是为以上情况发生时准备的。暂列金额可被"全部或部分"使用，但雇主不能通过变更或其他方式增加暂列金额的额度超出规定额度。

13.6　Daywork（计日工作）

For work of a minor or incidental nature（零星或附带性工作）, the Engineer may instruct that a Variation shall be executed on a daywork basis. The work shall then be valued in accordance with the Daywork Schedule included in the Contract, and the following procedure shall apply. If a Daywork Schedule is not included in the Contract, this Sub-Clause shall not apply.

Before ordering Goods for the work, the Contractor shall submit quotations to the Engineer. When applying for payment, the Contractor shall submit invoices, vouchers and accounts or receipts for any Goods.

Except for any items for which the Daywork Schedule specifies that payment is not due, the Contractor shall deliver each day to the Engineer accurate statements in duplicate（一式两份）which shall include the following details of the resources used in executing the previous day's work：

（a）the names, occupations and time of Contractor's Personnel,

（b）the identification, type and time of Contractor's Equipment and Temporary Works, and

（c）the quantities and types of Plant and Materials used.

One copy of each statement will, if correct, or when agreed, be signed by the Engineer, and returned to the Contractor. The Contractor shall then submit priced statements（估价报表）of these resources to the Engineer, prior to their inclusion in the next Statement under Sub-Clause 14.3 ［Application for Interim Payment Certificates］.

计日工是在施工过程中，完成雇主提出的工程合同范围以外的，按合同中约定的综合单价计价的零星项目或额外工作，一般用于工程量表中没有合适项目的零星附加工作或变更项目。如果在工程建设过程中出现了零星项目或附加工作，工程师可以下达变更指示要求承包商按计日工实施此类工作,并按照计日工作计划表和相关程序进行估价和支付,但合同中未包括计日工作计划表时不适用本款规定。

若计日工作需要购买物品,购买前承包商应向工程师提交报价单,承包商申请付款时应出示物品有关发票、凭证、账单或收据。除了计日工作计划表中规定暂时不需要支付的工作内容外,承包商应每天向工程师提交前一日工作中使用的资源清单,一式两份,清单内容包括承包商人员的姓名、工种和工作时间、施工设备和临时工程的类别、型号和使用时间,永久设备和材料的使用数量和类别。工程师在核实每份报表的准确性后应签字认同,并退回一份由承包商留存。承包商应根据工程师核定的计日工作报表进行计价,计价后再提交给工程师一份,然后将此类计价包括在第14.3款[期中支付证书]所述的月报表中申请付款。

计日工通常包含在工程表中的一项暂定金额内,其费率和价格表一般作为工程量表的附件包括在合同中。在国际工程招标中,招标文件通常有计日工表列出有关施工人员工种、施工设备及施工材料等资料,要求投标人报出单价,同时明确规定每人或每类工种的计时费率、每类施工设备的计时费率、每类施工材料的应付款,作为计日工作的支付依据。上述费率一般是"一揽子"费率,即不允许选择性地接受其中部分项目的费率取值而拒绝接受其他项目的费率取值。

13.7 Adjustments for Changes in Legislation(因法律改变的调整)

The Contract Price shall be adjusted to take account of any increase or decrease in Cost resulting from a change in the Laws of the Country (including the introduction of new Laws and the repeal or modification of existing Laws) or in the judicial or official governmental interpretation of such Laws, made after the Base Date, which affect the Contractor in the performance of obligations under the Contract.

If the Contractor suffers (or will suffer) delay and/or incurs (or will incur) additional Cost as a result of these changes in the Laws or in such interpretations, made after the Base Date, the Contractor shall give notice to the Engineer and shall be entitled subject to (有权承担) Sub-Clause 20.1 [Contractors Claims] to:

(a) an extension of time for any such delay, if completion is or will be delayed, under Sub-Clause 8.4 [Extension of Time for Completion], and

(b) payment of any such Cost, which shall be included in the Contract Price.

After receiving this notice, the Engineer shall proceed in accordance with Sub-Clause 3.5 [Determinations] to agree or determine these matters.

工程项目施工周期一般较长,承包商投标时虽考虑了影响投标报价的因素,但可能会因施工期间相关法律变动(如税法的变动)而影响到工程的实际费用。在基准日期后因工程所在国的法律变动,或颁布新的法律,或废除、修改现有法律,或对现有法律原司法解释、官方说法变动,从而影响承包商合同义务的履行,应根据工程费用增减的具体情况相应调整合同价格。由于法律变动而致使承包商延误工期、产生额外费用,承包商可根据第20.1款[承包商的索赔]的规定向工程师发出索赔通知,索赔工期和费用。工程师收到索赔通知后应按照第 3.5 款 [确定] 的规定商定或确定索赔事宜。

　　法律调整的改变，承包商具有进行工期延长索赔的权利，也具有包括合理利润在内的费用补偿权利。承包商向工程师发出索赔通知后工程师表示同意或作出决定即可，无需进行协商确定。在支出额外费用后承包商可申请费用补偿，但本款未说明费用减少时的处理规定。

　　本款适用于因工程所在国的法律发生变动引起工期延误和费用增减的工程，工程所在国以外发生的法律变更不在本款管辖范围内，且并非所有法律的变动都会影响到承包商履行合同义务。实践中，影响承包商工程活动的法律主要有劳动法、社会保险法、健康安全法、环境保护法、海关法（尤其是关税变动），以及其他相关法律的变动。承包商应关注工程活动相关法律的变化与影响。

13.8　Adjustments for Changes in the Cost（因成本调整的改变）

　　In this Sub-Clause, "table of adjustment data（调整数据表）" means the completed table of adjustment data included in the Appendix to Tender. If there is no such table of adjustment data, this Sub-Clause shall not apply.

　　If this Sub-Clause applies, the amounts payable to the Contractor shall be adjusted for rises or falls in the cost of labour, Goods and other inputs to the Works, by the addition or deduction of the amounts（增减额）determined by the formulae（公式）prescribed in this Sub-Clause. To the extent that full compensation for any rise or fall in Costs is not covered by the provisions of this or other Clauses, the Accepted Contract Amount shall be deemed to have included amounts to cover the contingency（应急费用）of other rises and falls in costs.

　　The adjustment to be applied to the amount otherwise payable to the Contractor, as valued in accordance with the appropriate Schedule and certified in Payment Certificates, shall be determined from formulae for each of the currencies in which the Contract Price is payable. No adjustment is to be applied to work valued on the basis of Cost or current prices. The formulae shall be of the following general type:

$$Pn = a + b\frac{Ln}{Lo} + c\frac{En}{Eo} + d\frac{Mn}{Mo} + \cdots$$

　　Where:

　　"Pn" is the adjustment multiplier（调整乘数）to be applied to the estimated contract value in the relevant currency of the work carried out in period "n", this period being a month unless otherwise stated in the Appendix to Tender;

　　"a" is a fixed coefficient（固定系数）, stated in the relevant table of adjustment data, representing the non-adjustable portion in contractual payments;

　　"b", "c", "d", ... are coefficients representing the estimated proportion of each cost element related to the execution of the Works, as stated in the relevant table of adjustment data; such tabulated cost elements may be indicative of resources such as labour,

13 Variations and Adjustment（变更和调整）

equipment and materials；

"*Ln*"，"*En*"，"*Mn*"，… *are the current cost indices*（现行成本指数）*or reference prices*（参考价格）*for period* "*n*"，*expressed in the relevant currency of payment*，*each of which is applicable to the relevant tabulated cost element on the date* 49 *days prior to the last day of the period*（期间最后一天前第 49 天）（*to which the particular Payment Certificate relates*）；*and*

"*Lo*"，"*Eo*"，"*Mo*"，… *are the base cost indices*（基准成本指数）*or reference prices*，*expressed in the relevant currency of payment*，*each of which is applicable to the relevant tabulated cost element on the Base Date.*

The cost indices or reference prices stated in the table of adjustment data shall be used. If their source is in doubt，*it shall be determined by the Engineer. For this purpose*，*reference shall be made to the values of the indices*（指数值）*at stated dates*（*quoted in the fourth and fifth columns respectively of the table*）*for the purposes of clarification of the source*；*although these dates*（*and thus these values*）*may not correspond to the base cost indices.*

In cases where the "*currency of index*（指数对应的货币）" （*stated in the table*）*is not the relevant currency of payment*，*each index shall be converted into the relevant currency of payment at the selling rate*（卖出汇率）， *established by the central bank of the Country*， *of this relevant currency on the above date for which the index is required to be applicable.*

Until such time as each current cost index is available，*the Engineer shall determine a provisional index*（临时指数）*for the issue of Interim Payment Certificates. When a current cost index is available*，*the adjustment shall be recalculated accordingly.*

If the Contractor fails to complete the Works within the Time for Completion，*adjustment of prices thereafter shall be made using either*（ⅰ）*each index or price applicable on the date* 49 *days prior to the expiry of the Time for Completion of the Works*（工程竣工时间期满前第 49 天），*or*（ⅱ）*the current index or price*：*whichever is more favourable*（有利的）*to the Employer.*

The weightings（*coefficients*）*for each of the factors of cost stated in the table*（*s*）*of adjustment data shall only be adjusted if they have been rendered unreasonable*，*unbalanced or inapplicable*，*as a result of Variations.*

施工期间市场物价的变化会对工程项目的顺利进行产生影响。在 FIDIC 施工合同中，雇主承担物价上涨、价格浮动的风险，承包商有权根据合同条款的相关规定进行调价，以弥补承包商因市场价格变化所造成的损失。

本款的适用条件是投标函附录中附有已经填好数据的"调整数据表"。在投标函附录包含此类调整数据表的情况下，如果承包商在工程建设过程中所用的劳动力、货物以及其他成本的市场价格产生浮动，雇主支付给承包商的工程款应按照本款中的公式进行增减额调整。没有调整到的部分，应视为在中标合同金额内包含了该部分物价浮动的风险费。

雇主是否允许因物价变动而相应调整合同价格，取决于招标文件中是否存在调整数据

171

表,而调价公式也只适用于表中列明的劳动力、设备、材料等资源费用。可调整的款项由承包商在投标书内填写并在签订合同前与雇主谈判中确定,那些根据实际费用支出或现行价格估价的工程款项一律不予调整。如合同中已经规定了价格浮动条款,因价格浮动引起的价格调整属于合同款正常支付的部分,承包商不能以索赔名义要求费用补偿。

调价公式为

$$P_n = a + b\frac{L_n}{L_o} + c\frac{E_n}{E_o} + d\frac{M_n}{M_o} + \cdots \tag{13-1}$$

式中,

"P_n"为第 n 期间(除非投标函附录中另有规定,这个期间通常是一个月,以下简称"月")的调价系数,用该调价系数乘以第 n 月的估算工程进度款,即得到调价后的该月工程款,适用于各种支付货币,如果物价上涨则该系数大于 1,反之则小于 1;

"a"为调整数据表中规定的一个固定系数,代表合同支付中不调整的部分合同款,在国际工程中一般取 0.1~0.2;

"b"、"c"、"d"、…为调整数据表中规定的系数,代表与实施工程有关资源的每项费用因素的估算比例,包括劳务、设备和材料等资源;

"L_n"、"E_n"、"M_n"、…为第 n 月使用的现行费用指数或参照价格,取该期间(具体付款证书的相关期限)最后一日之前第 49 天当天适用的指数值,不同支付货币的费用指数或参考价格由相关表中的费用因素确定;

"L_o"、"E_o"、"M_o"、…为基本费用参数或参照价格,取基准日期当天适用的指数值,每种支付货币所对应的费用构成,应取相应的指数值。

本款对调价公式的系数作出了说明:

(1)调价公式应使用"调整数据表"中规定的费用指数或参数价格,如果指数来源不清楚,则由工程师决定取值。为澄清指数值的来源,工程师应当参照投标函附录中相应调整数据表所指日期的指数值,但此类日期和指数值不一定与基准成本指数一致。

(2)如果调整数据表中某指数对应的货币不是支付货币,则该指数应换算成相应支付货币,兑换率取工程所在国中央银行确定的该支付货币在要求日期当天的卖出汇率。

(3)在获取每种现行成本指数前,为了签发期中支付证书,工程师可以暂时确定一个临时指数,待得到现行成本指数后再重新计算调整。

(4)如果承包商未能在竣工时间内完成工程,则应利用竣工时间期满前第 49 天当天适用的指数或价格,或者利用现行指数或价格对合同价格作出调整,调价的指数值在二者间取对雇主有利的指数值。

(5)当由于工程发生变更导致调整数据表中的费用因素权重(系数)不合适时,应对此类权重(系数)予以调整。

结合第 13.7 款[因法律改变的调整]与本款的规定来看,"基准日期"(详细解释可参照第 1.1.3.1 款[基准日期])是十分重要的时间点。在基准日期后因法律改变或成本调整而对合同价格进行调整,这体现了国际工程中雇主和承包商分摊风险的特点。

【例 13.2】某国际工程项目,承包商项目进口一批机械设备于 2016 年 6 月 23 日抵达工程所在国 A 港口,集装箱装运的物资于 2016 年 7 月 5 日抵达该港口。此时,该国农业发展部进口了大批粮食,造成 A 港口异常拥挤和堵塞。为此,公路运输局下达行政指令,要求所有运输公司的运输车辆必须优先运送农业发展部进口的粮食。这使计划给承包商运送机械设备、物资的车辆都不得不转而运送粮食,致使承包商进口的机械设备和物资一直滞留在A港口不能如期运抵现场,产生滞港费、管理费和其他费用的额外支出以及调整数据表的调整,造成了严重的工期延误和资金损失。

由于上述非正常的行政指令干扰影响承包商的机械设备和物资进口计划,给承包商造成了工期和经济损失,这些都是一个有经验的承包商无法合理预见的。所以承包商应依据第13.8款［因成本调整的改变］和第19.1款［不可抗力的定义］的相关规定,向工程师提出索赔意向,并抄送雇主,在发生上述事件之时应依据第20.1款［承包商的索赔］中相关规定收集并保留同期记录和有关证据资料。

思考题

1. 简述变更权的定义和进行变更的途径。
2. 简述工程师变更工程的权利范围。
3. 承包商是否必须接收变更指令,为什么?
4. 承包商主动提出变更建议可能产生什么后果?
5. 简述承包商提出的变更建议获得批准后应履行的义务和应获得的收益。
6. 简述工程变更的程序。
7. 如何确定变更价款的适用货币和货币比例。
8. 简述暂列金额的定义、组成、使用条件及使用范围。
9. 简述计日工作实施程序和支付方法。
10. 哪些情况属于立法变动?
11. 简述因立法变动产生工期和费用调整的处理办法。
12. 因物价波动调整费用和工期的前提是什么?
13. 简述因物价波动调整费用和工期的款项范围。
14. 影响因物价波动调整费用的因素有哪些?

14 Contractor Price and Payment
（合同价格和付款）

本节的主要内容是 FIDIC 合同条件中的支付条款。支付条款是对工程款支付的货币、款额、方式以及支付时间的一系列规定，是工程合同的核心，是雇主按照合同规定向承包商支付工程款额，对承包商应承担的基本义务。合理的支付规定、完整清晰的支付程序，是承包商顺利获得工程款项的重要保证，也是合同双方合作顺利进行的重要保障。

本章要求：熟悉本合同条款中的关键术语的含义；

了解合同中合同价格的性质；

了解工程预付款的支付和付还；

了解期中付款证书和最终付款证书的申请和颁发；

了解工程材料和永久设备款的计算和支付方法；

了解合同中规定的支付时间和延误支付的处理办法；

了解合同中对支付货币汇率的规定以及其他规定。

14.1 The Contractor Price（合同价格）

Unless otherwise stated in the Particular Conditions:

(a) the Contract Price shall be agreed or determined under Sub-Clause 12.3 [Evaluation] and be subject to adjustments in accordance with the Contract;

(b) the Contractor shall pay all taxes（税金）*, duties*（关税）*and fees required to be paid by him under the Contract, and the Contract Price shall not be adjusted for any of these costs except as stated in Sub-Clause 13.7 [Adjustments for Changes in Legislation];*

(c) any quantities which may be set out in the Bill of Quantities or other Schedule are estimated quantities and are not to be taken as the actual and correct quantities:

(i) of the Works which the Contractor is required to execute, or

(ii) for the purposes of Clause 12 [Measurement and Evaluation]; and

(d) the Contractor shall submit to the Engineer, within 28 days after the Commencement Date, a proposed breakdown（建议分类细目）*of each lump sum price in the Schedules. The Engineer may take account of the breakdown when preparing Payment Certificates, but shall not be bound by it.*

合同价格是在工程招标投标阶段，雇主和中标人（承包商）根据合同条款及有关规定，签订工程合同时所确定的拟建工程价格总额，又称合同标定价格。在承包商正确地履行完合同义务，完成合同规定的建造任务后，工程师经过"测量和估价"（详细解释参见第12条〔测量与估价〕）后向承包商签发付款证书来确定雇主支付给承包商的金额，雇主应根据合同规定向承包商支付此款额。

上述款额通过用测量的实际工程量乘以相应费率或价格来确定,其中"相应费率或价格"的确定应遵循第12.3款[估价]的规定,同时按照合同规定进行调整。工程量表或其他资料表中列出的工程量只是估计工程量,不应视为要求承包商实际完成的工程量,同样不应视为用于第12条[测量和估价]规定下的工程量。工程量表中的工程量是估算值,而实际支付采用的工程量是按照第12条[测量和估价]规定实际测量所得的工程量。

合同价格应是综合考虑了各种费用后,工程项目合同最终确定的结算价格,包含各类税费。承包商应支付合同中要求其支付的各项税金、关税和费用。合同价格中已经包括此类费用,只有在第13.7款[因法律改变的调整]规定下因法律改变导致此类费用变化的情况下,合同价格才予以调整。

与中标合同款额不同,合同价格是雇主实际应付给承包商的最终工程款,在合同中呈现款项细目内容;而中标合同款额是承包商投标报价,经过评标和合同谈判后确定的一个暂时工程价格,是雇主在中标函中接受、认可承包商承建工程所需的费用。

雇主和承包商可就合同价格进行协商,并在专用条件中另作约定。如果在专用条件中另有规定,则以专用条件中对于合同价格的规定为准。

14.2 Advance Payment(预付款)

The Employer shall make an advance payment, as an interest-free loan(无息贷款)for mobilization(动员), when the Contractor submits a guarantee(保函)in accordance with this Sub-Clause. The total advance payment, the number and timing of installments(分期付款)(if more than one), and the applicable currencies and proportions, shall be as stated in the Appendix to Tender.

Unless and until the Employer receives this guarantee, or if the total advance payment is not stated in the Appendix to Tender, this Sub-Clause shall not apply.

The Engineer shall issue an Interim Payment Certificate for the first installment after receiving a Statement (under Sub-Clause 14.3 [Application for Interim Payment Certificates]) and after the Employer receives (i) the Performance Security in accordance with Sub-Clause 4.2 [Performance Security] and (ii) a guarantee in amounts and currencies equal to the advance payment. This guarantee shall be issued by an entity and from within a country (or other jurisdiction(司法管辖区)) approved by the Employer, and shall be in the form annexed to the Particular Conditions or in another form approved by the Employer.

The Contractor shall ensure that the guarantee is valid and enforceable until the advance payment has been repaid, but its amount may be progressively reduced by the amount repaid by the Contractor as indicated in the Payment Certificates. If the terms of the guarantee specify its expiry date, and the advance payment has not been repaid by the date 28 days prior to the expiry date, the Contractor shall extend the validity of the guarantee until the advance payment has been repaid.

The advance payment shall be repaid through percentage deductions in Payment

Certificates. Unless other percentages are stated in the Appendix to Tender：

(a)deductions shall commence in the Payment Certificate in which the total of all certified interim payments (excluding the advance payment and deductions and repayments of retention)exceeds ten per cent (10%)of the Accepted Contract Amountless Provisional Sums；and

(b)deductions shall be made at the amortisation rate（摊还比率）of one quarter (25%)of the amount of each Payment Certificate (excluding the advance payment and deductions and repayments of retention) in the currencies and proportions of the advance payment, until such time as the advance payment has been repaid.

If the advance payment has not been repaid prior to the issue of the Taking-Over Certificate for the Works or prior to termination under Clause 15 [Termination by Employer], Clause 16 [Suspension and Termination by Contractor]or Clause 19 [Force Majeure](as the case may be（视情况而定）), the whole of the balance then outstanding shall immediately become due and payable by the Contractor to the Employer.

工程项目承包中，开工准备期间，承包商一般需要投入大量启动资金。为确保工程顺利开展，FIDIC合同条件规定雇主应向承包商支付一定数额的预付款，以确保承包商在工程前期资金流动顺畅。雇主支付工程预付款的相关规定如下：

（1）雇主应向承包商支付一笔无息预付款用于承包商启动工程建设，其总额、分期预付的次数和时间安排（如次数多于一次）、适用货币及货币比例，应按投标函附录中的规定执行。承包商应在收到预付款前提交一份预付款保函。

（2）本款的规定不适用于雇主未收到承包商的预付款保函，或投标书附录中未列明预付款总额的情况。即雇主支付预付款的前提条件是承包商已提交预付款保函，且投标书附录中列明预付款总额的额度、分期支付次数、分期支付时间、支付货币及货币比例等。

（3）工程师首次发出分期付款的期中付款证书前提是：1）承包商向工程师提交第14.3款［期中付款证书的申请］中规定的报表；2）承包商向雇主提交第4.2款［履约担保］中规定的履约担保；3）承包商向雇主提交一份金额与货币种类与预付款一致的预付款保函，这份预付款保函应由雇主批准的国家（或地区）机构开具，并符合专用条件中所附或雇主认可的格式。

本款在说明预付款支付规定后，同样也规定了承包商偿还程序：

（1）在完全偿还预付款前，承包商应保证预付款保函一直有效且可兑现，预付款保函担保的额度可以随预付款逐步付还而减少。

（2）如果预付款保函存在有效期，且承包商在该有效期届满前28天还未完全付还预付款，则承包商应延长保函的有效期直至全部付还预付款为止。

（3）预付款应按每次付款的百分比在付款证书中扣减，如果扣减的百分比没有在投标书附录中注明，则按以下方式扣减：1）当期中付款证书的累计款额超过中标合同款额与暂列金额的差的10%时，则开始从期中付款证书中扣减；2）每次从付款证书中扣减的金额数为该付款证书的25%，且扣减金额的货币比例与支付预付款的货币比例相同，直到**预付款全部付还为止。预付款**付还的起扣额度以及每次付还的扣减额度，均不包括预付款本身与保留金的扣减和归还。

14 Contractor Price and Payment（合同价格和付款）

（4）如果在颁发工程接收证书前，或者根据第 15 条［由雇主终止］、第 16 条［由承包商暂停和终止］、第 19 条［不可抗力］的规定不得不终止预付款付还的情况下，承包商还未全部付还预付款，承包商应立即偿还剩余预付款。

FIDIC 合同强调预付款保函的作用是确保一旦承包商未能履约或者未能全部履约，雇主可向承包商提出索赔并要求其返还预付款。预付款保函可约束承包商在收到预付款后，按合同规定履行预付款付还义务。

在确定预付款归还条件后，计算每期应付还的预付款额度可采用下式：

$$R = \frac{A(C/aS)}{(b/a)S}$$

式中，

"R" 表示期中付款证书累计付还的预付款总数；

"A" 表示预付款的总额度；

"C" 表示期中付款证书中累计的应付工程款总数，该数额的确定方式取决于合同规定，取值范围为 $aS < C < bS$；

"S" 表示中标合同金额；

"a" 表示期中付款总额累计达到整个中标合同金额开始扣减预付款的百分数；

"b" 表示当期中付款累计额度等于中标合同金额的百分数，达到该百分数时预付款必须全部付还。

14.3 Application for Interim Payment Certificates（期中付款证书的申请）

The Contractor shall submit a Statement in six copies to the Engineer after the end of each month, in a form approved by the Engineer, showing in detail the amounts to which the Contractor considers himself to be entitled, together with supporting documents which shall include the report on the progress during this month in accordance with Sub-Clause 4.21 [Progress Reports].

The Statement shall include the following items, as applicable, which shall be expressed in the various currencies in which the Contract Price is payable, in the sequence listed:

(a) the estimated contract value of the Works executed and the Contractor's Documents produced up to the end of the month (including Variations but excluding items described in sub-paragraphs (b) to (g) below);

(b) any amounts to be added and deducted for changes in legislation and changes in cost, in accordance with Sub-Clause 13.7 [Adjustments for Changes in Legislation] and Sub-Clause 13.8 [Adjustments for Changes in Cost];

(c) any amount to be deducted for retention（应扣减的任何保留金额）, calculated by applying the percentage of retention stated in the Appendix to Tender to the total of the above amounts, until the amount so retained by the Employer reaches the limit of Retention Money (if any) stated in the Appendix to Tender;

(d) any amounts to be added and deducted for the advance payment and repayments in accordance with Sub-Clause 14.2 [Advance Payment];

(e) any amounts to be added and deducted for Plant and Materials in accordance with Sub-Clause 14.5 [Plant and Materials intended for the Works];

(f) any other additions or deductions which may have become due under the Contract or otherwise, including those under Clause 20 [Claims, Disputes and Arbitration]; and

(g) the deduction of amounts certified in all previous Payment Certificates.

期中付款是工程建设过程中根据承包商完成的工程进度及工程量给予的临时付款。在每个月末后，按照工程师规定的格式，承包商可以向工程师提交申请期中支付的报表，一式六份，并需详细说明承包商认为其有权获得付款的款项，以及出示第4.21款[进度报告]规定的相关进度报告等证明材料。承包商提交期中支付申请的时间为"after the end of each month（每个月末）"，相应地，承包商提交的证明材料即为当月的月报告。FIDIC合同没有规定承包商可以提交申请的确切时间，但以月为计时单位，承包商相对容易计算工程价值，即用工程量表中的单价乘当月完成的实际工程量。

承包商申请期中付款的报表应包括以下内容并按顺序排列：

（1）估算截止该月底完成的工程价值以及编制的承包商文件的合同价值，包括变更款，但不再列举以下各项包括的内容；

（2）按照第13.7款[因法律改变的调整]和第13.8款[因成本改变的调整]的规定应进行调价的任何款额；

（3）保留金按照投标函附录中规定的百分比与上述两项款额之和的乘积扣减，逐步扣减到投标函附录规定的保留金限额；

（4）按第14.2款[预付款]规定支付的预付款或已付还的预付款；

（5）按第14.5款[拟用于工程的永久设备和材料]的规定，为施工设备和材料增加或减少的款项；

（6）根据第20条[索赔、争端和仲裁]的规定得以追加或扣减的其他款项；

（7）前期支付证书确认扣除的款项。

理解上述报表的内容时需注意如下几点：

（1）承包商应估算当月实际完成的工程实体量和合同价值。合同价值包括工程所有相关价值事项，即当月实际完成的构成工程实体价值的所有项目，既包括承包商完成的工程内容（包括开办费、照管费和已发生的暂列金额），也包括分包商完成的一切与构成工程实体有关的工程项目。

（2）保留金需按合同规定逐步扣减至合同规定的限额。根据FIDIC合同条件的规定，保留金应从首次付款证书开始按每期支付工程款的10%扣留，直到累计扣留达到合同总额的5%为止，即保留金的限额为合同总价的5%。

（3）因生产设备和材料而产生的费用应当予以增减。在购入生产设备或材料时可能存在该物品需独立付款，有时承包商会要求雇主按照该付款要求来支付款项，就产生了第14.5款中的特殊付款方式。

14.4 Schedule of Payments（付款计划表）

If the Contract includes a schedule of payments specifying the instalments（分期付款）*in which the Contract Price will be paid, then unless otherwise stated in this schedule:*

(a) *the instalments quoted in this schedule of payments shall be the estimated contract values for the purposes of sub-paragraph (a) of Sub-Clause 14.3 [Application for Interim Payment Certificates];*

(b) *Sub-Clause 14.5 [Plant and Materials intended for the Works] shall not apply; and*

(c) *if these instalments are not defined by reference to the actual progress achieved in executing the Works, and if actual progress is found to be less than that on which this schedule of payments was based, then the Engineer may proceed in accordance with Sub-Clause 3.5 [Determinations] to agree or determine revised instalments, which shall take account of the extent to which progress is less than that on which the instalments were previously based.*

If the Contract does not include a schedule of payments, the Contractor shall submit non-binding（无约束的）*estimates of the payments which he expects to become due during each quarterly*（季度的）*period. The first estimate shall be submitted within 42 days after the Commencement Date. Revised estimates shall be submitted at quarterly intervals, until the Taking-Over Certificate has been issued for the Works.*

付款计划表是雇主给予承包商的按期付款承诺。雇主和承包商可在合同中列明付款计划表，确定分期付款的次数和时间，也可在工程进行过程中分阶段（如按季度）列出付款计划。

如果合同中包含付款计划表，其中详细规定了合同价格的分期支付方法，则应按照以下操作进行分期支付：(1) 承包商按第14.3款［期中付款证书的申请］的规定申请期中付款证书时，付款计划表中规定的分期付款额即为估算的合同价值，即该月完成的工程价值和承包商所编制的承包商文件的价值；(2) 第14.5款［拟用于工程的永久设备和材料］规定的生产设备和材料费用不包含在内；(3) 如编制付款计划表时依据的工程进度计划与实际进度不符，且实际进度慢于付款计划表中的进度计划，工程师可依据具体情况相应调整付款计划表。

如果合同中未包括付款计划表，承包商应提交工程季度用款估算书，但此估算书不具有约束力。首次提交估算书的时间应在开工日期后42天内，之后每季度提交一次修改的季度估算书。

在工程建设进度稳定的情况下，工程进度款的支付可按照付款进度表进行。但工程实际进度偏离计划进度，付款计划表也应当进行修改。本款并未说明当工程实际进度快于计划进度时，付款计划表如何修改。本款赋予了工程师调整付款计划的权利，承包商不应在工程实际进度落后于计划进度时仍坚持雇主按计划表付款。

14.5 Plant and Materials intended for the Works（拟用于工程的生产设备和材料）

If this Sub-Clause applies, Interim Payment Certificates shall include, under sub-paragraph (e) of Sub-Clause 14.3, (i) an amount for Plant and Materials which have been sent to the Site for incorporation in the Permanent Works, and (ii) a reduction when the contract value of such Plant and Materials is included as part of the Permanent Works under sub-paragraph (a) of Sub-Clause 14.3 [Application for Interim Payment Certificates].

If the lists referred to in sub-paragraphs (b)(i) or (c)(i) below are not included in the Appendix to Tender, this Sub-Clause shall not apply.

The Engineer shall determine and certify each addition if the following conditions are satisfied:

(a) The Contractor has:

(i) Kept satisfactory（保存）records (including the orders, receipts, Costs and use of Plant and Materials) which are available for inspection, and

(ii) submitted a statement of the Cost of acquiring and delivering the Plant and Materials to the Site, supported by satisfactory evidence;

And either:

(b) The relevant Plant and Materials:

(i) are those listed in the Appendix to Tender for payment when shipped（转运），

(ii) have been shipped to the Country, en route to the Site, in accordance with the Contract; and

(iii) are described in a clean shipped bill of lading（清洁装运提单）or other evidence of shipment, which has been submitted to the Engineer together with evidence of payment of freight（运费）and insurance, any other documents reasonably required, and a bank guarantee in a form and issued by an entity approved by the Employer in amounts and currencies equal to the amount due under this Sub-Clause: this guarantee may be in a similar form to the form referred to in Sub-Clause 14.2 [Advance Payment] and shall be valid until the Plant and Materials are properly stored on Site and protected against loss, damage or deterioration;

or

(c) The relevant Plant and Materials:

(i) are those listed in the Appendix to Tender for payment when delivered to the Site, and

(ii) have been delivered to and are properly stored on the Site, are protected against loss, damage or deterioration, and appear to be in accordance with the Contract.

The additional amount to be certified shall be the equivalent of eighty percent of the

14 Contractor Price and Payment（合同价格和付款）

Engineer's determination of the cost of the Plant and Materials (including delivery to Site), taking account of the documents mentioned in this Sub-Clause and of the contract value of the Plant and Materials.

The currencies for this additional amount shall be the same as those in which payment will become due when the contract value is included under sub-paragraph (a) of Sub-Clause 14.3 [Application for Interim Payment Certificates]. At that time, the Payment Certificate shall include the applicable reduction which shall be equivalent to, and in the same currencies and proportions as, this additional amount for the relevant Plant and Materials.

本款要求投标书附录列明所需预付费或运至现场后付费的有关生产设备（本款提到的"设备"均指永久设备）和材料。在此适用前提下，本款规定了工程材料设备款的计算方法和支付方式。按照第14.3款［期中付款证书的申请］的规定，期中付款证书中应包括用于预支已运至现场的永久设备和材料的部分款项，且当此类生产设备和材料构成永久工程的一部分时从预支款项中扣减。

当满足以下条件时，工程师应确定和确认向承包商预付设备和材料款：

（1）承包商已经准备好了一切符合要求、可供工程师随时检查的有关记录，包括该材料设备的订单、收据、金额和用途等资料。

（2）承包商已经提交了生产设备和材料的采购费用以及运送至现场的运费报表，并附有符合要求的证明材料。

（3）此类生产设备和材料是投标书附录中列明需预付费的设备材料。

（4）此类生产设备和材料按照合同规定已经运至工程所在国且已经在送往现场的路上。

（5）此类生产设备和材料有装运的清单或其他装运证明，连同运费、保险费支付证明和其他合理要求的证明文件，已经全部提交给了工程师。除此之外，承包商还需出具一份材料设备款保函，该保函的有效期应确保生产设备和材料在现场妥善存放并采取相应保护措施。

如果不能同时满足（3）、（4）、（5）三项条件，则必须同时满足以下（6）、（7）两项条件。

（6）此类生产设备和材料是投标书附录中列明需在装运至现场后付款的设备材料。

（7）此类生产设备和材料已装运至现场并且已经妥善存放，做好有效保护措施。

雇主应在一定条件下向承包商支付设备和材料预付款以协助承包商解决因采购大量设备材料而影响资金周转的问题，前提是此类设备和材料将用于永久工程。上述（3）、（4）、（5）三项可以简单理解为"款到发货"，这需要结合国际贸易市场上"信用证支付方式"来理解，即承包商下订单时需开具采购合同等额的银行信用证，以得到雇主预支付的设备材料款。一般情况下，只有承包商的银行账户有足够的存款，银行才能开出信用证，承包商才能凭借此保函从雇主处获取预付款，相互约束。上述（6）、（7）两项可以简单理解为"货到付款"。如，在实际大型机电安装项目中，永久设备采购费高昂，为了减轻承包商的资金压力，雇主往往不会在设备全部安装好后才付款，雇主可能分成若干次支付，每次支付实际采购款的一个百分数。

设备和材料预付款的支付货币，与其构成永久工程的一部分后应获得的支付货币相同。预付款额度为设备和材料购置时实际发生费用的 80%，由工程师根据承包商提交的证明材料及合同价值确定设备和材料的实际费用。此类预付款应在付款证书中相应扣减，扣减金额与预付金额的计算方法相同，且采用相同的货币和货币比例。专用条款中也可以约定其他扣减方式，如每次预付的设备和材料款在付款后的约定时间内（最长不超过 6 个月），每个月平均扣减等。

14.6　Issue of Interim Payment Certificates（期中付款证书的颁发）

　　No amount will be certified or paid until the Employer has received and approved the Performance Security. Thereafter, the Engineer shall, within 28 days after receiving a Statement and supporting documents, issue to the Employer an Interim Payment Certificate which shall state the amount which the Engineer fairly determines to be due, with supporting particulars.

　　However, prior to issuing the Taking-Over Certificate for the Works, the Engineer shall not be bound to issue an Interim Payment Certificate in an amount which would (after retention and other deductions) be less than the minimum amount of Interim Payment Certificates (if any) stated in the Appendix to Tender. In this event, the Engineer shall give notice to the Contractor accordingly.

　　An Interim Payment Certificate shall not be withheld for any other reason, although:

　　(a) if any thing supplied or work done by the Contractor is not in accordance with the Contract, the cost of rectification or replacement may be withheld until rectification or replacement has been completed; and/or

　　(b) if the Contractor was or is failing to perform any work or obligation in accordance with the Contract, and had been so notified by the Engineer, the value of this work or obligation may be withheld until the work or obligation has been performed.

　　The Engineer may in any Payment Certificate make any correction or modification that should properly be made to any previous Payment Certificate. A Payment Certificate shall not be deemed to indicate the Engineer's acceptance, approval, consent or satisfaction.

　　承包商应向工程师提交各项符合规定的报表资料，证明当月已实际完成的工程价值和应付款（详细解释参见第 14.3 款［期中付款证书的申请］）。工程师收到报表后应对承包商完成的工程内容的质量、数量以及各款项进行核查，如有疑问可要求承包商共同参与复核。工程师应在收到承包商的期中付款申请报表和证明材料后 28 天内，向雇主发出期中付款证书，说明应付金额并附详细说明。确认期中付款证书无误后按第 14.7 款［付款］的规定，雇主应向承包商执行期中付款（即支付进度款），但在雇主收到并认可承包商的履约担保之前，有权不对期中付款证书进行确认、不向承包商支付款额。

　　工程师在下述情况下，可不签发付款证书或扣留承包商报表中部分金额：

（1）如果一次期中付款证书金额扣除保留金等应扣款项后，净值小于投标书附录期中付款证书的最低额度，则工程师无需开具该期中付款证书，该款额接转下月，超过最低额度后一并支付，同时相应通知承包商；

（2）承包商提供的货物或实施的某项工作不符合合同要求时，工程师可以扣发相应的修正或重置费用，直到修正或重置工作完成；

（3）承包商未能按照合同规定执行工作或履行义务，并且工程师已经通知承包商执行工作或履行义务时，工程师可以扣发属于该部分工作的价值款项，直到承包商执行工作或履行义务。

在上述（2）、（3）项规定中，当承包商工作不符合合同要求或不执行合同要求的工作时，工程师有权扣留相关期中付款款项。尽管在上述两种情况下，工程师可以扣发部分款项，但不得以任何理由扣发期中付款证书。如，在浇筑混凝土时出现质量问题，工程师有权扣发混凝土浇筑工作的进度款，即从相关期中付款证书中暂时扣留这部分工作相应的款额，延迟到承包商解决这个质量问题后发放，而无权扣留该期中付款证书。

工程进度款支付证书属于临时支付证书，工程师有权对以前签发过的证书中出现的错误、遗漏或重复进行更正或修改，经过核查后将增加或扣减的金额纳入本次付款证书中。虽然工程师有权对承包商提交的期中付款申请报表及证明材料进行复核，甚至扣留部分款项，但并不代表工程师接受或者认可该付款申请及证明材料中所有的具体内容。即工程师签发期中付款证书仅表明工程师同意支付该进度款，并不代表其完全认同承包商完成的工作质量或其他。由于付款问题具有复杂性，工程中常常存在预付款、设备材料费预支等情况，在此情况下不存在此类"工程师接受、批准、同意或满意"的问题。故本款声明期中付款证书仅代表工程师对款项的认同，而非对全部付款项目的批准。

14.7 Payment（付款）

The Employer shall pay to the Contractor：

(a) the first instalment of the advance payment within 42 days after issuing the Letter of Acceptance or within 21 days after receiving the documents in accordance with Sub-Clause 4.2 [Performance Security] and Sub-Clause 14.2 [Advance Payment], whichever is later；

(b) the amount certified in each Interim Payment Certificate within 56 days after the Engineer receives the Statement and supporting documents; and

(c) the amount certified in the Final Payment Certificate within 56 days after the Employer receives this Payment Certificate.

Payment of the amount due in each currency shall be made into the bank account, nominated by the Contractor, in the payment country (for this currency) specified in the Contract.

FIDIC合同中，向承包商付款时，工程师开具付款证书，最终由雇主支付款额。本款主要对雇主支付工程款额的时间进行了规定：

（1）首次预付款应为雇主签发中标函后42天内，或承包商提交履约保证和预付款保函、预付款报表及相关证明材料后 21 天内，二者中取时间较晚的日期；

（2）在工程师收到承包商的期中付款申请报表和证明材料后 56 天内，雇主应将期中付款证书中证明的款额支付给承包商；

（3）雇主收到最终付款证书后 56 天内，应向承包商支付证书确定的款额。

雇主向承包商支付的每种货币对应的应付款额，均应汇入承包商在合同中列明的工程所在国的境内指定账户。付款到境外账户一般会产生国家外汇及金融管理问题，故在招标投标阶段及合同谈判时合同双方应就银行账户所在国问题进行明确说明，以确保付款问题不影响工程的顺利进行。

如付款期限超出本款的规定，应按照第 14.8 款 [延误的付款] 中规定的要求处理。

14.8　Delayed Payment（延误的付款）

If the Contractor does not receive payment in accordance with Sub-Clause 14.7 [Payment], the Contractor shall be entitled to receive financing charges（融资费用）compounded monthly on the amount unpaid during the period of delay. This period shall be deemed to commence on the date for payment specified in Sub-Clause 14.7 [Payment], irrespective（不考虑）(in the case of its sub-paragraph (b)) of the date on which any Interim Payment Certificate is issued.

Unless otherwise stated in the Particular Conditions, these financing charges shall be calculated at the annual rate of three percentage points above the discount rate（贴现率）of the central bank in the country of the currency of payment, and shall be paid in such currency.

The Contractor shall be entitled to this payment without formal notice or certification, and without prejudice to any other right or remedy.

支付工程款是雇主最根本的义务。如雇主没有按照第 14.7 款 [付款] 的规定向承包商支付工程款，承包商有权就未收到的工程款收取融资费用（即资金利息），从第 14.7 款 [付款] 规定的应付款日期开始按月计算复利，且无需再向雇主发出通知或出具证明。计算融资费用的利率按支付货币国家中央银行的贴现率加上 3%，且支付融资费用的货币也应当与应支付的货币相同。

如果雇主延误支付，承包商除有权获得该笔雇主应支付款额和融资费用外，还可享有其他权利和补偿，如暂停、甚至终止合同（见第 16 条 [承包商的暂停与终止]）。

14.9　Payment of Retention money（保留金的支付）

When the Taking-Over Certificate has been issued for the Works, the first half of the Retention Money shall be certified by the Engineer for payment to the Contractor. If a Taking-Over Certificate is issued for a Section or part of the Works, a proportion of the Retention Money shall be certified and paid. This proportion shag be two-fifths (40%) of the proportion calculated by dividing the estimated contract value of the Sec-

tion or part, by the estimated final Contract Price.

Promptly after the latest of the expiry dates of the Defects Notification Periods, the outstanding balance of the Retention Money shall be certified by the Engineer for payment to the Contractor. If a Taking-Over Certificate was issued for a Section, a proportion of the second half of the Retention Money shall be certified and paid promptly after the expiry date of the Defects Notification Period for the Section. This proportion shall be two-fifths (40%) of the proportion calculated by dividing the estimated contract value of the Section by the estimated final Contract Price.

However, if any work remains to be executed under Clause 11 [Defects Liability], the Engineer shall be entitled to withhold certification of the estimated cost of this work until it has been executed.

When calculating these proportions, no account shall be taken of any adjustments under Sub-Clause 13.7 [Adjustments for Changes in Legislation] and Sub-Clause 13.8 [Adjustments for changes in-cost].

保留金是按合同规定从承包商应得的工程进度款中相应扣减的一笔金额。设置保留金的目的是约束承包商严格履行合同义务，确保在工程保修期间承包商及时修复工程缺陷。缺陷责任期内，如果承包商未在工程师规定的时间修复缺陷工程部位，则雇主雇用他人完成该修复工作后所支付的费用从保留金中扣除。

如果工程未进行区段划分，则雇主应将所有保留金分两次支付给承包商，签发工程接收证书时支付一半，整个工程缺陷通知期满时支付剩下的一半。如果工程按区段划分，则保留金分三次支付，该单位工程签发接收证书时支付40%，该单位工程缺陷通知期满时支付40%，待最后一个单位工程缺陷通知期满后支付剩余20%。但如果是最后一个单位工程则只需要支付两次，签发接收证书时支付40%，缺陷通知期满后支付剩余60%。

根据第11条［缺陷责任］的规定，如果承包商仍有工作未完成，此时工程师有权在该项工作完成之前不签发该项工作的支付证书。该"未完成的工作"主要指签发接收证书后发现的工程缺陷，由于该缺陷部分的工程款已支付，工程师有权从本应支付的保留金中将该缺陷部分维修所需费用暂时扣留。

计算保留金支付金额时，比例的确定不考虑法律和费用变化导致的调价。

14.10 Statement of Completion（竣工报表）

Within 84 days after receiving the Taking-Over Certificate for the Works, the Contractor shall submit to the Engineer six copies of a Statement at completion with supporting documents, in accordance with Sub-Clause 14.3 [Application for Interim Payment Certificates], showing:

(a) the value of all work done in accordance with the Contract up to the date stated in the Taking-Over Certificate for the Works,

(b) any further sums which the Contractor considers to be due, and

(c) an estimate of any other amounts which the Contractor considers will become due *to him under the Contract. Estimated amounts shall be shown separately in this Statement at completion.*

The Engineer shall then certify in accordance with Sub-Clause 14.6 [Issue of Interim Payment Certificates].

承包商应在收到工程接收证书后84天内，按第14.3款［期中付款证书的申请］中规定的要求，向工程师提交竣工报表和证明材料，一式六份。竣工报表应列明：（1）到工程接收证书中指明的竣工日期为止，承包商按照合同要求已完成工程的最终价值；（2）承包商认为雇主到期应支付的其他款项，如要求的索赔款、应退还的部分保留金等；（3）承包商认为根据合同要求，雇主应支付的所有款项的估算总额（工程师还未审核同意），并在竣工结算表中单独列出，以便工程师签发付款证书。

工程师收到竣工报表后，应按照第14.3款［期中付款证书的申请］中的规定，对报表和证明材料及承包商的其他支付要求进行审查，并在收到竣工报表后28天内完成付款证书的签发。

承包商在竣工报表中可向雇主提出合同期满时需要支付的费用，以及工程款的估算额，以便雇主掌握仍需要支付的工程款数额，从而做好资金准备。

14.11 Application for Final Payment Certificate（最终付款证书的申请）

Within 56 days after receiving the Performance Certificate, the Contractor shall submit, to the Engineer, six copies of a draft final statement（最终报表草案）*with supporting documents showing in detail in a form approved by the Engineer：*

(a) the value of all work done in accordance with the Contract, and

(b) any further sums which the Contractor considers to be due to him under the Contract or otherwise.

If the Engineer disagrees with or cannot verify any part of the draft final statement, the Contractor shall submit such further information as the Engineer may reasonably require and shall make such changes in the draft as may be agreed between them. The Contractor shall then prepare and submit to the Engineer the final statement as agreed. This agreed statement is referred to in these Conditions as the "Final Statement".

However if, following discussions between the Engineer and the Contractor and any changes to the draft final statement which are agreed, it becomes evident that a dispute exists, the Engineer shall deliver to the Employer (with a copy to the Contractor) an Interim Payment Certificate for the agreed parts of the draft final statement. Thereafter, if the dispute is finally resolved under Sub-Clause 20.4 [Obtaining Dispute Adjudication Board' Decision] or Sub-Clause 20.5 [Amicable settlement], the Contract shall then prepare and submit to the Employer (with a copy to the Engineer) a Final Statement.

工程缺陷通知期满后，雇主需要将合同价格剩余的款额全部支付给承包商。在此之前，承包商需按照以下规定提交最终付款证书的申请：

（1）承包商应在收到履约证书后56天内，按照工程师批准的格式，向工程师提交最终报表草案，一式六份，同时附有证明材料。最终报表草案应列明：承包商根据合同要求完成的全部工作的价值；承包商认为雇主仍需要向其支付的款额，如剩余保留金及缺陷通知期内发生的索赔费用。

（2）如果工程师对最终报表草案存在异议，承包商应按工程师的要求提交补充证明材料，待工程师审核后与承包商协商，对最终报表草案进行适当的补充或修改后形成最终报表。

（3）如果工程师和承包商无法对最终报表草案协商一致，工程师应先就最终报表草案中无争议的部分向雇主开具期中付款证书，并呈送承包商一份。争议部分按照第20.4款［取得争端裁决委员会的决定］或第20.5款［友好解决］中的规定处理，承包商根据处理结果编制最终报表，提交给雇主并抄送工程师。

在上述第（3）项中，工程师就最终报表草案中"无争议的部分"向雇主开具期中付款证书，此处应当按期中付款证书的相关规定来处理此付款问题。一般情况下由工程师根据承包商报送的最终报表开具最终付款证书，雇主根据最终付款证书向承包商支付工程款（详细解释参见第14.13款［最终付款证书的颁发］）。由于工程合同争端的主体是雇主和承包商（详细解释参见第20.4款［取得争端裁决委员会的决定］或第20.5款［友好解决］），故就最终报表草案中"争议部分"的处理结果，承包商直接向雇主提交最终报表，抄报工程师即可。

14.12　Discharge（结清证明）

When submitting the Final Statement, the Contractor shall submit a written discharge which confirms that the total of the Final Statement represents full and final settlement of all moneys due to the Contractor under or in connection with the Contract. This discharge may state that it becomes effective when the Contractor has received the Performance Security and the outstanding balance of this total, in which event the discharge shall be effective on such date.

承包商在申请最终支付款项时，不但应提交最终报表，而且应提交一份书面结清证明，作为一种附加确认。结清证明应确认最终报表中的总额即为雇主应支付给承包商的全部、最终合同结算款额。雇主给予承包商履约保证，承包商对应地给予雇主结清证明，这是双方合同义务完全履行完毕的相互证明文件。只有当承包商收到履约保证和合同款余额时，结清证明才具有效力。实际工程中，承包商收到合同款余额的时间往往比收回履约保证的时间晚，此时结清证明应在合同款余额收回的日期当天生效。本款虽然未说明结清证明的提交对象，但根据第14.13款［最终付款证书的颁发］的规定来推定，结清证明应由承包商向工程师提交。

14.13　Issue of Final Payment Certificate（最终付款证书的颁发）

Within 28 days after receiving the Final Statement and written discharge in accordance with Sub-Clause 14.11 [Application for Final Payment Certificate] and Sub-Clause

14.12 [Discharge], the Engineer shall issue, to the Employer, the Final Payment Certificate which shall state:

(a) the amount which is finally due, and

(b) after giving credit to the Employer for all amounts previously paid by the Employer and for all sums to which the Employer is entitled, the balance (if any) due from the Employer to the Contractor or from the Contractor to the Employer, as the case may be.

If the Contractor has not applied for a Final Payment Certificate in accordance with Sub-Clause 14.11 [Application for Final Payment Certificate] and Sub-Clause 14.12 [Discharge], the Engineer shall request the Contractor to do so. If the Contractor fails to submit an application within a period of 28 days, the Engineer shall issue the Final Payment Certificate for such amount as he fairly determines to be due.

在承包商按照第14.11款［最终付款证书的申请］和第14.12款［结清证书］的规定提交最终报表和结清证明后28天内，工程师应向雇主开具最终付款证书，并说明雇主最终应支付的款额，以及在扣除已支付的款额、有权得到的款额后仍需支付的款额和仍可得的款额。

承包商未按规定申请最终付款证书时，工程师应要求承包商提出申请。如承包商在28天期限内仍未提交申请，工程师应自行合理决定最终支付金额并签发相应的最终付款证书。实质上，最终付款证书的核算内容基本只有"预留金"。如果工程预留金最后并无争议或变更，在承包商不提交最终付款证书申请的情况下，工程师可按合同规定核算预留金，并在28天后签发最终付款证书。

14.14 Cessation of Employer's Liability（雇主责任的终止）

The Employer shall not be liable to the Contractor for any matter or thing under or in connection with the Contract or execution of the Works, except to the extent that the Contractor shall have included an amount expressly for it:

(a) in the Final Statement and also

(b) (except for matters or things arising after the issue of the Taking-Over Certificate for the Works) in the Statement at completion described in Sub-Clause 14.10 [Statement at Completion].

However, this Sub-Clause shall not limit the Employer's liability under his indemnification obligations（保障义务）, or the Employer's liability in any case of fraud（欺骗）, deliberate default（有意违约）or reckless misconduct（轻率的不当行为）by the Employer.

一般情况下，当雇主向承包商退回履约保证，即说明承包商的合同义务已经履行完毕。除了最终报表和竣工报表包含的相应款项的相关事宜外（竣工报表可以不包括接收证书签发后发生的事宜），雇主不再对合同中其他任何事宜承担责任，即承包商的竣工报表和结清证明是雇主合同付款责任中止的承包商确认文件。

本款的规定不影响雇主在保障承包商方面的责任，也不影响因雇主不当行为而应承担的责任。

除了接收证书签发后发生的工作可以不包括在竣工报表中,对于没有包含在竣工报表和最终报表中的工作,雇主不再承担支付责任。参考第 14.11 款 [最终付款证书的申请] 的规定,雇主责任的终止有以下情形:(1) 如果工程师与承包商商定了最终报表中的款额,雇主在向承包商支付完最终付款证书中所示款额后,即为履行完合同义务;(2) 如果工程师与承包商对最终报表草案中的款额未达成一致,雇主在支付完无争议部分的款额以及争端裁定的款额后,即为履行完合同义务;(3) 承包商须在竣工报表中列明其认为雇主应支付的款项,包括到期的款项、未到期款项的估算以及索赔款,因为一旦漏项,即使在最终报表中补充,工程师也不一定认可(签发接收证书后增加的工作除外)。

14.15　Currencies of Payment(支付的货币)

The Contract Price shall be paid in the currency or currencies named in the Appendix to Tender. Unless otherwise stated in the Particular Conditions, if more than one currency is so named, payments shall be made as follows:

(a) if the Accepted Contract Amount was expressed in Local Currency only:

(i) the proportions or amounts of the Local and Foreign Currencies, and the fixed rates of exchange to be used for calculating the payments, shall be as stated in the Appendix to Tender, except as otherwise agreed by both Parties;

(ii) payments and deductions under Sub-Clause 13.5 [Provisional Sums] and Sub-Clause 13.7 [Adjustments for Changes in Legislation] shall be made in the applicable currencies and proportions; and

(iii) other payments and deductions under sub-paragraphs (a) to (d) of Sub-Clause 14.3 [Application for Interim Payment Certificates] shall be made in the currencies and proportions specified in sub-paragraph (a)(i) above;

(b) payment of the damages specified in the Appendix to Tender shall be made in the currencies and proportions specified in the Appendix to Tender;

(c) Other payments to the Employer by the Contractor shall be made in the currency in which the sum was expended by the Employer, or in such currency as may be agreed by both Parties;

(d) if any amount payable by the Contractor to the Employer in a particular currency exceeds the sum payable by the Employer to the Contractor in that currency, the Employer may recover the balance of this amount from the sums otherwise payable to the Contractor in other currencies; and

(e) if no rates of exchange are stated in the Appendix to Tender, they shall be those prevailing on the Base Date and determined by the central bank of the Country.

雇主在招标文件中一般要求投标人的投标价格以工程所在国流通的币种表示。但在国际工程中,由于国际工程的参与方可能来自多个国家,投标人往往会在投标文件中提出某些外币需求。因此工程实际支付中常会涉及大量货币汇兑问题。

合同价格应以投标函附件中指定的一种或多种货币支付。当工程合同采用一种以上货币支付且专用条件中无其他说明时：

（1）如果中标合同金额仅用当地币表示，则

1）当地币和各外币的支付数额或比例，以及计算支付款时采用的固定费率，均应按投标书附录中的规定执行，或由双方另行商定；

2）根据第 13.5 款［暂列金额］和第 13.7 款［因法律改变的调整］规定的付款，即暂定金额和因法律改变产生的调价，均应按照适用的货币和货币比例支付；

3）支付期中付款时，除因法律改变产生的调价外，凡是属于第 14.3 款［期中付款证书的申请］中前四项规定所列的内容，均应按照上述 1）项的规定执行。

（2）投标书附录中规定的损害赔偿费应以投标书附录中规定的货币以及货币比例支付。

（3）承包商应支付给雇主的其他费用，应按照雇主当时所花费的货币来支付，或者由双方另行商定。

（4）如果承包商应支付给雇主的某种货币的款额，超过雇主按该货币支付给承包商的款额，承包商可从雇主以其他币种支付的款额中收回其中的差额。

（5）如果投标书附录中未规定汇率，则使用的汇率应为由工程所在国中央银行确定的基准日期当天的汇率。

外币兑换率应在投标书附录中进行规定，如果投标书附录中无此规定，则按工程所在国中央银行确定的基准日期当天的汇率计算。

思考题

1. 简述合同价格的定义、性质及确定办法。
2. 工程预付款的支付前提是什么？
3. 工程师首次发出分期付款的期中付款证书需具备什么条件？
4. 简述工程预付款的支付和付还程序。
5. 简述期中付款证书的申请程序及报表内容。
6. 简述分期付款的支付范围。
7. 简述向承包商预付设备和材料款的条件。
8. 简述工程材料设备款的计算方法和支付方式。
9. 简述期中付款证书的颁发程序。
10. 简述工程师可不签发付款证书或扣留部分金额的情况。
11. 简述雇主支付工程款的时间延误支付的处理办法。
12. 简述保留金的支付方法。
13. 简述竣工报表的提交时间和内容。
14. 简述承包商申请最终付款证书的程序。
15. 简述最终报表草案中"争议部分"的处理办法。
16. 结清证明何时生效？

17. 简述最终付款证书的颁发时间及其说明内容。
18. 雇主责任的终止有哪些情形？
19. 简述合同价格的支付办法。
20. 如何确定所应支付的外币的汇率？

15 Termination by Employer（由雇主终止）

作为合同当事人，雇主和承包商均有义务按照合同的约定履行合同，但出于自身原因或对方违约等情况下，雇主和承包商均具有终止合同的权利。FIDIC 施工合同条件通用条款的 15 条和 16 条分别说明了由雇主和承包商终止合同条件、程序、影响及相关后续工作。

本章要求：了解雇主有权终止合同的情形；

了解雇主终止合同的程序；

了解雇主终止合同后如何对承包商已完成的工作进行估价和支付。

15.1 Notice to Correct（通知改正）

If the Contractor fails to carry out any obligation under the Contract, the Engineer may by notice require the Contractor to make good the failure and to remedy it within a specified reasonable time.

工程建设过程中，如果承包商未履行合同中规定其应当履行的义务，工程师可通知其改正，并要求承包商在规定的合理时间内完成该义务。

工程建设是工程各参与方履行合同约定义务的过程。对于雇主而言，一般在招标投标阶段采用资格预审来排除不合格承包商。签订工程合同后，如果承包商在合同履行过程中不按合同规定执行义务，显然不能任由其继续违约，雇主有权终止合同。但雇主在选择终止合同前应给予承包商改正的机会。工程师应以书面通知的形式向承包商给予"警告"，要求承包商限期改正，否则就将终止合同。

15.2 Termination by Employer（由雇主终止）

The Employer shall be entitled to terminate the Contract if the Contractor:

(a) fails to comply with Sub-Clause 4.2 [Performance Security] or with a notice under Sub-Clause 15.1 [Notice to Correct],

(b) abandons the Works or otherwise plainly demonstrates the intention not to continue performance of his obligations under the Contract,

(c) without reasonable excuse fails:

(i) to proceed with the Works in accordance with Clause 8 [Commencement, Delays and Suspension], or

(ii) to comply with a notice issued under Sub-Clause 7.5 [Rejection] or Sub-Clause 7.6 [Remedial Work], within 28 days after receiving it,

(d) subcontracts the whole of the Works or assigns（转让）the Contract without the re-

15 Termination by Employer（由雇主终止）

quired agreement,

(e) becomes bankrupt（破产）or insolvent（无力偿债）, goes into liquidation（停业清理）, has a receiving or administration order made against him, compounds with his creditors, or carries on business under a receiver, trustee or manager for the benefit of his creditors, or if any act is done or event occurs which (under applicable Laws) has a similar effect to any of these acts or events, or

(f) gives or offers to give (directly or indirectly) to any person any bribe, gift, gratuity, commission or other thing of value, as an inducement or reward:

(i) for doing or forbearing to do any action in relation to the Contract; or

(ii) for showing or forbearing to show favour or disfavour to any person in relation to the Contract, or if any of the Contractor's Personnel, agents or Subcontractors gives or offers to give (directly or indirectly) to any person any such inducement or reward as is described in this sub-paragraph (f). However, lawful inducements and rewards to Contractor's Personnel shall not entitle termination.

In any of these events or circumstances, the Employer may, upon giving 14 days' notice to the Contractor, terminate the Contract and expel the Contractor from the Site. However, in the case of sub-paragraph (e) or (f), the Employer may by notice terminate the Contract immediately.

The Employer's election to terminate the Contract shall not prejudice any other rights of the Employer, under the Contract or otherwise.

The Contractor shall then leave the Site and deliver any required Goods, all Contractor's Documents, and other design documents made by or for him, to the Engineer. However, the Contractor shall use his best efforts to comply immediately with any reasonable instructions included in the notice (i) for the assignment of any subcontract, and (ii) for the protection of life or property or for the safety of the Works.

After termination, the Employer may complete the Works and/or arrange for any other entities to do so. The Employer and these entities may then use any Goods, Contractor's Documents and other design documents made by or on behalf of the Contractor.

The Employer shall then give notice that the Contractor's Equipment and Temporary Works will be released to the Contractor at or near the Site. The Contractor shall promptly arrange their removal, at the risk and cost of the Contractor. However, if by this time the Contractor has failed to make a payment due to the Employer, these items may be sold by the Employer in order to recover this payment. Any balance of the proceeds shall then be paid to the Contractor.

承包商发生下列违约行为时，雇主有权终止合同：

（1）承包商未遵守第 4.2 款［履约担保］的规定，未在收到中标函 28 天内向雇主提交履约保证或者未能使履约保证持续有效；或承包商未遵守第 15.1 款［通知改正］的规定，未能根据合同规定履行义务，且在工程师发出通知要求限期改正后仍然不履行合同义务。

(2) 承包商放弃工程,或者有明确的意愿表示不再继续履行合同义务。

(3) 在没有合理解释的情况下,承包商未能遵守第8条[开工、延误和暂停]的规定,拖延开工;或根据第7.5款[拒收]和第7.6款[修补工作]的相关规定,承包商在收到工程师关于质量问题方面的通知后28内未进行整改。

(4) 未经雇主同意,承包商擅自将整个工程分包或将整个合同转让给他人。

(5) 承包商处于破产、无力偿还债务、停业清算或其他无法控制其财产的类似状况。

(6) 承包商或承包商人员、代理商、分包商直接或间接向工程有关人员行贿,诱导其做出不当行为或不实言论,但是承包商给予承包商人员的合法奖励不在此列。

当任何上述(1)~(6)项所述情况发生后,雇主可以在终止合同前14天向承包商发出通知,要求承包商离开现场。但如果发生上述(5)、(6)项所述情况,雇主可以立即终止合同。雇主对合同的终止,不影响雇主根据合同应享有的其他权利。

合同终止后,承包商应立即撤离现场,按工程师的要求将有关物品、承包商文件以及其他设计文件提交给工程师。承包商仍应按雇主的通知,尽最大努力协助雇主进行分包合同转让、保护人员和财产安全以及保护工程本身的安全。雇主可以自行或安排他人继续完成工程,且有权使用原承包商提交的有关物品、文件。雇主应通知承包商,将承包商的设备和在现场或附近的临时工程返还给承包商,由其自费运走,风险自负。如果承包商还有应支付给雇主的款额未付清,则雇主有权出售承包商的设备和临时工程,并在扣除欠款后应将余额返还给承包商。

本款对雇主终止合同的情况给出了完整清晰的规定。雇主终止合同的原因可以分为两种:承包商在工程上表现出的违约情况或承包商公司出现重大经济危机。对于上述第(6)项关于"贿赂"的处理原则,FIDIC合同表现出了非常严格的处罚措施,即立即终止合同。实际上,对于工程建设过程中"贿赂"事项的发生、定性、处理并不简单,但如此清晰明确的合同规定对于承包商及其雇员、分包商来说,都是一种有力的制约。

15.3 Valuation at Date of Termination (终止日期时的估价)

As soon as practicable after a notice of termination under Sub-Clause 15.2 [Termination by Employer] has taken effect, the Engineer shall proceed in accordance with Sub-Clause 3.5 [Determinations] to agree or determine the value of the Works, Goods and Contractor'Documents, and any other sums due to the Contractor for work executed in accordance with the Contract.

在雇主根据第15.2款[由雇主终止]的规定向承包商发出的合同终止通知生效后,工程师应尽快按照第3.5款[确定]的规定,确定工程、货物和承包商文件的价值,以及根据合同规定承包商应得的所有款项。

本款要求工程师对承包商按照合同完成的全部工作的价值进行估价。该"全部工作"主要指承包商实际完成的工程、采购的永久设备和材料、为工程编制的有关文件和设计图纸等。

15.4 Payment after Termination （终止后的付款）

After a notice of termination under Sub-Clause 15.2 (Termination form the Employer) has taken effect, the Employer may:
　　(a) proceed in accordance with Sub-Clause 2.5 [Employer's Claims],
　　(b) withhold（扣留）further payments to the Contractor until the costs of execution, completion and remedying of any defects, damages for delay in completion (if any), and all other costs incurred by the Employer, have been established, and/or
　　(c) recover from the Contractor any losses and damages incurred by the Employer and any extra costs of completing the Works, after allowing for any sum due to the Contractor under Sub-Clause 15.3 [Valuation at Date of Termination]. After recovering any such losses, damages and extra costs, the Employer shall pay any balance to the Contractor.

在根据第15.2款[由雇主终止]的规定发出的合同终止通知生效后，雇主可以采取下列措施来处理承包商应得的工程款项：
　　（1）对于合同终止导致雇主遭受的损失，可以按照第2.5款[雇主的索赔]的规定向承包商提出索赔；
　　（2）在计算出完成工程的费用之前，扣发本应向承包商支付的一切款项；
　　（3）在整个工程完成的费用确定后，从承包商处收回雇主因合同终止遭受的一切损失，其中包括雇主为完成剩余工程多支付的费用、工程未按照原计划完工导致雇主遭受的竣工延误损失等；
　　（4）在从终止合同后工程师估价的工程款中扣除上述款项后，将余额支付给承包商。
　　合同终止后，雇主通常需要雇用其他承包商继续施工。由于工程实施的连续性被打断，完成整个工程的费用一般会高于原承包商的投标价格，完成工程的最终工期也会迟于原定竣工日期，这些均为合同终止会给雇主带来的损失。雇主应在工程完成后计算出原合同终止后遭受的损失，从原承包商工程款中扣除。但"损害赔偿"有时无法用统一标准来界定，由此会引起雇主和承包商对于此款项额度的争议。除了扣发合同终止时本应向承包商支付的工程款项外，雇主仍暂扣承包商的履约保证和已经扣发的部分保留金，雇主可以按照履约保证的规定向担保银行提出赔偿请求。

15.5 Employer' Entitlement to Termination （雇主终止的权利）

The Employer shall be entitled to terminate the Contract, at any time for the Employer' convenience, by giving notice of such termination to the Contractor. The termination shall take effect 28 days after the later of the dates on which the Contractor receives this notice or the Employer returns the Performance Security. The Employer shall not terminate the Contract under this Sub-Clause in order to execute the Works himself or to arrange for the Works to be executed by another contractor.

After this termination, the Contractor shall proceed in accordance with Sub-Clause 16.3 [Cessation of Work and Removal of Contractor's Equipment] and shall be paid in accordance with Sub-Clause 19.6 [Optional Termination, Payment and Release].

工程进行过程中，如果雇主自身出现较大的财务危机或该工程项目在某些方面不可行，导致雇主无力继续工程的建设或雇主认为停止建设才能防止损失进一步扩大，雇主同样有权终止合同。

雇主可以"出于自身利益"的考虑，随时通知承包商终止合同。在承包商收到终止通知后，或者在雇主返还履约保证后第28天生效，取较晚的日期为准。但如果雇主是为了自行实施工程建设或雇用他人实施，本款不适用。终止合同后，承包商应根据第16.3款［停止工作和承包商设备的撤离］的规定执行，雇主按照第19.6款［自主选择终止、付款和解除］的规定向承包商支付工程款。

本款中涉及的合同终止是由于雇主自身原因造成的，此时由于合同终止产生的损失和后果也由雇主承担，如向承包商支付因合同终止使承包商遭受的损失赔偿等。

思考题

1. 如果承包商未履行合同中规定其应当履行的义务或违约，应当如何处理？
2. 简述雇主有权终止合同的情形。
3. 简述雇主终止合同的程序以及合同终止后承包商应尽的义务。
4. 雇主终止合同后如何对承包商已完成的工作进行估价和支付？
5. 简述雇主终止合同的权利范围及可能承担的后果。

16 Suspension and Termination by Constractor（由承包商暂停和终止）

当承包商违约导致雇主终止合同，雇主可以扣发应支付给承包商的工程款项，可以扣押承包商所有在现场的设备、临时工程，可以扣留履约保函，以保护雇主的权益。当雇主违约，尤其是当雇主出现严重财务危机时，承包商同样享有采取相应措施保护自身权益的权利。

本章要求：了解雇主发生哪些行为时承包商有权暂停工作；
了解雇主发生哪些行为时承包商有权终止合同；
了解承包商终止合同后的义务；
了解终止合同后承包商可获得的赔偿。

16.1 Contractor's Entitlement to Suspend Work（承包商暂停工作的权利）

If the Engineer fails to certify in accordance with Sub-Clause 14.6 [Issue of Interim Payment Certificates] or the Employer fails to comply with Sub-Clause 2.4 [Employer's Financial Arrangements] or Sub-Clause 14.7 [Payment], the Contractor may, after giving not less than 21 days' notice to the Employer, suspend work (or reduce the rate（速度） of work) unless and until the Contractor has received the Payment Certificate, reasonable evidence or payment, as the case may be and as described in the notice.

The Contractor's action shall not prejudice his entitlements to financing charges under Sub-Clause 14.8 [Delayed Payment] and to termination under Sub-Clause 16.2 [Termination by Contractor].

If the Contractor subsequently receives such Payment Certificate, evidence or payment (as described in the relevant Sub-Clause and in the above notice) before giving a notice of termination, the Contractor shall resume normal working as soon as is reasonably practicable.

If the Contractor suffers delay and/or incurs Cost as a result of suspending work (or reducing the rate of work) in accordance with this Sub-Clause, the Contractor shall give notice to the Engineer and shall be entitled subject to Sub-Clause 20.1 [Contractor's Claims] to：

(a) an extension of time for any such delay, if completion is or will be delayed, under Sub-Clause 8.4 [Extension of Time for Completion], and

(b) payment of any such Cost plus reasonable profit, which shall be included in the Contract Price.

After receiving this notice, the Engineer shall proceed in accordance with Sub-Clause 3.5 [Determinations]to agree or determine these matters.

如果雇主由于自身的财务危机而影响支付能力或拖延承包商应得的工程款，给承包商造成极大的经济困难，影响工程的顺利进行，承包商可按照本款的规定，通过下列措施来保护自己的权益：

（1）如果工程师未能按照第14.6款［期中付款证书的颁发］的规定，在规定时间内签发付款证书，或者雇主未能在规定时间内提供资金证明（详见第2.4款［雇主的资金安排］的规定）或支付工程款（详见第14.7款［付款］的规定），承包商在向雇主发出通知21天后，有权放慢工作进度或暂停工作进展，直到收到付款证书、雇主资金证明或工程款。承包商暂停工作时，仍享有获得延误工程款的融资费用以及终止合同的权利。

（2）如果承包商在发出终止合同通知前，已经收到了上述各类证书、证明或付款，则承包商应尽快恢复工作。

（3）如果承包商因放慢工作速度或暂停工作，而造成工期延长或费用损失，承包商有权向工程师发出通知，根据第20.1款［承包商的索赔］的规定索赔，要求延长竣工日期（详见第8.4款［竣工日期的延长］的规定）和费用补偿，索赔费用时可要求雇主将该费用损失和合理利润计入合同价格中进行支付。工程师收到该索赔通知后，应按第3.5款［确定］的规定予以商定或确定。

工程合同中雇主最根本的义务是在规定时限内向承包商支付工程款。一旦雇主在支付工程款方面违反合同规定，承包商享有四种权利：放慢工作速度；暂停工作进展；获得延误工程款的融资费用（利息等）、工期索赔及费用补偿（加上相应利润）；终止合同（详见第16.2款［由承包商终止］的规定）。

实际上，由于雇主原因导致工程暂停还有其他情况，比如雇主与政府协调不力导致工程证照不齐、政府临时管制导致工程无法施工等。对于承包商来说，上述由于"雇主或当局（如政府）"导致工程暂停的情况，都是工程建设过程中需要面对的风险。FIDIC施工合同中，只有雇主不按规定支付工程款时，承包商才有权利"主动"暂停工作。

16.2　Termination by Contractor（由承包商终止）

The Contractor shall be entitled to terminate the Contract if:

(a) the Contractor does not receive the reasonable evidence within 42 days after giving notice under Sub-Clause 16.1 [Contractor's Entitlement to Suspend Work]in respect of a failure to comply with Sub-Clause 2.4 [Employer's Financial Arrangements],

(b) the Engineer fails, within 56 days after receiving a Statement and supporting documents, to issue the relevant Payment Certificate,

(c) the Contractor does not receive the amount due under an Interim Payment Certificate within 42 days after the expiry of the time stated in Sub-Clause 14.7 [Payment] within which payment is to be made (except for deductions in accordance with Sub-Clause 2.5 [Employer's Claims]),

(d) the Employer substantially fails to perform his obligations under the Contract,

(e) the Employer fails to comply with Sub-Clause 1.6 [Contract Agreement] or Sub-Clause 1.7 [Assignment],

(f) a prolonged suspension affects the whole of the Works as described in Sub-Clause 8.11 [Prolonged Suspension], or

(g) the Employer becomes bankrupt or insolvent, goes into liquidation, has a receiving or administration order made against him, compounds with his creditors, or carries on business under a receiver, trustee or manager for the benefit of his creditors, or if any act is done or event occurs which (under applicable Laws) has a similar effect to any of these acts or events.

In any of these events or circumstances, the Contractor may, upon giving 14 days' notice to the Employer, terminate the Contract: However, in the case of subparagraph (f) or (g), the Contractor may by notice terminate the Contract immediately.

The Contractor's election to terminate the Contract shall not prejudice any other rights of the Contractor, under the Contract or otherwise.

承包商有权在下列情况发生时,终止合同:

(1) 雇主不提供资金证明,承包商发出暂停工作的通知后42天内,承包商仍然未收到任何合理证明;

(2) 工程师在收到承包商提交的报表及证明材料后56天内未签发有关付款证书;

(3) 根据第14.7款[付款]的规定,在期中付款证书到期后42天内,承包商仍未收到该付款证书所指的雇主应付款项(按照第2.5款[雇主的索赔]规定扣除的部分除外);

(4) 雇主严重不履行合同规定的义务;

(5) 雇主不按合同规定签署合同协议书(详细解释参见第1.6款[合同协议书]),或违反合同转让的规定(详细解释参见第1.7款[权益转让]);

(6) 按照第8.11款[拖长的暂停]的规定,如果由于非承包商责任暂停工程超过84天,并且在承包商要求复工的请求下28天内工程师未给予许可,而该工程部分的暂停影响到整个工程的进行;

(7) 雇主处于破产、无力偿还债务或停业清算等严重财务危机的状况。

当上述(1)~(7)项所述情况发生后,承包商可以在向雇主发出通知14天后终止合同。但如果上述(6)、(7)项所述情况发生后,承包商可以立即终止合同。承包商对合同的终止,不影响其根据合同应享有的其他任何权利。

由于雇主违约导致承包商终止合同,尤其是当雇主出现严重财务危机时,承包商应采取保护自己权益的措施。本款虽然规定承包商可以享有多项权利,但赋予承包商的保护措施却有限。在国际工程中,承包商投标决策时应考虑的重要内容就是项目资金来源,即雇主的支付能力。

16.3 Cessation of Work and Removal of Contractor's Equipment (停止工作和承包商设备的撤离)

After a notice of termination under Sub-Clause 15.5 [Employer's Entitlement to Termination], Sub-Clause 16.2 [Termination by Contractor] or Sub-Clause 19.6 [Optional

Termination, Payment and Release] has taken effect, the Contractor shall promptly:

(a) cease all further work, except for such work as may have been instructed by the Engineer for the protection of life or property or for the safety of the Works,

(b) hand over Contractor's Documents, Plant, Materials and other work, for which the Contractor has received payment, and

(c) remove all other Goods from the Site, except as necessary for safety, and leave the Site.

在合同终止通知（详见第15.5款［雇主终止的权利］、第16.2款［由承包商终止］、第19.6款［自主选择终止，付款和解除］的规定）生效后，承包商应尽快停止一切进一步的工作，但为了保护生命财产安全或工程安全，工程师指定承包商继续进行的工作除外。同时，承包商应向雇主移交已得到付款的文件、生产设备、材料或其他工作，从现场运走除了安全所需之外的所有物品，并撤离现场。

即合同终止后，承包商应及时运走除了安全所需的、属于自己的所有相关设备及材料。

16.4 Payment on Termination（终止时的付款）

After a notice of termination under Sub-Clause 16.2 [Termination by Contractor] has taken effect, the Employer shall promptly:

(a) return the Performance Security to the Contractor,

(b) pay the Contractor in accordance with Sub-Clause 19.6 [Optional Termination, Payment and Release], and

(c) pay to the Contractor the amount of any loss of profit or other loss or damage sustained by the Contractor as a result of this termination.

在根据第16.2款［由承包商终止］的规定发出合同终止通知后，雇主应立即将履约担保退还给承包商。按照第19.6款［自主选择终止、付款和解除］的规定，雇主应向承包商支付已完成工程、已采购永久设备和材料的相应款项，并承担承包商人员、设备、临时工程遣返回国的费用。同时，雇主还应向承包商赔偿因合同终止遭受的利润损失。

思考题

1. 简述承包商暂停工作的情形。
2. 雇主未按时支付工程款或违约时承包商如何保护自身权益？
3. 简述承包商有权终止合同的情形。
4. 分别说明雇主和承包商在承包商终止合同后应履行的义务。

17 Risk and Responsibility (风险与职责)

本条从保障免责事项、承包商的照管责任、雇主风险及其后果、第三方维权以及合同当事人的责任限度出发，对合同当事人双方各自所需承担的责任、义务及风险进行了"原则性规定"，明确双方在 FIDIC 施工合同中的责任划分。合同当事人对其中所涉及职责的争议，常导致索赔事件的发生。

本章要求：了解承包商和雇主互为保障的内容；

　　　　　　了解承包商对工程的照管职责；

　　　　　　了解雇主的风险以及风险后果；

　　　　　　了解工程所涉及的知识产权和工业产权以及保护措施；

　　　　　　了解合同双方的赔偿责任限度。

17.1 Indemnities (保障)

The Contractor shall indemnify and hold harmless the Employer, the Employer's Personnel, and their respective agents, against and from all claims, damages, losses and expenses (including legal fees and expenses) in respect of:

(a) bodily injury, sickness, disease or death, of any person whatsoever arising out of or in the course of or by reason of the Contractor's design (if any), the execution and completion of the Works and the remedying of any defects, unless attributable to any negligence, wilful act or breach of the Contract by the Employer, the Employer's Personnel, or any of their respective agents, and

(b) damage to or loss of any property, real or personal (other than the Works), to the extent that such damage or loss:

　　(i) arises out of or in the course of or by reason of the Contractor's design (if any), the execution and completion of the Works and the remedying of any defects, and

　　(ii) is attributable to any negligence, wilful act or breach of the Contract by the Contractor, the Contractor's Personnel, their respective agents, or anyone directly or indirectly employed by any of them.

The Employer shall indemnify and hold harmless the Contractor, the Contractor's Personnel, and their respective agents, against and from all claims, damages, losses and expenses (including legal fees and expenses) in respect of (1) bodily injury, sickness, disease or death, which is attributable to any negligence, wilful act or breach of the Contract by the Employer, the Employer's Personnel, or any of their respective agents, and (2) the matters for which liability may be excluded from insurance cover, as described in sub-paragraphs (d)(i), (ii) and (iii) of Sub-Clause 18.3 [*Insurance Against Injury to*

Persons and Damage to Property].

本款是关于保障和保证不受损害事项的规定，或称免责条款，旨在保障合同对方"免受规定事项所导致的任何索赔、损害赔偿、损失或开支（包括法律费用和开支）带来的伤害"，即限制或免除合同当事人在规定事项下的责任。

在承包商的设计和施工过程中，出现下列两种情况时，承包商应保证雇主及其一切相关人员免于承担此类事件导致的索赔、损害赔偿费、损失和开支：

（1）如果出现了任何人员伤亡或患病，除非此类事件是由雇主及其相关人员渎职、恶意行为或违约行为导致。

（2）如果由于承包商及其人员的渎职、恶意行为或违约行为，导致任何财产、不动产或动产（工程本身除外）受到损害或损失。

相应地，如果由于雇主及其相关人员的渎职、恶意行为或违约行为导致人员伤亡或患病，以及发生了第18.3款［人身伤害和财产损害险］规定的意外责任事件，雇主也应保证承包商及其一切相关人员免于承担这类事件导致的索赔、损害赔偿费、损失和开支。

保障合同对方"免受规定事项所导致的任何索赔、损害赔偿、损失或开支（包括法律费用和开支）带来的伤害"，不但要求责任方承担一切由"免责"事项引发的后果，同时要求保证"免除"合同另一方在此类事件中可能受到的"任何伤害"。承包商的"免责"责任包括"人员和财产保护"，而雇主的"免责"责任只包括"人员保护"。这主要是因为在工程施工过程中，承包商的"财产"一般不会由于雇主原因导致损失，且按照第17.2款［承包商对工程的照管］中的规定，承包商对工程具有照管权，由此雇主对承包商"财产"方面不应承担任何责任。

上述工程中的大部分风险属于合同要求承包商投保的内容（详见第18条［保险］的规定）。当此类事情发生时，承包商一般可以从保险公司处获得赔偿。但对于保险内容没有覆盖或覆盖不足的情况，则由责任方自行承担。

17.2 Contractor's Care of the Works（承包商对工程的照管）

The Contractor shall take full responsibility for the care of the Works and Goods the Commencement Date until the Taking-Over Certificate is issued (or is deemed to be issued under Sub-Clause 10.1 [Taking Over of the Works and Sections]) for the Works, when responsibility for the care of the Works shall pass to the Employer. If a Taking-Over Certificate is issued (or is so deemed to be issued) for any Section or part of the Works, responsibility for the care of the Section or part shall then pass to the Employer.

After responsibility has accordingly passed to the Employer, the Contractor shall take responsibility for the care of any work which is outstanding on the date stated in a Taking-Over Certificate, until this outstanding work has been completed.

If any loss or damage happens to the Works, Goods or Contractor's Documents during the period when the Contractor is responsible for their care, from any cause not listed in Sub-Clause 17.3 [Employer's Risks], the Contractor shall rectify the loss or damage at the Contractor's risk and cost, so that the Works, Goods and Contractor's Documents con form with the Contract.

The Contractor shall be liable for any loss or damage caused by any actions performed by the Contractor after a Taking-Over Certificate has been issued. The Contractor shall also be liable for any loss or damage which occurs after a Taking-Over Certificate has been issued and which arose from a previous event for which the Contractor was liable.

工程实施过程中需要对工程现场及已完工程进行照管,以防工程及相关物品受到损失(如偷盗、人为破坏等)。

本款对承包商的工程照管权进行了以下规定:

(1) 从开工到工程接收证书的签发,承包商应对工程及相关物品的照管承担全部责任。

(2) 工程接收证书签发后,照管责任移交给雇主;单位工程或部分工程的接收证书签发后,照管责任虽然移交给了雇主,但承包商仍需负责对未完成工程的照管,直至任何扫尾工作完成。

(3) 如在承包商照管工程期间,由于第17.3款[雇主的风险]中所列风险以外的原因,工程、物品、承包商文件发生损失或损害,承包商应承担一切责任。

(4) 如在接收证书签发后,由于承包商原因导致工程或物品受到损失,承包商应为该损失负责;如在接收证书签发后工程和物品发生的损失,是由于接收证书签发之前承包商负责的原因所致,承包商仍须对该损失负责。

承包商的工程照管权自工程开工之日起,至颁发工程接收证书(或按照第10.1款[工程和单位工程的接收]的规定视为颁发)止。承包商对已完工和未完工的工程均负有照管责任。任何在承包商照管期间非雇主原因造成的工程损害,均由承包商承担风险和费用。

17.3 Employer's Risks (雇主的风险)

The risks referred to in Sub-Clause 17.4 below are:

(a) war, hostilities (whether war be declared or not), invasion, act of foreign enemies,

(b) rebellion, terrorism, revolution, insurrection, military or usurped power, or civil war, within the Country,

(c) riot, commotion or disorder within the Country by persons other than the Contractor's Personnel and other employees of the Contractor and Subcontractors,

(d) munitions of war, explosive materials, ionising radiation or contamination by radio-activity, within the Country, except as may be attributable to the Contractor's use of such munitions, explosives, radiation or radio-activity,

(e) pressure waves caused by aircraft or other aerial devices traveling at sonic or supersonic speeds,

(f) use or occupation by the Employer of any part of the Permanent Works, except

as may be specified in the Contract,

(g) design of any part of the Works by the Employer's Personnel or by others for whom the Employer is responsible, and

(h) any operation of the forces of nature which is Unforeseeable or against which an experienced contractor could not reasonably have been expected to have taken adequate preventative precautions.

工程中应由雇主承担的风险有：

（1）战争、敌对行动（不论是否发生战争）、入侵、外敌行动等；

（2）工程所在国内部发生叛乱、恐怖主义、革命、暴乱、军事政变或篡夺政权、内战等动乱；

（3）非承包商、承包商人员、分包商、分包商人员在工程所在国引起的动乱；

（4）工程所在国内由于战争军火、爆炸性材料、放射性物质造成的离子辐射或污染等造成的威胁，除了承包商本身使用此类物资导致的情况之外；

（5）飞机及其他飞行装置造成的压力波；

（6）除合同规定外雇主使用或占有的部分永久工程；

（7）由雇主或雇主指定人员负责的工程设计；

（8）一个经验丰富的承包商无法合理预见并采取措施防范的任何自然力的作用。

由雇主承担的风险，大致可分为政治风险、社会风险、污染及外力风险、雇主行为风险等，除此之外还有雇主的经济风险（详见第13.8款［因成本调整的改变］、第14.15款［支付货币］的规定）、法律风险（详见第13.7款［因法律改变的调整］的规定）等。

【例17.1】在某国一公路项目工程中，合同双方签订EPC合同。工程施工过程中，当地村民以工程阻碍出行为由阻止承包商继续施工，要求承包商必须增加人行天桥解决村民的出行问题。承包商出于时间和成本考虑未答应村民的要求，当地村民因此问题未解决扰乱现场施工致使承包商数日无法正常施工。承包商因此遭受的工期延误、费用损失可否向雇主索赔？

本案例应分两种情况来考虑：

第一种情况，工程并未影响当地村民的日常出行，则上述案例情况属于第17.3款［雇主的风险］规定的"非承包商、承包商人员、分包商、分包商人员在工程所在国引起的动乱"，属于雇主风险。承包商可根据第17.4款［雇主风险的后果］、第18.2款［工程和承包商的设备保险］等条款的规定向雇主索赔。

第二种情况，工程确实影响当地村民的日常出行。参看第4.10款［现场数据］、第4.14款［避免干扰］等条款的规定，承包商在投标时就应当对现场周边环境进行调查，应当预见上述案例所示情况并在报价中加以考虑，因而这种风险也由承包商承担。

17.4 Consequences of Employer's Risks（雇主风险的后果）

If and to the extent that any of the risks listed in Sub-Clause 17.3 above results in loss or damage to the Works, Goods or Contractor's Documents, the Contractor shall promptly give notice to the Engineer and shall rectify this loss or damage to the extent required by the Engineer.

If the Contractor suffers delay and/or incurs Cost from rectifying this loss or dam-

age, the Contractor shall give a further notice to the Engineer and shall be entitled subject to Sub-Clause 20.1 [Contractor's Claims] to:

(a) an extension of time for any such delay, if completion is or will be delayed, under Sub-Clause 8.4 [Extension of Time for Completion], and

(b) payment of any such Cost, which shall be included in the Contract Price. In the case of sub-paragraphs (f) and (g) of Sub-Clause 17.3 [Employer's Risks], reasonable profit on the Cost shall also be included.

After receiving this further notice, the Engineer shall proceed in accordance with Sub-Clause 3.5 [Determinations] to agree or determine these matters.

一旦发生第17.3款［雇主的风险］中列明的任何雇主风险，并对工程及相关物品或承包商文件造成损失或损害，承包商应立即向工程师发出通知，并根据工程师的要求进行修复或补救。因修复此类损失或损害延误的工期或增加的成本，承包商应进一步通知工程师，有权根据相关规定进行工期和费用索赔，如因雇主行为风险（第17.3条款［雇主的风险］中第6、7项）导致承包商遭受工期或费用损失，承包商有权向雇主索赔相应利润。

第17.3条款［雇主的风险］中"战争、敌对行动及工程所在国内部动乱"与第19条［不可抗力］的规定及处理原则相近。在FIDIC合同条件下，事件属于"雇主风险"还是"不可抗力"，关键是承包商是否在合同中提出此类事件由雇主承担风险。对于承包商来说，"雇主风险"和"不可抗力"理论上的不同，在于承包商是否能获得融资费用的补偿。

【例17.2】某承包商以5000万美元总价中标一国际工程项目，与雇主签订了工程施工合同，合同工期为36个月（扣除雨季）。施工期间，工程所在国发生了大规模骚乱，武装分子闯进了项目工地，大肆抢夺，幸未造成人员伤亡，但抢走了一辆丰田吉普车、一辆三菱双排座皮卡车、一套光学测量仪、一台电源稳压装置和部分放在车上的一些日常所用的劳动工具。政府出动了正规部队进行围剿，事件才得到平息，致使工地停工一周。承包商清算损失财物价值后欲向雇主索赔工期及费用。

参考第13.3款［雇主的风险］及本款［雇主风险的后果］的相关规定，雇主应承担诸如社会动乱等政治风险，如果该政治风险对工程、物品或承包商文件造成损失，承包商有权进行工期和费用索赔。在上述案例中，工程所在国内部的社会动乱致使承包商停工一周并损失财产若干，承包商应立即通知工程师并按工程师的要求修正此类损失或损害，由此修复工作产生的费用或工期延误，承包商应向工程师作进一步汇报，提出索赔后由工程师确定。虽然此类风险是雇主风险，引发的后果主要由雇主承担，这并不意味着承包商不负担任何相关义务。相反，承包商应有义务在风险发生后立即通知工程师，并按工程师的指令实施补救，与这些义务相应的才是承包商获得索赔工期和费用的权利。

17.5 Intellectual and Industrial Property Rights（知识产权与工业产权）

In this Sub-Clause, "infringement" means an infringement (or alleged infringement) of any patent, registered design, copyright, trade mark, trade name, trade secret or other intellectual or industrial property right relating to the Works; and "claim" means a claim (or proceedings pursuing a claim) alleging an infringement.

Whenever a Party does not give notice to the other Party of any claim within 28 days of receiving the claim, the first Party shall be deemed to have waived any right to in-

demnity under this Sub-Clause.

The Employer shall indemnify and hold the Contractor harmless against and from any claim alleging an infringement which is or was:

 (*a*)*an unavoidable result of the Contractor's compliance with the Contract*, *or*

 (*b*)*a result of any Works being used by the Employer*:

  (*i*)*for a purpose other than that indicated by*, *or reasonably to be inferred from*, *the Contract*, *or*

  (*ii*)*in conjunction with any thing not supplied by the Contractor*, *unless such use was disclosed to the Contractor prior to the Base Date or is stated in the Contract.*

The Contractor shall indemnify and hold the Employer harmless against and from any other claim which arises out of or in relation to (*i*)*the manufacture*, *use*, *sale or import of any Goods*, *or* (*ii*)*any design for which the Contractor is responsible.*

If a Party is entitled to be indemnified under this Sub-Clause, *the indemnifying Party may* (*at its cost*)*conduct negotiations for the settlement of the claim*, *and any litigation or arbitration which may arise from it. The other Party shall*, *at the request and cost of the indemnifying Party*, *assist in contesting the claim. This other Party* (*and its Personnel*)*shall not make any admission which might be prejudicial to the indemnifying Party*, *unless the indemnifying Party failed to take over the conduct of any negotiations*, *litigation or arbitration upon being requested to do so by such other Party.*

"侵权"是侵犯（或被指侵犯）与工程有关的任何专利权、注册设计及设计方案、版权、商标、商号商品名称、商业机密等知识产权或工业产权。"索赔"是就上述侵犯知识产权或工业产权的行为，指被侵权的一方向侵权方为赔偿而进行的诉讼。如果一方在收到对方的侵权赔偿后 28 天内，未向对方发出索赔通知，则该方（指第一方）应被视为放弃了本款规定的任何保障。

雇主对承包商的侵权保障，在下列情况下，承包商不承担侵权责任，由雇主负责侵权赔偿：

（1）如果承包商的侵权是履行合同义务不可避免的，由此产生侵权索赔；

（2）如果雇主不遵从合同中规定或合同隐含规定的目的使用工程，而导致侵权索赔；

（3）如果合同中未规定，或未在基准日期前向承包商说明，在此情况下雇主使用工程，同时使用了非承包商提供的物品，从而导致侵权索赔。

相应地，承包商对雇主的侵权保障，在下列两种情况下，雇主不承担责任，由承包商负责侵权赔偿：

（1）与工程建设有关的任何使用（制造、使用、销售或进口）物品导致了侵权索赔；

（2）由承包商负责的工程设计导致了侵权索赔。

如果一方根据本款规定有权受到保障，但引起谈判、诉讼或仲裁的侵权索赔由该保障方负责，则该保障方应自费组织与提出侵权索赔的权利人进行谈判、诉讼或仲裁的相关事宜。在处理过程中，如果保障方要求另一方协助并负担该另一方因协助产生的费用时，该另一方应协助其对侵权索赔进行答辩。在答辩时，该另一方不得做出对保障方不利的承认，除非在该另一方要求保障方对此类事件谈判或协助谈判的情况下，保障方未参与，即未接办任何谈判、诉讼或仲裁事宜。

例如，如果有第三权利方向承包商提出侵权索赔，且引起索赔的原因本应由雇主负责，雇主应替承包商进行赔偿谈判，同时可以要求承包商协助。但如果雇主在本应负责的情况下不参与谈判事宜，则承包商可以答应该第三权利方提出的索赔请求，但由雇主支付给其赔偿金。

本款规定了在工程建设过程中，雇主和承包商各自负责的侵权责任。本款对"知识产权和工业产权"侵权问题的解决方式，属于第 17.1 款［保障］中的"免责"责任。承包商使用雇主文件以及雇主使用承包商文件，所涉及的知识产权与工业产权问题，已在第 1.10 款［雇主使用承包商文件］及第 1.11 款［承包商使用雇主文件］中详细规定，而本款涉及的侵权问题是指由第三权利方主张的知识产权或工业产权。虽然 FIDIC 合同规定，由合同当事人使用第三权利方所属权利而引起的争议，使用方应保证合同对方"免责"，但是 FIDIC 合同同样规定了在"免责"前提下，"免责"方协助解决问题的责任。

17.6 Limitation of Liability（责任限度）

Neither Party shall be liable to the other Party for loss of use of any Works, loss of profit, loss of any contract or for any indirect or consequential loss or damage which may be suffered by the other Party in connection with the Sub-Clause 16.4 ［Payment on Termination］and Sub-Clause 17.1 ［Indemnities］.

The total liability of the Contractor to the Employer, under or in connection with the Contract other than under Sub-Clause 4.19 ［Electricity, Water and Gas］, Sub-Clause 4.20 ［Employer's Equipment and Free-Issue Material］, Sub-Clause 17.1 ［Indemnities］ and Sub-Clause 17.5 ［Intellectual and Industrial Property Rights］, shall not exceed the sum stated in the Particular Conditions or (if a sum is not so stated) the Accepted Contract Amount.

This Sub-Clause shall not limit liability in any case of fraud, deliberate default or reckless misconduct by the defaulting Party.

理解合同当事人的责任限度时需注意如下几点：

（1）合同当事人使用工程中的损失（即工程使用功能方面的损失），利润损失，合同损失，或是一切其他与合同有关、直接或间接引发的损失，合同双方中责任方对受害方的赔偿责任，仅限于第 16.4 款［终止时的付款］和第 17.1 款［保障］中的规定。

本项虽然适用于合同双方，但主要适用于雇主对承包商的最大赔偿责任，即当雇主违约时，承包商最多可获得的因雇主违约导致终止合同时的赔偿，以及雇主对承包商的保障等经济责任。

（2）除根据第 4.19 款［电、水和燃气］、第 4.10 款［雇主设备和免费供应的材料］、第 17.1 款［保障］、第 17.5 款［知识产权和工业产权］的规定外，承包商对雇主的全部责任不超过专用条件中规定的限额，若专用条件中没有规定则不得超过中标合同金额。

本项明确了承包商的总责任限度，即除了承包商应支付雇主提供的水电和燃气费、雇主的设备使用费，给予雇主保障的经济责任，知识产权等方面的保障之外，承包商的总责任应按专用条件中的规定为限,若无规定则以中标合同金额为限。

(3) 如果违约方存在欺诈、故意违约或不轨行为,则本款不限制责任方在此情况下的一切责任。

本条规定的是合同当事人一方在执行合同过程中的最大赔偿责任。但合同规定的赔偿限度与相关适用法律相违背时,合同的规定不具有约束力。

思考题

1. 简述雇主和承包商互为保障的内容及免责范围。
2. 简述承包商的工程照管权的定义、期限、责任范围。
3. 简述雇主风险的分类和具体情形。
4. 试比较雇主风险和不可抗力的差异和区别方法。
5. 简述工程中所涉及的知识产权和工业产权。
6. 分别说明雇主和承包商的侵权责任及侵权保障。
7. 简述责任限度的定义,及合同当事人的赔偿责任限度。

18 Insurance（保险）

风险贯穿在国际工程实施的整个过程之中，因此，风险管理也是整个工程管理的一个重要组成部分。工程建设过程中面临的高风险导致工程保险成为风险方法的重要手段。国际工程中，为了避免某些风险可能带来的巨大损失对工程做出不利影响，工程合同一般要求对工程以及相关事项进行保险。

本章要求：了解合同对保险的总体要求；
　　　　　　了解工程、设备以及承包商的设备的保险要求；
　　　　　　了解对第三方人员以及财产的保险要求；
　　　　　　了解对承包商的人员的保险要求。

18.1 General Requirements for insurances（有关保险的一般要求）

In this Clause, "insuring Party（保险方）" means, for each type of insurance, the Party responsible for effecting and maintaining the insurance specified in the relevant Sub-Clause.

Wherever the Employer is the insuring Party, each insurance shall be effected with insurers and in terms approved by the Employer. These terms shall be consistent with any terms agreed by both Parties before the date of letter of Acceptance. This agreement of terms shall take precedence over the provisions of this Clause.

Wherever the Employer is the insuring Party, each insurance shall be effected with insurers and in terms consistent with the details annexed to the Particular Conditions.

If a policy is required to indemnify joint insured, the cover shall apply separately to each insured as though a separate policy had been issued for each of the joint insured. If a policy indemnifies additional joint insured, namely in addition to the insured specified in this Clause, (i) the Contractor shall act under the policy on behalf of these additional joint insured except that the

Employer shall act for Employer's Personnel, (ii) additional joint insured shall not be entitled to receive payments directly from the insurer or to have any other direct dealings with the insurer, and (iii) the insuring Party shall require all additional joint insured to comply with the conditions stipulated in the policy.

Each policy insuring against loss or damage shall provide for payments to be made in the currencies required to rectify the loss or damage. Payments received from insurers shall be used for the rectification of the loss or damage.

The relevant insuring Party shall, within the respective periods stated in the Appendix to Tender (calculated from the Commencement Date), submit to the other Party:

(a) evidence that the insurances described in this Clause have been effected, and

(b) copies of the policies for the insurances described in Sub-Clause 18.2 [Insurance for Works and Contractor's Equipment] and Sub-Clause 18.3 [Insurance against Injury to Persons and Damage to Property]

When each premium is paid, the insuring Parry shall submit evidence of payment to the other Party. Whenever evidence or policies are submitted, the insuring Party shall also give notice to the Engineer.

Each Party shall comply with the conditions stipulated in each of the insurance policies. The insuring Party shall keep the insurers informed of any relevant changes to the execution of the Works and ensure that insurance is maintained in accordance with this Clause.

Neither Party shall make any material alteration to the terms of any insurance without the prior approval of the other Parry. If an insurer makes (or attempts to make) any alteration, the Party first notified by the insurer shall promptly give notice to the other Party.

If the insuring Party fails to effect and keep in force any of the insurances it is required to effect and maintain under the Contract, or fails to provide satisfactory evidence and copies of policies in accordance with this Sub-Clause, the other satisfactory may (at its option and without prejudice to any other right or remedy) effect insurance for the relevant coverage and pay the premiums due. The insuring Party shall pay the amount of these premiums to the other Party, and the Contract Price shall be adjusted accordingly.

Nothing in this Clause limits the obligations, liabilities or responsibilities of the Contractor or the Employer, under the other terms of the Contract or otherwise. Any amounts not insured or not recovered from the insurers shall be borne by the Contractor and/or the Employer in accordance with these obligations, liabilities or responsibilities. However, if the insuring Party fails to effect and keep in force an insurance which is available and which it is required to effect and maintain under the Contract, and the other Party neither approves the omission nor effects insurance for the coverage relevant to this default, any moneys which should have been recoverable under this insurance shall be paid by the insuring Party.

Payments by one Party to the other Party shall be subject to Sub-Clause 2.5 [Employer's Claims] or Sub-Clause 20.1 [Contractor's Claims], as applicable.

本款主要说明办理保险时的投保条件；保险单的性质；非保险方的知情权；双方遵守保险单的义务；保险方没有按规定投保的补救方法等。本款规定的是有关保险的总体要求，无论承包商或者雇主作为保险方，都应遵守。

在本款中，"保险方"是指根据相关条款的规定投保各种类型的保险并保持其有效的一方。FIDIC 施工合同条件中规定，保险可以由雇主来办理，也可以由承包商来办理，具体合同中的保险方应根据项目具体情况确定，可以在专用条件或投标函附录中明确规定。

在国际工程中，通常承包商为投保方，但也有雇主和承包商分别负责保险一定范围的情况。目前，国际上的一些大型工程，当承包商较多时，雇主方更愿意去统一办理涉及工程的某些险种，如：工程一切险，承包商只需为其人员和施工设备办理保险即可。对雇主来说，此做法不但可以降低保险费，而且还可以便于统一管理。至于具体由哪一方负责投保，这取决于雇主在招标时的总体策略和项目的实际情况。本款没有明确规定哪一方为投保方，因此具体的投保方应在专用条件相应条款中明确。

若承包商作为保险方，应按照雇主批准的承保人及条件办理保险。这些条件应与中标函颁发日期前达成的条件保持一致，且此达成一致的条件优先于本条的各项规定，若商定的投保条件与本款规定不一致，以双方商定为准。若雇主作为保险方，应按照专用条件后所附详细说明的承保人及条件办理保险。如果某一保险单被要求对联合被投保人进行保障，则任何一方在发生与自己有关的投保事件时，均可单独运用保单，提出索赔。其效力应和向每一联合被投保人颁发了一张保单的效力一致。若保单中被保险人同时为雇主和承包商双方，且保单中还包括其他被保险人，如：分包商、工程师、工程其他参与方或相关人员，雇主可为雇主人员进行保险索赔，其他情况由承包商负责处理，其他被保险人无权直接与保险公司处理索赔事宜。

投保方应要求保单中的其他被保险人遵守保单的规定。在涉及财产损失赔偿时，为防范损失或损害，对于所办理的每份保单应规定按照修复损失所需的货币种类进行补偿。从承保人处得到的赔偿金应用于修复和弥补上述损失或损害，专款专用。

在投标函附录中规定的各个期限内（从开工日期算起），相应的保险方应向另一方提交保险已生效的证明以及所办理的保单的副本。保险方在支付每一笔保险费后，应将支付证明提交给另一方。在提交此类证明或投保单的同时，保险方还应将此类提交事宜通知工程师。双方都应遵守保单的规定。

一旦工程实施过程中情况发生变化，与投保时提供给保险公司的不一样，投保方应通知保险公司，作出相应安排，以便保单持续有效。合同双方都不得单方面对保险单作出较大修改。保险方应将工程实施过程中发生的任何有关的变动通知给承保人，并确保保险条件与本款的规定一致。没有另一方的事先批准，任一方都不得对保险条款作出实质性的变动。如果承保人作出（或预作出）任何实质性的变动，承保人先行通知的一方应立即通知另一方。若保险公司提出修改，先得到通知的一方应立即通知另一方。当工程的情况发生变化，与投保时提供给保险公司的工程信息不一致时，应及时通知保险公司，并对原保单作出相应修改。如果需要追加保险事项，则可提出附加申请，作为原保险的一部分，并由保险公司以批单（endorsement）的形式确认。另外，若发生保险索赔情况，应按保单的规定，及时通知保险公司，同时保护好事故现场和记录，以便保险公司的理赔估算师（adjuster）评定损失。

如果保险方未能按合同要求办理保险并使之保持有效，或未能按本款要求提供令另一方满意的保险生效证明和保险单的副本，则另一方可以（按他自己的决定且不影响任何其他权利或补救的情况下）为此类违约相关的险别办理保险并支付应交的保险费。保险方应向另一方支付此类保险费的款额，同时合同价格应作相应的调整。

本条规定不限制合同的其余条款或其他文件所规定的承包商或雇主的义务、职责或责任。即使办理了保险，合同双方的义务和责任仍应认真履行，并不因保险而减少。任何未保险或未能从承保人处收回的款额，应由承包商或雇主根据上述义务、职责或责任相应负担。但是，如果保险方未能按合同要求办理保险并使之保持有效，并且另一方没有批准将其作为一项工作的删减，也没有为此类违约相关的险别办理保险，则任何通过此类保险本可收回的款项应由保险方支付给另一方。若发生未能从保险公司得到赔付的情况，则双方根据合同的义务和责任来承担该损失。若由于一方的过失，发生不能从保险公司得到赔偿的情况，则损失由该方承担，若由于投保方没有办理本应办理的保险，则本应能从保险公司办理获得的赔偿，应由投保方赔付。

一方向另一方进行的支付必须遵循第 2.5 款【雇主的索赔】或第 20.1 款【承包商的索赔】（如适用）的规定。

本款中出现的相关保险术语，解释如下：

保单（insurance policy）：保单是保险人（公司）根据投保人的投保申请和两方的协商所签发的保险凭证，是保险合同的核心部分，包括的内容由：被保险人名称、保险标的、责任范围、保险金额、保险期限、保险费以及缴费方式。

投保人（insurance applicant）：投保人是向保险公司申请保险的一方，一般为被保险人。

被保险人（insured）：被保险人是发生保险范围的事件后，其损失可以从保险公司索偿的那一方，是保险的受益人。

联合被保险人（joint insured）：联合保险人是一个保单中的共同受益人。在保险业中，保险公司允许在同一个保单中加入两个甚至更多受益人。在国际工程保险中，通常一个保险单中的受益人包括承包商和雇主，有的也包括分包商和工程师。他们统称联合被保险人。

18.2 Insurance for Works and Contractor's Equipment（工程和承包商设备的保险）

The insuring Party shall insure the Works, Plant, Materials and Contractor's Documents for not less than the full reinstatement cost including the costs of demolition. removal of debris and professional fees and profit. This insurance shall be effective from the date by which the evidence is to be submitted under sub-paragraph (a) of Sub-Clause 18.1 [General Requirements for Insurances], until the date of issue of the Taking-Over Certificate for the Works.

The insuring Party shall maintain this insurance to provide cover until the date of issue of the Performance Certificate, for loss or damage for which the Contractor is liable arising from a cause occurring prior to the issue of the Taking-Over Certificate, and for loss or damage caused by the Contractor in the course of any other operations (including those under Clause 11 [Defects Liability]).

The insuring Party shall insure the Contractor's Equipment for not less than the full replacement value, including delivery to Site. For each item of Contractor's Equipment, the insurance shall be effective while it is being transported to the Site and until it is no longer required as Contractor's Equipment.

Unless otherwise stated in the Particular Conditions, insurances under this Sub-Clause:

(a) shall be effected and maintained by the Contractor as insuring Party,

(b) shall be in the joint names of the Parties, who shall be jointly entitled to receive payments from the insurers, payments being held or allocated between the Parties for the sole purpose of rectifying the loss or damage,

(c) shall cover all loss and damage from any cause not listed in Sub-Clause 17.3 [Employer's Risks],

(d) shall also cover loss or damage to a part of the Works which is attributable to the use or occupation by the Employer of another part of the Works, and loss or damage from the risks listed in sub-paragraphs (c), (g) and (h) of Sub-Clause 17.3 [Employer's Risks], excluding (in each case) risks which are not insurable at commercially reasonable terms, with deductibles per occurrence of not more than the amount stated in the Appendix to Tender (if an amount is not so stated, this sub-paragraph (d) shall not apply), and

(e) may however exclude loss of, damage to, and reinstatement of:

(i) a part of the Works which is in a defective condition due to a defect in its design, materials or workmanship (but cover shall include any other parts which are lost or damaged as a direct result of this defective condition and not as described in sub-paragraph (ii) below),

(ii) a part of the Works which is lost or damaged in order to reinstate any other part of the Works if this other part is in a defective condition due to a defect in its design, materials or workmanship,

(iii) a part of the Works which has been taken over by the Employer, except to the extent that the Contractor is liable for the loss or damage, and

(iv) Goods while they are not in the Country, subject to Sub-Clause 14.5 [Plant and Materials intended for the Works].

If, more than one year after the Base Date, the cover described in sub-paragraph (d) above ceases to be available at commercially reasonable terms, the Contractor shall (as insuring Party) give notice to the Employer, with supporting particulars. The Employer shall then (i) be entitled subject to Sub-Clause 2.5 [Employer's Claims] to payment of an amount equivalent to such commercially reasonable terms as the Contractor should have expected to have paid for such cover, and (ii) be deemed, unless he obtains the cover at commercially reasonable terms to have approved the omission under Sub-Clause 18.1 [General Requirements for Insurances].

工程本身、相关永久设备、材料以及承包商的施工设备是工程保险的核心内容。就工程本身、永久设备、材料以及承包商的设备各项的保险，本款作出了详细规定。

保险方应为工程、永久设备、材料以及承包商的文件投保，该保险的最低限额应不少于全部复原成本，包括补偿拆除和移走废弃物以及专业服务费和利润。

此类保险的有效期应一直保持到签发履约证书的日期为止，即：应自根据第18.1款［有关保险的总体要求］提交证明之日起，至颁发工程的接收证书之日止保持有效。对于颁发接收证书前发生的由承包商负责的原因以及承包商在进行任何其他作业（包括第11条［缺陷责任］所规定的作业）过程中造成的损失或损坏，保险方应将此类保险的有效期延至履约证书颁发的日期。

保险方应为承包商的设备投保，该保险的最低限额应不少于全部重置价值（包括运至现场）。此类保险覆盖的范围是：对于每项承包商的设备，该保险应保证其运往现场的过程中以及设备停留在现场或附近期间，均处于被保险之中，直至不再将其作为承包商的设备使用为止。除非专用条件中另有规定，否则本款规定的保险：（1）应由承包商作为保险方办理并使之保持有效；（2）应以合同双方联合的名义投保，联合的合同双方均有权从承保人处得到支付，仅为修复损失或损害的目的，该支付的款额由合同双方共同占有或在各方间进行分配；（3）应补偿除第17.3款［雇主的风险］所列雇主的风险之外的任何原因所导致的所有损失和损害；（4）还应补偿由于雇主使用或占用工程的另一部分而对工程的某一部分造成的损失或损害，以及第17.3款［雇主的风险］所列雇主的风险所导致的损失或损害（对于每种情况，不包括那些根据商业合理条款不能进行保险的风险），每次发生事故的扣减不大于投标函附录中注明的款额；（5）将不包括下述情况导致的损失、损害，以及将其恢复原状：（i）工程的某一部分由于其设计、材料或工艺的缺陷而处于不完善的状态（但是保险应包括直接由此类不完善的状态（下述（ii）中的情况除外）导致的工程的任何其他部分的损失和损害），（ii）工程的某一部分所遭受的损失或损害是为了修复工程的任何其他部分所致，而此类其他部分由于其设计、材料或工艺的缺陷而处于不完善的状态，（iii）工程的某一部分已移交给雇主，但承包商负责的损失或损害除外，（iv）根据第14.5款［用于永久工程的永久设备和材料］，货物还未运抵工程所在国时。

如果在基准日期后超过一年时间，上述（4）所述保险由于商业合理条件（commercially reasonable terms）而无法再获得，则承包商（作为保险方）应通知雇主，并提交详细证明文件。雇主应该随即（1）有权根据第2.5款［雇主的索赔］，获得款额与此类商业合理条件相等的支付，作为承包商为此类保险本应作出的支付，以及（2）被认为（除非他依据商业合理条件办理了保险）已经根据第18.1款［有关保险的总体要求］，批准了此类工作的删减。

国际工程保险市场中，较为常见的几类基本保险险种有：建筑工程一切险（Construction All Risks）、安装工程一切险（Erection All Risks）、雇主责任险（Employer's Liability Insurance）、第三人责任险（Third Party Liability Insurance）等，通常投保建筑工程一切险和安装工程一切险时常附加第三人责任险。保险人投保时，可以根据实际情况和保险公司协商，对标准保单和保险条件进行灵活修改，增加或删除某些内容。实际工程中，除少数工程会单独对承包商设备投保外，此类保险可包含在建筑工程一切险中。

18.3 Insurance against Injury to Persons and Damage under to Property（人身伤害和财产损害险）

The insuring Party shall insure against each Party's liability for any loss, damage, death or bodily injury which may occur to any physical property (except things insured Sub-Clause 18.2 [Insurance for Works and Contractor's Equipment]) or to any person (except persons insured under Sub-Clause 18.4 [Insurance for Contractor's Personnel]), which may arise out of the Contractor's performance of the Contract and occurring before the issue of the Performance Certificate.

This insurance shall be for a limit per occurrence of not less than the amount stated in the Appendix to Tender, with no limit on the number of occurrences. If an amount is not stated in the Appendix to Tender, this Sub-Clause shall not apply.

Unless otherwise stated in the Particular Conditions, the insurances specified in this Sub-Clause:

(a) shall be effected and maintained by the Contractor as insuring Party,

(b) shall be in the joint names of the Parties,

(c) shall be extended to cover liability for all loss and damage to the Employer's property (except things insured under Sub-Clause 18.2) arising out of the Contractor's performance of the Contract, and

(d) may however exclude liability to the extent that it arises from:

(i) the Employer's right to have the Permanent Works executed on, over, under, in or through any land, and to occupy this land for the Permanent Works,

(ii) damage which is an unavoidable result of the Contractor's obligations to execute the Works and remedy any defects, and

(iii) a cause listed in Sub-Clause 17.3 (Employer's Risks), except to the extent that cover is available at commercially reasonable.

工程实施过程中，可能会引起项目以外的财产和人员损失或伤亡，合同中通常要求办理相关保险以防范此类风险的发生。

保险方应为履行合同引起的，并在履约证书颁发之前发生的任何物资和财产（第18.2款[工程和承包商的设备的保险]的规定被投保的物品除外）的损失或损害，或任何人员（根据第18.4款[承包商人员的保险]规定的被投保的人员除外）的伤亡引起的每一方的责任办理保险。该保险每一次事故的最低限额应不少于投标函附录中规定的数额，对于事故的数目并无限制。如果在投标函附录中没有注明此类金额，则本款将不再适用。

除非专用条件中另有规定，本款中规定的保险：(1) 应由承包商作为保险方办理并使之保持有效；(2) 应以合同双方联合的名义投保；(3) 应保证弥补由于承包商履行合同而导致的雇主的财产的一切损失和损害（根据第18.2款的规定被投保的物品除外），以及(4) 不承保下述情况引起的责任：(i) 雇主有权在任何土地上，越过该土地，在该土地之下、之内或穿过其间实施永久工程，并为永久工程占有该土地，(ii) 承包商履行实施工程并修补缺陷而导致的无法避免的损害，(iii) 第 17.3 款[雇主的风险]所列雇主的风险所导致的情况，根据商业合理条件可以投保的除外。

本款所规定的保险内容属于第三人责任险，各国的法律中，第三人责任险一般是法律强制要求办理的保险，目的在于保护因行为人对他人造成危害时，可使受侵害方的权益得到保障。对工程而言，第三人责任险主要是保障因施工作用影响到的公众的权益。对于第三人造成的损失可能是巨大的，因此，第三人责任险一般会规定一个每次发生此类风险事件的最低保险额度，而且不限次数。如：管道项目在管沟开挖爆破时，对附加的另一并行管道造成的影响，不论并行管道是属于雇主还是第三人，都属于第三人责任险的范围。

18.4　Insurance for Contractor's Personnel（承包商人员的保险）

The Contractor shall effect and maintain insurance against liability for claims, damages, losses and expenses (including legal fees and expenses) arising from injury, sickness, disease or death of any person employed by the Contractor or any other of the Contractor's Personnel.

The Employer and the Engineer shall also be indemnified under the policy of insurance, except that this insurance may exclude losses and claims to the extent that they arise from any act or neglect of the Employer or of the Employer's Personnel.

The insurance shall be maintained in full force and effect during the whole time that these personnel are assisting in the execution of the Works. For a Subcontractor's employees, the insurance may be effected by the Subcontractor, but the Contractor shall be responsible for compliance with this Clause.

承包商应为由于承包商或任何其他承包商的人员雇用的任何人员的伤害、疾病、病疫或死亡所导致的一切索赔、损害、损失和开支（包括法律费用和开支）的责任投保，并使之保持有效。雇主和工程师也应能够依此保险单得到保障，但此类保险不承保由雇主或雇主人员的任何行为或疏忽造成的损失和索赔。

此类人员协助实施工程的整个期间都要保持保险完全有效。对于分包商的雇员，此类保险可由分包商来办理，但承包商应负责使分包商遵循本款的要求。

本款规定的承包商应为其人员办理人身事故和疾病方面的保险，此类保险在工程保险中成为雇主责任险。

思考题

1. 简述合同对保险的总体要求。
2. 合同中的保险方有哪几类？不同保险方的投保有何区别？
3. 办理工程和承包商设备保险时，保险范围可以不包括的损失、损害情况有哪些？
4. 承包商人员的保险单中保障的人员范围有哪些？
5. 简述国际工程中常见的工程保险类别。

19 Force Majeure（不可抗力）

由于工程建设周期较长，发生不可抗力事件的可能性相对较大，不可抗力事件的发生也对工程的实施产生严重影响。

本章要求：了解不可抗力在本合同条件中被赋予的含义；
了解不可抗力发生后双方的责任；
了解不可抗力导致终止合同时的处理方法；
了解法律规定的导致解除履约的处理方法。

19.1 Definition of Force Majeure（不可抗力的定义）

In this Clause , "Force Majeure" means an exceptional event or circumstance：
(a) which is beyond a Party's control ,
(b) which such Party could not reasonably have provided against before entering into the Contract ,
(c) which , having arisen , such Party could not reasonably have avoided or overcome , and
(d) which is not substantially attributable to the other Party.
Force Majeure may include , but is not limited to , exceptional events or circumstances of the kind listed below , so long as conditions (a) to (d) above are satisfied：
(i) war , hostilities (whether war be declared or not) , invasion , act of foreign enemies ,
(ii) rebellion , terrorism , revolution , insurrection , military or usurped power , or civil war ,
(iii) riot , commotion , disorder , strike or lockout by persons other than the Contractor's Personnel and other employees of the Contractor and Sub-contractors ,
(iv) munitions of war , explosive materials , ionising radiation or contamination by radio-activity , except as may be attributable to the Contractor's use of such munitions , explosives , radiation or radio-activity , and
(v) natural catastrophes such as earthquake , hurricane , typhoon or volcanic activity.

由于国际上对"不可抗力"的理解并不完全一致，因此，只有在合同中严格界定其含义，才能在不可抗力事件发生后，高效处理其产生的后果，避免产生争议。

"不可抗力"是指如下所述的特殊事件或情况：（1）一方无法控制的；（2）在签订合同前该方无法合理防范的；（3）情况发生时，该方无法合理回避或克服的；（4）该事件本质上不是由于合同另一方造成的。

只要满足上述（1）至（4）段所述的条件，不可抗力可包括（但不限于）下列特殊事件或情况：

（i）战争、敌对行动（不论宣战与否）、入侵、外敌行动；

（ii）叛乱、恐怖活动、革命、暴动、军事政变或篡夺政权，或内战；

（iii）暴乱、骚乱、混乱、罢工或停业，完全局限于承包商的人员以及承包商和分包商的其他雇员中间的事件除外；

（iv）军火、炸药、离子辐射或放射性污染，由于承包商使用此类军火、炸药、辐射或放射性的情况除外；

（v）自然灾害，如地震、飓风、台风或火山爆发。

本款用四个条件来限定不可抗力的内涵，列出了常见的不可抗力事件。规定的内容与国际通行规定一致，且更完整和明晰。FIDIC对"不可抗力"的定义具有广泛的代表性，若此定义与合同使用法律不一致，合同双方应在合同条款中加以修改和说明。

19.2　Notice of Force Majeure（不可抗力的通知）

If a Party is or will be prevented from performing any of its obligations under the Contract by Force Majeure, then it shall give notice to the other Party of the event or circumstances constituting the Force Majeure and shall specify the obligations, the performance of which is or will be prevented. The notice shall be given within 14 days after the Party became aware, or should have become aware, of the relevant event or circumstance constituting Force Majeure.

The Party shall, having given notice, be excused performance of such obligations for so long as such Force Majeure prevents it from performing them.

Notwithstanding any other provision of this Clause, Force Majeure shall not apply to obligations of either Party to make payments to the other Party under the Contract.

本款规定受到不可抗力影响的一方有通知另一方的义务。如果由于不可抗力，一方已经或将要无法依据合同履行他的任何义务，则该方应将构成不可抗力的事件或情况通知另一方，并具体说明已经无法或即将无法履行的义务、工作。

由于不可抗力事件的影响面可能较广，且后果具有持续性，不可抗力事件还可能造成信息沟通和交流困难，甚至中断。为了不损害一方的实际利益，本款规定受到不可抗力影响的一方应在注意到（或应该开始注意到）构成不可抗力的相应事件或情况发生后14天内发出通知。

在发出通知后，一方应在此类不可抗力持续期间免除此类义务的履行。不论本条中其他款作何规定，不可抗力的规定不适用于任一方依据合同向另一方进行支付的义务。这说明合同一方不能以不可抗力为借口，拒绝向另一方支付按合同支付的款项。如果因不可抗力导致支付困难，可以暂缓支付，但应按照合同其他条款的规定支付利息，且不影响另一方按合同行使其权益。

19.3 Duty to Minimise Delay（将延误减至最小的义务）

Each Party shall at all times use all reasonable endeavours to minimise any delay in the performance of the Contract as a result of Force Majeure.

A Party shall give notice to the other Party when it ceases to be affected by the Force Majeure.

发生不可抗力事件后，每一方都应尽力履行合同规定的义务，以减少由于不可抗力导致的任何延误。当不可抗力的影响终止时，一方应通知另一方。本款规定的目的是防止发生不可抗力事件后某一方的投机行为。合同一方可能出于某种意图，对不可抗力事件消极处理，从中获得某种利益，造成不可抗力导致的损失扩大，整个工程成本增加。本款规定各方应将造成的延误降低到最小程度，而没有规定各方应采取措施将费用损失降低。这是因为大多数情况下不可抗力事件导致的费用损失由雇主承担，如果对费用方面加以限制，可能有助于承包商为了自身利益而采取消极的态度处理不可抗力事件。

19.4 Consequences of Force Majeure（不可抗力的后果）

If the Contractor is prevented from performing any of his obligations under the Contract by Force Majeure of which notice has been given under Sub-Clause 19.2 [Notice of Force Majeure], and suffers delay and/or incurs Cost by reason of such Force Majeure, the Contractor shall be entitled subject to Sub-Clause 20.1 [Contractor's Claims] to:

(a) an extension of time for any such delay, if completion is or will be delayed, under Sub-Clause 8.4 [Extension of Time for Completion], and

(b) if the event or circumstance is of the kind described in sub-paragraphs (i) to (iv) of Sub-Clause 19.1 [Definition of Force Majeure] and, in the case of sub-paragraphs (ii) to (iv), occurs in the Country, payment of any such Cost.

After receiving this notice, the Engineer shall proceed in accordance with Sub-Clause 3.5 [Determinations] to agree or determine these matters.

由于不可抗力，承包商如无法依据合同履行他的任何义务，且已根据第19.2款[不可抗力的通知]，发出了相应的通知，由于承包商无法履行此类义务而使其遭受工期的延误和（或）费用的增加，则根据第20.1款[承包商的索赔]，承包商有权：

（1）根据第8.4款[竣工时间的延长]的规定，就任何此类延误获得延长的工期，如果竣工时间已经（或将要）被延误，以及（2）获得任何此类费用的支付款额，如果发生了如第19.1款[不可抗力的定义]中（i）～（iv）所描述的事件或情况，以及如果在工程所在国发生了如（ii）～（iv）中所述的事件或情况。

在收到此类通知后，工程师应根据第3.5款[决定]表示同意或作出决定。

本款规定可以看出不可抗力事件发生后，风险基本上是由雇主承担。但若不可抗力属于自然灾害，承包商有权提出工期索赔，而无权提出费用索赔，此时雇主和承包商应各承担一部分损失。

FIDIC 施工合同条件中规定，若发生影响承包商的不可抗力事件，承包商应直接将情况通知给雇主，而不是工程师。但承包商关于不可抗力的索赔则仍需要向工程师提出，由工程师审核。实际工程中，为了便于处理不可抗力事件，一般在发生不可抗力事件时，承包商应同时向雇主和工程师发出通知，而不应只通知雇主。

19.5　Force Majeure Affecting Subcontractor（不可抗力影响分包商）

If any Subcontractor is entitled under any contract or agreement relating to the works to relief from force majeure on terms additional to or broader than those specified in this Clause, such additional or broader force majeure events or circumstances shall not excuse the Contractor's non-performance or entitle him to relief under this Clause.

如果根据有关工程的任何合同或协议，分包商有权在附加的或超出本款规定范围之外的不可抗力发生时解除其义务，则在此类附加的或超出的不可抗力事件或情况发生时，承包商应继续工作，且无权根据本款解除其履约义务。

实际工程中，分包合同中的规定一般比主合同严格。大多数情况下，分包合同中不可抗力范围及其相关规定与主合同一致。但有时承包商会在工程分包时多承担一部分风险，从而降低分包合同的合同价格。此时，分包合同规定的不可抗力的外延会比主合同大，导致承包商对分包商的责任超过雇主按照主合同对承包商的责任。发生不可抗力事件后，承包商则常以分包商向其索赔为由，向雇主提出索赔，从而获得利益。

19.6　Optional Termination, Payment and Release（自主选择终止，付款和解除）

If the execution of substantially all the Works in progress is prevented for a continues period of 84 days by reason of Force Majeure of which notice has been given under Sub-Clause 19.2 [Notice of Force Majeure], or for multiple periods which total more than 140 days due to the same notified Force Majeure, then either Party may give to the other Party a notice of termination of the Contract. In this event, the termination shall take effect 7 days after the notice is given, and the Contractor shall proceed in accordance with Sub-Clause 16.3 [Cessation of Work and Removal of Contractor's Equipment].

Upon such termination, the Engineer shall determine the value of the work done and issue a Payment Certificate which shall include:

(a) the amounts payable for any work carried out for which a price is stated in the Contract;

(b) the Cost of Plant and Materials ordered for the Works which have been delivered to the Contractor, or of which the Contractor is liable to accept delivery: this Plant and Materials shall become the property of (and be at the risk of) the Employer when paid for by the Employer, and the Contractor shall place the same at the Employer's disposal;

(c) any other Cost or liability which in the circumstances was reasonably incurred by the Contractor in the expectation of completing the Works;

(d) the Cost of removal of Temporary Works and Contractor's Equipment from the Site and the return of these items to the Contractor's works in his country (or to any other destination at no greater cost); and

(e) the Cost of repatriation of the Contractor's staff and labour employed wholly in connection with the Works at the date of termination.

不可抗力事件造成的后果有时非常严重，若其对工程的影响时间过长，对雇主而言，继续该工程无价值或可能招致更大损失；对承包商而言，继续等待工程恢复施工会失去其他项目的机会，本款提出了解决这一问题的原则和方法：

如果由于不可抗力，导致整个工程的施工无法进行已经持续了84天，且已根据第19.2款[不可抗力的通知]发出了相应的通知，或如果由于同样原因停工时间的总和已经超过了140天，则任一方可向另一方发出终止合同的通知。在这种情况下，合同将在通知发出后7天终止，同时承包商应按照第16.3款[停止工作及承包商的设备的撤离]的规定执行。一旦发生此类终止，工程师应决定已完成的工作的价值，并颁发包括下列内容的支付证书：

（1）已完成的且其价格在合同中有规定的任何工作的应付款额；

（2）为工程订购的，且已交付给承包商或承包商有责任去接受交货的永久设备和材料的费用：当雇主为之付款后，此类永久设备和材料应成为雇主的财产（雇主为之承担风险），并且承包商应将此类永久设备和材料交由雇主处置；

（3）为完成整个工程，承包商在某些情况合理导致的任何其他费用或负债；

（4）将临时工程和承包商的设备撤离现场并运回承包商本国设备基地的合理费用（或运回其他目的地的费用，但不能超过运回本国基地的费用）；

（5）在合同终止日期将完全是为工程雇用的承包商的职员和劳工遣返回国的费用。

19.7　Release from Performance under the Law（根据法律解除履约）

Notwithstanding any other provision of this Clause, if any event or circumstance outside the control of the Parties (including, but not limited to, Force Majeure) arises which makes it impossible or unlawful for either or both Parties to fulfil its or their contractual obligations or which, under the law governing the Contract, entitles the Parties to be released from further performance of the Contract, then upon notice by either Party to the other Party of such event or circumstance:

(a) the Parties shall be discharged from further performance, without prejudice to the rights of either Party in respect of any previous breach of the Contract, and

(b) the sum payable by the Employer to the Contractor shall be the same as would have been payable under Sub-Clause 19.6 [Optional Termination, Payment and Release] if the Contract had been terminated under Sub-Clause 19.6.

除非本条另有规定，如果发生的事件或情况属于（但不限于）不可抗力，合同双方无法控制，使任一方（或合同双方）履行他的合同义务已变为不可能或非法，或者根据本合同适用的法律，合同双方均被解除进一步的履约义务，但是不影响由于任何以前的违约任一方享有的权利。如果合同是依据第19.6款[可选择的终止、支付和返回]的规定终止的，雇主支付给承包商的金额应与根据第19.6款终止合同时支付给承包商的金额相同。

思考题

1. 简述不可抗力的类型和范围。
2. 简述不可抗力事件发生后承包商应采取的处理措施。
3. 简述不可抗力事件发生后雇主应采取的必要措施。
4. 说明不可抗力对工程可能造成的影响。

20 Claim, Disputes and Arbitration
（索赔、争端和仲裁）

合同当事人在订立施工合同时，通过各项合同条款对合同风险进行了分担，承包商在投标报价及安排工期时应将自身承担的风险考虑进去。对于雇主承担的风险，一旦风险发生承包商则有权提出索赔。FIDIC施工合同通用条件的很多条款中明确规定或隐含了承包商的索赔权。索赔事项的处理由工程师按合同规定、与双方沟通协商后确定。如果承包商不同意工程师的确定结论，发生争端，可向争端裁定委员会提出异议。若争端仍未解决，可向合同中指定的仲裁委员会提出仲裁。本条详述了索赔和程序；争端的解决方式；争端裁决委员会的构成、性质和运作机制；仲裁的条件、规则和程序。

本章要求：了解承包商的索赔程序；
　　　　　　了解争端仲裁委员会的构成、性质和运作机制；
　　　　　　了解仲裁的前提条件、规则和程序。

20.1 Contractor's Claims（承包商的索赔）

If the Contractor considers himself to be entitled to any extension of the Time for Completion and/or any additional payment, under any Clause of these Conditions or otherwise in connection with the Contract, the Contractor shall give notice to the Engineer, describing the event or circumstance giving rise to the claim. The notice shall be given as soon as practicable, and not later than 28 days after the Contractor became aware, or should have become aware, of the event or circumstance.

If the Contractor fails to give notice of a claim within such period of 28 days, the Time for Completion shall not be extended, the Contractor shall not be entitled to additional payment, and the Employer shall be discharged from all liability in connection with the claim. Otherwise, the following provisions of this Sub-Clause shall apply.

The Contractor shall also submit any other notices which are required by the Contract, and supporting particulars for the claim, all as relevant to such event or circumstance.

The Contractor shall keep such contemporary records as may be necessary to substantiate any claim, either on the Site or at another location acceptable to the Engineer. Without admitting the Employer's liability, the Engineer may, after receiving any notice under this Sub-Clause, monitor the record-keeping and/or instruct the Contractor to keep further contemporary records. The Contractor shall permit the Engineer to inspect all these records, and shall (if instructed) submit copies to the Engineer.

Within 42 days after the Contractor became aware (or should have become aware) of the event or circumstance giving rise to the claim, or within such other period as may be proposed by the Contractor and approved by the Engineer, the Contractor shall send to the Engineer a fully detailed claim which includes full supporting particulars of the basis of the claim and of the extension of time and/or additional payment claimed. If the event or circumstance giving rise to the claim has a continuing effect:

(a) this fully detailed claim shall be considered as interim;

(b) the Contractor shall send further interim claims at monthly intervals, giving the accumulated delay and/or amount claimed, and such further particulars as the Engineer may reasonably require; and

(c) the Contractor shall send a final claim within 28 days after the end of the effects resulting from the event or circumstance, or within such other period as may be proposed by the Contractor and approved by the Engineer.

Within 42 days after receiving a claim or any further particulars supporting a previous claim, or within such other period as may be proposed by the Engineer and approved by the Contractor, the Engineer shall respond with approval, or with disapproval and detailed comments. He may also request any necessary further particulars, but shall nevertheless give his response on the principles of the claim within such time.

Each Payment Certificate shall include such amounts for any claim as have been reasonably substantiated as due under the relevant provision of the Contract. Unless and until the particulars supplied are sufficient to substantiate the whole of the claim, the Contractor shall only be entitled to payment for such part of the claim as he has been able to substantiate.

The Engineer shall proceed in accordance with Sub-Clause 3.5 [Determinations] to agree or determine (i) the extension (if any) of the Time for Completion (before or after its expiry) in accordance with Sub-Clause 8.4 [Extension of Time for Completion], and/or (ii) the additional payment (if any) to which the Contractor is entitled under the Contract.

The requirements of this Sub-Clause are in addition to those of any other Sub-Clause which may apply to a claim. If the Contractor fails to comply with this or another Sub-Clause in relation to any claim, any extension of time and/or additional payment shall take account of the extent (if any) to which the failure has prevented or prejudiced proper investigation of the claim, unless the claim is excluded under the second paragraph of this Sub-Clause.

本款主要规定了承包商提交索赔通知的时间限制、承包商对工程师指示保持同期记录的要求、承包商提交索赔报告的内容要求和时间限制、工程师批复索赔报告的时间限制及其他规定。

如果承包商根据本合同条件的任何条款或合同的其他规定，认为他有权获得任何竣工时间的延长和（或）任何附加款项，应通知工程师，说明引起索赔的事件或情况。该通知应尽快发出，并应不迟于承包商开始注意到（或应该开始注意到）这种事件或情况之后

28 天。

如果承包商未能在 28 天内发出索赔通知，竣工时间将不被延长，承包商将无权得到附加款项，并且雇主将被解除有关索赔的一切责任。否则本款以下规定应适用。

承包商还应提交一切与此类事件或情况有关的任何其他通知（如果合同要求），以及索赔的详细证明报告。

承包商应在现场或工程师可接受的其他地点保留同期记录，这些记录是证明任何索赔的必要资料。工程师在收到根据本款发出的上述通知后，在不必事先承认雇主责任的情况下，可监督此类记录，并（或）可指示承包商保持进一步的同期记录。承包商应允许工程师审查所有此类记录，并应向工程师提供复印件（如果工程师指示的话）。

在承包商开始注意到，或应该开始注意到，引起索赔的事件或情况之日起 42 天内，或在承包商可能建议且由工程师批准的此类其他时间内，承包商应向工程师提交一份足够详细的索赔，包括一份完整的证明报告，详细说明索赔的依据以及索赔的工期和（或）索赔的金额。

如果引起索赔的事件或情况具有连续影响：

（1）该全面详细的索赔应被认为是临时的；

（2）承包商应该按月提交进一步的临时索赔，说明累计索赔工期和（或）索赔款额，以及工程师可能合理要求的此类进一步的详细报告；

（3）在索赔事件所产生的影响结束后的 28 天内（或在承包商可能建议且由工程师批准的此类其他时间内），承包商应提交一份最终索赔报告。

在收到索赔报告或该索赔的任何进一步的详细证明报告后 42 天内（或在工程师可能建议且由承包商批准的此类其他时间内），工程师应表示批准或不批准，不批准时要给予详细的评价。他可能会要求任何必要的进一步的详细报告，但他应在这段时间内就索赔的原则作出反应。

每一份支付证明应将根据相关合同条款应支付并已被合理证实的此类索赔金额纳入其中。如果承包商提供的详细报告不足以证明全部的索赔，则承包商仅有权得到已被证实的那部分索赔。

根据本款规定，承包商提交索赔的程序要求较严格，索赔的每个环节一旦超过时间限制，则承包商就会丧失索赔权。实际工程中，雇主和工程师可能会对时间限制放宽，但作为承包商而言，遵守合同规定的各项时间限制，是成功索赔的基础。

工程师应根据第 3.5 款［确定］，表示同意或作出决定：（i）根据第 8.4 款［竣工时间的延长］的规定延长竣工时间（在其终止时间之前或之后）（如果有），以及（或者）（ii）根据合同承包商有权获得的附加款项（如果有）。

本款同时对工程师回应索赔有时间限制，但并未规定工程师未遵守规定的后果。但可以推定，承包商违反时间限定会丧失索赔权，工程师违反时间限定则可认为其批准了索赔要求。

除本款的规定外，还有许多其他条款适用于索赔。如果承包商未能遵循本款或其他有关索赔的条款的规定，则在决定竣工时间的延长和（或）额外款项时，要考虑这种未遵循（如果有）已妨碍或影响索赔调查的程度，除非根据本款第二段该索赔已被排除。

20.2 Appointment of the Dispute Adjudication Board（争端裁决委员会的任命）

Disputes shall be adjudicated by a DAB in accordance with Sub-Clause 20.4 [Obtaining Dispute Adjudication Board's Decision]. The Parties shall jointly appoint a DAB by the date stated in the Appendix to Tender.

The DAB shall comprise, as stated in the Appendix to Tender, either one or three suitably qualified persons ("the members"). If the number is not so stated and the Parties do not agree otherwise, the DAB shall comprise three persons.

If the DAB is to comprise three persons, each Party shall nominate one member for the approval of the other Party. The Parties shall consult both these members and shall agree upon the third member, who shall be appointed to act as chairman.

However, if a list of potential members is included in the Contract, the members shall be selected from those on the list, other than anyone who is unable or unwilling to accept appointment to the DAB.

The agreement between the Parties and either the sole member ("adjudicator") or each of the three members shall incorporate by reference the General Conditions of Dispute Adjudication Agreement contained in the Appendix to these General Conditions, with such amendments as are agreed between them.

The terms of the remuneration of either the sole member or each of the three members, including the remuneration of any expert whom the DAB consults, shall be mutually agreed upon by the Parties when agreeing the terms of appointment. Each Party shall be responsible for paying one-half of this remuneration.

If at any time the Parties so agree, they may jointly refer a matter to the DAB for it to give its opinion. Neither Party shall consult the DAB on any matter without agreement of the other Party.

If at any time the Parties so agree, they may appoint a suitably qualified person or persons to replace (or to be available to replace) any one or more members of the DAB. Unless the Parties agree otherwise, the appointment will come into effect member declines to act or is unable to act as a result of death, disability, resignation or termination of appointment.

If any of these circumstances occurs and no such replacement is available replacement shall be appointed in the same manner as the replaced person was required to have been nominated or agreed upon, as described in this Sub-Clause.

The appointment of any member may be terminated by mutual agreement of both Parties, but not by the Employer or the Contractor acting alone. Unless other agreed by both Parties, the appointment of the DAB (including each member) shall expire when the discharge referred to in Sub-Clause 14.12 [Discharge] shall be come effective.

争端应由争端裁决委员会（DAB）根据第 20.4 款[获得争端裁决委员会的决定]进行裁决。合同双方应在投标函附录规定的日期内，共同任命争端裁决委员会（DAB）。该争端裁决委员会应由具有恰当资格的成员组成，成员人数可为一名或三名（具体情况由投标函附录中规定）。如果投标函附录中没有规定成员人数，且合同双方没有其他的协议，则争端裁决委员会应包含三名成员，其中由合同双方各提名一位且征得对方同意的成员，再由合同双方与这两名成员商定第三位成员（作为主席）。若合同中包含了意向性成员的名单，则成员应从该名单中选出，除非他不能或不愿接受争端裁决委员会的任命。合同双方与 DAB 成员中的每一个人的协议书应编入争端裁决协议书的通用条件中。DAB 成员报酬的支付条件，可由合同双方在协商任命条件时共同商定，且每一方应负责支付酬金的一半。合同双方同意的任何时候，他们可以共同将有争端的事宜提交给争端裁决委员会，由其给出意见或建议。无合同当事人一方的同意，另一方不得向争端裁决委员会征求建议。合同双方同意的情况下，他们可任命一名（或多名）合格人选替代争端裁决委员会的任何一个或多个成员。除非合同双方另有协议，只要某一 DAB 成员拒绝履行其职责或由于死亡、伤残、辞职或其委任终止等原因而不能尽其职责，该任命即生效。若发生了上述情况，而没有可替换的人员，委任替换人员的方式与本款中规定的任命或商定被替换人员的方式相同。

任何成员的委任只有在合同双方同意的情况下才能终止，雇主或承包商各自的行动不能终止委任。除非双方另有协议，在第 14.12 款[结清单]提及的结清单即将生效时，争端裁决委员会（包括每一个成员）的任期即告期满。

20.3 Failure to Agree Dispute Adjudication Board（对争端裁决委员会未能取得一致）

If any of the following conditions apply, namely：

(a) the Parties fail to agree upon the appointment of he sole member of the DAB by the date stated in the first paragraph of Sub-Clause 20.2,

(b) either Party fails to nominate a member (for approval by the other Party) of a DAB of three persons by such date,

(c) the Parties fail to agree upon the appointment of the third member (to act chairman) of the DAB by such date, or

(d) the Parties fail to agree upon the appointment of a replacement person within 42 days after the date on which the sole member or one of the three members declines to act or is unable to act as a result of death, disability, resignation termination of appointment,

then the appointing entity or official named in the Appendix to Tender shall, upon request of either or both of the Parties and after due consultation with both Parties appoint this member of the DAB. This appointment shall be final and conclusive. Each Party shall be responsible for paying one-half of the remuneration of the appoint entity or official.

如果下列条件中任一条件适用，即：

（a）合同双方未能在第20.2款第一段说明的日期就争端裁决委员会的唯一成员的委任达成一致意见，

（b）合同中任一方未能在此日期，为由三名成员组成的争端裁决委员会提名一名人员（可为另一方接受的），

（c）合同双方未能在此日期，就第三位成员（担任主席）的委任达成一致意见；或者，

（d）合同双方在唯一成员或三名成员中的一名成员拒绝履行其职责，或由于死亡、伤残、辞职或其委任终止而不能尽其职责之日后42天内，未能就替代人选的任命达成一致意见，

则专用条件中指定的机构或官方应根据合同一方或双方的要求，并在与合同双方适当协商后，提名该争端裁决委员会成员。该任命应是最终的和具有决定性的。每一方应负责支付该指定的机构或官方的酬金的一半。

20.4 Obtaining Dispute Adjudication Board's Decision（取得争端裁决委员会的决定）

If a dispute (of any kind whatsoever) arises between the Parties in connection with, or arising out of, the Contract or the execution of the Works, including any dispute as to any certificate, determination, instruction, opinion or valuation of the Engineer, either Party may refer the dispute in writing to the DAB for its decision, with copies to the other Party and the Engineer. Such reference shall state that it is given under this Sub-Clause.

For a DAB of three persons, the DAB shall be deemed to have received such reference on the date when it is received by the chairman of the DAB.

Both Parties shall promptly make available to the DAB all such additional information further access to the Site, and appropriate facilities, as the DAB may require for purposes of making adecision on such dispute. The DAB shall be deemed to be not acting as arbitrator(s).

Within 84 days after receiving such reference, or within such other period as may be proposed by the DAB and approved by both Parties, the DAB shall give its decision, which shall be reasoned and shall state that it is given under this Sub-Clause. The decision shall be binding on both Parties, who shall promptly give effect to it unless and until it shall be revised in an amicable settlement or an arbitral award as described below. Unless the Contract has already been abandoned, repudiated or terminated, the Contractor shall continue to proceed with the Works in accordance with the Contract.

If either Party is dissatisfied with the DAB's decision, then either Party may, within 28 days after receiving the decision, give notice to the other Party of its dissatisfaction. If the DAB fails to give its decision within the period of 84 days (or as other-

wise approved) after receiving such reference, *then either Party may, within 28 days after this period has expired, give notice to the other Party of its dissatisfaction.*

In either event, this notice of dissatisfaction shall state that it is given under this Sub-Clause, and shall set out the matter in dispute and the reason (s) for dissatisfaction. Except as stated in Sub-Clause 20.7 [Failure to Comply with Dispute Adjudication Board's Decision] and Sub-Clause 20.8 [Expiry of Dispute Adjudication Board's Appointment], neither Party shall be entitled to commence arbitration of a dispute unless a notice of dissatisfaction has been given in accordance with this Sub-Clause.

If the DAB has given its decision as to a matter in dispute to both Parties, and no notice of dissatisfaction has been given by either Party within 28 days after it received the DAB's decision, then the decision shall become final and binding upon both Parties.

如果在合同双方之间产生起因于合同、或实施过程、或与之相关的任何争端，包括对工程师的任何证书的签发、决定、指示、意见或估价的任何争端，任一方可将此类争端以书面形式提交争端裁决委员会，由其裁定，并将副本抄送另一方和工程师，并说明争端的提交是根据本款作出的。

对于由三名成员组成的争端裁决委员会，当争端裁决委员会主席收到此类提交时，即认为争端裁决委员会收到了此类提交。合同双方应立即向争端裁决委员会提供为对此类争端进行裁决为目的而需要的所有附加资料、进一步的现场通道和适当的设施。

争端裁决委员不应被视为仲裁人。在争端裁决委员会收到上述争端事宜的提交后84天内，或在争端裁决委员会建议并由双方批准的其他时间内，争端裁决委员会应作出合理决定，并应声明该决定是根据本款作出的。该决定对双方都有约束力，合同双方应立即执行争端裁决委员会作出的决定，除非此类决定按下文规定在友好解决或仲裁裁决中得以修改。除非合同已被放弃、撤销或终止，否则承包商应继续按照合同实施工程。如果合同双方中任一方对争端裁决委员会的裁决有疑义，则可在收到该决定的通知后第28天内或此前将其疑义通知对方。如果争端裁决委员会的决定未能在其收到疑义通知后84天（或其他批准的时间）内作出，那么合同双方中的任一方均可在上述期限期满后28天之内将其疑义通知对方。在上述任一情况下，写有疑义的通知应说明是根据本款发出的，且该通知应指明争端事宜及疑义的理由。除非依据本款发出此类通知，否则将不能对争端进行仲裁，但第20.7款［未能遵守争端裁决委员会的决定］和第20.8款［争端裁决委员会的委任期满］所述的情况除外。任何一方若未按本款发出表示疑义的通知，均无权就该争端要求开始仲裁。如果争端裁决委员会已将其对争端作出的决定通知了合同双方，而双方中的任一方在收到争端裁决委员会的决定的第28天或此前未将其疑义事宜通知对方，则该决定应被视为最终决定并对合同双方均具有约束力。

20.5 Amicable both Settlement（友好解决）

Where notice of dissatisfaction has been given under Sub-Clause 20.4 above, both Parties shall attempt to settle the dispute amicably before the commencement of arbitration. However, unless both Parties agree otherwise, arbitration may be commenced on or after the fifty-sixth day after the day on which notice of dissatisfaction was given, even if no attempt at amicable settlement has been made.

按上述第 20.4 款规定已发出表示疑义的通知后，合同双方在仲裁开始前应尽力以友好的方式解决争端。除非合同双方另有协议，否则仲裁将在表示疑义的通知发出后第 56 天或此后开始，即使双方未曾作过友好解决的努力。

20.6 Arbitration（仲裁）

Unless settled amicably, any dispute in respect of which the DAB's decision (if any) has not become final and binding shall be finally settled by international arbitration. Unless otherwise agreed by both Parties:

(a) the dispute shall be finally settled under the Rules of Arbitration of the International Chamber of Commerce,

(b) the dispute shall be settled by three arbitrators appointed in accordance with these Rules, and

(c) the arbitration shall be conducted in the language for communications defined in Sub-Clause 1.4 [Law and Language].

The arbitrator(s) shall have full power to open up, review and revise any certificate, determination, instruction, opinion or valuation of the Engineer, and any decision of the DAB, relevant to the dispute. Nothing shall disqualify the Engineer from being called as a witness and giving evidence before the arbitrator(s) on any matter whatsoever relevant to the dispute.

Neither Party shall be limited in the proceedings before the arbitrator(s) to the evidence or arguments previously put before the DAB to obtain its decision, or to the for dissatisfaction given in its notice of dissatisfaction. Any decision of the DAB shall be admissible in evidence in the arbitration.

Arbitration may be commenced prior to or after completion of the Works. The obligations of the Parties, the Engineer and the DAB shall not be altered by reason of any arbitration being conducted during the progress of the Works.

除非通过友好解决，否则如果争端裁决委员会有关争端的决定（如有时）未能成为最终决定并具有约束力，那么此类争端应由国际仲裁机构最终裁决。除非合同双方另有协议，否则：

(a) 该争端应根据国际商会的仲裁规则被最终解决；(b) 该争端应由按本规则指定的三位仲裁人裁决；(c) 该仲裁应以第 1.4 款[法律和语言]规定的日常交流语言作为仲裁语言。

仲裁人有全权公开、审查和修改工程师的任何证书的签发、决定、指示、意见或估价，以及任何争端裁决委员会有关争端事宜的决定。工程师不会失去被作为证人以及向仲裁人提供任何与争端有关的证据的资格。合同双方的任一方在上述仲裁人的仲裁过程中均不受以前为取得争端裁决委员会的决定而提供的证据或论据或其不满意通知中提出的不满理由的限制。在仲裁过程中，可将争端裁决委员会的决定作为一项证据。工程竣工之前或之后均可开始仲裁。但在工程进行过程中，合同双方、工程师以及争端裁决委员会的各自义务不得因任何仲裁正在进行而改变。

20.7 Failure to Comply with Dispute Adjudication Board's Decision（未能遵守争端裁决委员会的决定）

In the event that:
(a) neither Party has given notice of dissatisfaction within the period stated in Sub-Clause 20.4 [Obtaining Dispute Adjudication Board's. Decision],
(b) the DAB's related decision (if any) has become final and binding, and
(c) a Party fails to comply with this decision,
then the other Party may, without prejudice to any other rights it may have, refer the failure itself to arbitration under Sub-Clause 20.6 [Arbitration]. Sub-Clause 20.4 [Obtaining Dispute Adjudication Board's Decision] and Sub-Clause 20.5 [Amicable Settlement] shall not apply to this reference.

如果下述情况发生：
（a）合同双方中的任一方均未在第 20.4 款[获得争端裁决委员会的决定]规定的期限内向争端裁决委员会发出表示不满的通知，
（b）该争端裁决委员会的有关决定（如有时）已成为最终决定并且具有约束力，
（c）合同一方未遵守此类决定，
则合同的另一方在不损害其拥有的其他权利的情况下，可将不执行决定的行为提交第 20.6 款[仲裁]中规定的仲裁。且此时，第 20.4 款[获得争端裁决委员会的决定]和第 20.5 款[友好解决]的各项规定均不适用。

20.8 Expiry of Dispute Adjudication Board's Appointment（争端裁决委员会任命期满）

If a dispute arises between the Parties in connection with, or arising out of, the Contract or the execution of the Works and there is no DAB in place, whether by reason of the expiry of the DAB's appointment or otherwise:
(a) Sub-Clause 20.4 [Obtaining Dispute Adjudication Board's Decision] and Sub-Clause 20.5 [Amicable Settlement] shall not apply, and
(b) the dispute may be referred directly to arbitration under Sub-Clause 20.6 [Arbitration].

如果合同双方之间产生了起因于或相关于合同或工程的实施过程的某一争端，而此时不存在一个争端裁决委员会（there is no DAB in place）（无论是因为争端裁决委员会的任命已到期还是因为其他原因）：

(a) 第 20.4 款[获得争端裁决委员会的决定]和第 20.5 款[友好解决]的各项规定均不适用，

(b) 该争端应根据第 20.6 款[仲裁]，直接通过仲裁最终解决。

思考题

1. 简述承包商索赔的基本程序。
2. 简述雇主和承包商争端的解决方式和途径。
3. 何谓争端裁决委员会？其人员构成有何规定？
4. 雇主和承包商应如何正确对待争端裁决委员会的决定？